# Augustine and World Religions

# Augustine in Conversation: Tradition and Innovation

Series Editors: John Doody and Kim Paffenroth

This series produces edited volumes that explore Augustine's relationship to a particular discipline or field of study. This "relationship" is considered in several different ways: some contributors consider Augustine's practice of the particular discipline in question; some consider his subsequent influence on the field of study; and others consider how Augustine himself has become an object of study by their discipline. Such variety adds breadth and new perspectives—*innovation*—to our ongoing conversation with Augustine on topics of lasting import to him and us, while using Augustine as our conversation partner lends focus and a common thread—*tradition*—to our disparate fields and interests.

**TITLES IN THE SERIES**

*Augustine and Politics*
Edited by John Doody, Kevin L. Hughes, and Kim Paffenroth

*Augustine and Literature*
Edited by Robert P. Kennedy, Kim Paffenroth, and John Doody

*Augustine and History*
Edited by Christopher T. Daly, John Doody, and Kim Paffenroth

*Augustine and Liberal Education*
Edited by Kim Paffenroth and Kevin L. Hughes

# Augustine and World Religions

Brian Brown, John Doody, and
Kim Paffenroth

LEXINGTON BOOKS

A division of
ROWMAN & LITTLEFIELD PUBLISHERS, INC.
*Lanham • Boulder • New York • Toronto • Plymouth, UK*

LEXINGTON BOOKS

A division of Rowman & Littlefield Publishers, Inc.
A wholly owned subsidiary of The Rowman & Littlefield Publishing Group, Inc.
4501 Forbes Boulevard, Suite 200
Lanham, MD 20706

Estover Road
Plymouth PL6 7PY
United Kingdom



British Library Cataloguing in Publication Information Available

**Library of Congress Cataloging-in-Publication Data**

Augustine and world religions / [edited by] Brian Brown, John Doody, and Kim Paffenroth.
p. cm.
ISBN-13: 978-0-7391-2579-3 (cloth : alk. paper)
ISBN-10: 0-7391-2579-6 (cloth : alk. paper)
ISBN-13: 978-0-7391-2580-9 (pbk. : alk. paper)
ISBN-10: 0-7391-2580-X (pbk. : alk. paper)
1. Augustine, Saint, Bishop of Hippo. 2. Christianity and other religions. I. Brown, Brian, 1948- II. Doody, John, 1943- III. Paffenroth, Kim, 1966-
BR65.A65A85 2008
261'.2092--dc22 2008010154

Printed in the United States of America

∞™ The paper used in this publication meets the minimum requirements of American National Standard for Information Sciences—Permanence of Paper for Printed Library Materials, ANSI/NISO Z39.48-1992.

# Contents

## II. Augustine and Non-Western Religions

# Introduction

## Brian Brown, John Doody, and Kim Paffenroth

At the beginning of the twenty-first century, interreligious dialogue would seem at least as desirable as it would have been in Augustine's own time, at the beginning of the fifth century. Indeed, as the world grows ever more connected and ever more aware of its diversity, such dialogue would seem far more necessary, not less. But the very necessity of such dialogue, it seems, may diminish its depth and its honesty. If it is already agreed from the beginning that the only allowable conclusion is that we *must* get along, that we really are all worshiping the same God and to recognize or advocate any differences between our faiths is tantamount to open warfare and violence, then there is little room for discussion, let alone disagreement. There may be, moreover, very little room for real, heartfelt belief or commitment. Interreligious or interfaith encounters seem to descend to this level frequently, as little more than mutual congratulation and vague goodwill—or, at least, inoffensiveness—without real engagement.

It is in this context that perhaps the bishop of Hippo, if he cannot exactly come to the rescue—as flawed as his own practice of interreligious dialogue was—can at least remind us of ways and perspectives that we might be lacking or overlooking. For whatever else one can say of Augustine, he was always informed about his opponents and their beliefs. Ironically, he almost certainly knew more about the various non-Christian religions and Christian schisms of his day than do all those U.S. congresspeople who recently could not, in the most basic terms, articulate the difference between "Sunni" and "Shi'ite": we may (and many often do) pillory Augustine for being "intolerant," but how useful or real can our "tolerance" be, when we lack the vaguest idea of what others believe? And how could we strive for deeper levels of engagement, such as "respect," if such basic knowledge is lacking? If understanding and knowledge are the keys and the basis for dialogue and respect, then we would have much to learn from Augustine. And as several of our essays show, there is much in his thought that finds impressive and illuminating analogues in other faith traditions.

Such knowledge and respect seem amply illustrated in Augustine's enormous work, *The City of God*. Hardly the model of ecumenicity—for it seeks throughout to prove the superiority of Christianity over other beliefs—along the way it nonetheless has a great many respectful *and accurate and informed* things to say about non-Christians. For Augustine, Roman (pagan) virtues are not false or hypocritical but merely incomplete and lacking in a proper final goal. Pagans are often more virtuous than their Christian counterparts and neighbors, and this admission by Augustine is not grudging, but rather a shame-faced encouragement for his readers to emulate the pagans (in this one way at least). In general, the lesson Augustine wants to take away from pagan virtue is similar to the point Paul makes in Romans 9–11, a passage to which several of our essays make reference: if many virtuous non-Christians may be cut off from God—and Augustine, it must be noted, is as uncertain as Paul as to their final fate (*CD* 1.35)—the only appropriate response for Christian believers is emphatically *not* smug, self-righteous condemnation—despite the stereotype of such Christian intolerance so prevalent today—but only awe at God's power and inscrutability.

Even more important, perhaps, Augustine provides us with a powerful and *positive* purpose for interreligious dialogue—and, moreover, a goal that is, itself, religious. For if the goal of dialogue is merely mutual nonaggression—as necessary and desirable as this might be for our species' physical survival—then, it should be admitted, such dialogue serves only a negative purpose—to restrain base, violent urges. And, it seems, there is a certain unstated and slightly intolerant assumption in such modern justifications for interreligious dialogue—namely, that there really will be no reason to engage in such discussions once people's religious urges are sufficiently curbed or domesticated, thereby stopping their bad (religious) violence. From this modern, cynical perspective, religion is really the problem, and tolerance is not a part of religion but rather its solution or cure—a cure brought from outside of religion by enlightened, human reason. Moreover, there is no room here for anything resembling "respect" for religion, as much as moderns pay lip-service to the ideal, for one hardly respects that for which one blames all the species' woes. But Augustine hints at a much more authentically, even uniquely religious justification for examining and dialoguing with other religions. One studies such things because, quite simply, they contain true ideas about God: Augustine claims that within non-Christian writings there are "some truths in regard even to the worship of the One God" and these the Christian is to take away from such writings, as though they were the "gold and silver . . . dug out of the mines of God's providence" (*On Christian Doctrine* 2.40.60; cf. *Conf.* 7.9.13–14). For Augustine, the real reason to study and dialogue with other religions would be so that one could better understand and worship God. That, more than modern fears of violence and annihilation—as justifiable and frightening as they may be—would seem the only authentically Christian, the only really *religious* reason to study what our essayists have so passionately and insightfully presented.

We have divided our analysis into two groups of essays. The first considers Augustine's direct interaction and theorizing about the real (and competing) religions of his day—Roman paganism (with the usual caveats about the non-monolithic nature of such an entity) and Judaism. These essays are primarily historical and seek to navigate and elaborate the tricky, ambiguous relationship that Augustine saw between Christianity and these two entities with which it shared much in terms of common background and goals, and yet from which it increasingly saw itself as distinct or even antagonistic. Since in our modern world the relationship between Judaism and Christianity is still problematic, those essays that deal with Augustine's thoughts on Jews and Judaism are clearly relevant to us today. And though Roman paganism is not a living world religion in our time, there are many ways in which it can be seen as equivalent in our modern world to the prevailing, secular culture. Since the modern Christian responses to secular culture are so varied and questionable—from categorical rejection, to easy tolerance, to enthusiastic embracing and identity—Augustine's thoughts again prove timely.

The second section takes a very different approach—that of comparative theology. These essays compare specific points of Augustinian theology with equivalent or analogous concepts in several of the world's other religions. The results are a fascinating and fruitful way to encourage dialogue on common points between our various faiths. These essays are exciting examples of how understanding contributes to real respect and dialogue, much to the benefit of both participants.

Beginning our collection, Olivier Dufault examines the vague category of "magic," ancient and modern. He argues that since Augustine, magic in European culture has been used as a cultural marker which identifies its bearer as a marginal individual. In our sources, this has been used mostly as an accusation. Modern cases of identification with magic show that, in certain social contexts, this marker can be used by the bearer himself. He then attempts to transpose this example to antiquity in an attempt to find out who might have been attracted by such an identity back then.

There next follows a reprint of a classic study, in which we see Paula Fredriksen revealing the complexity of Augustine's attitudes and beliefs concerning Israel—both the historical Israel described in the Bible and, more problematically and difficultly, the contemporary and unconverted Israel of Augustine's own time.

In a similar vein, Franklin Harkins aims in his essay to provide a detailed analysis of Augustine's mature teaching on Jews and Judaism against the twofold contextual backdrop of: (1) the preceding tradition of early Christian thought; and (2) the interreligious world of late-antique North Africa. Inheriting from early Christian texts stock images of the Jews as a blind and faithless people having been rejected by God in favor of Christians, Augustine combines them to produce a unique and perduring portrait commonly known as the doctrine of Jewish witness. Having been exiled and scattered throughout the world, Jews serve as unwitting witnesses to the truth of Christianity by blindly carrying about their own sacred scriptures—proof that Christians have not forged the prophecies concerning Christ. Augustine's mature doctrine of Jewish witness is most fully and properly understood, it is argued, in the context of the competitive but relatively peaceful interactions between Jews and Christians in the bishop's late-antique North Africa.

In his essay, Paul Joseph LaChance contributes to the search for the literary unity of the *Confessions*, as well as investigating Augustine's relationship with pagan ideas. The author argues that the *Confessions* may be read as a re-narration of Virgil's epic in which Augustine converted Virgil's pagan view of historical progress and virtue into a Christian view centered on Christ and the Church. By bringing together his classical education with his Christian formation, Augustine the Bishop of Hippo forged a literary outlet for his new voice.

Taking up again the issue of Augustine's relation to Judaism, C. C. Pecknold's essay examines recent debates about Augustine's "hermeneutical Jew." By first arguing that Augustine's sacramental understanding of scriptural semiotics is a consequence of his Christology (theo-semiotics), the author suggests that Augustine's incarnational hermeneutic for scriptural interpretation should regulate how we understand his construction of Jewish identity and difference, and should direct contemporary Augustinian theology as well. Through a rereading of *Tractatus adversus Iudaeos*, Pecknold claims that the hermeneutical differences between Jews and Christians must be learned and sustained through exegetical conversations with actual Jews rather than imaginary, constructed, or hermeneutical ones.

Beginning our investigation of the possible interface between Augustinian thought and some non-Western religions, Michael Barnes' essay starts with the observation that, however it is interpreted, the Buddhist account of the human person as *anatman*, lacking a substantial sense of self, opens up certain resonances with the central paradox of Christianity—that one must lose the self in order to find it. This soteriological theme is explored through a detailed analysis of a Theravadin Buddhist text, the *Samanññaphala Sutta*, with its central theme of the "fruits of being a recluse," the stages of progress on the way to enlightenment. A more contemporary account of Buddhist practice raises questions about how "way"—practice and performance—are to be configured with "wilderness"—the everyday world of experience through which the practitioner passes. In exploring the question of how progress on any spiritual path is possible—how a vision of truth is to be maintained in the middle of things—recourse is made to Augustinian spirituality and particularly to Augustine's own account of the mystery of time—past, present, and future configured in a single life.

Beginning with Augustine's strong opinions about pagan religion and culture, and his firm conviction about the superiority of the Christian religion and culture, Francis X. Clooney shows how Augustine models a contested erudition—respectable and serious, but at the same time also vulnerable in light of other readings of the same texts. Clooney first examines books VIII and IX of the *City of God*, where Augustine reads with care, though not uncontroversially, the *God of Socrates* of Apuleius and the *Apuleius* attributed to Hermes Trismegistus, and then goes on to suggest that Augustine thus exemplifies a practice of apologetic reading that can be traced throughout Church history, including in the period of colonial, missionary encounters with Asian religions. Heuristic similarities are illustrated with reference to how three Jesuits in colonial India—Frs. de Nobili, Bouchet, and Meurin, respectively, in the seventeenth, eighteenth, and nineteenth centuries—appropriated Hindu texts for the sake of Christian mission, and the questions their reading practices raise.

Drawing connections between Augustine and Buddhism, Leo Lefebure shows how both Shakyamuni Buddha in the Lotus Sutra and Augustine acknowledge that ultimate wisdom cannot be expressed or understood in human concepts, but they look to the interpretation of concrete images and narratives for practical transformation of human life. The Lotus Sutra and Augustine both warn that our ordinary self-consciousness is warped. In very different cosmological contexts, both reject any claim of adequacy for a detached, speculative understanding of ultimate reality and aim instead at the practical goal of healing and renewing human existence. Buddhist wisdom leads to compassion, and Augustine's Christian wisdom leads to charity.

Returning to an examination of Hindu thought, Reid Locklin reconsiders Augustine's theology of grace and election, particularly as articulated in his *Reply to Simplicianus*, by placing it into dialogue with the non-dualist teaching of the Hindu teacher, Adi Shankaracharya, particularly as articulated in his commentary on the Mundaka Upanishad. Shankara, no less than Augustine, refused to view the final end of human life as something produced by finite means; final liberation follows, instead, from the intrinsic nature (*sva-bhava*) of God the divine self. Yet Shankara also retains a paradoxical sense of human agency, embodied in the idea of the "fittingness" or "eligibility" (*adhikara*) that qualifies prospective disciples to receive the word of liberation in a fruitful way. Though there is much in Shankara's account that Augustine would certainly reject, the tension this Hindu teacher creates between strong affirmation and even stronger denial of human agency in the attainment of final liberation offers a useful framework within which to reconsider Augustine's own affirmations and denials as he attempts to work out the inscrutable and irresistible gift of God's grace.

Finally, Aaron Stalnaker shows the similarities of Augustine and the early Confucian figure Xunzi in their sophisticated and insightful accounts of spiritual exercises, which both make central to their religious visions, offering detailed analyses and advocacy of particular practices. This essay, after setting the stage with general discussions of their accounts of human life, focuses on a striking thematic difference between the two: the contrast between Augustine's "inside-out" approach to personal formation, typified by his laudatory emphasis on confessional prayer, and Xunzi's "outside-in" approach, typified by his insistence on the great value of communal ritual practice, understood expansively so as to encompass all realms of life. It then develops this fundamental contrast in strategy by exploring their differing evaluations of honesty and pretence within religious self-cultivation.

To borrow and adapt from Shakespeare, we come to understand Augustine, not to praise him. We have also tried to understand—on their own terms, as well as in relation to Christianity—several dialogue partners with Augustine on diverse and important points of belief. But by understanding these various thinkers, we may find that there is something there to praise—and more importantly, things to question and blame in our own hearts and minds—as we strive to further a real dialogue between the various religions of our world.

# I

# AUGUSTINE'S RELATION TO JUDAISM AND ROMAN RELIGIONS

# 1

# Augustine and the Invention of Magical Dissent

Olivier Dufault

*Any kind of organized revolution against the Party, which was bound to be a failure, struck her as stupid. The clever thing was to break the rules and stay alive all the same. He wondered vaguely how many others like her might be in the younger generation—people who had grown up in the world of the Revolution, knowing nothing else, accepting the Party as something unalterable, like the sky, not rebelling against its authority but simply evading it, as a rabbit dodges a dog.*

George Orwell, *1984*

## INTRODUCTION

Augustine was not the first to theorize magic, but his own definition, scattered across many treatises, is undoubtedly the most politically explicit and the most influential. The aim of this paper is to illustrate how the binary framework he established—in which he opposed magic to religion, the past to the present, the personal to the social—was kept alive until now through gradual metamorphoses. Furthermore, I propose to look at contemporary magic-users as providing comparative material which can help us discover who might have self-identified as magicians in antiquity.

Ultimately, I am suggesting that, at least from Augustine on, the theorization as well as the use of magic was more often than not associated with cultural revolutions, or, less dramatically, with social dissent. This view is partly due to our lack of first-hand accounts from sorcerers and the highly normative tone of the sources. As noticed by many historians, no extant ancient author claims for himself the title of "sorcerer" (*goes* or *magos* in Greek, *magus* in Latin). On the contrary, our sources are almost always accusing others of doing magic—a notable exception being Apuleius, who defended himself from an accusation, and Plato and Plotinus, who could discuss it in more neutral terms.[1] Accordingly, it might seem tautological to describe magic as a subversive category or as a category for the "other" since all we can get from our sources are accounts of other people's activities. Historians of antiquity have been toying with this idea quite a bit already, studying magic, as Richard Gordon said, "with everybody talking at once," meaning that what we can study is the multiple rhetorical uses of magic, not a hypothetical concept. This perspective has not yet been fully explored.[2] Although it produced very interesting sociopolitical analysis, it has the tendency to deny the existence of real sorcerers.[3] While our sources are extremely biased, and while we can assume that it was not to the advantage of anybody to portray himself as a sorcerer, I argue that such a category was still attractive to certain individuals. Since Augustine, magic in European culture has been used as a cultural marker which identifies its bearer as a marginal individual. In our sources, this has been used mostly as an accusation. Modern cases of identification with magic show that, in certain social contexts, this marker can be used by the bearer himself. Even though the Late Antique Greco-Roman culture might seem impossible to compare with our own, I believe that if we are comparing different uses of the category of "magic," the culture gap between us and Augustine is much smaller than between us and most of the ethnographical material coming from contemporary, but linguistically and culturally remote cultures. I propose thus to transpose modern examples to antiquity in an attempt to map out a sociological structure that made the identification with magic possible.

## MAGIC IN ANTIQUITY

Pliny stands as a pivotal source for the history of magic in the Roman world. He represents a state of magic theory which is midway between the late Republican conception and late imperial one, as detailed by Augustine. For Pliny, magic is found in two places, Rome's past and foreign practices. As such, Pliny stands as a predecessor to Augustine, who would take on these two characteristic and add a third sociolinguistic criterion to the theory of magic.

From Republican times to Pliny the Elder, the Latin term of *magia* became more polemical and more general. During the last centuries of the Republic, the context where the words *magus* and *magia* were used was unclear, and it is difficult to assess whether it refers to actual Persian priests and their ritual techniques or, more normatively, to a ritualistic attitude.[4] A century later, Pliny still historically derived the notion of magic from Persia but he also clearly enlarged the breadth of the concept, so much so that it now included the practices of Gauls, Britons, and even historical Romans.[5]

For Pliny, the practice of magic surrounded Rome. Magic spread from the Persians among the Gauls, most notably through the work of the druids. The Gauls, he glosses, call "their mages" druids—a clear indication of the level of abstraction the word now had acquired.[6] The Britons practice it as well, he says, and they are so good at it that they could almost have taught it to the Persians.[7] However, magic is practiced not only by the Britons and the Gauls, but by all the people of the world. He even associates it with Pythagoras, Empedocles, Democritus, and Plato and ridicules them for that reason.[8] Magic has spread across the whole universe and Romans could not be thanked enough to have stamped it out.[9] There is probably no clearer indication of the high degree of imprecision—and of corresponding applicability—the concept of magic had acquired by the time of Pliny.

In what would become a constant habit for later western scholars, Pliny interprets his own past as being replete with magical and superstitious practices. Indeed Pliny's interpretation of Rome's ancient practice of magic recalls Frazer's evolutionary and ethnocentric explanation of magic in the opening pages of the *Golden Bough*. Thus, at the time of Pliny in the first century C.E., magic became more abstract and more applicable to strange and unpleasant people, not only geographically but historically as well. In the old Roman code of the Twelve Tables, he finds two instances of magical practice. Moreover, he adduces as a proof that Romans used magic by referring to a *senatus consultum* (a decree of the senate) of 94 B.C.E. which interdicted the immolation of human beings, which is a clear indication for him that such "extraordinary rites" were accomplished at the time.[10]

In terms of efficacy, Pliny is quite clear that magic is bogus and produces no concrete results.[11] In terms of practice, Pliny is rather confusing. In book 30, the only book of his *Natural History* solely dedicated to magic, he defines it as a sort of parasitic art, "first born from medicine," which was then augmented by the "powers of religion" and finally "mixed with the divinatory arts."[12] We could be tempted to see magic for Pliny as a textual tradition which was handed down by the first Persian *magi*. In that sense, magic in antiquity would be a set of recipes found in books attributed to "real" Persian mages like Ostanes, Zarathoustra, and so forth. It could thus be argued that Pliny only considered magical what he read in books which he thought ultimately came from the Persian *magi*. Magic would thus be what he found in Persian doctrine and this would greatly simplify the task of understanding how Pliny separates magic from astrology, medicine, and religion. The argument is convincing principally because Pliny historically explains that magic mushroomed out of Persia. But even more persuasive is the fact that he does not call magic what we would assume would be interpreted as such at the time. For example, in a digression on the power of words, he speaks of curses (*defixiones*) and love potions as generally conceived as having power, but not specifically as magical devices.[13] On the contrary, he lists them with other traditional prayers used by Romans. Now, as much as it may seem strange from our modern perspective, the explicit association of magic (*magia*) with curses (*defixiones*) or love charms (*incantamenta amatoria, philtra*) is hard to find in Latin sources. Moreover, when classical authors such as the "new poets" (Tibullus, Catullus, Propertius), Cicero, or Virgil mention magic, it is always in reference to Persia.[14] Similarly, it is also surprising that Pliny writes about many activities which would be later on described as magic without making that claim.[15]

As Fritz Graf noted, however, Pliny's description of magic is revolutionary. While he does not represent the full extent of the later evolution of magic theory, Pliny stands on the cusp between the older ethnological definition and a later universal one. To understand Pliny as illustrating the future form which magic would take in Greco-Roman thought, it is important to note first that Pliny's most extensive treatments of magic are found in sections of his *Natural History* dedicated to medicine, and not in his geographical/ethnological book on Asia and Persia. More precisely, these discussions are included in books on cures derived from parts of the human body, "a subject replete with boundless difficulties at the very outset." These problems, it seems, come from the association that Pliny makes between magic and the use of body parts:

> Say, Osthanes, who was it that first devised these practices [cannibalism]; for it is thee that I accuse, thou uprooter of all human laws, thou inventor of these monstrosities; devised, no doubt, with the view that mankind might not forget thy name! Who was it that first thought of devouring each member of the human body? By what conjectural motives was he induced? What can possibly have been the origin of such a system of medicine as this? Who was it that thus made the very poisons less baneful than the antidotes prescribed for them? Granted that barbarous and outlandish tribes first devised such practices, must the men of Greece, too, adopt these as arts of their own?[16]

Pliny's explicit association of magic and cannibalism is key here in understanding his construction of a "universal magic." Eating human flesh has always been a representation of savageness in Greco-Roman texts, at least since Homer's story of the man-eating and milk-drinking Polyphemos, the Cyclops of the *Odyssey*. It is also frequently found in historic or geographic works describing extremely remote or extremely uncivilized nations.[17] Pliny associates magic and cannibalism first in book 28 only to repeat this theme so often that any cannibalistic act seems to have been part of a magical ritual.

Less than a century later, Apuleius would be accused of practicing *magia* on various grounds, which reorganize most of what Pliny described as *superstitiones* or *magia* under the new umbrella term of magic.[18] It is important to note, however, that Pliny is not particularly concerned about establishing a clear distinction between what belongs to the domain of magic and what belongs to proper "religion." This is a later concern. What Augustine would add to the debate is not only the sense that some practices, or *religiones*, are wrong, but that they constitute a polar opposite to the right *religiones*, thus introducing a radically new interpretation of religion, one which has been more or less the standard in European cultures since then. However, like Augustine three centuries later, Pliny understood magic historically. For both of them, magic in their culture was thought as a thing of the past. This similitude probably reflects a similar problem: finding, in a world where the traditional and the immutable rules, how to justify the respectability of a nation for which the historical record constantly reminds the reader that his own culture is evolving. In the hands of the Roman elite, theorizing about magic was one way of normalizing Roman culture. The expansion of the concept of magic which occurred around the turn of the millennium furnished to Romans like Pliny another tool to shape Roman identity. At the same time, similar things were happening with the concept of *superstition*.

## EVOLUTION OF THE TERMS

There is a current historical narrative that sees the Occident's pagan past as inherently tolerant of other religions. This, the narrative says, is mostly due to polytheism, which is inherently inclusive. This is particularly popular among Neopagans, who often subscribe—whether in the mode of professional historians or not—to the "Burning Time" narrative. In this reading of history, the late medieval and early modern witch hunts were aimed specifically at stamping out the last vestiges of paganism. As we will see later, this particular story opposes a magical and inclusive past to a modern and constrained present.[19] Following the same lines, can we explain the expansion of the category of magic by a corresponding growth of religious intolerance in antiquity? Or, should we rather say that the concept of religious toleration was alien to Romans, and that the expansion of the concepts of magic and superstition was rather a symptom of the change in elite self-representation—a new Roman identity which now fully assumed imperialism? Indeed, facing the radical patriotism of a man such as Pliny, who believed the whole world to be possessed by magic—with the exception of the Romans, of course—one wonders if the Romans were really as tolerant of other religions as is usually believed.

According to Denise Grodzynski, who studied the evolution of the term *superstitio* from the third century B.C.E. to the fifth century C.E., Romans under the Republic were not particularly tolerant, but they recognized foreign religious practices as such (*religiones*) and not as magic or superstition (*magia, superstitiones*).[20] For Peter Garnsey, too, Romans did not "tolerate" foreign gods. They assimilated, destroyed, or simply left them behind.[21] Understanding tolerance as the conscious acceptance of an otherwise disapproved moral, political, or religious attitude, Garnsey claims that the traditional concept of a tolerant Paganism is misguided. Instances of Roman "inclusion" or "toleration" of foreign cults can often look like aggressive religious tactics. For example, the appropriation of the Phrygian meteorite and the cult of the Magna Mater in Rome during their conflict with Carthage is strikingly similar to the practice of *evocatio*, in which Romans co-opted the particular deity of an enemy by offering an identical or superior cult.[22] Even if we can thus claim that *toleration* was not an option for Romans, we can still see that the concept of *superstitio* changed its meaning during the Empire. Under the Republic, authors like Cicero, Varro, and Livy used *religio* for other people's national cults as well as for their own cult. Cicero is very clear on this point when he says that "each nation has its religion and we have ours."[23] Even Livy, who never missed an opportunity to attack the adoption of foreign cults, used *religiones* to describe new cults introduced into the Roman pantheon.[24] These cults were not *superstitiones* by themselves but were adopted because of *superstitio*, that is, because of an excessive fear of the divine. Thus it seems that, while some *religio* were good and others were bad, the concept of *superstitio* was not yet a general term covering all disapproved *religio*.

I argue that this phenomenon was produced by a change in the way the elite related to the Roman Empire, rather than how they understood *superstitio*. By including foreign people in the Roman Empire, the unwanted religions which came with them were judged with the same severity as if they had been practiced in Rome. Strangers were perhaps far away and indeed strange, but their cults were now a Roman business. Grodzinsky claims that the change in attitude toward *superstitio* started with the younger Pliny's letters to the emperor Trajan concerning Christians. In this new paradigm, *religio* ceased to be used for other religious cults and *superstitio* became the standard category for alien rites.[25] It is also possible, however, that the term did not change its meaning but that it is rather the elite's identity which was modified by Roman imperialism. By expanding their notion of Roman identity, the Roman elites applied their religious category to the whole known world, now under the Roman Empire. We can already see in the *Natural History* of Pliny the Elder, that the definition of magic underwent a similar change. The fact that under the Empire, Romans did not recognize another religion as a *religio* but as a *superstitio* does not necessarily entail that the meaning of *superstitio* changed, but perhaps rather that Romans started applying these categories to other cultures now under the rule of Rome. In that sense, the expansion of the categories of magic and superstition does not show a growing intolerance but rather a fuller approval and understanding of Rome's empire and a further affirmation of its imperialism.[26] During the first three centuries of the Roman Empire, the concepts of magic and superstition followed the changes in the culture of the Roman elite. The category of magic was already an important social marker although it wasn't explicitly thought of in that way. It is only with Augustine that the culture-making characteristic of magic would be put clearly into light.

## AUGUSTINE

In the Latin world, reflections on magic did not change much until Augustine. In fact, our most extensive Latin source between Pliny and Augustine is Apuleius' *Apologia*, where the concept of magic was used quite vaguely. Pointing to the same expansion of the concept, the compilation of Gregorius, a legal scholar of the late third century C.E., shows that *malefici* (a term which was used synonymously with sorcerer) now got its own rubric called *de maleficis et Manichaeis*. The creation of a new legal rubric combining *malefici* and Manicheans probably shows that the association of magic with religious deviance was now well accepted and could be legitimized by legal terms.[27]

Although Pliny's theorization of magic is rather different than Augustine's, we can see how their motivations were remarkably similar. Pliny's discussion of magic revealed that magic followed the contours of Roman society—whether viewed according to nations (as in the case of Persians, Gauls, and Britons) or according to time (with Rome's own past). Augustine's own theory recast magic and religion in a sociological mold so influential that it is still commonly used today. Since the theory of Augustine's magic has been well covered elsewhere, I will only sum up these earlier arguments.

Robert Markus first pointed to the important implications of Augustine's sociolinguistic theory of magic. He observed that Augustine separated sorcery from sacraments by the radically different communities to which they catered.[28] Later on, Fritz Graf and then I argued that Augustine's involvement in this question was partly caused by the lack of a clearly demarcated line between miracles and magic tricks.[29] According to Augustine, while *magi* seem to do things that are similar to what saints do, they do it for a different end (*diverso fine*) and according to a different law (*diverso iure*).[30] In a remarkably systematic way, Augustine presented magic as a language, that is, as a convention which has no other power than to express ideas between individuals. Magic's "law" is based on "pacts of signs agreed with demons by contract."[31] Moreover, Augustine used a linguistic analogy to make clear that magical signs acted exactly like language, and that, as language, they had no power in and of themselves:

> *Bêta*, which has only one sound, is the name of a letter for the Greeks and the name of a vegetable for the Latins . . . . Thus all these signs are understood according to the convention of the society, and, as the conventions differ, they are understood differently. Men did not agree upon them because they already had a meaning but they received their meaning because they agreed on them.[32]

In the end, what truly defines magic is not a particular set of practices or a disputed notion of *superstitio*, but it is the self-centered person's intention to belong to a community of demons which manifests itself when he uses their language and their signs.[33] Augustine could also have used such crude language to talk about the sacraments but he preferred another way of putting the matter. He rather insisted on "Christian freedom," the fact that Christians are not following the signs themselves, as do pagans and Jews, but the meaning of the signs.[34] That is not to say that Augustine was not worried about orthodox cult. On the contrary, Augustine wrote a long treatise on baptism that radically forbade re-baptism, and accepted the baptism of heretical priests. In *On Baptism*, we can see the same linguistic and contractual theories at work, here explaining the working of a sacrament. As in magic, where demons create prodigies in response to private contracts (*privatos contractus*), Augustine understood that in the Church miracles were performed through its public law (*publicam iustitiam*).[35] Allegorizing the story of Jacob's sons, born of a handmaiden but nonetheless legitimate, he explained that it is the Church, "Christ's spouse," which empowers baptism through the practice of sacraments, and not the priests: "Therefore she herself bears them in her own womb and in the womb of her handmaids, by virtue of the same sacraments, as though by virtue of the seed of her husband."[36] Thus, as with the power of Jesus' name to exorcise, which has power whoever uses it, a baptism is still a baptism, even if given by impure persons.[37] The point, in Augustine's sacramental theology, is not that these rituals are effective in themselves; it is that they are the signs of an agreement with God, as the magical act is the sign of an agreement with demons. Miracles are thus divided in three groups—those done by magicians through private contracts with demons, those done by good Christians through public law, and those done by bad Christians through the *signs* of this law.[38] What constitutes orthodoxy, heresy, and magic is thus ultimately sociological for Augustine.[39]

Unlike Augustine, earlier Christian writers generally considered paganism as a simple superstition.[40] This was notably taken over by the remarkably vague law of 341 which interdicted *superstitio* and "the madness of sacrifices."[41] Being particularly powerful in the hands of imperial authorities, the ambiguity of *superstitio* was, however, problematic because anybody could be the target of such an accusation. In terms of ritual efficacy, nothing clearly separated "magical" practice from "Christian" practice, and nothing could then explain why exorcising with certain words was considered as magic but that exorcising with the name of Jesus was not.[42]

Augustine's rhetoric introduced a major change into early Christian apologetics. The Roman intellectual elite usually considered *superstitio* as powerless and futile.[43] Consequentially, *superstitio* could not be invoked in the case of contested "religious evidence," that is, in the case of extraordinary events which got so much attention from pagans and Christians that they could not be dismissed by any group. Merely considering pagan miracles as *superstitiones* could not explain their efficacy. We can hear an echo of these controversies in a passage of the *City of God* which explains how to refute pagans contesting the existence of Christian miracles.[44] Augustine's argument is that since many extraordinary things already happen everywhere in the world, why would one refuse to accept Christian miracles? For example, why would anybody refuse to believe that bodies could be consumed eternally in hell when, on earth, salamanders thrive in fire? Pagans, he says, could refute such claims by pointing to the pagan miracles described in the same books of marvels used to uphold the Christian position. These people, he says, "may add what has the appearance of argument and say 'If you believe such things as these, believe what is recorded in the same books, that there was or is a temple of Venus in which a candelabrum set in the open air holds a lamp, which burns so strongly that no storm or rain extinguishes it, and which is therefore called, like the stone mentioned above, the asbestos or inextinguishable lamp.'"[45] Astute polemists like Augustine and the pagan philosopher Porphyry of Tyre knew the importance of recognizing the other party's miracles and absorbed them in their own cosmology by explaining them on their own terms.[46]

A good example of this practice is Augustine's *On the divination of demons*. Summing up a discussion he had on the destruction of the famous temple of Serapis in Alexandria, he explained how pagan divination worked through the agency of demons, that is, that divination and magic are the same thing. Doing so, he also included the thoughts and doubts of the young Christians with whom he was speaking. Their chain of thought is very interesting because it shows that the logic of Christian history cannot reconcile the existence of the pagan past with the Christian present, where God had explicitly forbidden polytheism.[47] Augustine's interlocutors could not consider that official pagan rituals were being performed to this day, and thus understood them as "the things done in the night." That is to say that these Christians considered contemporary paganism as magic, not as an alien and autonomous religion. The first half of the *City of God* can be considered as a more sophisticated version of the same idea.

With the help of magic, Augustine made *thinking* about the existence of any other religion impossible. Moreover, his definition of magic also carried the Roman Empire's pagan past as well as its contemporary religious deviants into the *Christian* world of magic. Augustine's definition of magic is sociological—in the modern sense—because it explicitly ascribes the practice of magic to a particular community of persons, and not to a set of practices, a religion or a world-view.

## MODERN DESCRIPTIONS OF MAGIC

Looking at modern anthropological and historical work on magic, it is surprising to see that there is no scholar who really thinks outside of Augustine's theoretical framework. A hundred years ago, Tylor and Frazer developed theories which were basic elaborations of the historical definition of magic seen in Augustine, where magic is an old and bad practice.[48] For Mauss, magic was the manifestation of the antisocial: "it is, and we want it to be anti-religious."[49] Mauss's theory is also similar to Augustine's in that he does not want to look at particular practices but "the place that they occupy in the totality of social customs."[50] As we have seen, Augustine similarly described magic according to its place in society (that is, as antisocial contracts), and not according to its physical manifestation. Indeed, characterizing magic as, say, the use of words of power would have also meant attacking Christian practice itself. Also similar is the fact that, while presenting this theory, Mauss and Augustine clearly ascribe the practice of magic to alien—or alienated—populations. As with Augustine, Mauss chose a sociological explanation which made the assimilation of magic and religion possible—and problematic. At the end of his essay, Mauss saves religion from complete irrationality by proposing a parallel definition which opposes structured and metaphysical rituals (religion) to pragmatic and unstructured rituals (magic). No matter how

Mauss might have framed this dichotomy, by the very fact that he thinks there should be one, he follows Augustine's path. Mauss looked for specific instances of magic, and naturally found them. By using the binary category magic/religion, he pasted the Christian paradigm on foreign cultures only to "realize" that one fundamental aspect of their theology—the notion of *mana*—was magical. Moreover, the magical rites which he ascribes to the notion of *mana* are seen, as in *On the Divination of Demons*, as the immature stage of fully religious behavior.[51]

It is not my goal to debunk once again Mauss, Frazer, Tylor, or other important anthropological works. They have long been criticized for their ethnocentrism and most anthropologists now are aware that the category of magic is not exportable. What seems to be impossible to dispel, however, is the social dichotomy which was introduced in the concept, as we can see with Augustine. Closer to us, in *Purity and Danger*, Mary Douglas defined witchcraft as an "antisocial psychic power with which persons in relatively unstructured areas of society are credited."[52] Augustine's definition of magic doesn't seem to be going away, despite many modern attempts at dismissing it. Like Jonathan Z. Smith said, "Just say no" is not going to do the trick,[53] especially when studying the ancient Mediterranean world, where the use of magic—as a concept as well as an art—seems to flow seamlessly. Whoever goes on to search for "magic" will find it, because it is exactly what Augustine, Mauss, and everybody until now said—the symbol of the private, the antisocial, the unknown. In other words, there is nothing to debunk in what these ethnographers said about the ancient Mediterranean world because they—and we—are simply *using* the concept of magic and creating subcultures through its practice or its observation and theorization. Defining magic in Occidental history as such, it is tempting to deny the existence of *magi* and simply study the accusation of magic as a cultural process. Nothing rules out the possibility that no matter how vile the category of sorcerer could have been, some people might have desired to identify with it nonetheless. I suggest that contemporary practitioners of magic give us a case study for thinking about the sociological framework which would have created such individuals in antiquity.

## MODERN PRACTITIONERS OF MAGIC

Among modern magic-users, it seems that a consensus can be drawn from the way they relate with the rest of society. From the "occult terrorism" of anarchist Hakim Bey (a.k.a. Peter Lamborn Wilson), to the cosmos-worship of Neopagans, one can see a constant dissatisfaction with the current state of societies and politics. Moreover, this dissatisfaction is often accompanied with a radical distrust of revolution or any attempt at changing "the System."

One of Hakim Bey's favorite weapons against modern institutions is the "occult assault," that is, sending to TV execs and writers "objects as exquisite and disturbing as surrealist 'boxes,' containing beautiful but 'illegal' images of sexual pleasure, and intricate spiritual symbolism . . . made with real artistic fervor and the highest inspiration." Completely obsessed with the cursed objects, the victims should quit their jobs or else they would stay and "learn to fight against the Eye of Babylon from within the idol's belly," while their company is taken over by a group of "Shiite terrorist sorcerers," the "Libyan Voodoo Hit Squad, or something of the sort."[54] Other options include cursing the premises of the MUZAK Company, or the *New York Post* with the "Malay Black Djinn Curse."[55] One could even say that the practice of magic *is* the manifestation of his own alienation: "If Post-Modernism offers us the melancholic freedom to pick and browse the ruins of the Past and salvage whatever shards we may find amusing, why not dig up once again (surrealist archaeology) some of the shattered relics of resistance, revolt . . . even revolution? Can these antiques ever prove dangerous again? Can we evade or even oppose the Final Enclosure—and learn to create our own Outside?"[56]

Although Hakim Bey endorses a full frontal occult assault on various institutions, he is clearly against any form of martyrdom. And learning his lesson from his antique Christian revolutionary ancestors, he perhaps understood that martyrdom can also be a powerful tool for revolution. As with a certain representation of Neopaganism, Hakim Bey is not looking for revolution per se, but in living a life of revolt, living against a vision of society which is so powerful that the only frontal assault possible is the occult one.[57]

Hakim Bey is not the only one proposing a complete disenfranchisement from modern society coupled with the practice of freeform magic. Much less caustic than Hakim Bey, Wiccans and Neopagans in general can also be said to be creating their own "Outside." One could say that by the simple fact that they associate with real magic—an idea which mainstream culture finds amusing, but certainly not worthy of serious commitment—Wiccans already pull themselves out of society. Glen Shuck's analysis of the myth of the "Burning Times" also supports this idea. The "Burning Times" is a name given to the Wiccan reading of the early-modern witchcraft trials, which became a foundation myth for Wiccans.[58] Margaret Murray's 1921 book *The Witch Cult in Western Europe* is a key element of this narrative. Her theory is that the persecution of witches during the late medieval and early modern period was actually an attempt at destroying the last remnant of paganism.[59] This theory was then amplified by Gerald Gardner's *Witchcraft Today* (with an introduction by

Margaret Murray) which now stands for many as the foundational work of Wicca.[60] For Shuck, Wiccans keep the "Burning Times" in mind as a "narrative of resistance," which helps them live a life outside the occidental world order: "Call it patriarchy, bureaucracy, capitalism, or whichever label one prefers, it represents the forced assimilation of individuals into an economy that circumscribes meaningful dissent and individual difference."[61] This particular world-view generated moral criticism which only furthers the point that their position is radically at odds with normal society. As Hakim Bey was accused of indulging in narcissistic "lifestyle anarchism" by anarchist and activist Murray Bookchin,[62] Shuck also defends Neopaganism from similar attacks. Shuck refuses to see the "Burning Times" as a narrative of victimization, and he focuses his energies on illustrating how Neopagans strive to live in a "comfortable" state of rebellion rather than proposing a new world order. Far from being a problem, this lack of a clear social project is extremely important for Shuck who sees in Wicca's resistance to "reified social movements"—understood by critics as a narcissistic indifference to social ills—a commitment to the preservation of the difference between individuals and subcultures.[63]

My point is not to criticize these movements for their political position, but to show that these groups are marginalizing themselves. Criticisms such as Bookchin's "life-style anarchism" as well as Heath and Potter "extreme rebellion" only manifest this, from an external and moral point of view:

> Because the everyday acts of symbolic resistance that characterize countercultural rebellion are not actually disruptive to "the system," anyone who follows the logic of countercultural thinking through to its natural conclusion will find herself drawn into increasingly extreme forms of rebellion. The point at which the rebellion becomes disruptive generally coincides with the point at which it becomes genuinely antisocial. And then you're not so much being a rebel as you are simply being a nuisance.[64]

Hakim Bey, for his part, clearly favors the uprising—the *temporary autonomous zones*—over the revolution and adduces "Foucault, Baudrillard, et al." in supporting his decision to live a "revolution of everyday life."[65] How radical and subversive Hakim Bey's thought might seem, he is not alone and many other people more or less involved in art hold similar beliefs. For graphic novel artist Grant Morrison, becoming a magician is revolutionary in itself. But echoing his relativistic position regarding magic itself, he is very cautious about any sweeping generalization of "the System." As with Bey's "ontological anarchism," Morrison suggests we consider "the System" as the sorcerer's playground, not as his enemy.[66]

The same could be said of Genesis Breyer P-Orridge, who met William Burroughs and Brion Gysin and holds them as sorcerers, or "creative/cultural alchemists." Like P-Orridge, Burroughs and Gysin honored the words of Hassan-I-Sabah, the old man of the mountain: "nothing is true, everything is permitted." With such a relativistic world-view, it becomes clearer why P-Orridge holds magic—a sort of cultural engineering science—as an evolution of human life which would be "non-destructive and anathema to polarization" as well as central to "our survival with ethical honor." The art-magic of Genesis Breyer P-Orridge is effective only if one considers that the world is a mental construct. In that sense, the words of the infamous Hassan-I-Sabah make magic an essential art for anybody living in a world where the meaning of any history, of any memory, is up for grabs. Once again, the use of magic in modern life is coupled with a total rejection of external narratives, past and present.

This is exactly how the heroine of *1984* saw the world and lived a life of lip-service, although constantly profiting from the Party. What I am describing is a type of anarchism that partly or radically rejects the world order and which does not express itself outwardly by a will to reform but inwardly (if it does), in ways that are often described as "mystical" or "spiritual."

There seems to be a correlation between rebellion and magic—not necessarily because magic is a powerful tool, but rather because it is associated with the indefinite, the unstructured, and the unknown. Augustine came up with a theory of magic explaining the pagan past as well as its contemporary manifestations. By doing so, he was transporting practices and people out of a religious denomination and into a conceptual void, symbolized by magic. Similarly, Marcel Mauss understood magic as a world-view working solely through social categories and not experimental ones. That is, through social *distance*, the stranger an object is to society, the more magical power one should expect from it.[67] Even though it seems now that Mauss was explaining occidental religion rather than universal magic, the similar emphasis on social category and irrationality is very similar to Augustine's views. Far from saying that they were right, or that "magic" in itself should be given a general definition, I am suggesting that modern magical enthusiasts echo Augustine and Mauss' definition of magic by associating themselves with magic, which these two thinkers recognized as essentially antisocial. Ultimately, my interest is in history, and not social critique.[68] Considering that the current association of magic and antisocial sentiment indeed comes from late antiquity, could it be possible to find individuals in antiquity who, consciously or not, chose for themselves to follow the path of magic, as a fitting existence for their antisocial lifestyle? The collection of ancient ritual texts now known as the *Greek Magical Papyri* offers a good starting point. While these are traditionally thought of as representing the craft of Greco-Egyptian sorcerers, the manuscripts rarely mention magic itself (*goeteia*, *mageia*) and do not seem to imply that they are presenting "magical ritual," as being different from "religious rituals." The case, however, is not that simple. Many rituals are recipes for *defixiones* (curses) which not only look like magic to us but were also considered as such in antiquity. There is an instance where a papyri addresses its reader as an initiate (*ma[kari]e musta*) into *sacred* magic (*hiera mageia*).[69] Knowing that the practice of magic is not something which is openly spoken of, why would a scribe call his doctrine a sort of magic, even if it is "holy"? A comparison with modern association with magic, which is also often considered "holy," would force us to reconsider the idea that magic was completely relative. But, in keeping with the social dimension of the definition of magic, this comparison enables us to understand how certain individuals were attracted by its practice, and thus, by its social connotations.

## NOTES

1. Plato, *Symposium*, 202E; Plotinus, *Enneads*, 4.4.30–45. However, this doesn't stop them using the term in the usual accusatory way elsewhere in their works.

2. Two good examples of this kind of studies are Jens Braarvig, "Magic: Reconsidering the Grand Dichotomy," *in* D. R. Jordan, H. Montgomery, and E. Thomassen, eds., *The world of ancient magic: papers from the first International Samson Eitrem Seminar at the Norwegian Institute at Athens, 4–8 May 1997* (Athens: Norwegian Institute at Athens, 1999) 21–54; R. L. Gordon, "Imagining Greek and Roman Magic," in B. Ankarloo and S. Clark, eds., *Witchcraft and Magic in Europe: Ancient Greece and Rome*. The Athlone History of Witchcraft and Magic in Europe 2 (London: Athlone, 1999) 159–276.

3. See, for example, Naomi Janowitz, *Magic in the Roman World, Pagans, Jews and Christians* (Philadelphia: Routledge, 2001), and idem, *Icons of Power* (University Park: Pennsylvania State Press, 2002).

4. See F. Graf, *La magie dans l'Antiquité gréco-romaine* (Belles Lettres, 1994) 46–105. The original Persian high priests were known to the Greco-Roman world in part thanks to Herodotus. See Graf (1994) 60–61.

5. Other sources for the first century C.E. show signs of intolerance as well. This can explain how magic gradually became such a problem at the time of Pliny: expulsions of *mathematici* (astrologers) and *magi* (Tacitus, *Annals*, 2.32; Jerome, *Chronicle*, 28 av. J.-C.); accusations involving *magi* (Tacitus, *Annals*, 12.22; 12.59; 16.8; 16.30).

6. Pliny, 17.95: *Nihil habent Druidae — ita suos appellant magos — visco et arbore, in qua gignatur, si modo sit robur, sacratius*.

7. Ibid. 30.4.

8. Ibid. 30.2; 22.9; 24.99; 24.102.

9. Ibid. 30.4.

10. Ibid. 28.4–14 and 30.3. (*sacra prodigiosa*).

11. Ibid. 30.1 (*magicas uanitates; fraudulentissima artium*); 30.5 (*quae omnia aetate nostra princeps Nero uana falsaque comperit*). If one thing is clear about magic for Pliny, it is its deceitfulness. He repeatedly drives the point home showing that Nero had all the talent, the interest, and the leisure necessary to learn the magical arts but that he nonetheless abandoned it.

12. Ibid. 30.1.

13. Ibid. 28.4.19, curse (*Defigi quidem diris precationibus nemo non metuit*); love charms (*incantamentorum amatoria*).

14. Fritz Graf shows Pliny completely oblivious to curse magic, especially prominent in other sources of the same period (see Graf, 1994, p. 66). See Tacitus' striking description of the curse of Germanicus (*Annals*, 2.69): *reperiebantur solo ac parietibus erutae humanorum corporum reliquiae, carmina et devotiones et nomen Germanici plumbeis tabulis insculptum, semusti cineres ac tabo obliti aliaque malefica quis creditur animas numinibus infernis sacrari*. Note that the curses are glossed as *malefica* but not as *magia*.

15. Pliny, 28.3–5.

16. Ibid. 28.2.

17. Strabo, 4.5.4; 7.3.6–9; 11.2.1; Pomponius Mela, 3.36; 38; 59, Pliny, 4.80; 6.50–53.

18. Buying fish for a love-philter; praying to a skeleton-shaped statue; making a secret devotion to the *lararium* of a dead friend; using a beautiful boy as a medium; offering sacrifice of birds at night.

19. See Margaret Murray, *The Witch-Cult in Western Europe* (Oxford: Clarendon Press, 1921), which is often cited as the foundational work for this narrative. For a competing view, see Ronald Hutton, *The Triumph of the Moon* (Oxford: Oxford University Press, 1999). For a critique and a brief review of the controversy, see Richard Hutton, "Paganism and Polemic: The Debate over the Origin of Modern Pagan Witchcraft," *Folklore* 111.1 (2000) 103–117.

20. Denise Grodzynski, "Superstitio," *Revue des études anciennes* 76 (1974) 36–60.

21. Peter Garnsey, "Religious Toleration in Classical Antiquity," *in* W. Shiels, ed., *Persecution and Toleration*. Studies in Church History 21 (Oxford: Blackwell, 1984) 24–25.

22. For the introduction of the cult of Magna Mater, see Livy, 29.10, Dionysius of Halicarnassus, 2.19.15 (incidentally, Dionysius cites the introduction of *Magna Mater* in Rome as proof that Romans were suspicious of foreign rites and strictly regulated those which they accepted). For *evocatio*, see Pliny, 28.4.

23. *Pro Flacco*, 69. He also says in de *De legibus* (1.32; as well as *De divinatione* 2.148) that *superstitio* is an evil that is found in all nations.

24. 4.30.9; 25.1.6–12.

25. Denise Grodzynski, "Superstitio," *Revue des études anciennes* 76 (1974) 47.

26. On Roman "manifest destiny," see Cassius Dio 52.36.1–3. For other examples of the association of persecution or the creation of imaginary enemies/aliens with the centralization of power, see (among many others), M. Beard, J. North, and S. Price, *Religions of Rome* (Cambridge, UK: Cambridge University Press, 1998) 213; Michel Foucault, *Histoire de la folie à l'âge classique* (Paris: Gaillimard, 1972).

27. See James B. Rives, "Magic, Religion, and Law," in C. Ando and J. Rüpke, eds., *Religion and Law in Classical and Christian Rome*. Potsdamer Altertumswissenschaftliche Beiträge 15 (Stuttgart: Franz Steiner, 2006) 66.

28. Robert A. Markus, "Augustine on magic: A neglected semiotic theory," *Revue des Études Augustiennes* 40 (1994) 375–88.

29. Fritz Graf, "Augustine and Magic," *in* J. N. Bremmer and J. R. Veenstra, eds., *The Metamorphosis of Magic from Late Antiquity to the Early Modern Period* (Leuven: Peeters, 2002) 87–104; Olivier Dufault, "Magic and Religion in Augustine and Iamblichus" in E. Digeser and R. Frakes, eds., *Religious Identities in Late Antiquity* (Campbellville: Edgar Kent, 2006) 63–91.

30. Augustine, *De diversis quaestionibus 83*, 79.4.

31. Augustine, *De doctrina Christiana*, 2.20: *pacta quaedam significationum cum daemonibus placita atque foederata.*

32. Ibid. 2.24.

33. See Robert A. Markus, "Augustine on magic," *Revue des Études Augustiennes* 40 (1994) 381–84.

34. Augustine, *De doctrina Christiana*, 3.8–9.

35. Augustine, *De diversis quaestionibus 83*, 79.4.

36. Augustine, *De baptismo*, 1.10.14. See also 7.39.77, where Augustine explains how exorcism works with the same idea.

37. Ibid. 3.10.15.

38. Augustine, *De diversis quaestionibus 83*, 79.4: *magi per privatos contractus, boni christiani per publiciam iustitiam, mali christiani per signa publicae iustitiae.*

39. For a sociological interpretation of third-century baptism polemics, see J. Patout Burns, "On rebaptism: social organization in the third century church," *Journal of Early Christian Studies* 1 (1993) 367–403.

40. Tertullian, *Apology*, 24.2; Minicius Felix, *Octavius*, 24.10.

41. *Theodosian code*, 16.10.2.

42. See Augustine, *De diversis quaestionibus 83*, 79.4 and Luke, 9.49. On the same problem, see Origen, *Against Celsus*, 1.6.

43. Denise Grodzynski, "Superstitio," *Revue des études anciennes* 76 (1974) 41.

44. Augustine, *City of God*, 21.1–8.

45. Augustine, *City of God*, 21.6.

46. Porphyry copied down an oracle acknowledging the divinity of Jesus (in Augustine, *City of God*, 19.23), but disapproving of Christians worshipping him.

47. *On the Divination of Demons*, 5. See also, *City of God* (19.23.4), where Augustine adduced Moses' laws to support that (*Exodus* 22.20: "Those who sacrifice to the gods will be destroyed, unless they sacrifice solely to God").

48. See Murray and Rosalie Wax, "The Notion of Magic," *Current Anthropology* 4 (1963), 495–518.

49. Marcel Mauss, *Sociologie et anthropologie* (Paris: Presses Universitaires de France, 1950) 15 (from the *Année Sociologique*, 1902–1903).

50. Idib. p. 16.

51. Ibid. p. 134; 129.

52. Mary Douglas, *Purity and Danger* (Philadelphia: Routledge, 1966) 127.

53. Jonathan Z. Smith, "Trading Places," in M. Meyer and P. Mirecki, *Ancient Magic and Ritual Power* (Leiden: Brill, 2001) 27.

54. Hakim Bey, "Media Hex," in Richard Metzger, *The Book of Lies* (2003), p. 338.

55. Hakim Bey, *T.A.Z.* (Autonomedia, 2003) 57 (the editor "anti-copyrighted" the work and the full text is thus legally available on the Internet). For a political

critique of Hakim Bey's "art-sabotage" or "poetic terrorism" as "culture-jamming," see Joseph Heath and Andrew Potter, *Nation of Rebels* (New York: HarperCollins, 2004) Chap. 5.

56. Hakim Bey, *T.A.Z.*, p. xii.

57. For the establishment of a culture through the creation of victimhood narratives, cf. Elizabeth Castelli, *Martyrdom and Memory, Early Christian Culture Making* (New York: Columbia University Press, 2004). Although the early Christian obsession with martyrology seemed to have completely rejected the mundane world, it clearly succeeded in giving a narrative radically opposed to the Roman world, even though through that process it also finally reproduced the Roman order.

58. Glen Shuck, "The Myth of the Burning Times and the Politics of Resistance in Contemporary America," *Journal of Religion and Society* [http://purl.org/JRS] 2 (2000).

59. Cf. Richard Hutton, " Paganism and Polemic The Debate over the Origin of Modern Pagan Witchcraft," *Folklore* 111.1 (2000) 103–17.

60. It is a hotly debated subject whether witchcraft was reinvented (by Gardner, or others), or simply resurfaced in mainstream media. For the position which sees Wicca as a new religion, and mainly deriving from Gardner's work, see Hutton (1999); Aidan Kelly, *Crafting the Art of Magic* (Woodbury: Llewellyn Publications, 1991). In Gardner's own *Witchcraft Today* (New York: Citadel Press, 2004) he claims to have been initiated by a witch coven. This reprint of the 1954 work still has a blurb on Gardner in the inner cover page describing him as a *member of one of the ancient covens of the Witch Cult which still survive in England*).

61. Shuck (2000), par. 19.

62. Murray Bookchin, *Social Anarchism or Lifestyle Anarchism* (Oakland: AK Press, 1995) 19–28.

63. Shuck (2000), par. 8.

64. Heath and Potter, *Nation of Rebels*, 158.

65. Hakim Bey (2003), p. 126.

66. Grant Morrison, "Pop Magic!" in Richard Metzger (2003), p. 25.

67. Mauss (1950), p. 114.

68. As for the debate whether one should endorse a life-style of dissent or not, see Joseph Heath and Andrew Potter (2004); Murray Bookchin, *Social Anarchism or Lifestyle Anarchism* (Oakland: AK Press, 1995); Bronislaw Szerszynski and Emma Tomalin, "Enchantment and its uses: religion and spirituality in environmental direct action," in J. Purkis and J. Bowen, eds., *Changing Anarchism* (Manchester: Manchester University Press, 2004) 199–229.

69. H. D. Betz, "Magic and Mystery in the Greek Magical Papyri," in C. A. Faraone and D. Obbink, eds., *Magika Hiera* (Oxford: Oxford University Press, 1991) 248, with reference to "Papyri Graecae Magicae," 1.127.

# 2

# *Secundum Carnem:* History and Israel in the Theology of St. Augustine

Paula Fredriksen

## INTRODUCTION

In his classic study of history and society in the theology of Augustine, Robert Markus brilliantly laid out the threefold secularization of history, empire, and church that came to define Augustine's mature theology of the *saeculum*.[1] The Christian, argued Augustine, now lived in a world of ambiguity. The True Church was not the church of the perfect: rather, in the age before the End, it must abide as a *corpus permixtum*, containing both sinner and saint.[2] The empire, neither demonic before 312 nor holy thereafter, lacked any absolute religious significance.[3] And events in the present—be they positive (such as the free and universal proclamation of the Gospel) or negative (famine, earthquake, or the fall of Rome)—were eschatologically opaque: they could not be matched with scriptural prophecy to indicate anything of the divine plan.[4] However certain in their faith, Christians could never be certain of their circumstances. Their circumstances, therefore, could never be constitutive of their identities.

Augustine's theology of the *saeculum*, in brief, challenged traditional constructions of Christian identity. But prior to and coherent with this theology, sharing many of the same stimuli and sources, lay another of Augustine's daring revisions: that of his views on Israel *secundum carnem*, on the Law and its observances, on Jews and Judaism, that emerged in the late 390s in the course of his refutation of Manichaeism. Augustine, interestingly, could not go so far in "secularizing" the idea of Israel and the image of the Jew as he could the concepts of church, empire, and history. But his new perspective on historical Israel as God's Chosen, and current Israel as Christ's witness, complicated and thus enriched the church's identity as Israel *secundum spiritum*. In a world where ambiguity obscured the Ultimate, Israel remained history's polestar.

## DUALIST AND CATHOLIC ANTI-JUDAISM

Neither his own former Manichaeism nor the perspectives of Catholic tradition would have prepared the way for Augustine's theology of Israel. Their highly developed negative critique of the Old Testament and, correspondingly, their polarized reading of Paul, were two major weapons in the Manichees' anti-Catholic arsenal. It had accounted for some of their appeal for the young Augustine, who, repulsed by the low literary quality of Scripture, passed directly over to their camp.[5] "[They] deceived me with such questions as: Whence comes evil? And is God bounded by a bodily shape and has he hair and nails? And are those [patriarchs] to be esteemed righteous who had many wives at the same time and slew men and offered sacrifices of living animals?"[6] This destructive criticism was an effective missionary technique exercised in public debate.[7] Unversed in the techniques of interpretation, the unlearned remained susceptible to Manichaean criticisms of the Old Testament as absurd, arbitrary, repulsive.[8]

Many of these objections to the Jewish Scriptures were ancient, found initially in the pagan critique of the Hellenistic synagogue.[9] But Manichees could appeal to an impeccable Christian authority for their renunciation of Judaism and its Scriptures: the letters of Paul. The Apostle held a central place in Manichaean teaching, having expounded with unerring clarity the absolute distinction between good and evil, spirit and flesh, the Law and the Gospel, the inner and outer man.[10] Seemingly positive remarks about the Law and the prophets found in the Epistles, they maintained, could only be the result of later interpolations:[11] Paul's condemnation of circumcision, food laws, and other aspects of Jewish observance was unambiguous and uncompromising. Indeed, the Catholic insistence on retaining both testaments was not only perverse, it was inconsistent and hypocritical. What point holding on to the books of the Law while disregarding its precepts?[12]

Orthodox tradition had had centuries, by Augustine's time, to rehearse its response to this dualist reading of Paul with its concomitant rejection of the Old Testament: these arguments had been mounted systematically already in the mid-second century both by Marcion and by Valentinus and other gnostics. Interestingly, the responses of Orthodox antidualists—Justin, Tertullian, Origen—though in defense of the church's appropriation of Jewish Scriptures, themselves comprise arguments *adversus Iudaeos*.[13] Defending the Christian validity of the Old Testament, these authors deflected much of the dualist-Paulinist critique of the Creator God and his Law onto the Jewish people themselves.[14] What was "bad" in the Law—most often, specific observances: Sabbath, food laws, sacrifices, circumcision—was there because of what was "bad" in the Jews: a carnal mentality (which prevented them from understanding their own Scriptures correctly, that is, allegorically, and thus as revealing Christ) and hardness of heart.

Catholic tradition had resolved the tensions it brought on itself in retaining Jewish Scriptures while renouncing Judaism by reading the Jewish past as a history, largely, of failure—failure to understand, failure to perform. With a view toward Augustine's ultimate revision, I would like to attend here to five particular themes in this patristic reading: (1) God's intention in giving the Law, and (2) its status, especially (3) the commandment to circumcise; (4) the murder of Christ as the culminating act sealing the Jews' rejection; and (5) Jewish political desuetude as proof of this rejection.

The respective Jewish and Christian revelations, insisted Catholics against dualists, were not mutually exclusive but sequential. The Good God had given the (Jewish) Law, but he had always intended that Law to be temporary. "We do not think that there is one God for us, another for you," Justin—with Marcion and Valentinus doubtless in mind—informed his Jewish interlocutor Trypho; but "the Law promulgated on Horeb is now old, and belongs to you alone," and he cited Jeremiah 31:31 in support of his scheme.[15] The Law's observance, thus, is obviously not incumbent upon Christians: "There is now another covenant, and another law has come forth from Zion" (*Dial.* 24). Temporary, onerous, the old Law had been given to—inflicted, rather, on—the Jews alone. Why? "On account of your transgressions and the hardness of your hearts" (18).[16]

The perverse literal-mindedness with which the Jews insisted on observing these (punitive) mandates was nowhere more blatantly manifest than in their fixation on fleshly circumcision. Given to Abraham as a sign, it was intended by God to mark off the Jewish nation, to isolate it for its singular punishments as murderers of Christ.[17] Even after the coming of Christ, then, Jews failed to see this fundamental mistake: literal—which is to say, carnal—observance of the Law had never been God's goal. *True* circumcision was always of the foreskin of the heart (18, and frequently); *true* Sabbath, the Sabbath in Christ (12); *true* baptism, not the interminable Jewish immersions, but the baptism of Life (19). Interpretatively, spiritually, religiously—in every imaginable way—the Jews had missed the point. In their obdurate perverseness they declined to understand even the most public proclamation of divine censure for their error: the destruction of the Temple, and their banishment from Jerusalem (16). If they do not understand, the world does: Israel is not Jews, but the Church (123).[18]

## AUGUSTINE, ALLEGORY, AND THE BIBLE

In his *Confessions,* Augustine reports that his allegiance to Manichaeism had been troubled almost from the beginning. Even in Carthage, in the first flush of enthusiasm, he had recoiled from its elaborate mythology ("manducabam, non avide quidem")[19]; in Italy, its theory of Judaizing interpolations of New Testament texts struck him increasingly as unpersuasive and desperate.[20] But the force of their critique of the Old Testament and their powerful reading of Paul continued to hold him.[21] When his shift of allegiance came, it came through a new philosophical understanding of the nature of evil, and a new intellectual understanding of the necessity of spiritual hermeneutics. The one he owed to the *libri platonicorum;* the other, to Ambrose of Milan.

> And it was a joy to hear Ambrose, who often repeated to his congregation as if it were a rule he was most strongly urging upon them, the text: "the letter kills, but the spirit gives Life" (2 Cor 3:6). And he would go on to draw aside the veil of mystery and lay open the spiritual meaning of things which, taken literally, would have seemed to teach falsehood.[22]

In the writing campaign that followed this period in Milan and Cassiciacum, Augustine returned frequently to the benefits of allegory in combating Manichaean readings of Scripture. His "first ecclesiastical pamphlet," the *De Genesi contra Manichaeos,*[23] is a sustained application of those techniques of interpretation learned, at a distance, from Ambrose. In *De utilitate credendi,* written shortly thereafter, he lamented that such techniques were not more broadly known to the faithful: were they, much of the force of the Manichaean critique would be lost.[24] Yet, for all his self-conscious appreciation of allegory, Augustine evidently was not content to rest with it. Not long after the composition of the *De Genesi contra Manichaeos,* he abandoned that mode of exegesis and embarked on the first of his commentaries on Genesis *ad litteram* (393), in an effort to investigate "the great secrets of natural things . . . according to their historical character."[25] As with so many of his writings from this period, this project too remained unfinished. A great intellectual uncertainty settled upon Augustine in the 390s. What was the problem?

At the risk of simplifying a notoriously complex man, I would characterize the fundamental intellectual issue confounding Augustine as his uncertainty about how to read the Bible.[26] The highly philosophical vision of Christianity won in Milan had not sustained him back in Africa, where he was confronted, intimately and publicly, with the biblical culture of both his own church and its opponents.[27] Augustine's early priesthood marked out a six-year-long Jabbok, a time when he wrestled with the text of the Bible; with his post-Manichee, post-Milanese convictions about physical creation, divine justice, and human freedom, with his view of his own past. But if he limped through this period, he did not limp thereafter. The 390s end in a great burst of self-confident creativity with the staccato composition of this theological *novum*, the *Ad Simplicianum* (396), its autobiographical companion piece, the *Confessions* (397), and the massive refutation of Latin Manichaeism, the *Contra Faustum* (398).

Of all the various factors facilitating this spectacular conclusion to Augustine's intellectual paralysis, I would like to consider, briefly, one: his encounter with Tyconius.[28] In his *Liber regularum*, Tyconius had laid out principles of exegesis that were strikingly indifferent to and independent of the Alexandrian allegory represented by Ambrose. Tyconius sought, rather, to walk through "the immense forest of prophecy" by understanding Scripture not philosophically, hence allegorically, but typologically—hence historically.[29] In pursuit of his goal, he construed *all* of Scripture, New Testament and Old, as "the Law": *lex fidei demonstratrix*.[30] Disowning any sharp rupture between the two dispensations, insisting that the dynamics of law and faith, will and grace are constant across nations, times, and individuals, Tyconius disclosed in the Bible a continuous and consistent record of God's saving acts in history.

Augustine owed much to Tyconius: his strategies against millenarian interpretations of traditionally millenarian scriptures[31]; his view of the church as a *corpus permixtum;* his understanding of salvation as a process at once linear and interior that came of their mutual meditation on Romans.[32] The kernel of his threefold secularization was nourished by Tyconius's work.[33] More immediately, Tyconius's insistence on the redemptive value of the Law, and his persistently historical typologizing of Scripture, inspired Augustine to a renewed, exhaustive attack on the "Manichaean blasphemy": the thirty-three books of the *Contra Faustum*.[34]

## ISRAEL, THE LAW, AND THE JEWS

As we saw earlier, earlier Catholic writers had strongly linked their antiheretical and anti-Jewish polemic, despite—or, paradoxically, because of—the anti-Judaism of their dualist opponents. Augustine himself can certainly echo, on occasion, much of their sentiment. His *arguments*, however, are quite strikingly different, not least of all because of his interpretation *ad litteram* and the historicizing hermeneutics acquired, in part through Tyconius. To compare these two different Catholic responses to the theological challenge of Judaism, let us review Augustine on the five themes that we isolated previously in earlier patristic polemic.

Why had God given the Law? To lead to faith: the two stand on a single continuum of God's saving acts within both public and private history.[35] Providential, not punitive, the Law was indeed, as Paul himself had proclaimed in Romans 9:1–5, a benefit and a privilege (*C. Faust.* 12.3). While many of its precepts, "appropriate rather than good in themselves," were due to the proverbially stony Jewish heart (18.4), the status of the Law was perpetual and enduring, since it referred in its entirety, whether directly or indirectly, to Christ (12.7). This Christ—"not the Christ of their [the Manichees'] own making, but the Christ of the Hebrew prophets" (12.4)—had removed the veil obscuring the Law, but the Law itself remained. "The same Law that was given by Moses became grace and truth in Jesus Christ" (22.6). Thus "the Apostle himself, . . . speaking of the advantages of the Jews, mentions this as one, that they had the giving of the Law. If the Law had been bad, the Apostle would not have referred to it in praise of the Jews" (12.3).

But surely the Jews' literal-mindedness in observing the Law had never been as God intended: were they not condemned by the overwhelming evidence of their own carnal interpretations? Not at all, countered Augustine, on the contrary. "The Jews were right in practicing these things"—the sacrifices, the immersions, the times and seasons; the fault lay with their failure "to distinguish the time of the New Testament, when Christ came, from the time of the Old" (12.9). *God had not said one thing and meant another* (the first definition of *allos-agoreuein!*): literal observance was exactly what he had had in mind. By keeping to these observances, the entire people of Israel "was like a great prophet," foretelling Christ not only in word (that is, the Scriptures) but also in deed ("in his quae faciebant," 22.24). Their actions, apt and pious, conformed to their times.[36]

True of the Sabbath, true of immersions and sacrifices, and true most compellingly of fleshly circumcision itself. That very fact which the Manichees ridiculed and abhorred, the Apostle himself named the seal of the righteousness of faith (6.3). Augustine explodes with impatience at Manichaean squeamishness over God's sovereign decision to seal in the flesh of the circumcised penis his covenant of redemption with the children of Abraham:

> It is mere prurient absurdity to find fault with the sign of human regeneration appointed by that God, to whom all things are pure, to be put on the organ of human generation. . . . If you ask, as you often do, whether God could not find some other way of sealing the righteousness of the faith, the answer is, Why not this way, since all things are pure to the pure, much more to

> God?. . . As for you, you must try not to blush when you are asked whether your God had nothing better to do than to entangle part of his nature with these members that you revile so much. These are delicate subjects to speak of, on account of the penal corruption attending the propagation of man. They are things which call into exercise the modesty of the chaste, the passions of the impure, and the justice of God. (6.3)

The Manichaean aversion to fleshly circumcision had blinded them to the promise of redemption embodied and prefigured in and by that circumcision: the fleshly resurrection of Christ (6.3, 19.9). Had Jews understood the commandment to circumcise *secundum spiritum* and not *secundum carnem* (as Justin and others had criticized them for not doing), neither they nor the Law they were privileged to carry would have prefigured the fundamental mystery of Christianity itself: the revelation of God in the flesh, through Christ's Incarnation, and the redemption of humanity through his Resurrection. The fullness of the myriad Jewish observances—Sabbath, circumcision, sacrifices—were thus *sacramenta:* "[signa] cum ad res divinas pertinent."[37] Their being enacted in the flesh was precisely the point.

Thus in keeping the Law *secundum carnem,* the Jews had witnessed to divine truth. But with the coming of Christ, the mystery prefigured in the Law had been revealed: no one, Jews included, should any longer preserve the letter of the Law.[38] That the Jews should have continued to do so was, Augustine concluded, a great mystery. God had blinded them; and only God knew why. The sins on account of which they had merited this blindness were "hidden, . . . known only to God."[39] It could not, therefore, be the penalty for their most manifest role in killing Christ. But here, again, God brought it about that the Jewish insistence on the letter of the Law worked to providential ends. The Law sealed them with the mark of Cain: like Cain, they lived as fugitive fratricides, driven out from their native land but under the protection of God (12.12–13). And as long as they wrongly construe their heavenly mandate to keep the Law, they serve in perpetuity, till the end of the age, as witness to the Church:

> Those who do not receive these truths in their heart for their own good nonetheless carry in their hands, for our benefit, the writings in which these truths are contained. And the unbelief of the Jews increases rather than lessens the authority of these books, for this blindness is itself foretold. They testify to the truth by their not understanding it. (16.21)[40]

## JUDAISM AND CHRISTIAN IDENTITY

These grand theological themes, sounded with great authority in the *Contra Faustum,* will swell to a crescendo in books 15 to 18 in Augustine's mature masterwork, the *City of God*. In keeping with my opening remarks on secularization and identity, however, I would like to turn away from Augustine's Big Ideas to consider, briefly, one small application of them: his argument with Jerome over Galatians 2.

Augustine and Jerome had fallen out over the nature of the argument between Peter and Paul in Antioch (Gal 2:11–14). Jerome, in his commentary, had suggested that the apostles' quarrel had been a pretense enacted for the edification of the community; Augustine protested that this imputation of polite deceit to Scripture undermined its authority.[41] In 397, continuing in this line, Augustine added another challenge: What had been wrong, *in any case,* with these apostles, though Christian, keeping these commandments as Jews? Paul, he insisted, had kept the Law, though he did not hope in it for salvation. (Though once the Law had indeed been necessary for salvation, Augustine observed: the example of the Maccabean martyrs teaches this.[42]) Further, Paul had permitted other Jewish Christians to keep the Law, preserving their "ancestral traditions": why, then, would he have reprimanded Peter for so doing? The issue was, purely and simply, whether Gentiles should have to keep the Law. They did not. Thus Peter was truly corrected, and Paul truly reported the incident, which was to be understood as a straightforward account of an actual dispute.[43]

Responding several years later, Jerome does the rhetorical equivalent of hitting Augustine with everything but the kitchen sink:[44] Origen and other authorities supported Jerome (75.4); Augustine's interpretation virtually advocated Judaizing (75.5); Acts gives evidence that Peter already knew full well that the Law was overthrown (75.7–11); Augustine was claiming that fear of the Jews made Peter and Paul hypocrites vis-à-vis the Gospel, and that Paul was a Judaizer—on and on. And as for those Jews who challenged the aptness of Jerome's new translation of Jonah—"your Jews," as he calls them—clearly they either did not know Hebrew, or else they lied: no surprise, huffed Jerome, since it was well known that Jews willingly corrupted even the Hebrew text of Scripture just to spite Christians (75.19–22).[45]

Augustine responded to Jerome's bullying in *Ep.* 82 (ca. 405).[46] The calm confidence with which he restates his position gives the measure of the extent to which he viewed in historical perspective the Jewish attachment to Jewish law—not just Peter's and Paul's, but even that of Jesus himself. Paul had always and everywhere vigorously denied that Gentiles should observe the Law like the Jews: but Scripture abounds with examples where Paul himself, as a Christian and a Jew, kept the Law.[47] The first apostolic generation had been right to keep the Law, lest any Gentile Christian, not seeing its essential connection to Christ, think that the Law, like idols, was to be despised.[48] Jesus himself had received circumcision—not *fallaciter* by his parents, nor because, as an eight-day-old infant, he could not defend himself. He sent the cured leper to a priest "as Moses commanded" (cf. Mk 1:40–44); he himself worshiped at the Temple on the great Jewish feast days. Jesus, in brief, had lived full-heartedly as a Law-observant Jew.[49] As for the international Jewish conspiracy covertly altering Hebrew biblical texts in order to spite Jerome, Augustine politely concludes, "Would you be so kind as to point out what Jews ever did this?" (82.34).[50]

## CONCLUSION

Augustine was neither a philo-Semite nor a civil libertarian. Current Jewish religious practice repulsed him, and he condemned in strongest terms any Christian flirtation with the observances of the Law.[51] The privileged place in defining Christian community that he granted Israel *secundum carnem*—in interesting contrast to what he was prepared to grant to Manichees, Donatists, or Pelagians—arose out of the dynamics of his theology of history, and his specific battles in defense of the Old Testament against the Manichees. Real Jews had little to do with it.[52]

We cannot, as a consequence, know very much about contemporary Jewish communities or fourth- and fifth-century Jewish/Christian relations in North Africa on the basis of Augustine's writings about them. His references to "real" Jews are random and superficial; his interactions, where he mentions them, for the most part are strikingly neutral.[53] Again, compared with the legal pressure he was prepared to bring to bear on Christian opponents, his principled exemption of Jews from religious coercion might seem striking. It is and it is not. The Jews' protected status was deeply traditional, written for centuries into that extremely conservative social force, Roman law.[54] What was new was the theological spin he put on it.[55]

Augustine's theology of Judaism countered, in powerful and imaginative ways, the Manichaean arguments against Catholicism. It incidentally affirmed a new kind of Christian identity. By so embedding Jewish legal observance in history, Augustine in effect demythologized, and so secularized, its implications: carnal praxis was not a huge and enduringly indictable moral failing, but divinely mandated action appropriate to those earlier times. Further, by understanding this practice as incarnate prophetic enactment, Augustine domesticated it for Catholic doctrine, relating ancient Jewish observances to current Christian beliefs by way of conformation rather than contrast. His construction of Christian identity consequently neither generated nor required an image of the Jew as a religious antitype.

A certain mildness, accordingly, characterizes much of his discussion of Jews and Judaism. Some Jews may be moved by God to convert to Christ, but that is of no eschatological significance: the community as such will remain Jews till the close of the age (*C. Faust.* 12.12). The Church is the True Israel? Sure, says Augustine: but when people hear "Israel" they think, for good reason, "Jews." Leave the name, then, to them, and avoid confusing matters.[56]

The one place where the Jews retained their old pariah status, and where Augustine stands close to the older anti-Jewish tradition, is on the issue of Jewish political powerlessness. In his view, the consequences of the years 70 and 135 were absolute and eternal: the Jews, like Cain, can never go home again.[57] Perpetual political desuetude, a people forever without their land, is for Augustine both a quotidian reality and, uncharacteristically, an eschatological fact. This is the one glaring exception to his otherwise stalwart historical agnosticism: empires might come and go, ecclesiastical power wax and wane, but broken Jewish temporal power, tied as it was in the evangelical passion narratives and in christological readings of the classical prophets to the Jewish rejection of Christ, was, by theological necessity, set forever. His general secularization of these other political and social communities notwithstanding, then, Israel *secundum carnem* stood apart. The Jews as a people continued uniquely, even in postbiblical times, to express unambiguously the oracles of God.

## NOTES

1. R. A. Markus, *Saeculum: History and Society in the Theology of St. Augustine* (Cambridge, 1970). He summarizes these themes in chap. 6. The present chapter is a reprint of an essay by the same name in *The Limits of Ancient Christianity. Essays on Late Antique Though and Culture in Honor of R.A. Markus*, W. Klingshirn and M. Vessey, eds. (Ann Arbor: University of Michigan Press, 1999) 26–41; reprinted by permission of the University of Michigan Press.

2. On the eschatological ambiguity of the church in the world, Markus, *Saeculum*, 105–32.

3. Ibid., 45–104.

4. Ibid., 1–44.

5. *Confessiones (Conf.)* 3.5–6, ed. J. J. O'Donnell, *Augustine: Confessions*, vol. 1 (Oxford, 1992); cf. 5.10–11, where Augustine, though now dissatisfied with the Manichees, is still held by the force of their critique of Scripture.

6. *Conf.* 3.7.12, trans. F. J. Sheed, *The Confessions of St. Augustine* (New York, 1943).

7. "Nam bene nosti quod reprehendentes Manichaei catholicam fidem, et maxime Vetus Testamentum discerpentes et dilaniantes, commovent imperitos," *De utilitate credendi (De util. cred.)* 2.4 (*PL* 42, 67). The opportunity the Manichees offered the young Augustine to best unlearned Catholics in public debate was also no small part of their appeal, *De duabus animabus* 9.11 (*PL* 42, 102); see now R. Lim, *Public Disputation, Power, and Social Order in Late Antiquity* (Berkeley and Los Angeles, 1995), esp. 70–108.

8. On the fourfold sense of Scripture, known only to the erudite few, as an effective defense against this critique, *De util. cred.* 3.5 (*PL* 42, 68–69); absurdity of man in God's image (hence the jibe about God's beard and nails), e.g., *De Genesi contra Manichaeos* 1.17.27 (*PL* 34, 186); *Conf.* 3.7; cf. *Contra Faustum Manichaeum (C. Faust.)* 22.4 (*CSEL* 25.1, 593–94); arbitrariness (Why, all of a sudden, did God choose to create? what had he been doing beforehand?), *De Genesi contra Manichaeos* 1.2.3 (*PL* 34, 174–75); *Conf.* 11.10.12. For an overview of the Manichaean critique of Judaism, see P. Alfaric, *L'Évolution intellectuelle de saint Augustin* (Paris, 1918), 174–92; of their critique of the OT in particular, F. Decret, *Aspects du manichéisme dans l'Afrique romaine: Les controverses de Fortunatus, Faustus et Felix avec saint Augustin* (Paris, 1970), 123–49.

9. This polemic remains embedded in, e.g., Origen, *Contra Celsum (C. Celsum)*, trans. H. Chadwick (Cambridge, 1953).

10. On the authority of Paul for Mani, H. D. Betz, "Paul in the Mani Biography (Codex Manichaicus Coloniensis)," in *Codex Manichaicus Coloniensis: Atti del Simposio Internazionale...1984*, ed. L. Cirillo and A. Roselli (Cosenza, 1986), 215–34; J. Ries, "Saint Paul dans la formation de Mani," in *Le epistole paoline nei Manichei, i Donatisti e il primo Agostino*, ed. J. Ries et al. (Rome, 1989), 7–27; in western Manichaeism generally, F. Decret, "L'utilisation des épîtres de Paul chez les Manichéens d'Afrique," in *Le epistole paoline*, 29–83; Alfaric, *L'Évolution intellectuelle*, 207–8. On interpolations, Decret, *Aspects*, 174–76. On the view of Paul that Augustine would have held as a Manichee, C. P. Bammel, "Pauline Exegesis, Manichaeism, and Philosophy in the Early Augustine," in *Christian Faith and Greek Philosophy in Late Antiquity: Essays in Tribute to George Christopher Stead*, ed. L. R. Wickham and C. P. Bammel (Leiden, 1993), 1–25.

11. Cf. Faustus's qualified acknowledgment of Rom 1:3, on Christ's descent from David *secundum carnem*: "Verumtamen si eius est prior illa sententia [Rom 1:3], nunc emendata est [i.e., by 2 Cor 5:16]: sin fas non est Paulum inemendatum dixisse aliquid umquam, ipsius non est," *C. Faust.* 11.1 (*CSEL* 25.1, 314).

12. E.g., *C. Faust.* 32.

13. See esp. J. G. Gager, *The Origins of Anti-Semitism: Attitudes toward Judaism in Pagan and Christian Antiquity* (Oxford, 1983), 160–73.

14. See esp. D. Efroymsen, "The Patristic Connection," in *Antisemitism and the Foundations of Christianity*, ed. A. Davies (New York, 1979), 98–117: Efroymsen notes that the largest block of Tertullian's anti-Jewish material is found not in his treatise *Adversus Iudaeos*, but in his masterwork *Adversus Marcionem*, 100. On Christian anti-Judaism as Orthodoxy's response to Christian dualists, Gager, *Origins*, 160–73.

The *adversus Iudaeos* tradition itself, while obviously relevant to the line I am pursuing, cannot concern us directly here. The classic studies are A. L. Williams, *Adversus Judaeos: A Bird's-Eye View of Christian Apologiae until the Renaissance* (Cambridge, 1935); B. Blumenkranz, *Die Judenpredigt Augustins* (Paris, 1973; orig. pub. 1946); M. Simon, *Verus Israel* (Paris, 1948). In this continuing context of charged debate, with different groups of Christians contesting for the construction of Christianity, and Jews and Christians debating which community held true title to the Scriptures, and thus to the designation "Israel," we also find pagans (e.g., Celsus, Porphyry) engaged in active criticism of all groups: see Bammel's insightful discussion of the ways that African Manichaeism would have satisfied particular pagan theological objections to Christianity and to Judaism, "Pauline exegesis," 8–10.

15. *Dialogus cum Tryphone Iudaeo* 11, ed. G. Archambault, *Dialogue avec Tryphon*, 2 vols. (Paris, 1909); trans. based on M. Dods, *The Writings of Justin Martyr and Athenagoras*, vol. 2 of the *Ante-Nicene Christian Library*, ed. A. Roberts and J. Donaldson (Edinburgh, 1867), repr. in *ANF*, vol. 1.

16. Similarly, says Justin, God proscribed certain meats (20) and imposed the Sabbath "as a sign, on account of your unrighteousness and that of your fathers" (21); he mandated sacrifices "for the sins of your own nation and their idolatries" and permitted the building of the Temple "that you . . . might not worship idols" (22); the commands to observe the Sabbath, and other things were "on account of your hardness of heart" (27).

17. "For the circumcision according the flesh, which is from Abraham, was given for a sign; that you may be separated from other nations, and from us; and that you alone may suffer what you now justly suffer [Justin evidently intends the measures taken after the Bar Kochba revolt of 132–135 (1)]; and that your land may be desolate and your cities burned with fire; and that strangers may eat your fruit in your presence, and not one of you may go up to Jerusalem. For you are not recognized among the rest of men by any other mark than your fleshly circumcision. . . . Accordingly, these things have happened to you in fairness and justice, for you have slain that Just One and his prophets before him; and now you reject those who hope in him, and in him who sent him" (16). Justin further argues the wrong-headedness of fleshly circumcision in 19 (Adam and other men before Abraham were not circumcised) and in 23 (women cannot be circumcised, yet they can be made righteous; thus, circumcision is not necessary for righteousness).

18. My description synopsizes Justin's argument, much of which reappears in book 3 of Tertullian's *Adversus Marcionem*. Origen, in his concluding essay on biblical exegesis in the fourth book of the *Peri Archon*, likewise diagnosed the root reason for Jewish obduracy as the failure to understand the spiritual—which is to say, allegorical—sense of Scripture. Justin directed his dialogue against the Jews (represented by Trypho), but he aimed as well at Marcion and Valentinus (chap. 11, 35). Tertullian's anti-Marcionite text incorporated much of what had appeared earlier in his *Adversus Iudaeos*. In the background of Origen's *Peri Archon* stand Marcionites and Valentinian gnostics; of the *C. Celsum*, the pagan critique of Christianity: but specifically anti-*Jewish* arguments lay scattered throughout. Finally, many of the themes we can designate as ostensibly antidualist reappear in the first book of Cyprian's *Ad Quirinum (Testimoniorum libri)* against the Jews. Anti-heretical and anti-Jewish polemic—despite the strong anti-Judaism of these same heretics themselves—were strongly and closely linked.

19. *Conf.* 3.6.10.

20. *Conf.* 5.11; cf. *De util. cred.* 3.7 (*PL* 42, 69–70).

21. The intellectual struggle recorded throughout books 5 through 7 owes much to the forcefulness with which the Manichees had put the question of the issue of God's body as presented in the OT, e.g., 5.10.19: "They [the Manichees] had turned me against [your church]: and it seemed to me degrading to believe that you had the shape of our human flesh"; 6.4.5: "Thus I was ignorant how this im-

age of yours could be"; 7 passim, on God's implication in the problem of evil if he is indeed the Creator.

22. *Conf.* 6.4.6. P. Brown, *Augustine of Hippo: A Biography* (Berkeley and Los Angeles, 1967), 79–114, for a vivid review of Augustine's life in this period; P. Courcelle, *Recherches sur les Confessions de Saint Augustin* (Paris, 1950), 98–132, for a reconstruction of the chronology of those sermons of Ambrose that can be dated to Augustine's stay in Milan.

23. Brown's characterization, *Augustine of Hippo,* 134. Augustine began the commentary in Italy in 389, but completed it once back in Africa.

24. *De util. cred.* 2.4–4.10 (*PL* 42, 67–73).

25. "Secundum historicam proprietatem," *Retractationes* 1.18 (*CCSL* 57, 54).

26. There were other issues as well, of course, not least of them his being worn out. This period was prefaced by wrenching personal losses and drastic changes of circumstance: by 391, Augustine had lost his mother, his son, and his best friend, Nebridius, to death. Augustine himself had terminated his fifteen-year common-law marriage, abandoned his career, committed himself to celibacy and to Catholic Christianity, left Italy and its cosmopolitan Catholicism for a life of retirement in North Africa as a *servus dei,* and been suddenly inducted into the clergy at Hippo. (The *Confessions* [397] is, among many other things, his successful attempt to locate himself in his own life.)

His writing subsequently foundered: the early and mid-390s are littered with the fitful productions of a man with writer's block (J. J. O'Donnell's apt diagnosis: see his *Augustine: Confessions,* vol. 1, xlii–xliii). Besides abandoning the style of exegesis attempted in *De Genesi contra Manichaeos* (388/9) and his subsequent effort *ad litteram* (393/4), he left his commentary on Romans after completing only the first book (395). *De doctrina christiana,* begun in 396, was left until 428; the *De diversis quaestionibus* and the *Propositiones* on Romans were transcripts of small lectures given on various occasions.

27. His plunge into the study of Paul in particular was precipitated in no small part by his public debate with Fortunatus, who, defeat notwithstanding, certainly out-quoted Augustine vis-à-vis the NT and esp. the epistles, e.g., *Contra Fortunatum Manichaeum* 3, 7, 17, 19, 20, 21 (*PL* 42, 114, 115, 120, 121, 122, 124). See P. Fredriksen, "*Excaecati Occulta Justitia Dei:* Augustine on Jews and Judaism," *Journal of Early Christian Studies* 3 (1995): 299–324, at 302–4, for an analysis of this debate.

28. We can securely date Augustine's reading of Tyconius's *Liber regularum* to 397, when he enthusiastically endorsed the work in correspondence with Aurelius of Carthage (*Ep.* 41.2 [*CSEL* 34.2, 83]). I have argued, on the basis of similarities in Tyconius's and Augustine's reading of Paul, that Augustine had already read the *Liber* during his earlier cycle of work on Romans in 394. See P. Fredriksen, "Beyond the Body/Soul Dichotomy: Augustine on Paul against the Manichees and the Pelagians," *Recherches Augustiniennes* 23 (1988): 87–114, at 99–101.

29. The text of Burkitt's scientific edition (Cambridge, 1894) is now reprinted with facing English translation by W. S. Babcock, *Tyconius: The Book of Rules,* Society of Biblical Literature Texts and Translations (Atlanta, 1989). For the "prophetiae immensam silvam," *Rules,* prol. (ed. Babcock, 2).

30. Rule 3, "de promissis et lege" (ed. Babcock, 32); see also the editor's observation, 33 n. 6: The goal of the Law is the salvation of Israel, it is the means by which Israel is driven to faith.

31. See P. Fredriksen, "Apocalypse and Redemption in Early Christianity: From John of Patmos to Augustine of Hippo," *Vigiliae Christianae* 45 (1991): 151–83, and nn. 40–54 reviewing earlier literature on this topic.

32. Fredriksen, "Body/Soul," 99–101.

33. Recognized—exceptionally—by Markus, *Saeculum*, 56; also 115. On the otherwise all-but-universal misreading of Tyconius as an apocalyptic thinker despite his being a source for Augustine's own antiapocalyptic thought, see P. Fredriksen, "Tyconius and the End of the World," *Revue des Études Augustiniennes* 28 (1982): 59–75.

34. Ed. *PL* 42, 207–518, and *CSEL* 25.1, 249–797; trans. based on R. Stothert, *Writings in Connection with the Manichaean Heresy*, vol. 5 of *The Works of Aurelius Augustinus*, ed. M. Dods (Edinburgh, 1872).

35. Augustine articulated this conviction through his schematization of history and individual development into four stages: *ante legem, sub lege, sub gratia,* and *in pace*—the characteristic teaching of his notes on Romans, the *Propositiones*.

36. See Gerald Bonner's brief but excellent discussion of the consequences of Augustine's new sense of history and historical process for his anti-Manichaean critique, *St. Augustine of Hippo: Life and Controversies*, rev. ed. (Norwich, 1986), 218–24: "this conception . . . is Augustine's great argument against Manichaean attacks on Old Testament morality and must be accounted one of his major discoveries," 222. Cf. *Conf.* 3.7.12–13, on understanding the observance of the Law historically, "though the Law itself is the same always and everywhere."

37. *Ep.* 138.7 (*CSEL* 44, 131); of the Law and its ordinances, e.g., *C. Faust.* 19.13, 16; *Adnotationes in Iob* 30 (*CSEL* 28.2, 572–76); *Enarrationes in Psalmos* 73.2 (*CCSL* 39, 1005–7); 74.12 (*CCSL* 39, 1033–34); *Ep.* 102.2, 12 (*CSEL* 34.2, 545–46, 554–55); *Contra Iulianum opus imperfectum* 1.124 (*CSEL* 85.1, 137–38).

38. A frequently sounded theme, e.g. *C. Faust.* 6.2, where Augustine comments that literal observance (in this instance, circumcision) was nonetheless "certainly suited to past time." On those who currently Judaize, be they Jew or Gentile, *Ep.* 82.18 (*CSEL* 34.2, 369–70).

39. "ex aliis occultis peccatis Deo cognitis, venire iustam poenam huius caecitatis . . . et [Jeremias] ostendit occulti eorum meriti fuisse ut non cognoscerent," *C. Faust.* 13.11.

40. On the origins of Augustine's idea of Jews as a witness people, see Fredriksen, "*Excaecati*."

41. *Ep.* 28.3–5 (*CSEL* 34.1, 107–12), ca. 394/95.

42. *Ep.* 40.6 (*CSEL* 34.2, 75–77).

43. "Otherwise, the Holy Scripture, which has been given to preserve the faith of generations to come, would be wholly undermined and thrown into doubt, if the validity of lying were once admitted," *Ep.* 40.5 (*CSEL* 34.2, 75), trans. based on W. Parsons, *Saint Augustine: Letters*, vol. 1 (New York, 1951). The Jewish *malum* that Paul renounced was not the Law, but the belief that the Law was necessary for Gentiles (40.6). For a recently edited sermon preached at this time on this same theme, see F. Dolbeau, "Sermons inédits de saint Augustin prêchés en 397 (2e série)," *Revue Bénédictine* 102 (1992): 52–63; for a review of the entire correspon-

dence on Galatians, with interesting observations on its relevance to the Donatist controversy, R. S. Cole-Turner, "Anti-heretical Issues and the Debate over Galatians 2:11–14 in the Letters of St. Augustine to St. Jerome," *Augustinian Studies* 11 (1980): 155–65.

44. Aug., *Ep.* 75 (*CSEL* 34.2, 280–324) = Jerome, *Ep.* 112 (*CSEL* 55, 367–93).

45. Cf. *Ep.* 71.3.5 (*CSEL* 34.2, 253), on the near riot that broke out at a service when the bishop of Oea introduced Jerome's new translation of Jonah.

46. *CSEL* 34.2, 351–87.

47. He adduces Acts 16:3, circumcising Timothy (who was half-Jewish); Acts 18:18, Paul's Nazirite vow at Cenchrae; Acts 21:18–26, Paul's offering of blood sacrifices at the Temple in Jerusalem. I note here that Augustine is a much more tough-minded student of the historical Paul than the vast majority of his modern counterparts in New Testament studies, who continue to insist that, in becoming a follower of Jesus, Paul had renounced the works of the Law. Two recent wrong readings, to quote Gal 2:7, H. D. Boyarin, *A Radical Jew: Paul and the Politics of Identity* (Berkeley and Los Angeles, 1993), and N. T. Wright, *Climax of the Covenant: Christ and the Law in Pauline Theology* (Minneapolis, 1992).

48. A powerful passage, *Ep.* 82.9–15.

49. Another powerful passage, *Ep.* 82.19. Augustine was unaware that the Jesus Seminar would later settle by vote that such passages are Judaizing interpolations; but he was familiar with the argument.

50. He had persistently dismissed Manichaean fantasy on this score; cf. his later remarks, *De civitate Dei* 15.11 (*CCSL* 48, 467–68).

51. In this letter in particular, *Ep.* 82.18.

52. For the full argument, Fredriksen, "*Excaecati,*" esp. 320–24.

53. E.g., inquiring after the meaning of a Hebrew word in the Gospels, *De sermone domini in monte* 1.9.23 (*PL* 34, 1240–41); settling a legal dispute between a Jew and an episcopal colleague, *Ep.* 8* (*CSEL* 88, 41–42). See Blumenkranz, *Judenpredigt*, 59–68.

54. See esp. A. Linder, *The Jews in Roman Imperial Legislation* (Detroit, 1987); more discursively, J. Juster, *Les Juifs dans l'Empire Romain*, 2 vols. (Paris, 1914).

55. *C. Faust.* 12–13.

56. *Ep.* 196.8–11 (*CSEL* 57, 221–25).

57. *C. Faust.* 12.12; more dramatic, and with specific reference to the Jewish War in 70, *De civitate Dei* 18.46 (*CCSL* 48, 644).

On 1 May 1897, responding to the impending meeting of the First Zionist Congress, the Jesuit paper *Civiltà Cattolica* observed that, "according to the Sacred Scriptures, the Jewish people must always live dispersed and wandering among the other nations, so that they may render witness to Christ not only by the Scriptures . . . but by their very existence. As for a rebuilt Jerusalem, which could become the center of a reconstituted state of Israel, we must add that this is contrary to the prediction of Christ Himself"—the argument is pure Augustine. Quotation from S. I. Minerbi, *The Vatican and Zionism: Conflict in the Holy Land, 1895–1925*, trans. A. Schwarz (Oxford, 1990), 96.

# 3

# Unwitting Witnesses: Jews and Judaism in the Thought of Augustine

Franklin T. Harkins

## INTRODUCTION

Augustine of Hippo is most commonly known by modern students of Christian history for various aspects of his thought that determined the subsequent theological tradition in significant ways—for example, his powerful and pointed critique of human pride in the *Confessions*, his anti-Manichean understanding of being as good and evil as nothing, his anti-Pelagian emphasis on the necessity of grace for human salvation, and his fundamental formulations of the doctrines of original sin and predestination. Among such profound and perduring contributions to Christian thought and life stands Augustine's generally less well-known teaching on Jews and Judaism. To the extent that students and even scholars of Augustine study his ideas on the Jews, they tend to do so piecemeal and tangentially, considering them merely as a function of some other aspect of his thought such as his theology of history or theory of biblical reading.

This essay aims to serve both student and scholar by moving this significant yet relatively understudied aspect of Augustine's thought from the periphery to the center. We seek to accomplish this by providing a detailed analysis of Augustine's mature doctrine on the Jews against the twofold contextual backdrop of: (1) the preceding tradition of Christian thinking about Jews and Judaism; and (2) the interreligious world of late-antique

North Africa in which Augustine's teaching developed. Toward this end, in the first section we offer an overview of Christian anti-Jewish thought from the late-first through the early-fifth century. By briefly considering such early Christian texts as the Gospels of Matthew and John, *The Epistle of Barnabas*, Melito of Sardis' *On the Passover*, and John Chrysostom's *Discourses against Judaizing Christians*, we seek to establish the fundamental themes of the tradition that Augustine would receive and the polemical extremes of this tradition that he would reject. Having established this historical and theological background, the second section provides a detailed consideration of what is commonly known as Augustine's doctrine of Jewish witness. By offering a close reading of several of the bishop's later writings that reveal his thought on Jews and Judaism, we seek to present a fuller and more coherent account of the mature doctrine of Jewish witness than Augustinian scholarship has heretofore provided.

The crux of Augustine's teaching is that the Jews, having been exiled and scattered throughout the world, serve as unwitting witnesses to the truth of Christianity by preserving and carrying about their sacred legal and prophetic books. Although the Jews themselves do not read and understand their scriptures rightly, the ubiquitous presence of these texts provides important testimony in the face of pagan detractors that Christians have not forged the prophecies concerning Christ. In the third and final part of this essay we seek to further elucidate Augustine's teaching on Jews and Judaism by rooting it firmly in the interreligious context in which the bishop lived and worked. Here we offer archeological, epigraphic, and textual evidence for the presence of thriving Jewish communities in late-antique North Africa with which Christians interacted and even competed. The references Augustine makes in his sermons to actual Jews shed additional light on significant aspects of the bishop's mature doctrine of Jewish witness.

## EARLY CHRISTIAN TEACHING ON JEWS AND JUDAISM

From its earliest beginnings, Christianity has sought to define and understand itself in relationship to the Judaism out of which it arose. As early as the late first century, for example, the writer of the Gospel of Matthew aimed to teach Jewish Christians in Antioch that the Good News of Jesus Christ was not a negation of their Jewish heritage but rather the authentic fulfillment of it. From the opening genealogy to the formula quotations to the final commissioning of the disciples, the evangelist presents Jesus as the fulfillment of Israel's history and prophetic scriptures, on the one hand, and an authoritative teacher of these selfsame scriptures who will be present in and with the church until the end of the age, on the other.[1]

The anti-Pharisaism, supersessionism, and deicide charge that will come to characterize Christian thinking about Jews and Judaism are found for the first time here in Matthew. Matthew's Jesus variously describes and critiques the Pharisees, rival claimants to the heritage of Judaism, as: "a brood of vipers" (3:7–10); overly legalistic (9:10–13; 15:12–14); hypocrites (ch. 23); blind, deaf, dumb, and obdurate (13:10–17); and murderers of God's servants and his very Son (21:33–45). The evangelist's denunciation of his Jewish rivals reaches a crescendo in the Passion Narrative (chs. 26–27), where (27:25) "the people as a whole," in response to Pilate's refusal to condemn Christ to death, answer "His blood be on us and on our children!"[2] This statement and the words with which Christ concludes the parable of the wicked tenants, namely, "Therefore, I tell you, the kingdom of God will be taken away from you and given to a people that produces the fruits of the kingdom" (21:43), were generally read by early Christian exegetes as teaching that the Jews, by virtue of their rejection and crucifixion of the Lord, had been stripped of their special status as the people of God and replaced by the church.

In several significant ways the Gospel of John serves to advance and heighten the anti-Jewish polemic found in Matthew. Written at the turn of the first century, John recounts a kind of religious divorce between the followers of Jesus and the adherents of Pharisaic Judaism in which the former were "put out of the synagogue" for confessing Jesus as Israel's long-awaited Messiah (7:13; 9:22; 12:42; 15:18–22; 16:2–4; 19:38). The Gospel of John may be read as the *Magna Charta* for the centuries-long conflict between the church and synagogue.[3] The fourth Gospel's reputation as the most anti-Jewish of the canonical narratives is largely attributable to the evangelist's antagonistic posture toward "the Jews" (*hoi ioudaioi*), a descriptor he uses some seventy times. Whereas John's phrase "the Jews" variously refers to the people of Judea, the synagogue leadership, the chief priests, scribes, and Pharisees, the overall impression it may make on the reader (and did, in fact, make on most early Christian interpreters) is that all Jews without distinction opposed Jesus and continue to oppose his followers.[4]

A high Christology marks the fourth Gospel and shapes the relationship between the Johannine Jesus and the Johannine community, on the one hand, and "the Jews," on the other.[5] According to the prologue (1:1–18), Jesus is the eternal and life-giving divine *Logos* who became incarnate in order to enlighten all people. He is also "the Lamb of God who takes away the sin of the world" (1:29, 35–37). Unlike the synoptic gospels, John has Jesus crucified on the day of preparation for the Passover (19:14, 31) at noon, the exact time at which the sacrificial lambs were slaughtered in the temple. Thus, John's Jesus is not only the very Wisdom of God who enlightens all who receive his words, but also the true Lamb of God who enlivens all who believe in him (3:16). And yet Jesus' own people failed to accept him. Those who did receive and believe in Christ, by contrast, became "children of God" (1:11–12). Whereas the Law was given through Moses, "grace and truth came through Jesus Christ" (1:17).

At several points in John's narrative, Jesus criticizes the Jews and their leaders for their lack of spiritual understanding and faith. For example, after explaining to the puzzled Pharisee Nicodemus (who literally comes to Jesus in the darkness of night) that one must be born anew of water and the Spirit in order to enter the kingdom of God, Jesus declares (3:10), "Are you a teacher of Israel, and yet you do not understand these things?" Jesus goes on to affirm that those like Nicodemus who have not believed in him loved darkness rather than light "because their deeds were evil" and are "condemned already" (1:11–21). Subsequently, Jesus teaches that the Jews who have not believed in him seek to kill him because they have neither understood nor accepted his word (8:37–59). Rather than being children of God or of Abraham, "[y]ou are from your father the devil, and you choose to do your father's desires," John's Jesus polemically proclaims (8:44). The stark contrast between the faithful followers of Christ and the perfidious Jews continues until Jesus' passion and death, on which John's Jews insist "because he has claimed to be the Son of God" (19:7). As we will soon see, based on this Johannine portrait of the Jews and their synagogue as the demonic enemies of Christ and his church, early Christian thinkers such as John Chrysostom developed a more virulent strain of anti-Judaism than that found in Augustine.[6]

In the second century, several of the anti-Jewish themes propounded in the Gospels of Matthew and John were adopted and adapted in *The Epistle of Barnabas* and Melito of Sardis' *On the Passover*, both of which served to shape Christian exegesis and anti-Judaism in the patristic period. Although of unknown authorship, *The Epistle of Barnabas* was first attributed by Clement of Alexandria (c.150–215) to Barnabas, the apostle and missionary companion of St. Paul. This early attribution of apostolic authorship (hence, authority) likely explains the presence of *Barnabas* in Codex Sinaiticus, a fourth-century manuscript containing the canonical scriptures.[7] That *Barnabas*, dated to the period 70–150, was found as a part of this codex of scriptural texts strongly suggests the work's important status and wide use in the early church. Furthermore, the fundamental concern of *Barnabas* elucidates why and how the epistle may have been used in early Christianity.

In the midst of an unspecified crisis, the author of *Barnabas* exhorts his Christian readers to a careful study of divine scriptures and aims to impart knowledge (*gnosis*) concerning how these scriptures are to be properly read and understood.[8] He finds himself writing in "evil days," likely a reference to the bitter and incessant struggle in the late first and early second century between the followers of Jesus and their Jewish counterparts over Israel's inheritance and potential Gentile proselytes.[9] The sacred scriptures of Judaism and their meaning were at the heart of this conflict. As such, the author of *Barnabas* seeks to demonstrate that the Law and the Prophets of the Hebrew canon are, in fact, Christian scriptures whose real meaning is that spiritual one revealed and fulfilled in Christ. Simply stated, the Jewish scriptures must be read allegorically. Therefore, according to *Barnabas*, to the extent that the Jews have understood their own scriptures literally and carnally, they have misunderstood them. Citing several prophetic texts, *Barnabas* maintains that God has "swept away" the outward and physical offerings and oblations demanded by the Law, replacing them with commands that inculcate inward and spiritual sacrifices.[10] The author of *Barnabas* uses the scriptures of the Jews against the very Jewish readers he seeks to counter. In so doing, he sets a precedent that Augustine will follow in developing his own teaching on Jews and Judaism.

In his allegorical and typological rereading of various passages of Hebrew scripture, the author of *Barnabas* mounts a scathing critique of the Jews as a people who have been divinely rejected by virtue of their rejection of the divinely given Law. At Sinai Moses broke the tablets of stone (representing God's unique covenant with the Israelites), he maintains, because the Jews departed from the Law of God in favor of idols. "[T]hat Covenant of theirs was smashed to pieces, so that the seal of the Covenant of Jesus the Beloved might be stamped on our own hearts, together with the hope that accompanies faith in Him."[11] The Jews have not only rejected God's Law explicitly through idolatry, however, according to *Barnabas*. Their rejection of the divine ordinances manifests itself simply in their unwillingness or inability to hear or read them rightly (i.e., allegorically or typologically). Having explained the scapegoat and heifer as types of Christ and his salvific crucifixion, the writer of *Barnabas* concludes: "To ourselves [as Christian readers] it is plain enough that these were the true reasons for doing things in this way; but to them it was all dark, because their ears were deaf to the voice of the Lord."[12] According to *Barnabas*, whereas the God-forsaken Jews are spiritually blind and deaf, the Lord has circumcised the hearts and ears of His new people "so that we might hear His word and believe."[13]

In allegory, then, *The Epistle of Barnabas* provided the apostolic church with the hermeneutical key for unlocking the true meaning of the scriptural witness. The spiritual reading exemplified in *Barnabas*, with its attendant anti-Jewish implications, shaped the exegetical imagination and theological practice of subsequent Christian thinkers, from Melito of Sardis (d. c.190) to Origen of Alexandria (c.185–c.254) to Augustine.[14]

Melito of Sardis' homily *On the Passover* (*Peri Pascha*), dated to 167–68, typifies early Christian spiritual, particularly typological, interpretation. Here Melito provides a rhetorically powerful reading of the Jewish Passover (Exodus 12) as a type or prefiguration of Christ and his sacrifice. He argues that the literal Passover lamb of the Old Testament was but a preliminary model or sketch of the real Passover lamb spoken of in the New Testament. Just as with a building project, when the reality or antitype arrives, the model or type is destroyed because it is no longer useful.[15] This hermeneutic of Old Testament type replaced by New Testament antitype determines Melito's understanding of the relationship not only between Law and Gospel, but also between Jews and Christians. He proclaims:

> So the type was honorable prior to the truth's coming, and the figure was astonishing prior to its interpretation. That is, the people was honorable before the church arose, and the Law was astonishing before the gospel was brought to light. But when the church arose and the gospel stood forward, the type became an empty thing because it had handed its power over to the truth, and the Law was fulfilled because it had handed its power over to the gospel. . . . [T]he Law was fulfilled when the gospel had been brought to light, and the people was made an empty thing when the church had been raised up.[16]

Melito's supersessionist notion of changing "mysteries" and changing peoples with the changes in time throughout salvation history is a theme that Augustine will develop in his *Tractatus adversus Iudaeos*. Melito's *On the Passover* also stands as a significant signpost on the road to Augustine because it testifies to increasing rivalry between actual Jews and Christians beginning in the second century, and, as a consequence, to the increasing ferocity of Christian anti-Jewish polemic. Archaeological and documentary evidence suggests that the Jewish community in second-century Sardis was well-established, substantial (constituting about ten percent of the population), and influential.[17] Thriving, the Jews likely posed a threat to Bishop Melito's relatively small, fledgling Christian community.

In the face of the more prosperous religion, Melito seeks, in *On the Passover*, to encourage his Christian hearers by defining and strengthening their own collective identity over against Judaism.[18] He does this most clearly and powerfully by contrasting "us" (Christians, presumably), for whom the true Passover lamb was sacrificed, with "you" (Israel and her descendants), whom Melito boldly blames for sacrificing the salvific victim.[19] By means of a series of striking contrasts, Melito calls Israel to task for rejecting and killing the Lord: "Why, O Israel, did you do this new misdeed? You dishonored the one who honored you. You have held in low esteem the one who esteemed you. You have denied the one who confessed you. You have renounced the one who publicly called out your name. You have done to death the one who gave you life. What have you done, O Israel?"[20] Melito continues in vivid detail to recount precisely what Israel has done:

> On the eve of the Lord's sacrifice you prepared sharp nails and false witnesses and bonds and scourges and sour wine and gall and a sword and calamity, as though for a murderous robber. When you had laid scourges to his body and thorns on his head, you bound his good hands, which had formed you out of earth, and fed with gall that good mouth which had fed you with life, and you did your Lord to death on the great feast. . . . O wicked Israel, why did you carry out this fresh deed of injustice, bringing new sufferings upon your Lord—your master, your creator, your maker . . . ?[21]

Grappling with the unfathomable injustice of God's chosen people having chosen to destroy God, Melito brings his caustic critique to a climax: "He who hung the earth in place is hanged. He who fixed the heavens in place is fixed in place. He who made all things fast is made fast on the tree. The Master is insulted. God is murdered. . . . O unheard of murder, O unheard of injustice!"[22] With these words, Melito for the first time explicitly introduces the deicide charge into the burgeoning tradition of Christian anti-Jewish teaching. It is not simply Jesus the man, nor even Jesus the Messiah whom the Jews rejected and killed; rather, it is God Himself, the very source of all life.

Early Christian anti-Judaism arrived at its polemical peak approximately two hundred years later in the homilies of the "golden-mouthed" preacher of Antioch, John Chrysostom (c.347–407). As in second-century Sardis, the synagogue in fourth-century Antioch threatened the faith and practice of Chrysostom's Christian flock. Unlike Melito's Sardis, however, Christians constituted a majority of the Antiochene population in Chrysostom's day. Thus, it was not the sheer size or influence of Jewish community that posed the principal threat to Christianity in fourth-century Antioch. Rather, it was the common tendency toward religious syncretism and Judaizing among Christians themselves.[23] Apparently no small number of Chrysostom's congregants observed Jewish law, attended synagogue, participated in Jewish feasts, sought cures from rabbis, and swore oaths before the Jewish tribunal in the synagogue.[24] It was against these Christian Judaizers that Chrysostom, beginning in August 386, preached a series of homilies traditionally entitled *Against the Jews* (*Kata Ioudaiōn; Adversus Iudaeos*), but more aptly named *Discourses against Judaizing Christians*.[25]

In his *Discourses*, Chrysostom combines several of the stock images of early Christian anti-Judaism (e.g., Jewish carnality, blindness, obduracy; deicide; divine rejection and replacement by the church) with novel and more scathing accusations to produce what has been described as "the most vituperative and vindictive attack on the Jews from Christian antiquity."[26] Reminiscent of Melito's *On the Passover*, Chrysostom calls the Jews "pitiable and miserable" because, after having received so many blessings from heaven, they rejected the very source of these gifts, Christ himself.[27] They are a stiff-necked people who refused to take up the easy yoke of Christ. Instead, like "brute animals," the carnal Jews ate and drank so much that they became obstinate, failing to accept Christ's yoke or pull the plow of his teaching.[28] In response, Chrysostom elevates anti-Jewish polemic to an unprecedented height (or nadir, more properly) when he explains that the sub-human Jews ought to be murdered: "Although such beasts are unfit for work, they are fit for killing. And this is what happened to the Jews: while they were making themselves unfit for work [through gluttony and drunkenness], they grew fit for slaughter. This is why Christ said: 'But as for these my enemies, who did not want me to be king over them, bring them here and slay them' [Lk 19:27]."[29]

Chrysostom also rails against those Christians who are "sick with the Judaizing disease."[30] Struggling to understand why followers of Christ would share customs and practices with those who killed him, Chrysostom declares: "Consider, then, with whom they are sharing their fasts. It is with those who shouted: 'Crucify him, Crucify him' [Lk 23:21], with those who said: 'His blood be upon us and upon our children' [Mt 27:25]. . . . Is it not strange that those who worship the Crucified keep common festival with those who crucified him? Is it not a sign of folly and the worst madness?"[31] These words make clear that Chrysostom, like most ancient and medieval Christian exegetes, understands the statement of blood-guilt in Mt 27:25 as evidence that all Jews of all times and places, not simply certain ones in first-century Jerusalem, are responsible for killing Christ.

This is but one reason for the Antiochene preacher's hatred of the synagogue, which he also understands as a demonic den. "For, tell me," Chrysostom asks rhetorically, "is not the dwelling place of demons a place of impiety . . . ? Here the slayers of Christ gather together, here the cross is driven out, here God is blasphemed, here the Father is ignored, here the Son is outraged, here the grace of the Spirit is rejected. Does not greater harm come from this place since the Jews themselves are demons?"[32] In response to those Judaizing Christians who imagine that the synagogue is a holy place because it is where the holy books of the Law and the Prophets are housed, Chrysostom turns the tables and names this as the primary cause of his loathing the synagogue. He proclaims: "Will any place where these books are be a holy place? By no means! This is the reason above all others why I hate the synagogue and abhor it. They have the prophets but do not believe them; they read the sacred writings but reject their witness—and this is a mark of men guilty of the greatest outrage."[33] He offers the analogy of seeing a venerable man dragged off into a tavern or den of thieves where he is abused and violated. Surely one would not hold the tavern in high esteem, Chrysostom argues, simply because the illustrious man is inside. Rather, precisely because the noble man is mistreated in this place, the place itself would and should be detested.[34] So, too, should Christians hate the synagogue because the Jews brought the books of Moses and the prophets, esteemed men, inside and dishonored them by denying that they speak of Christ and his advent.[35] "[W]e must hate both them and their synagogue all the more because of their offensive treatment of those holy men," Chrysostom caustically concludes.[36]

Whereas Augustine concurs with Chrysostom (and Melito and *Barnabas* before him) that the Jews failed correctly to read (and therefore honor) their sacred texts, the bishop of Hippo diverges rather sharply from the vile and potentially destructive conclusions Chrysostom draws. Indeed, as we will see in the following section, central to Augustine's considerably less virulent doctrine is the claim that Jews, qua Jews, play a necessary role in Christendom and, as such, must be preserved and protected. This example illustrates the way in which the foregoing outline of early Christian thought on Jews and Judaism intends to serve as a backdrop against which we might more clearly see the particular contours of Augustine's teaching. Let us now turn to Augustine, careful to note the ways in which he draws on and departs from the preceding tradition.

## AUGUSTINE'S DOCTRINE OF JEWISH WITNESS

Augustine's original and lasting contribution to the Christian understanding of Jews and Judaism is what is commonly known as his doctrine of Jewish witness.[37] There is no single place in his corpus where Augustine sets forth his teaching in all of its particulars. Rather, as we will see, fleshing out his doctrine on the Jews requires combing through a number of his writings and combining the various elements to reconstruct a coherent whole. Jeremy Cohen has begun much of this meticulous research and reconstruction by enumerating six component parts of Augustine's mature doctrine of Jewish witness, namely: (1) Jewish survival in exile represents their punishment for rejecting Jesus Christ; (2) Jewish blindness and disbelief fulfill biblical prophecy and confirm the truth of Christianity; (3) Although Jews do not read their sacred books rightly, that they carry them about serves as testimony that Christians have not forged the prophecies concerning Christ; (4) That Jews continue to observe the Law and practice Judaism under Roman rule also serves as testimony for the truth of Christianity; (5) Psalm 59:11 (Vulg. 58:12), "Slay them not," is a prophetic policy-statement affirming that Christians must allow Jews to live as Jews, albeit in a dispersed and subjugated state; and (6) Although Christian missionizing among the Jews is not urgent (as Jewish conversion will occur in due course), nevertheless Judaism must be refuted in the effort to vindicate Christianity.[38]

Cohen notes that whereas the first three elements make their initial appearance in works dated to the end of the fourth century (e.g., *Contra Faustum*, 397; *De consensus evangelistarum*, c. 400), Augustine does not provide the fullest formulations of his doctrine until the second decade of the fifth century in such works as *Ennarationes in Psalmos* (Ps 58 dated to 413–15), *Epistula* 149 (c. 415), *De civitate Dei* (414–25), *De fide rerum invisibilium* (420–25), and *Tractatus adversus Iudaeos* (429–30).[39] The following pages seek to provide a detailed treatment of Augustine's mature doctrine of Jewish witness as gleaned particularly from these later writings.

One of Augustine's earliest partial formulations of the doctrine of Jewish witness appears in his *Exposition on Psalm* 56, dated to the period 395–408. Here Augustine understands the words of Ps 56:4, *Dedit in opprobrium conculcantes me* ("Those who trampled on me he has consigned to disgrace") as a reference to the punishment that God has meted out to the Jewish people for killing Christ.[40] The Jews "trampled on me," says Augustine's Christ, and as a consequence God has "consigned [them] to disgrace." Augustine elaborates:

> The Jews raged against Christ, and persecuted him in their pride—but where? In the city of Jerusalem. In the stronghold of that kingdom about which they were so conceited, there they raised their arrogant heads against him. But after the Lord's passion they were uprooted, and they lost the kingdom where they had refused to acknowledge Christ as king. Consider how completely they have been consigned to disgrace: they have been scattered throughout all nations, with no stability anywhere, and nowhere any secure home.[41]

*Saeuierunt Iudaei in Christum, superbierunt in Christum.* It is noteworthy that Augustine begins his teaching on the Jews here—with a violent image of their prideful raging against Christ. Pride (*superbia*), which Augustine understands as the original and archetypal sin, lay at the heart of the Jews' violation of Christ and their subsequent divine punishment.[42] In their pride, the Jews rejected Jesus as their messiah, their king. In their blindness, they did not know that he was God (*Deum non intellexerunt*).[43] On account of these grave sins of spiritual blindness, infidelity, and deicide, the Jews have been expelled by the Romans from Jerusalem and their holy land. In *De civitate Dei*, Augustine explains:

> But the Jews who killed him and refused to believe in him, to believe that he had to die and rise again, suffered a more wretched devastation at the hands

of the Romans and were utterly uprooted from their kingdom, where they had already been under the dominion of foreigners. They were dispersed all over the world—for indeed there is no part of the earth where they are not to be found.[44]

Augustine understands Jewish survival, in a dispersed and subjugated state within Christendom, as evidence of divine rejection of the Jews, on the one hand, and acceptance of Christians, on the other. Furthermore, both God's repudiation of the Jews on account of their spiritual blindness and His replacement of them with a more faithful people fulfill scriptural prophecies, Augustine believes. In *De fide rerum invisibilium,* for example, he maintains that the very authors of Hebrew scripture foretold that the Jewish people would not understand the prophecies of Christ, and that God would punish them for their ignorance.[45] Augustine writes:

> However, because of those others [i.e., unbelieving Jews], whom for more hidden reasons he [i.e., God] would abandon, he had foretold long before, through the prophet, *For food they offered me gall and gave me vinegar to drink. May their table become a trap for them, an occasion of vengeance and a stumbling-block. May their eyes grow dim so that they are unable to see, may their back be always bent* [Ps. 68:22–24].[46]

For the bishop of Hippo, scriptures such as this serve as convincing evidence of Christian supersessionism. Ironically, those whose poor spiritual eyesight prevents them from seeing Christ as the fulfillment of their own prophetic texts are condemned to even greater blindness, thereby themselves becoming the fulfillment of certain prophecies. Meanwhile, those with clear eyesight, precisely by virtue of their visual acuity, bring other prophecies to fulfillment—namely, those pertaining to the growth of the church.[47]

The conspicuous growth of the Catholic Church as a counterpoint to divine rejection of the Jews is at the heart of Augustine's purpose and principal argument in *De fide rerum invisibilium.* Here Augustine seeks to answer strict empiricists who despise Christianity because it requires one to have faith in things that cannot be seen.[48] His detractors wish to know whether there are any visible proofs for the realities proposed by the Christian religion. Are there empirical reasons that might bolster Christian faith? Does Christianity have credibility? The one sensible datum in support of Christian belief that Augustine offers is the growth of the church throughout the world, which the bishop understands as a fulfillment of Old Testament prophecies. To his skeptical opponents, Augustine writes:

> The Church herself addresses you with words of maternal love: 'I, whose ongoing fruitfulness and growth throughout the whole world you admire, once

did not exist as you see me now, but *in your offspring all the nations will be blessed* (Gen 22:18). By conferring a blessing on Abraham, God was at the same time promising me; in consequence of the blessing given to Christ, I am spread through all the nations. The sequence of generations testifies that Christ is the seed of Abraham. . . . And look: you see and are amazed at the fact that all nations are blessed in Christ, that is, in the seed of Abraham, and still you are afraid to believe in Christ'[49]

The expansion and existence of the church throughout the world represents a visible fulfillment of the divine promise to Abraham and his descendants. Augustine makes clear here that on the historical timeline between the patriarchal promises and the visible church of the early fifth century stands Jesus Christ, himself the fulfillment of Old Testament prophecy. And although Augustine's readers could not personally see Christ in his earthly life and the ways he fulfilled the scriptures, they certainly can see the universal church as a realization of God's promises. It is this sight of present fulfillment of scripture, Augustine proposes, that should encourage the reader to believe unseen things of the Christian religion that represent past fulfillments of prophecy (e.g., that a virgin conceived and bore a son [Is. 7:14]).[50]

In understanding scriptural prophecies as foretelling Christ and the church, Augustine shows himself a faithful heir to *Barnabas* and Melito. Like his early Christian predecessors, the late-antique North African bishop believes that the spiritually deft reader, in contrast to the blind Jewish one, will see the Old Testament as a Christian collection of books and interpret them as such. The particular relationship of the Jews to their own books is an integral component of Augustine's doctrine of Jewish witness and will be considered in greater detail below. What is important for our present purposes is Augustine's emphasis on the church as visible verification of both the reliability of scriptural prophecies and God's replacement of a faithless people with a faithful one. For Augustine, the *ecclesia* stands as evidence that the kingdom of God has, in fact, been taken away from the barren Jews and given to the more fruitful Christians, as Christ himself promised (Mt 21:43).

The theme of Jewish repudiation and Christian replacement as a fulfillment of scripture guides Augustine's reflections in the *Tractatus Adversus Iudaeos* (429–30). Much like Chrysostom's *Discourses on Judaizing Christians*, Augustine's *Adversus Iudaeos* is a sermon whose threefold purpose is, in order of importance, to instruct Christians, to combat Judaizing practices, and to offer a polemic against Jews and Judaism.[51] The primary scriptural text on which Augustine intends to comment in his sermon is St. Paul's consideration in Romans 11 of the "mystery" of God's rejection of part of Israel in order that the Gentiles might enter into salvation. Augustine opens *Adversus Iudaeos* by glossing the Apostle's words, "Note then the kindness and the severity of God: severity toward those who have fallen, but God's kindness toward you, provided you continue in his kindness; otherwise you will be cut off" (11:22). Our glossator writes: "Assuredly he said this about the Jews who, as branches of that olive tree which was fruitful in its root of the holy patriarchs, have been broken off on account of their unbelief, so that, because of the faith of the Gentiles, the wild olive was grafted on and shared in the richness of the true olive tree after the natural branches had been cut off."[52]

Throughout the *Adversus Iudaeos*, Augustine follows St. Paul (11:17–18) in enjoining his Christian hearers to receive God's kindness humbly, not boasting over the branches that have been broken off. *Superbia* does not befit those whom God has chosen. Quite to the contrary, Augustine explicitly states that it was the "unbelieving pride" (*infidelis superbia*) of the native branches that was broken off in order that the "faithful humility" (*fidelis humilitas*) of the wild olive might be engrafted.[53] The Jews fail to recognize themselves in St. Paul's words, Augustine notes, citing this as yet another manifestation of the blindness that prevents them from reading sacred writings rightly. The bishop explains:

> When these scriptural words are quoted to the Jews, they scorn the Gospel and the Apostle; they do not listen to what we say because they do not understand what they read. Certainly, if they understood what the prophet, whom they read, is foretelling: 'I have given you to be the light of the Gentiles, that you may be salvation even to the farthest part of the earth' [Is 49:6] they would not be so blind and so sick as not to recognize in Jesus Christ both light and salvation.[54]

The Jews have been rejected and replaced because of their faithless inability to see Christ as the fulfillment of their own scriptures.

Not only can the Jews not see Christ in their scriptures, however. Augustine also affirms that they cannot see themselves there. Jews reading their scriptures are like blind people looking into a mirror—whereas they cannot recognize themselves, others can see them reflected in the sacred writings.[55] The Jews wish to find themselves in the positive scriptural references to God's holy and faithful people. Yet their faithless rejection of Christ means that they themselves have become the fulfillment of altogether different scriptural texts, according to Augustine, a clear-sighted Christian. He declares:

> When you [Jews] hear: "Come and let us go up to the mountain of the Lord, and to the house of the God of Jacob" [Is 2:3] say: "We are the house of Jacob," so that like blind men you may dash against the mountain, and with your face badly bruised you smash your head the worse. If you sincerely

> want to say: "We are they" [the house of Jacob], say it when you hear: "for the wickedness of my people was he led to death" [Is 53:8]. This is said about Christ whom you, in your parents, led to death [*vos in parentibus vestris duxistis ad mortem*]. . . . In these and other prophetic words of this kind say: "We are they." Without any doubt you are, but you are so blind that you say you are what you are not, and do not recognize yourselves for what you really are.[56]

Although Augustine does not here explicitly invoke the people's proclamation of blood-guilt in Matthew's Gospel (27:25), we can certainly imagine it in his mind as he penned the words "vos in parentibus vestris duxistis ad mortem." The Jews of Augustine's time (and, presumably, of all times) are guilty of killing Christ by virtue of their parents, whom the bishop understands as actually having committed the crime. The Jews of fifth-century Roman North Africa are, according to Augustine, just as blind, faithless, and wicked (and therefore fulfill prophecies such as Isaiah 53:8 just as well) as those of first-century Palestine. We will offer a more detailed consideration of actual Jews in Augustine's North Africa and in his sermons in the following section of this essay.

Augustine again affirms that Jewish infidelity simultaneously fulfills biblical predictions and promotes Christianity in his *Letter* 149, written to Paulinus of Nola circa 415.[57] Paulinus had written to Augustine (*Letter* 121) seeking clarification on the interpretation of various difficult passages of scripture. One such passage about which Paulinus seems to have been particularly troubled was St. Paul's words concerning the Jews in Romans 11:28, "As regards the gospel they are enemies of God for your sake; but as regards election they are beloved, for the sake of their ancestors." What could the Apostle possibly mean, Paulinus apparently asked, in affirming that the Jews are both enemies of God and beloved?

Paulinus' query provides Augustine the opportunity to reflect on the "inscrutabilia iudicia et inuestigabiles uiae" (Rom 11:33) of God's predestinating and providential will.[58] Although they do not understand why God rejects some people, believers should not doubt God's wisdom in this action. God did not make the reprobate evil, though He foreknew that they would become evil. Augustine explains: "For his plan is too deeply hidden by which he makes good use even of the evil for the betterment of the good [*etiam malis bene utitur ad prouectum bonorum*], revealing the marvels of the omnipotence of his goodness even in this. For just as it is a mark of their wickedness to make bad use of his good works, so it is a mark of his wisdom to make good use of their bad works." [59] In Augustine's view, humans in general have made bad use of the free will with which God benevolently created them. Specifically, their changeable wills have turned away from the unchangeable God in favor of inferior changeable creatures.[60] Jewish blindness to Christ and deicide are functions and particular manifestation of this general human misuse of free will. However, as with other sins, God makes good use of these evils *ad prouectum bonorum*, for the advancement of the good. In his comments on St. Paul's words, "As regards the gospel they are enemies of God for your sake," Augustine explains: "The price of our redemption is, of course, the blood of Christ who certainly could be killed only by enemies. This exemplifies that use of the evil for the betterment of the good [*usus malorum in prouectum bonorum*]."[61]

Augustine concludes his answer to Paulinus' question by briefly considering why St. Paul says that the Jews, in addition to being the enemies of Christ, are also divinely beloved (Rom 11:28). The Apostle's text makes clear that they are beloved on account of their ancestors, which statement Augustine reads as a reference to the patriarchal promises that, he believes, have been fulfilled in Christ.[62] Furthermore, Augustine notes, St. Paul earlier affirms that blindness has been produced only "in a part of Israel" (Rom 11:25). "He said, *in a part*, because not all were blinded; after all, there were some from them who came to know Christ [*qui Christum cognouerunt*]," Augustine avers.[63] It is this part of the Jewish people who recognized Christ as the fulfillment of their prophecies that St. Paul calls *dilecti propter patres*. Those who have not recognized Christ, on the other hand, continue to live as Jews—and God uses them, as Jews, in certain specific ways for the advancement of the good.

The most important role that Jews, qua Jews, play in God's plan for the promotion of the good is that of book-bearers. That the Jews carry their own sacred texts as a testimony to the truth of Christianity lies at the heart of Augustine's doctrine of Jewish witness. In his *Exposition on Psalm 56*, Augustine explains this indispensable function the Jews fulfill within Christendom:

> But the Jews survive still, and for a special purpose: so that they may carry our books, to their own confusion [*ut libros nostros portent ad confusionem suam*]. When we want to prove to the pagans that Christ's coming was prophesied, we produce these scriptures. But possibly pagans obstinately opposed to the faith might have alleged that we Christians had composed them, fabricating prophecies to buttress the gospel we preach. They might have thought that we were trying to pass off our message by pretending that it had been foreshadowed in prophecy. But we can convince them of their error by pointing out that all those scriptures which long ago spoke of Christ are the property of the Jews. Yes, the Jews recognize these very writings. We take books from our enemies to confute other enemies![64]

Augustine calls Jewish scriptures "our books" (*libros nostros*) for two related reasons. First, these sacred texts contain prophecies that find their fulfillment in Christ. Secondly, assuming that they are read in this way (which Augustine understands as the only correct way, of course), they serve to bolster the Christian faith against its pagan detractors. Thus, for Augustine (as for *Barnabas* and Melito before him), whereas these writings are Jewish in name and origin, they are in reality Christian.

The Jewish inability to read the sacred writings that they carry neither precludes nor inhibits their role as witnesses to Christianity. Spiritual blindness and scriptural illiteracy are certainly shameful for the Jews themselves. But, as Augustine makes clear in *Letter* 149, Jewish blindness is an evil that God uses to promote the good. It is, as we have seen, a fulfillment not only of scripture but also of the divine providential plan. Thus, it is as a gloss on Psalm 56:4 ("those who trampled on me he has consigned to disgrace") that the bishop writes:

> In what sort of disgrace do the Jews find themselves? A Jew carries the book which is the foundation of faith for a Christian [*Codicem portat Iudaeus, unde credat christianus*]. Jews act as book-bearers for us [*librarii nostri*], like the slaves who are accustomed to walk behind their masters carrying their books [*quomodo solent serui post dominos codices ferre*], so that while the slaves sink under the weight, the masters make great strides through reading [*ut illi portando deficiant, illi legendo proficiant*].[65]

Augustine's Latin succinctly and starkly contrasts Jews and Christians vis-à-vis the books of scripture. Jews carry the books, whereas Christians read them. The Jews have become *librarii nostri*, by which phrase Augustine means "our scribes or copyists" (from *librarius*) or "our bookcases" (from *librarium*), or both. The Jews produce, preserve, and protect the prophetic books that prefigure and predict Christ. They are the slaves of Christian masters, blindly bearing books they cannot decipher. By hauling their heavy load of codices, Jews become weak and fail. By contrast, Christians advance by reading.

For Augustine, the growth of the church is perhaps the most conspicuous manifestation of this Christian progress. We have seen that the late-antique bishop understands the expansion of the church throughout the world as evidence of both supersessionism and the reasonableness of Christian faith. It is also the ultimate purpose, this side of the beatific vision, for which the Jews carry their scriptures. In *De civitate Dei* 18.47, Augustine considers whether, prior to the advent of Christ, anyone outside Israel belonged to the City of God. He answers in the affirmative, citing the example of Job, but maintains that heavenly citizenship was granted only to those who by means of a divine revelation came to believe that the one mediator between God and humankind, Jesus Christ, would come at some future time. Augustine recognizes that the prophecies of Christ found in non-Jewish sources constitute less than ideal grounds on which to believe. Pagans will surely suppose them to be Christian fabrications. Consequently, the Jewish scriptures provide the surest means of refuting intelligent pagans in an argument over the central claims of Christianity.[66] Furthermore, as the bishop explains, the witness of the Jewish scriptures is a proven means of ecclesial expansion: "For the expulsion of the Jews from their own home, and their dispersal throughout the world with a view to this testimony has resulted in the increase of the Church of Christ in every quarter of the globe."[67]

Because of their important testimonial role in support of Christianity, it is God's will that the Jews should continue to live as Jews, Augustine believes. In advocating the preservation of Jews qua Jews, the bishop of Hippo diverges sharply from his Antiochene contemporary, John Chrysostom. Whereas Chrysostom finds scriptural support for his view that the Jewish enemies of Christ should be slaughtered ("But as for these my enemies, who did not want me to be king over them, bring them here and slay them" [Lk 19:27]), Augustine understands the words of Ps 58:12, "Slay them not, lest they forget your law; disperse them in your might," as revealing God's will that the Jews continue to live and give unwitting witness to Christianity. In *De fide rerum invisibilium*, Augustine explains:

> Therefore it has come about instead that they [i.e., the Jews] would not be destroyed, lest this same sect be completely obliterated, but that, having been scattered throughout the world, they would bring these prophecies which tell of God's grace to us [*sparsa est per terras, ut portans in nos collatae gratiae prophetias*]. The outcome of this is both a more robust refutation of unbelievers and a widespread source of good to us [*ad conuincendos firmius infideles nobis ubique prodesset*]. You must take to heart this very point I am making, as has been prophesied: *Do not slay them, lest they forget your law; disperse them by your power* (Ps 58:12).[68]

The Jews must not be slaughtered, Augustine avers, precisely in order that they might be everywhere useful to Christians (*nobis ubique prodesset*) by carrying the prophecies of grace for those who follow Christ (*portans in nos collatae gratiae prophetias*).

Augustine goes on to explain that the diaspora Jews have not completely forgotten the scriptures they have read and heard, although they do fail to understand them properly. If they were to utterly forget the Law and the Prophets, the bishop asserts, they would metaphorically be slain—that is, they would cease to be Jews and, as non-Jews, could not be useful (*Iudaei prodesse non possent*).[69] The first point worthy of note here is that, in contrast to Chrysostom's advocacy of murdering the Jews, Augustine veers from a literal reading of Ps 58:12, which prohibits slaying the Jews. In reading the verse metaphorically, Augustine keeps a discussion of even the possibility of the physical destruction of the Jews at bay. Second, Augustine makes clear once again that Jewish utility is not self-utility. The Jews do not have that faith in their own scriptures by which they might be saved. Rather, simply by retaining and carrying the memory or written record that they blindly preserve, the Jews help Christians and the Christian religion (*nos adiuuaremur memoria retinerent*).[70] The Jews neither recognize nor intend the indispensable role they play as testifiers to Christian truth. Quite to the contrary, in fact, the Jews aim to oppose Christianity. But God turns their intention on its head and makes them unwitting witnesses, as Augustine attests with rhetorical flare: "in uerbis contradictores, in libris suffragatores, in cordibus nostris hostes, in codicibus testes."[71]

Approximately a decade prior to his penning *De fide rerum invisibilium*, Augustine offered a more detailed treatment of Ps 58:12 in his *Exposition 2 on Psalm 58* (c. 413–15). From the opening lines of his sermon, the bishop intimates his concern to interpret "Slay them not" metaphorically or spiritually. Augustine encourages his Christian hearers to receive God's word (which he himself intends to proclaim) in such a way that it bears fruit in their lives.[72] Simply retaining the Law in one's mind is sufficient neither for perfection nor divine reward, Augustine maintains. For there are those who hold the Law in memory, but do not fulfill it in their lives (*Sunt enim qui tenent legem memoria, et non implant uita*).[73] These, of course, are the Jews. Developing a theme found in St. Paul and *Barnabas*, Augustine explains that Christians, by contrast, have had the Law divinely written on their hearts.[74] This internalization of the Law and a lived faith in what it proclaims are, for Augustine, among the most conspicuous marks distinguishing Christians, the friends of God, from Jews, enemies of the divine.

Although *inimici*, the Jews must nevertheless be allowed to live as Jews. On Ps 58:12, Augustine comments:

> The psalmist prayed that the Jewish nation might survive, and that through its survival the multitude of Christians might increase [*ut gens Iudaeorum maneret, et ea manente cresceret multitudo christianorum*]. And undoubtedly they do survive throughout all nations; they are still Jews, and have not lost their identity [*Iudaei sunt, nec destiterunt esse quod erant*]. That people has not made such concessions to the code of the Romans as to lose its Jewish character [*ut amiserit formam Iudaeorum*]. It is subject to the Romans, but in such a way as to hold onto its own laws, which are the laws of God [*ut etiam leges suas teneat, quae leges sunt Dei*].[75]

The bishop of Hippo advocates a Jewish survival that is not merely physical. His primary concern is to ensure the protection of Judaism as a religious reality. The Jews that have been dispersed throughout the world and subjected to Roman law have not ceased to be who they were, namely, bearers of the divine Law. They have not forsaken their fundamental identity as sacred codex carriers. In the face of strong pressures—

imperial, pagan, and even Christian—contemporary Jews have retained the *forma Iudaeorum*.

In Augustine's view, it is this basic identity of the Jews as book-bearers that the Psalmist, speaking on behalf of God Himself, advocates preserving when he writes, "Slay them not, lest they forget your law." It is this fundamental form of Judaism that is the *sine qua non* of the expansion of the church and the prosperity of the Christian religion. As such, Psalm 58:12 and the *forma Iudaeorum* that it seeks to safeguard lie at the heart of Augustine's understanding of the Jews as unwitting witnesses to the truth of Christianity.

The foregoing consideration of Augustine's mature teaching on Jews and Judaism raises important questions regarding historical context. Did the bishop's doctrine of Jewish witness arise out of his observation of or contact with actual adherents of Judaism in his late-antique North-African context, or was it merely theoretical or strictly theological? Did either Augustine himself or the Christian laity of Hippo Regius encounter the *forma Iudaeorum* and its role in ecclesial expansion, and if so, in what ways? Might Augustine's interactions with actual Jews in early-fifth-century Hippo have contributed to a less polemical, more palatable policy toward Jews than that of John Chrysostom? Although definitive answers to such questions remain beyond both the scope of this essay and the grasp of Augustinian scholarship to date, let us briefly consider the historical and textual evidence that Augustine's doctrine of Jewish witness did take shape in the context of interaction with actual Jews in late-antique North Africa.

## JEWS AND JUDAISM IN AUGUSTINE'S CONTEXT

Archeological and epigraphic evidence suggests that Jewish populations in late-antique North Africa were considerable numerically, diverse geographically, and influential religiously.[76] In the nineteenth century, for example, a Jewish cemetery containing several catacombs, each with about twenty graves, was unearthed at Gamarth near ancient Carthage.[77] The remains of a synagogue at ancient Naro, just 17 kilometers south of Carthage, has also been found.[78] The work of the Danish excavations in Carthage during the 1970s and 1980s suggests another synagogue in the northeastern quadrant of this city prior to and during the time of Augustine.[79] Additionally, Jewish tombstones inscribed in Latin have been discovered throughout central North Africa at such ancient sites as Cirta, Ausia, and Sitifis. One tombstone found at Sitifis, number 8640, is that of a baptized Jew and bears the Chi-Rho monogram.[80]

Such evidence lends credence to the view set forth by Bernhard Blumenkranz a half-century ago that Augustine lived, wrote, and preached in a context where the Jewish presence threatened Christianity, where the synagogue competed with the church for pagan converts, and where Augustine himself sought to persuade Jews to become Christians.[81] More recent scholarship, by contrast, maintains that Augustine's doctrine of Jewish witness took shape not in the context of the bishop's daily interactions with real Jews in Hippo Regius, but rather against the backdrop of various aspects of his theology—his understanding of biblical interpretation, terrestrial history, and human sexuality, for example.[82] Scholars such as Jeremy Cohen, Paula Fredriksen, and Marcel Dubois have argued that the Jew found in Augustine's works is not the real Jew whom the bishop would have met on the streets of Hippo, but rather the biblically constructed and "hermeneutically crafted" Jew whom Augustine devised as a servant of ecclesial self-definition, justification, and propagation.[83]

In an earlier article, I have attempted to nuance this acontextual view of Augustine's Jew by investigating the most contextual of the bishop's theological media, namely, his sermons.[84] I have argued that while it is undoubtedly true, as Cohen and Fredriksen have ably demonstrated, that Augustine's depiction of the Jews as blind and divinely rejected infidels is a theological construct that depends heavily on the New Testament and other early Christian writings (as we have also seen in the present essay), the bishop's homilies repeatedly refer to actual Jews in his late-antique North-African context. Furthermore, I have sought to show that it is precisely for real Jews and their potential proselytes, for the purpose of their conversion to Christ and his church, that Augustine spins the hermeneutically crafted Jew out of his allegorical interpretation of various scriptural stories.[85]

A brief consideration of the way in which actual Jews appear in the homilies of Augustine simultaneously suggests the competitive interreligious context in which the bishop developed his doctrine of Jewish witness and elucidates the lack of urgency with which Augustine advocates Jewish conversion to Christianity. In *Sermon* 4, preached either at Hippo or Carthage in late January sometime before 420, Augustine allegorizes the story of Isaac giving the primogenital blessing not to Esau, but rather to the younger son, Jacob (Gen 27). In the bishop's allegory, the older son Esau, whose name means "of the flesh" (*ex carnali*) represents the Jews, whereas Jacob represents the spiritual children, i.e., Christians.[86] Rebecca, who aided Jacob in procuring his older sibling's blessing, is a figure of Mother Church, who teaches Christians how to read the Old Testament spiritually and therefore receive the spiritual blessing that was materially promised to the Jews.[87] Isaac's dimness of vision represents the mental blindness which prevented the Jews from understanding their scriptures.

According to Augustine, Isaac did not become angry when Jacob deceived him precisely because the former was aware, by virtue of the fact that "he had the spirit of prophecy," of "this great mystery, this great sacrament" (*magnum mysterium, magnum sacramentum*) that he was symbolically enacting in granting the younger son the elder's blessing.[88]

Augustine further develops his allegory of this story in *Sermon* 5, preached during Lent sometime between 405 and 410. Here the bishop explains that Esau's natural hairiness signifies the Jew being covered in sins, whereas Jacob's putting on hairy skins (Gen 27:11–16) is a type of Christ and his church, bearing the sins of others.[89] It is precisely on account of the Jew's sinfulness that scripture says to the hairy Esau, "You shall be the slave of your brother" (Gen 27:40). Augustine explains to his hearers that these sacred words constitute a *mysterium* and, as such, have future referents:

> But the reason why these things were not fulfilled in the actual history of the two men is to make us understand that they were said of a future Jacob. The younger son received the first place [*accepit primatum*] and the elder son, the people of the Jews, lost the first place [*perdidit primatum*]. See how Jacob has filled the whole world, has taken possession of both nations and kingdoms. . . . And scattered through the world they [i.e., the Jews] have become as it were the keepers of our books [*Et sparsi per orbem terrarum, facti sunt quasi custodes librorum nostrorum*]; like slaves who carry their masters' books behind them when they go to the lecture room and sit outside themselves [*Quomodo serui, quando eunt in auditorium domini ipsorum, portant post illos codices et foris sedent*], that's what the elder son has become for the younger son. . . . In this way the elder serves the younger. Just see in what honor the Christian people are held [*cum quanta dignitate sit populus christianus*], and how the Jewish people are simply eclipsed [*in quanta defectione sit populus Iudaeorum*].[90]

With these rhetorically powerful words, Augustine sets forth (more or less explicitly) five of the six component parts of his mature doctrine of Jewish witness as enumerated by Cohen. The mode of existence of the Jews—scattered and servile—attests both to their divine punishment and to Christian reward. On account of their blindness and infidelity, the Jews have been rejected by God and replaced by Christians. Nevertheless, the Jews continue to carry their sacred books, thereby testifying to the historicity and authenticity of prophecies that find their fulfillment in Jesus Christ. Thus, in continuing to practice Judaism, the Jews ironically and unwittingly witness to the truth of the Christian religion. As such, for the sake of the church, Augustine intimates, Christians should allow Jews to remain Jews.

In spite of the vitally important role that Jews play in the continuation and expansion of the church, Augustine's doctrine allows for the possibility of and even seems to encourage Jewish conversion. The words of

Isaac that follow immediately upon "You shall be a slave to your brother," namely, "but when you break loose, you shall break his yoke from your neck" (Gen 27:40b) lead Augustine to a consideration of Jewish conversion in *Sermon* 5. The bishop takes Esau's "breaking loose" from the yoke of servitude to mean the Jew's free decision to become a Christian.[91] Just as many first-century Jews broke the servile yoke, so too can those Esaus in the time of Augustine, as the bishop hopefully observes:

> How many there are who undid the yoke from their necks and became our brothers! Notice how many Jews believed. And today, if you find a Jew, and proclaim to him the good news of the Lord Jesus Christ, and he believes [*Et modo, si quem iudaeum inueneris, et euangelizaueris illi dominum Iesum Christum, et crediderit*], won't he be undoing the yoke from his neck? And how many did this in the first days of the faith? Thousands. All who then believed, as we read [e.g., in Acts 2:41; 4:4; 5:14], from being slaves became brothers and fellow heirs.[92]

The conditional nature of Augustine's language here concerning actual Jews in his context (*si quem iudaeum inueneris, et euangelizaueris illi . . . et crediderit*) makes it difficult to know to what degree the bishop is encouraging his hearers to proselytize Jews, to what degree they might have been receptive to the Gospel, or even how common interactions between Jews and Christians would have been in early fifth-century Hippo Regius.

What is significant for our purposes, however, is how such passages point to a late-antique North African context of interreligious interaction in which Augustine formulated and promulgated his doctrine of Jewish witness. In *Sermon* 5 and other sermons, Augustine variously references actual Jews whom his Christian auditors likely encountered. In the midst of such Jewish-Christian encounters, the possibility of Jewish conversion surely existed and was not explicitly discouraged by Augustine. At the same time, the bishop seems not to take Christian proselytizing of Jews to be an urgent necessity. Rather, in several sermons Augustine gently encourages Jews to consider coming to Christ and his church (and gently encourages his Christian hearers to gently encourage potential converts from Judaism).[93] Although Jews did not, of course, represent the primary audience for Augustine's preaching, textual evidence suggests a Jewish presence at some of the bishop's homilies. For example, in *Sermon* 196, preached in Hippo on Christmas day sometime prior to 420, Augustine notes the exceptionally large assembly of Christians and Jews, and appeals to both groups to behave in the new year in a way pleasing to God, i.e., without judging or offending the other.[94]

This context of competitive but relatively peaceable interaction between Jews and Christians serves as an illuminating backlight for Augustine's doctrine of Jewish witness. The bishop's encouragement of positive relations between the Christian and Jewish hearers of his Christmas homily comports well with his understanding of Ps 58:12 as a divine safeguard against Christian coercion of Jewish conversion, to make no mention of the actual physical destruction of the Jews advocated by John Chrysostom. Whereas the blind and unfaithful Jews should be presented with and even refuted by the good news of Christ, according to Augustine, they also must be allowed to remain Jews. For it is only as Jews scattered throughout the world that they can serve the purpose for which God ultimately intends their wicked rejection of Christ—namely, to witness, however unwittingly, to the truth of Christianity by blindly carrying their own books and thereby to promote the growth of the Catholic Church.

## CONCLUSION

In this essay, we have sought to provide a full and coherent account of Augustine's mature teaching on Jews and Judaism by locating his thought within the dual context of early Christian anti-Judaism, on the one hand, and the interreligious world of late-antique North Africa, on the other. From such early Christian texts as the Gospels of Matthew and John, *The Epistle of Barnabas*, and Melito's *On the Passover*, Augustine inherited a supply of stock images of the Jews as a faithless people who rejected and even killed their long-awaited Messiah; a blind, deaf, and ignorant band who cannot read and understand their own scriptures; a nation exiled, scattered, and rejected by God on account of its perfidious wickedness and replaced by those who faithfully receive and follow Christ; and even the demonic enemies of Christ and his church. Augustine's Antiochene contemporary John Chrysostom combined these images to produce a malicious portrait of the Jews as brute beasts fit only for slaughter. Against Judaizing Christians for whom the synagogue was a good and sacred place on account of its role as preserver of the holy books of the Law and the Prophets, Chrysostom vehemently argued that Jewish rejection of the true meaning of these books necessitates Christian hatred of the synagogue and the inhabitants of this demonic den.

Augustine rearranged these same stock anti-Jewish images to produce a much less caustic collage. The centerpiece of Augustine's mature teaching is the affirmation that Jews must be allowed to remain Jews precisely because in their exiled and subjugated state they preserve and transport their own sacred texts throughout the world and, in this capacity, serve as unwitting witnesses to the truth of Christianity. In spite of their inability to read and comprehend their own books, the Jews nevertheless carry them for Christian readers who, in turn, make great strides by using these texts as proof that they themselves have not fabricated the prophecies concerning Christ. Such proof presumably counters and convinces pagan skeptics, ultimately leading to the growth of the church. Augustine's unique and subsequently influential contribution to early Christian thought on Jews is the significant positive role that the North African bishop gives them in God's providential plan *post Christum*. The notion that God makes good use of the evil for the advancement of the good acts as the theological engine that not only propels Augustine's doctrine of Jewish witness but also moves the relationship between Christians and Jews in a decidedly new and noticeably more positive direction.

We have attempted to sketch the beginnings of this transition by situating the doctrine of Jewish witness in Augustine's late-antique North Africa. Although archeological and epigraphic evidence suggests that the bishop lived and worked in a context where the synagogue competed with the church for pagan converts, Augustine's sermons reveal the general lack of urgency with which he encouraged Jewish conversion to Christianity. This comports well with Augustine's understanding that although Judaism must be refuted in an effort to vindicate Christianity, Jews must be allowed to continue to practice their religion. Indeed, Augustine reads Ps 58:12, "Slay them not, lest they forget your law," as revealing God's will that Christians throughout the world safeguard the *forma Iudaeorum*, the fundamental identity of the Jews as bearers of Christian books. It is only by means of such a safeguard that Jews and Christians can live peaceably together. And it is only by means of such a safeguard that Jews can serve as unwitting witnesses to Christian truth and, as such, promote ecclesial expansion.

The theological and practical influence of Augustine's mature doctrine of Jewish witness on medieval Christianity and its posture toward Jews and Judaism can hardly be overstated. About a century and a half after the death of Augustine, Gregory the Great (c.540–604) translated the doctrine of Jewish witness, in combination with Roman legal protection of the Jews and their religion, into official papal policy.[95] Pope Gregory famously formulated his policy of Jewish protection in *Epistle* 8 to Bishop Victor of Palermo (598). In response to the complaint of Palermo's Jewish community that Victor had seized their synagogue, consecrated it as a church, and confiscated Jewish books and religious ornaments, Gregory asserted: "Just as the Jews [*Sicut Iudaeis*] are not to be granted freedom in their synagogues greater than the law permits, so they should in no way suffer a violation of their rights."[96] During the High and Late Middle Ages, these words of Gregory became the opening sentence of a series of papal bulls providing legal protection for Jews within Christendom. From the twelfth through the fifteenth century, a total of twenty-three popes issued a *Sicut Iudaeis* bull, addressed "to all the Christian faithful" (*universis Christifidelibus*).[97] The basic features of the medieval *Sicut Iudaeis* bull were: (1) A guarantee of legal protection for the Jews, though with a restriction of privileges; (2) A decree against forced baptisms of Jews; (3) A prohibition against killing or physically harming the Jews; (4) A prohibition against disturbing Jewish worship and desecrating Jewish cemeteries; and (5) A caveat declaring that such protections will be guaranteed only for Jews who do not presume to plot against the Christian faith.[98]

The influence of Augustine's doctrine of Jewish witness on each of these features of official ecclesial policy in the Middle Ages is clear and crucial. Although some medieval Christian thinkers returned to the more antagonistic anti-Judaism of John Chrysostom and even developed new violently virulent strains, Augustine's doctrine of the Jews as unwitting witnesses to the truth of Christianity remained the most powerful and pervasive influence on Catholic thought and policy in the Middle Ages and beyond.

## NOTES

1. For an introduction to the Gospel of Matthew and these themes, see Luke T. Johnson, *The Writings of the New Testament: An Interpretation* (Philadelphia: Fortress Press, 1986), 172–96. It is noteworthy that Matthew is the only canonical Gospel in which the word "church" (*ekklesia*) appears (16:18 and 18:17). In terms of its purpose and use, Matthew may have served as a manual of instruction and discipline for the early Christian community in Antioch and beyond.

2. Unless otherwise noted, all English quotations of scriptural texts are those of the New Revised Standard Version (NRSV).

3. On the beginnings of the church-synagogue conflict, see James Parkes, *The Conflict of the Church and the Synagogue: A Study in the Origins of Antisemitism* (New York: Atheneum, 1985; orig. pub. 1934); and Edward H. Flannery, *The Anguish of the Jews: Twenty-Three Centuries of Antisemitism*, revised and updated edition (New York: Paulist Press, 1999; orig. pub. 1965), 28–46. On *Synagoga* and *Ecclesia* as allegorical representations of the Jewish-Christian encounter in medieval architecture, art, and literature, see Wolfgang Seiferth, *Synagoge und Kirche im Mittelalter* (München: Kösel-Verlag, 1964); and Bernhard Blumenkranz, "Géographie historique d'un theme de l'iconographie religieuse: les representations de *Synagoga* en France," in Pierre Gallais and Yves-Jean Riou, eds., *Mélanges offerts à René Crozet à l'occasion de son soixante-dixième anniversaire* (Poitiers: Société d'Études Médiévales, 1966), 1141–57.

4. On "the Jews" in John's Gospel, see U.C. von Wahlde, "The Johannine 'Jews': A Critical Survey," *New Testament Studies* 28 (1982) 33–60; Wayne A. Meeks, "Breaking Away: Three New Testament Pictures of Christianity's Separation from the Jewish Communities," in Jeremy Cohen, ed., *Essential Papers on Judaism and Christianity in Conflict: From Late Antiquity to the Reformation* (New York: New York University Press, 1991), 89–113; and Johnson, *The Writings of the New Testament*, 476–78.

5. On the high Christology of the New Testament in the context of Jewish Wisdom traditions, see Crispin H. T. Fletcher-Louis, "Wisdom Christology and the Partings of the Ways between Judaism and Christianity," in Stanley E. Porter and Brook W.R. Pearson, eds., *Christian-Jewish Relations through the Centuries* (London: T & T Clark, 2000), 52–68.

6. See, e.g., Guy G. Stroumsa, "From Anti-Judaism to Antisemitism in Early Christianity?" in Ora Limor and Guy G. Stroumsa, eds., *Contra Iudaeos: Ancient and Medieval Polemics between Christians and Jews* (Tübingen: J.C.B. Mohr, 1996), 1–26.

7. For an introduction to and English translation of *The Epistle of Barnabas*, see Andrew Louth, ed. and rev. trans., *Early Christian Writings: The Apostolic Fathers* (London: Penguin Books, 1987), 155–84.

8. *The Epistle of Barnabas* (hereafter *Barnabas*) 2 (Louth, 159–60). All quotations of *Barnabas* are those of Louth.

9. See W.H.C. Frend, *The Early Church* (Minneapolis: Fortress Press, 1982), 35–48.

10. See *Barnabas* 2, where he cites Isaiah 1:11–13, Jeremiah 7:22, and Zechariah 8:17 (Louth, 160).

11. *Barnabas* 4 (Louth, 162).

12. *Barnabas* 8 (Louth, 169).

13. *Barnabas* 9 (Louth, 169).

14. For a brief consideration of Origen on the spiritual and literal senses of scripture and his contribution to the threefold interpretive framework of history, allegory, and tropology, see Franklin T. Harkins, "*Historia*, Reading, and Restoration in the Theology of Hugh of St. Victor" (Ph.D. dissertation, University of Notre Dame, 2005), 172–85.

15. *On the Passover* 36–37. For an English translation, see Richard A. Norris, Jr., trans. and ed., *The Christological Controversy* (Philadelphia: Fortress Press, 1980), 33–47.

16. *On the Passover* 41–43 (Norris, 38).

17. See Mary C. Boys, *Has God Only One Blessing? Judaism as a Source of Christian Self-Understanding* (New York: Paulist Press, 2000), 48–53, esp. 52.

18. It is noteworthy that *On the Passover* is not a disputation that Melito used in debate against the Jews, but rather a homily, i.e., an exposition of scripture intended for a Christian audience. As such, its principal purpose seems to be to bolster the identity and confidence of his Christian hearers, albeit in contradistinction to Judaism (See Boys, *Has God Only One Blessing?*, 52–53).

19. See sections 67–99.

20. *On the Passover* 73 (Norris, 42).

21. *On the Passover* 78–79, 81 (Norris, 43–44).

22. *On the Passover* 96–97 (Norris, 46).

23. On Judaizing Christians in the interreligious context of Chrysostom's Antioch, see Robert L. Wilken, *John Chrysostom and the Jews: Rhetoric and Reality in the Late 4th Century* (Berkeley: University of California Press, 1983), 66–94; and the introduction to *Saint John Chrysostom, Discourses against Judaizing Christians*, Fathers of the Church vol. 68, trans. Paul Harkins (Washington, D.C.: Catholic University of America Press, 1979), xxi–lxii, esp. xxvi–xxxi (hereafter, FCh 68).

24. FCh 68.xxxix–xlii.

25. On the title of these sermons, see FCh 68.xxxi, n. 47.

26. Robert L. Wilken, *Judaism and the Early Christian Mind: A Study of Cyril of Alexandria's Exegesis and Theology* (New Haven: Yale University Press, 1971), 19. On Chrysostom's anti-Jewish invective, see also Marcel Simon, *Verus Israel. Étude sur les relations entre chrétiens et juifs dans l'empire romain (135–425)* (Paris: Éditions E. de Boccard, 1964), 256–63; and J. N. D. Kelly, *Golden Mouth: The Story of John Chrysostom – Ascetic, Preacher, Bishop* (Grand Rapids: Baker Books, 1995), 62–66.

27. *Discourse against Judaizing Christians* (hereafter, *Discourse*) I.2.1 (FCh 68.5).

28. *Discourse* I.2.4–5 (FCh 68.7–8). Cf. I.4.1 (FCh 68.14), where Chrysostom contrasts Christians, who are concerned with spiritual and eternal realities, with the carnal Jews. Of the latter, Chrysostom writes: "They live for their bellies, . . . gape for the things of this world, their condition is no better than that of pigs or goats because of their wanton ways and excessive gluttony. They know but one thing: to fill their bellies and be drunk . . . ."

29. *Discourse* I.2.6 (FCh 68.8).

30. *Discourse* I.1.5 (FCh 68.4).

31. *Discourse* I.5.1 (FCh 68.18).

32. *Discourse* I.6.3 (FCh 68.23). Cf. I.3.3: "If, then, the Jews fail to know the Father, if they crucified the Son, if they thrust off the help of the Spirit, who should not make bold to declare plainly that the synagogue is a dwelling of demons? God is not worshipped there. Heaven forbid! From now on it remains a place of idolatry" (FCh 68.11).

33. *Discourse* I.5.2 (FCh 68.19).

34. *Discourse* I.5.3 (FCh 68.19).

35. *Discourse* I.5.4 (FCh 68.19).

36. *Discourse* I.5.4 (FCh 68.19).

37. See Bernhard Blumenkranz, *Die Judenpredigt Augustins* (Paris: Études augustiniennes, 1973; orig. pub. 1946), which has become the foundational work on Augustine and the Jews; see also Bernhard Blumenkranz, "Augustin et les juifs: Augustin et le judaisme," *Recherches Augustiniennes* 1 (1958) 225–41; Jeremy Cohen, *Living Letters of the Law: Ideas of the Jew in Medieval Christianity* (Berkeley: University of California Press, 1999), 23–65; Paula Fredriksen, "Excaecati occulta justitia Dei: Augustine on Jews and Judaism," *Journal of Early Christian Studies* 3 (1995) 299–324; idem., "Divine Justice and Human Freedom: Augustine on Jews and Judaism, 392–398," in Jeremy Cohen, ed., *From Witness to Witchcraft: Jews and Judaism in Medieval Christian Thought* (Wiesbaden: Harrassowitz Verlag, 1996); and Marcel Dubois, "Jews, Judaism and Israel in the Theology of Saint Augustine: How He Links the Jewish People and the Land of Zion," *Immanuel* 22/23 (1989) 162–214. Jeremy Cohen provides a review of this literature in "'Slay Them Not': Augustine and the Jews in Modern Scholarship," *Medieval Encounters* 4 (1998) 78–92.

38. Cohen, *Living Letters*, 35–37 and Table I on 41.

39. Cohen, *Living Letters*, 37–38 and Table I on 41.

40. Unless otherwise noted, chapter and verse references of biblical texts will correspond to the Latin Vulgate version, and Latin scriptural quotations will be those provided in Augustine's own texts.

41. *Exposition of Psalm* (hereafter, *Exp. Ps.*) 56.9. English translation is from *Expositions of the Psalms 51–72*, The Works of Saint Augustine: A Translation for the

21st Century III/17, trans. Maria Boulding, O.S.B., ed. John E. Rotelle, O.S.A. (New York: New City Press, 2001), 109 (hereafter WSA III/17). Augustine's Latin reads: "Saeuierunt Iudaei in Christum, superbierunt in Christum; ubi? In ciuitate Ierusalem. Vbi enim regnabant, ibi tumebant, ibi ceruices erexerunt. Post passionem Domini eradicati inde sunt, et perdiderunt regnum, in quo regem Christum agnoscere noluerunt. Quemadmodum dati sunt in opprobrium, uidete: dispersit sunt per omnes gentes, nusquam habentes stabilitatem, nusquam certam sedem" (CCSL 39.699).

42. See also Augustine's discussion of Jewish pride in the context of the crucifixion in *Exposition 2 of Psalm 58*, sections 4–7 on the Psalmists words (v.13), "et conprehendantur in superbia sua" (WSA III/17.170–74; CCSL 39.747–51). On pride generally in Augustine's thought, see D. J. MacQueen, "Augustine on Superbia: The Historical Background and Sources of His Doctrine," *Mélanges de science religieuse* 34 (1977) 193–211; N. J. Torchia, "St. Augustine's Treatment of Superbia and Its Plotinian Affinities," *Augustinian Studies* 18 (1987) 66–80; and *Augustine through the Ages: An Encyclopedia*, gen. ed. Allan D. Fitzgerald, O.S.A. (Grand Rapids: Eerdmans, 1999), s.v. "Pride."

43. *Exp. Ps.* 56.9 (CCSL 39.699).

44. *City of God* 18.46. English translation is from *St. Augustine, Concerning the City of God against the Pagans*, trans. Henry Bettenson (London: Penguin Books, 1984), 827. Augustine's Latin reads: "Iudaei autem, qui eum occiderunt et in eum credere noluerunt, quia oportebat eum mori et resurgere, uastati infelicius a Romanis funditusque a suo regno, ubi iam eis alienigenae dominabantur, eradicati dispersique per terras (quando quidem ubique non desunt)" (CCSL 48.644).

45. *De fide rerum invisibilium* 6.9. "Nam eos non intellecturos ab eisdem prophetis ante praedictum est; quod ut cetera oportebat impleri et occulto, sed iusto iudicio dei meritis eorum poenam debitam reddi" (CCSL 46.15).

46. *Faith in the Unseen* 6.9. English translation is that of Matthew O'Connell in *Saint Augustine On Christian Belief*, The Works of Saint Augustine: A Translation for the 21st Century I/8, ed. Boniface Ramsey (New York: New City Press, 2005), 191–92. "[T]amen propter ceteros, quos occultioribus causis fuerat deserturus, per prophetam tanto ante praedixit: *Dederunt in escam meam fel et in siti mea potauerunt me aceto. Fiat mensa eorum coram ipsis in muscipulam et in retributionem et in scandalum. Obscurentur oculi eorum, ne uideant, et dorsum illorum semper incurua*" (CCSL 46.15–16).

47. In *De fide rerum invisibilium* 6.9, Augustine alludes to this line of thought, which he fleshes out throughout this work, when he writes: "Cum causae itaque nostrae praeclarissimis testimoniis circumquaque ambulant oculis obscuratis, ut per eos haec probentur, ubi et ipsi reprobentur" (CCSL 46.16).

48. Augustine opens his work thusly: "Sunt qui putant christianam religionem propterea ridendam potius quam tenendam, quia in ea non res quae uideatur ostenditur, sed fides rerum quae non uidentur hominibus imperatur" (CCSL 46.1).

49. *Faith in the Unseen* 3.5 (WSA I/8.187). "Ipsa uos ecclesia ore maternae dilectionis alloquitur: 'Ego, quam miramini per uniuersum mundum fructificantem atque crescentem, qualem me conspicitis, aliquando non fui, sed *in semine tuo benedicentur omnes gentes*. Quando deus Abrahae benedicebat, me promittebat: per omnes enim gentes in Christi benedictione diffundor. Semen Abrahae Christum

succedentium generationum ordo testatur. Quod ut breuiter colligam, Abraham genuit Isaac, Isaac genuit Iacob, Iacob genuit duodecim filios, ex quibus ortus est populus Israel. Iacob quippe ipse appellatus est Israel. In his duodecim filiis genuit Iudam, unde nomen est Iudaeorum, ex quibus nata est uirgo Maria, quae peperit Christum. Et ecce in Christo, id est in semine Abrahae, benedici omnes gentes uidetis et stupetis; et adhuc in eum credere timetis, in quem non credere, potius timere debuistis!" (CCSL 46.6–7).

50. See *Faith in the Unseen* 3.5–5.8 (WSA I/8.186–91; CCSL 46.6–15).

51. On the genre and purpose of Augustine's work, see *Augustine through the Ages*, s.v. "Adversus Judaeos."

52. *In Answer to the Jews* 1.1. English translation is that of Marie Liguori, I.H.M. in *Saint Augustine, Treatises on Marriage and Other Subjects*, ed. Roy J. Deferrari, Fathers of the Church vol. 27 (New York: Fathers of the Church, 1955), 391 (hereafter, FCh 27). Augustine's Latin reads: "Hoc dixit utique de Judaeis, qui tanquam rami ex illa olea, quae in sanctis Patriarchis tanquam in radice fructifera, propter infidelitatem fracti sunt; ut Gentium propter fidem insereretur oleaster, et fieret particeps pinguedinis oleae ramis naturalibus amputatis" (PL 42.51).

53. *In Answer to the Jews* 1.1. "Itaque illis Patriarchis in radice viventibus, et infidelis superbia naturalium ramorum justa Dei severitate confringitur, et fidelis humilitas oleastri gratia divinae bonitatis inseritur" (CCSL 42.51).

54. *In Answer to the Jews* 1.2 (FCh 27.392; language of quotation updated). "Sed quando Judaeis ista dicuntur, Evangelium Apostolumque contemnunt, et quod dicimus non audiunt; quoniam quod legunt, non intelligunt. Nam utique se intelligerent de quo praedixerit propheta, quem legunt, *Dedi te in lucem gentium, ita ut sis salus mea usque in fines terrae* (Isai. XLIX, 6); non sic caeci essent, non sic aegroti, ut in Domino Christo nec lucem agnoscerent, nec salutem" (PL 42.51–52).

55. In *Exp. Ps.* 56.9, Augustine writes: "In tale opprobrium dati sunt Iudaei; et impletum est quod tanto ante praedictum est: *Dedit in opprobrium conculcantes me* [Ps. 56:4]. Quale autem opprobrium est, fratres, ut hunc uersum legant, et ipsi caeci adtendant ad speculum suum? Sic enim apparent Iudaei de scriptura sancta quam portant, quomodo apparet facies caeci de speculo: ab aliis uidetur, ab ipso non uidetur. *Dedit in opprobrium conculcantes me*" (CCSL 39.700).

56. *In Answer to the Jews* 7.10 (FCh 27.405–406). "[C]um auditis, *Venite, ascendamus in montem Domini, et in domum Dei Jacob*; dicite, Nos sumus; ut caeci offendatis in montem; ubi collisa facie pejus perdatis frontem. Si vere vultis dicere, Nos sumus; ibi hoc dicite, ubi auditis, *Ab iniquitatibus populi mei ductus est ad mortem* (Isai. LIII, 8). De Christo enim dictum est, quem vos in parentibus vestris duxistis ad mortem. . . . In his atque hujusmodi propheticis vocibus dicite, Nos sumus; ubi sine ulla dubitatione vos estis: sed sic caeci estis, ut esse vos dicatis ubi non estis, et non vos agnoscatis ubi estis" (PL 42.58–59).

57. Scholars disagree on the precise date of *Epistula* 149. Jeremy Cohen gives a date of 414 (*Living Letters*, 41 Table I), whereas Robert Eno dates it to late 415 (*Augustine through the Ages*, s.v. "*Epistulae*," 302). Boniface Ramsey sets the date later still, to the end of 416 (*Letters 100–155 [Epistulae]*, The Works of Saint Augustine: A Translation for the 21st Century II/2, trans. Roland Teske, S.J., ed. Boniface Ramsey [Hyde Park: New City Press, 2003], 360).

58. *Letter* 149.2.18 (CSEL 44.364).

59. *Letter* 149.2.18 (WSA II/2.369). "[N]imis enim consilium eius in abdito est, quo etiam malis bene utitur ad prouectum bonorum etiam in hoc mirificans omnipotentiam bonitatis suae, quia, sicut illorum nequitiae est male uti bonis operibus eius, sic illius sapientiae est bene uti malis operibus eorum" (CSEL 44.364–65).

60. See *The Enchiridion on Faith, Hope, and Charity*, where Augustine writes, "[W]e must in no way doubt that the only cause of the good things that come our way is the goodness of God, while the cause of our evils is the will of a changeable good falling away from the unchangeable good" (8.23). Cf. *To Simplicianus* 1.2.18: "Sin in a human being is disorder or perversity, that is, an aversion to the more preferable Creator, and a conversion to the inferior creatures."

61. *Letter* 149.2.20 (WSA II/2.370). "[P]retium quippe redemptionis nostrae sanguis est Christi, qui utique non nisi ab inimicis potuit occidi. [H]ic est ille usus malorum in prouectum bonorum" (CSEL 44.365–66).

62. *Letter* 149.2.20 (WSA II/2.370). "[A]d hoc enim addidit 'propter patres', quia id, quod patribus promissum est, oportebat impleri, sicut circa finem epistulae ad Romanos ait: *Dico enim Christum ministrum fuisse circumcisionis propter ueritatem dei ad confirmandas promissiones patrum, gentes autem super misericordia glorificare deum* [15:8–9]" (CSEL 44.366–67].

63. *Letter* 149.2.19 (WSA II/2.369). "'[E]x parte' dixit, quia non omnes excaecati sunt; erant enim ex illis, qui Christum cognouerunt" (CSEL 44.365).

64. *Exp. Ps.* 56.9 (WSA III/17.110). "Propterea autem adhuc Iudaei sunt, ut libros nostros portent ad confusionem suam. Quando enim uolumus ostendere prophetatum Christum, proferimus paganis istas litteras. Et ne forte dicant duri ad fidem quia nos illas christiani composuimus, ut cum euangelio quod praedicamus finxerimus prophetas, per quos praedictum uideretur quod praedicamus; hinc eos conuincimus quia omnes ipsae litterae quibus Christus prophetatus est, apud Iudaeos sunt, omnes ipsas litteras habent Iudaei. Proferimus codices ab inimicis, ut confundamus alios inimicos" (CCSL 39.699–700).

65. *Exp. Ps.* 56.9 (WSA III/17.110). "In quali ergo opprobrio sunt Iudaei? Codicem portat Iudaeus, unde credat christianus. Librarii nostri facti sunt, quomodo solent serui post dominos codices ferre, ut illi portando deficiant, illi legendo proficiant" (CCSL 39.700).

66. *City of God* 18.47 (Bettenson, 829–30). "Sed quaecumque aliorum prophetiae de Dei per Iesum Christum gratia proferuntur, possunt putari a Christianis esse confictae. Ideo nihil est firmius ad conuincendos quoslibet alienos, si de hac re contenderint, nostrosque faciendos, si recte sapuerint, quam ut diuina praedicta de Christo ea proferantur, quae in Iudaeorum codicibus scripta sunt" (CCSL 48.646).

67. *City of God* 18.47 (Bettenson, 830). ". . . quibus auulsis de sedibus propriis et propter hoc testimonium toto orbe dispersis Christi usquequaque creuit ecclesia" (CCSL 48.646).

68. *Faith in the Unseen* 6.9 (WSA I/8.192). "Ideo factum est, ne sic delerentur, ut eadem secta omnino nulla esset, sed sparsa est per terras, ut portans in nos collatae gratiae prophetias ad conuincendos firmius infideles nobis ubique prodesset. Et hoc ipsum quod dico, accipite, quemadmodum fuerit prophetatum: *Ne occideris eos*, inquit, *ne quando obliuiscantur legem tuam; disperge eos in uirtute tua* [Ps. 58:12]" (CCSL 46.16).

69. *Faith in the Unseen* 6.9 (WSA I/8.192). "Non sunt ergo occisi in eo, quod non sunt, quae apud eos legebantur et audiebantur, obliti. Si enim scripturas sanctas, quamuis eas non intellegant, penitus obliuiscerentur, in ipso Iudaico ritu occiderentur, quia, cum legis et prophetarum nihil nossent, Iudaei prodesse non possent" (CCSL 46.16).

70. *Faith in the Unseen* 6.9 (WSA I/8.192). "Ergo occisi non sunt, sed disperse sunt, ut, quamuis in fide unde salui fierent non haberent, tamen unde nos adiuuaremur memoria retinerent. . . ." (CCSL 46.16).

71. *Faith in the Unseen* 6.9 (WSA I/8.192; CCSL 46.16).

72. *Exp. 2 Ps.* 58.1 (WSA III/17.167). "[H]oc est, ut quod ille donat, et nos reddimus (ille enim Dominus, nos serui sumus), sic accipiatis, ut sit fructus in auditione uestra de uita uestra. . . . Deus noster, sicut eum uidetis hanc terram uisitare imbribus sollemnibus, ita cor nostrum uerbo suo tamquam agrum suum uisitare dignatur; et de corde nostro fructus quaerit, quia nouit et quid ibi seminet, et quantum pluat" (CCSL 39.745).

73. *Exp. 2 Ps.* 58.2 (WSA III/17.167–68; CCSL 39.745).

74. *Exp. 2 Ps.* 58.2 (WSA III/17.168). "Ergo qui moribus praecepta Dei facit, et quodam modo uiuendo, semper in corde suo ne deleatur agit quod tenet, uiuendoque se commemorat quid ei in corde scriptum sit de lege Dei, ipse fructuose tenet legem Dei; ipse non inimicus deputabitur" (CCSL 39.745–46).

75. *Exp. 2 Ps.* 58.2 (WSA III/17.168). "[I]deo de illis dictum est: *Ne occideris eos, nequando obliuiscantur legis tuae*, ut gens Iudaeorum maneret, et ea manente cresceret multitudo christianorum. Per omnes gentes manent certe, et Iudaei sunt, nec destiterunt esse quod erant; id est, gens ista non ita cessit in iura Romanorum, ut amiserit formam Iudaeorum; sed ita subdita Romanis est, ut etiam leges suas teneat, quae leges sunt Dei" (CCSL 39.746).

76. For a fuller treatment of Jews and Judaism in Augustine's North Africa, see Franklin T. Harkins, "Nuancing Augustine's Hermeneutical Jew: Allegory and Actual Jews in the Bishop's Sermons," *Journal for the Study of Judaism* 36 (2005) 41–64, especially 44–49, on which the following consideration relies.

77. Haim Z. Hirschberg, *History of the Jews in North Africa*, 2 vols. (Leiden: E.J. Brill, 1974), 1:50.

78. Hirschberg, *History* 1:50–51.

79. On the Jewish community at Carthage in late antiquity and the Christian encounter with it, see John Lund, "A Synagogue at Carthage? Menorah-lamps from the Danish Excavations," *Journal of Roman Archaeology* 8 (1995) 245–262; W. H. C. Frend, "The Early Christian Church in Carthage," in J.H. Humphrey, ed., *Excavations at Carthage 1976 conducted by the University of Michigan*, vol. 3 (Ann Arbor, Mich.: University of Michigan Press, 1977), 21–40; and W.H.C. Frend, "Jews and Christians in Third Century Carthage," in *Paganisme, Judaïsme, Christianisme: Influences et affrontements dans le monde antique. Mélanges offerts à Marcel Simon* (Paris: Éditions E. de Boccard, 1978), 185–194.

80. Hirschberg, *History* 1:51. The inscriptions are in Gustav Wilmanns, René Cagnat, Johannes Schmidt, and Hermann Dessau, eds., *Inscriptiones Africae Latinae. Corpus Inscriptionum Latinarum*, vol. 8 (Berlin: G. Reimerum, 1881–1959), 1–5. Some were published by E. Diehl, *Inscriptiones Latinae Christianae Veteres*, 3 vols. (Berlin: Weidmann, 1925–1931). See also René Cagnat and Alfred Merlin with the

collaboration of Louis Châtelain, *Inscriptions latines d'Afrique (Tripolitaine, Tunisie, Maroc)* (Paris: E. Leroux, 1923); and Alfred Merlin, *Inscriptions latines de la Tunisie* (Paris: Presses Universitaires de France, 1944).

81. Blumenkranz, *Die Judenpredigt*; and Blumenkranz, "Augustin et les juifs."

82. See Fredriksen, "Excaecati occulta justitia Dei"; Cohen, *Living Letters*, 23–65; and Dubois, "Jews, Judaism, and Israel." For a fuller treatment of this literature, see Harkins, "Nuancing Augustine's Hermeneutical Jew," esp. 41–43.

83. Again see Fredriksen, "Excaecati occulta justitia Dei"; Cohen, *Living Letters*, 23–65; and Dubois, "Jews, Judaism, and Israel." On Augustine's "hermeneutically crafted" Jew, see Cohen, *Living Letters*, 13 and 42ff.; and Harkins, "Nuancing Augustine's Hermeneutical Jew," 42 n. 3.

84. Harkins, "Nuancing Augustine's Hermeneutical Jew."

85. For a detailed analysis of actual Jews in Augustine's sermons on the stories of Jacob's receiving Esau's primogenital blessing (Gen. 27), Christ giving sight to the man born blind (Jn. 9), Jacob wrestling with the angel at Peniel (Gen. 32), Christ cursing the fig tree (Mt. 21), and the parable of the prodigal son (Lk. 15), see Harkins, "Nuancing Augustine's Hermeneutical Jew," 49–63.

86. *Sermon* 4.11–12, in *Sermons on the Old Testament, 1–19*, The Works of Saint Augustine: A Translation for the 21st Century III/1, trans. Edmund Hill, O.P., ed. John E. Rotelle, O.S.A. (New York: New City Press, 1990), 190–92.

87. *Sermon* 4.13 (WSA III/1.192–93).

88. *Sermon* 4.21 (WSA III/1.196–97). Here Augustine avers: "Sine dubio Isaac ille, ut erat spiritu prophetico, nouerat quod agebatur, et ipse figurate agebat. Omnia ponit in magna altitudine sacramentorum" (CCSL 41.36). In *Sermon* 5 the bishop reiterates that Isaac was not angry that he had been deceived; quite to the contrary, Augustine's Isaac here declares of Esau, "Let his brother take that blessing from him, and to hell with him" (5.4 [WSA III/1.220]; "Tollat benedictionem illam frater ipsius, et sit in malis" [CCSL 41.54]).

89. *Sermon* 5.4 (WSA III/1.220; CCSL 41.54).

90. *Sermon* 5.5 (WSA III/1.221). "Sed ideo ista in historia non sunt impleta, ut intellegantur de futuro dicta Iacob. Minor filius accepit primatum, et maior filius, populus iudaeorum, perdidit primatum. Ecce Iacob impleuit terram, tenuit et gentes et regna. . . . Et sparsi per orbem terrarum, facti sunt quasi custodes librorum nostrorum. Quomodo serui, quando eunt in auditorium domini ipsorum, portant post illos codices et foris sedent, sic factus est filius maior minori. . . . Maior ergo minori seruit. Videte enim cum quanta dignitate sit populus christianus, et in quanta defectione sit populus Iudaeorum" (CCSL 41.55–56).

91. *Sermon* 5.4 (WSA III/1.220).

92. *Sermon* 5.5 (WSA III/1.221). "Quanti sunt qui soluerunt iugum a ceruice sua et facti sunt fratres nostri? Quanti iudaei crediderunt attendite. Et modo, si quem iudaeum inueneris, et euangelizaueris illi dominum Iesum Christum, et crediderit, nonne soluet iugum a ceruice sua? Et quanti hoc fecerunt primis temporibus fidei? Milia. Omnino qui tunc crediderunt, sicut legimus, et ex seruis facti sunt fratres et coheredes" (CCSL 41.56).

93. For examples of Augustine's gentle homiletical encouragement of Jewish conversion to Christianity, see Harkins, "Nuancing Augustine's Hermeneutical Jew," 53–56 and 59–63.

94. *Sermon* 196.4.

95. See Cohen, *Living Letters*, 73–94; and Edward A. Synan, *The Popes and the Jews in the Middle Ages* (New York: Macmillan, 1965), 35–50.

96. *Letter* 8.25 (CCSL 140A.546–47). On this and other letters in which Gregory provides protection for the Jews, see Jacob Rader Marcus, *The Jews in the Medieval World: A Sourcebook: 315–1791*, rev. ed. Marc Saperstein (Cincinnati: Hebrew Union College Press, 1999), 124–27; and Synan, *The Popes and the Jews*, 216–17.

97. See Solomon Grayzel, "The Papal Bull *Sicut Judeis*," in Meir Ben-Horin, Bernard D. Weinryb, and Solomon Zeitlin, eds., *Studies and Essays in Honor of Abraham A. Neuman* (Leiden: E.J. Brill, 1962), 243–80.

98. For the basic text of the bull in Latin and English see Grayzel, "The Papal Bull," 244–45.

# 4

✢

# A Christian *Aeneid*: Pagan and Christian Education in the *Confessions*

Paul Joseph LaChance

## INTRODUCTION

Augustine was a man of his books and sought in those books a way to understand and to articulate his own life and his world.[1] I suggest here that the texts that provided the narrative structure of Augustine's life in the *Confessions* were Virgil's *Aeneid* and the letters of St. Paul.[2] James J. O'Donnell notes that the *Confessions* came after a period of writer's block during which time Augustine tried his hand at various projects but could not find a framework or mechanism to carry off his own literary ambitions.[3] The difficulty Augustine had in completing his writing projects in the years before the *Confessions* points to a gap in his own Christian formation after his conversion. God had called him to a new life, but what exactly should that life look like? Augustine claimed in the *Confessions* that the writings of St. Paul were the catalyst for his conversion to Christianity, and that it was St. Paul more than any other author who was his authority in that ascetic, mystical, and joyful way of life to which he aspired most longingly. However, in the early years of his converted life, Augustine turned to Virgil in an effort to give voice to what his new life entailed.[4] Augustine had difficulty in reconciling his own education, philosophic worldview, and the demands of a Christian priest and, subsequently, bishop. It seems likely, therefore, that the success of the *Confessions* owes a great deal to the manner in which Augustine forged a rapprochement between his pagan cultural formation and his later Christian identity.[5] The Bishop of Hippo found his voice by transforming a classical pagan approach to the formation of character, conscripting it for the service of the Church. "Vergil's works" writes Sabine MacCormack, "had been integrated into the school curriculum and thence into the personal culture of every Latin speaker. Augustine himself was a participant in this tradition."[6] There can be little doubt that Augustine, who included Adeodatus in the philosophical conversations at Cassiciacum and who gave to his son a featured role as interlocutor in the book *The Teacher*, would have provided for his son the best available education in the customary form, including a careful study of Virgil.[7] But for Augustine Christianity required a new formation: *Nunc hic dies aliam vitam adfert, alios mores postulat*.[8] The older bishop reflected that he had "contributed nothing to that boy other than sin"[9] and was most grateful for the catholic formation the boy received. His membership in the Catholic Church kept him from becoming an initiate in the Manichean sect.[10]

At the level of religious belief and doctrine, Augustine had nothing in common with the ancient master of poetry. Besides noting the obvious difference between the pagan polytheist and Christian monotheist, we could point out that the Bishop of Hippo had little patience for ancestor worship, and rejected the notion of sin as contagion which may be contracted if one were, say, to drink from a spring venerated in pagan worship, to say nothing of the bodily nature and illicit behaviors of the gods. Virgil, however, did offer a powerful literary vision that unites a personal quest for virtue with larger public obligations, individual sin and weakness with ineluctable providence, and a moving viewpoint in which the hero's relationship to the gods changes as the hero develops.

St. Paul's efforts, notably in the Letter to the Romans, to explain why all peoples are in need of the healing power of Christ, provide a framework for gathering pagans, Jews, and Christians under the universal law of Providence and the grace of Christ (Romans 2:1–16; 3:29–30). The Pauline character of the *Confessions* lies in the unity of five central ideas. First, St. Paul affirmed that the law, because it is holy and righteous in itself, has the power to reveal sin (Romans 7:12), but knowing the law does not mean that one is capable of obeying the law. In fact, knowledge simply aggravates personal incontinence. The grace of Christ overcomes the will's divisiveness (Romans 8:3). Thus, Augustine contrasted his life, under the sway of human custom, subjected to the universal law, to his life in the Church, subjected to the grace of Christ. Second, as for St. Paul, the law serves a pedagogic purpose (Galatians 3:23), so for Augustine Providence, by the universal law, seeks to remove evil from the divine realm by providing opportunities for insight and correction. For St. Paul, the blindness and compounding wickedness that is the result of sin is itself instructive, in so far as it underlines the discrepancy between knowledge and action (Romans 2:1–4). Third, Augustine affirmed St. Paul's notion at Romans 1:19–21 that creation itself provides evidence for God and for the moral law. Quoting the Psalms, Augustine wrote, "From weariness our soul rises towards you, first supporting itself on the created order and then passing on to you yourself who wonderfully made it."[11] Fourth, the passage from creation and on to God is by way of Christ and the Spirit (Romans 8:1–2; Galatians 5:1). The soul cannot rise from sin on its own nor pass from the created to love and enjoyment of the uncreated without the Mediator. Augustine's ascent in Christ, then, is a return from the exile of sin empowered by Christ and the Spirit. Finally, St. Paul spoke of Jesus as Lord and of Christians as citizens of heaven (Philippians 3:20). N. T. Wright argues that in claiming Jesus as his Lord, St. Paul was quite explicitly saying that Caesar was not.[12] St. Paul adopted a traditional Jewish critique of pagan empire retelling the story of Israel to serve "as a counter-story to the by now standard imperial narrative of Roman history reaching its climax in Augustus Caesar."[13]

The *Aeneid* consists of an *Odyssey* and an *Iliad*. In the *Odyssey* half we follow Aeneas's wanderings from Troy, across the sea, and through the underworld, to Italy. The *Iliad* portion of the poem takes place in Italy where Aeneas plays his part in the founding of Rome by gaining victory over the forces of opposition. Virgil encompassed in one work the story of Aeneas and the story of Rome. Augustine's *Confessions* may be read in similar fashion. Augustine encompassed in one work his own personal history, in an autobiographical narrative, and the foundation of the Church in his meditations on St. Paul, the Psalms, and Genesis. In his re-narration of pagan virtue, Augustine transposed Virgil's themes from the migration of Greek culture to Italy into the pilgrimage of the Christian soul, and from Aeneas' founding of Rome to God's founding of the Church. The second half of the book narrates a return from the exile of sin rather than Virgil's martial and legal victory over strife and is a more complex and subtle fulfillment of the promises of the first half than we find in the *Aeneid*. Following the path of humility, Augustine is lifted up so that with the help of Christ and the Church he is able to discover in the second half of the book solutions to the difficulties he had narrated and discussed in the first half. Thus, there is an undercurrent of themes in the last six books that mirrors the themes narrated in the first six books.[14] The result is a new community, the city of God, which sees historical progress toward peace as founded on Christian virtue and hope in Christ. Peace must be the product of justice and Christian charity, but it does not mean the absence of all suffering. The structure of the *Confessions* may owe something to Virgil, but the language and meaning are those of scripture.

## VIRGIL'S *AENEID*

In the *Aeneid* we witness Aeneas's development from a "groping follower" to the "conscious and elect instrument, of the Providence that moves the worlds."[15] The dividing point is arguably the seventh book in which Virgil announces a grander theme and a greater work (*Maior rerum mihi nascitur ordo,/ Maius opus moveo*).[16] What, anecdotally, has been the least interesting part of Virgil's text to contemporary readers is, in the author's mind, the more important.

The second half of Virgil's epic completes the first but also carries the plot beyond the narrative of Aeneas's personal history to the history of Rome. Once in Italy, Aeneas plays his part in bringing about the glory of Rome. The action and meaning, however, are extended to encompass the world. The epic becomes universal in both time and space, and what is at stake is the eternal city of peace. That peace is founded on the defeat of strife by martial victory and law revealed by Jupiter in book 1:

> Cana Fides et Vesta, Remo cum fratre Quirinus
> Iura dabunt: dirae ferro et compagibus artis
> Claudentur Belli portae; Furor impius intus
> Saeva sedens super arma et centum vinctus aenis
> Post tergum nodis fremet horridus ore cruento.
>
> [And aged Faith and Vesta,
> together with the brothers, Romulus
> and Remus, shall make laws. The Gruesome gates
> of war, with tightly welded iron plates,
> shall be shut fast. Within, unholy Rage
> shall sit on his ferocious weapons, bound
> behind his back by a hundred knots of brass;
> he shall groan horribly with bloody lips.][17]

Aeneas arrives in Italy as the destined bringer of peace, but he must overcome forces opposed to peace under Roman hegemony. The first part of the poem opened on the storm-tossed sea with Aeneas's fleet subjected to Juno's mad ravings, and in the second, Italy is a new setting for the renewal of Juno's troublemaking. In Italy Juno enlists the aid of Turnus, inciting him to a jealous hatred of the Trojans. Aeneas's opponent in Italy lacks the hero's insight into the destiny of Rome and the ultimate victory of law over strife. Thus in Italy the Trojans are once again besieged but are destined not to fall a second time. They will conquer and, through strength of arms, greatness of character, and divine assistance, will wrest from the gods and humanity peace for Rome and for the world. The peace of Rome is certainly not guaranteed by human might alone, but divine assistance does come in martial form.

I would like to dwell for a moment on book 8, because of its relationship to the *Confessions*. A major theme in book 8 is strife: from Hercules's mythic struggle against the evil Cacus, to the political history of a golden age won and lost, to classical wars, to the psychological division of Aeneas's own troubled mind. The many forms of strife are woven into the images on a massive shield forged by Vulcan, whose erotic violence is quieted by the eternal love of Venus and subverted to good purpose, and the Cyclopes, whose contribution to Aeneas's fortunes causes the reader to question who really are the natural enemies of peace.[18] All of this is contrasted with a sense of the pastoral that seems to follow Aeneas through this and the next book. Shortly after arriving in the destined homeland we find Aeneas in a secluded spot, alone and restless. In his divided condition, Aeneas is visited by the river god Tiber who reveals to him the means by which he may conquer the warring Latins by enlisting other nations against Turnus's army.[19]

While the actual founding of Rome and the fulfillment of the grand destiny lies beyond the scope of the poem, Aeneas' part is paradigmatic for all those who follow in his line. He wins, through piety, valor, and devotion to civic duty, the reconciliation of gods and humanity. He learns through trial and error and the intervention of his father, Anchises, and his goddess-mother to follow the direction of Providence unhesitatingly. Aeneas embodies the Roman spirit. He preserves the duties of hospitality and piety. He sheds blood, not willingly, but out of necessity; though, if his passion *for* war is quelled, he retains his passion *in* war. Finally, he identifies his own happiness and destiny with the good of Rome. For a time Turnus stands in contrast to Aeneas. Turnus is committed to a destiny of his own and is not the instrument of destiny but the puppet of the gods. In the end, in a moment of personal awakening, Turnus relents.

## *ODYSSEY*: SIN AND LIFE UNDER THE ETERNAL LAW

Augustine made use of Virgil's own structure and imagery to create a Christian literature of sin, virtue, Providence, and the kingdom of God. In bringing together Virgil and St. Paul, Augustine modified the poet's literary design. He presented his own odyssey in dialectical terms governed by a sense of divine irony. Augustine's odyssey is only paradoxically a journey toward a homeland. His soul's wandering is a flight from God, which only God could transform into an unwitting movement toward God. His deliberate ascent is founded on the embrace of humility and the lessons of Christ's lowly humanity.

In the first part of the *Confessions*, the author's spiritual wanderings were, as were the wanderings of Aeneas, both providential and the products of the vicissitudes of human life. Among those vicissitudes of Augustine's life was the *Aeneid* itself, with its power to elicit sympathy for illicit behavior, together with the disvalues of his teachers and role models, who cared more for the *errores* of speech than of soul. Augustine however also drew attention to his own disordered desire. Augustine remains throughout the text, as is highlighted in book 10, a groping follower as well as a willing instrument of Providence. Throughout the first half of the text, Augustine wove together the natural goodness of creation and learning, their corruption according to human custom, and the use made of even that corruption by divine Providence.[20]

The first half of Augustine's text contains a tale of missteps, missed opportunities, and deep pathos. The action in the first six books of the *Aeneid* moves forward, that of the *Confessions* backwards. Augustine's narrated, younger self believed that he was moving toward God. However, the narrator dwells on experiences of bitterness, disappointment, and blindness to convince the reader of his steady decline in the first half of the text. The pattern is that of the law and grace in Paul's Letter to the Romans. Augustine saw himself in the condition of those who have the law written on their hearts but do not live by it. By the lights God had given him, Augustine should have known better, but failed to learn right. By failing to learn he condemned himself and became a victim of the universal law that in bitterness and disappointment showed him his sin, but not the way out of it.

The odyssey begins at birth, and, in some sense, before birth. Though Augustine maintained an agnostic position with respect to the origin of the human soul, he knew one thing both by observations of other infants and on the authority of Psalm 50(51)—that he was born in sin. From this bleak starting point things go from bad to worse, as the impressionable child is handed over to moral incompetents. Thus sin grows as individuals formed according to human customs measure their world and their God according to their own likes and dislikes. The result of his education and of the examples set before him was that Augustine learned to love more ardently what is of less value and to neglect the true love and goodness of God. One wants to believe that education is the beginning for something good for children, but Augustine stressed how what should have been a blessing was a curse. The study of grammar is important, and ought to provide the reader with the opportunity to learn virtue from salutary texts.[21] However, the manner in which grammar is taught—the disorienting and distorting scenes, like the tragedy of Dido, that evoke sympathy for misdeeds and, like theatrical performances of illicit behavior, that elicit satisfaction at the sufferings of a wretch—twist the good of grammar and literature to evil purpose. The missteps of teachers and pupils lead to disastrous consequences.

A further stage in the descending action is the corruption of the highest earthly blessing, friendship. Friendship itself possesses no natural or compulsory power to inculcate virtue apart from rectitude of the will. Friendship is a great gift benefiting those willingly subjected to filial correction, but harmful to those who are not: friendship may be a "dangerous enemy, a seduction of the mind."[22] Later in book 6 Augustine acknowledged that he loved his friends, without whom he could not be happy, imperfectly because he did not recognize that God was his happiness and not his friends.[23] Augustine lamented that in his youth there was no restraint imposed upon his disorder by the "exchange of mind with mind, which marks the brightly lit pathway of friendship."[24] Such restraint could have come from his parents (and both his father and mother are censured for not guiding him in the direction of marriage: "both of them, as I realized, were very ambitious for me").[25] Finally, restraint could have come from an encounter with the texts of scripture. He does encounter some saying from St. Paul concerning marriage chanted from his mother's lips,[26] though he successfully ignored it. In this book we do not see Augustine reading or conversing with anyone. In fact, Augustine accuses God of silence.[27]

Augustine illustrated, by his youthful theft of some second-rate pears, how sin vitiates nature's gifts. He wrote that his theft of the pears was without any other motive than the exercise of his own will. Under the pressure of his peers, he was seduced, not by the natural beauty of the fruit (in comparison to which his own fruit trees were more fine), but by his own power to act. The elder Augustine believed that his act was an imitation of divine freedom—the power to act contrary to law and without punishment. He saw in this act some fundamental selfishness, the desire to be God. This selfishness is also evident in the way one might reward oneself for one's virtue and thereby love God less.

In book 3 Augustine further describes the seductive character of the soul's powers. Love, Plato's *eros*, was, in Augustine's pagan tradition, a tremendous force attracting the soul to the good and elevating it above the life of the senses.[28] He wrote that he loved to be in love.[29] There is in this opening passage of book 3 a subtle contrast between this illicit motive, which will accept any base object, and that which ought to be the motive of love—goodness. Such a disorientation would not be possible if the human will were simply motivated by the goodness or beauty in things, as Augustine seems to have opined in his early life. As in the case of theatrical performances, passion is deformed by association with false or base objects and does not spontaneously find the good.

The disorientation of love has a debilitating effect on the mind. Augustine knew that incorruptibility was to be esteemed higher than corruptibility, yet he could not let his loving be directed by this principle. He had no appetite for the higher things,[30] and this false satiety prevented Augustine from deriving any benefit from his reading of Cicero's *Hortensius*.[31] Augustine explained that "from a self-concerned pride a false unity is loved in the part."[32] He knew Cicero was correct to counsel study of the whole of philosophy, but he loved more what his eyes showed him. Thus, he was unable to learn from the text that might have imposed a restraint on his desires and prevented him from falling in with the Manichees who fed his hunger for corporeal images. Further, his self-love or pride created for him certain difficulties, for instance the problem of divine justice, on which the Manichees capitalized. He was unable to learn from the lessons that were all around him (including the art of poetic composition of which he was a practitioner) that a single principle may admit of variation in diverse circumstances. (The explanation of this principle occurs in book 11 in the discussion of eternity and time.)

Augustine's flight from God reaches perhaps its deepest pathos in book 4. The distance between Augustine and God (though, of course, not between God and Augustine) underlines the pathos of Augustine's first great tragedy, the loss of his closest friend. Augustine could find no consolation in the God in whom he had come to believe.[33] Believing God to be what he is not, Augustine could not love the God he believed in.[34] Misconceiving God and his creatures, Augustine loved neither, though he desired both. Mistaking the part for the whole, the disordered soul loves changeable things, as Augustine did, as if they were unchangeable.[35] The problem begins with the fact that the senses are themselves incapable of grasping the whole, for unity is not given to the senses.[36] His own pride kept him from ascending beyond the senses. He knew himself to be mutable, so he preferred to think of God in the same way rather than to think of himself as being other than what God is.[37] Such a God affords no consolation nor any rest. The pathos of sin is complete. What remains is Augustine's contribution to the cultural decline.

In book 5 Augustine moves from Carthage to Rome and becomes an active participant in the propagation of human custom. Although we might feel sympathy with a young professor who seeks to advance from a situation in which the students are granted license to behave wildly to a more comfortable and respectable situation, it is not likely that the Bishop of Hippo would have seen in his action anything but selfishness and a flight from responsibility. Yet, the flight only led to new troubles; for the students in Rome did not like to pay their teachers, and Augustine wrote, "I cordially detested them, but not 'with the perfect hatred' (Ps 138:22); for I probably felt more resentment for what I personally was to suffer from them than for the wrong they were doing to anyone and everyone. . . . But at that time I was determined not to put up with badly behaved people more out of my own interest than because I wanted them to become good for your sake."[38] Augustine had lived up to the expectations of his early role models and become a player in the games of adults. In book 6 we see Augustine also contributing to the disorientation of his friend Alypius.

The result of this blind participation in human custom is the establishment of a philosophy that supports the neglect of intellect and God's light. In book 5 Augustine critiqued those natural philosophers who discovered truths about the universe but did not give themselves to God and reflect in piety on their own intellects or the source of their intelligence.[39] If they did happen to discover the God of Truth who enlightens the intellect, they did not worship him as God nor subject their own imaginings to the immutable standard of judgment in an awareness of their own natures and of their Creator. Augustine put himself in this class, recounting that his own wicked impiety was a contributing cause to his inability to think of God aright.[40] He found it more comforting to his pride to attribute sin not to himself but to some separate substance.

Augustine discovered that the expectation of self-reliance contributes not only to a misperception of the nature of evil, but also to a failure to properly apprehend the nature and advantages of belief. Under the influence of the Academics and of his own feelings of having been fooled once by the Manicheans, Augustine did not take advantage of the truth of God's immateriality as Ambrose taught. He would not make an act of belief in the truth of such a proposition by resting on the authority of Scripture, the Church, or even of Ambrose.[41] Only after his conversion in the garden in book 8 is Augustine able to trust God for continence and his Scriptures and Church for inspiration.

Sin and the communal effects of evil are not the only forces at work in the first half of the book. As members of the human community, individuals find themselves to various degrees on the right side or the wrong side of an eternal, divine law, which serves a pedagogical function and which they can never escape. All things in God's realm work providentially for the elimination of evil and the moral improvement of creatures. From the misguided punishments of his teachers,[42] to the bitterness he experienced in the satisfaction of his own disordered desires,[43] Augustine discerned the hand of Providence rescuing from sin those who have departed from God. The more miserable he was, the nearer he was to God.[44] The intimacy of Providence is imaged in the care bestowed on infants through the impulses of the caretakers.[45] Augustine also argued that the just punishment of illicit desire is a blindness to the good and indolence with respect to the means to attain it.[46] Although this penal blindness hampers the functioning of the gifts of intelligence and curiosity, it does not obviate them. He asserted that "free curiosity has a greater power to stimulate learning than rigorous coercion."[47] This natural motive is both unsettled by sin and channeled by discipline, if not by responsible adults then by the instructive hand of Providence.

This Providential care is part of the eternal law, and no one is without help or blame before the law. Although Augustine accused his custodians of failing in their duty, he criticized himself for not learning the lessons that punishments were meant to teach in spite of his teachers' intentions. These were the lessons that his True Teacher was teaching him.[48] Although Augustine's home failed to provide him with true friendships, providentially no one who has access to Scripture is without such true friends. Augustine claimed that he had the opportunity to learn from St. Paul; however, he failed to pay "more vigilant heed to your voice from the clouds."[49]

Providence was at work in his own studies. In book 5, when he encountered the natural philosophers, Augustine should have been released from the grip of ambition. Augustine had possessed a desire to rise higher in the Manichean sect. However, by the time he met Faustus, Augustine's own training in the liberal arts had provided him with sufficient knowledge of creation to protect his mind from Faustus' fabulous explanations of reality. His ambition for prominence momentarily checked, Augustine's overriding motive was philosophical curiosity. This lust was not quelled by the scientific knowledge of the natural philosophers, who investigated God without love and piety. Finally, Augustine was first drawn to Ambrose not for his wisdom but for his rhetorical technique, and his ambition associated with the Manichees is simply replaced by political ambition.

Even his desire for a comfortable life in pursuit of wisdom which, he thought, would help him to achieve self-mastery and happiness in this life, and which was met only by frustration, was the work of guiding Providence. As a result of his learning and his sadness Augustine is made aware of his sinful condition but lacks that power to raise himself above it. His persistent belief that happiness might consist in an earthly concord of love among friends prevented him from learning the lessons his unhappiness was meant to teach. He was also unable to discern this, because his pride led him to expect that continence ought to be within his own power, and to resist submitting himself to the counsels of Scripture and the Church in which he was a catechumen. However, the law of Providence, like the Law in St. Paul, offers instruction but does not offer the power to obey. This comes only with power of the Spirit poured forth into the human heart that enables one to live in imitation of the humility of Christ.[50]

## A HOMELAND, OF SORTS

Book 7 is a complex text. We have seen how Providence was at work in Augustine's studies. Now he explains how, with the help of the books of the Platonists, he was able to resolve "the principal and almost sole cause" of his error,[51] the belief that what is real must exist materially. He learned to think about existence not as the bodily substance of stuff as presented to the senses but as truth grasped in an affirmation that something depends on God for its being.[52] This intellectual conversion is the product of his intellectual ascent from bodily things, to the senses, to the mind that judges impressions, to the power of reasoning, to God who exists above the mind and enlightens the mind.[53] With this insight came an intellectual awakening including a discovery of self and the illumination of the mind, a solution to the problem of evil, and the beginnings of the contemplation of eternity. Thus, there is a change of "scene."

However, Augustine's insight did not grant him the power to enjoy eternity or to love God. Although certain that the conceptions he found in the books of the Platonists were true, Augustine confessed, "to enjoy you I was too weak."[54] The problem is not that Augustine's escape from the material world is incomplete and that the body itself holds him back. The problem is that the intellectual discovery does not overcome pride as the besetting problem: "Where was the charity which builds on the foundation of humility which is Christ Jesus? When would the Platonist books have taught me that?"[55] It was primarily his moral, not his ontological, attachment to the body that prevented the reversal of the descent by an ascent to God. Augustine's moral condition in this book is still one of presumption and pride.

Thus, since the books of the Platonists did not reveal the path to true happiness, he did not present this new scene as his proper homeland. It was, at best, an intellectual resting point or a halfway house. Augustine concluded his discussion of the Platonists by contrasting where he had arrived with where he was going:

> It is one thing from a wooded summit to catch a glimpse of the homeland of peace and not to find the way to it, but vainly to attempt the journey along an impracticable route surrounded by the ambushes and assaults of fugitive deserters with their chief, "the lion and the dragon" (Ps 90: 13). It is another thing to hold on to the way that leads there, defended by the protection of the heavenly emperor. There no deserters from the heavenly army lie waiting to attack. For this way they hate like a torture.[56]

Augustine's homeland, which Augustine/Aeneas does not recognize until he has arrived there, is not affirmation at a distance, but intimate affection for the truth. For this reason, the hero of Augustine's narrative does not know that he is at the threshold of a greater theme. He is aware only of the distance and the hostility between him and God—a distance and hostility, he will discover, of his own making.

Finally, in the seventh book, Augustine offered a schematic summary of the journey that awaits him in the second half of the text—an ascent of heart and mind to God along the path of humility modeled by Christ's humanity and empowered by the Eucharist. Here Augustine not only explains the role of the Mediator in Christian salvation, he also contrasts Christian revelation with the insight of the Platonists concerning the role of the Word in creation and Providence: "First you wanted to show me how you 'resist the proud and give grace to the humble' (1 Pet. 5: 5), and with what mercy you have shown humanity the way of humility in that your 'Word was made flesh and dwelt among' men" (John 1:14).[57] Then he writes,

> I sought a way to obtain strength enough to enjoy you; but I did not find it until I embraced "the mediator between God and man, the man Christ Jesus" (1 Tim 2:5), "who is above all things, God blessed for ever" (Rom 9:5). He called and said "I am the way and the truth and the life" (John 14:6). The food which I was too weak to accept he mingled with flesh, in that "The Word was made flesh" (John 1:14), so that our infant condition might come to suck milk from your wisdom by which you created all things. To possess my God the humble Jesus, I was not yet humble enough. I did not know what his weakness was meant to teach.[58]

The difference between the books of the Platonists and scripture, then, is the difference between presumption and confession, between apprehending truth and loving it with a humble and contrite heart. The books of the Platonists could only have pointed him away from the acceptance of the flesh of Christ as the key to human happiness and from participation in the sacraments—the divine assistance offered in accommodation to human minds and hearts. What Augustine needed strength for was not simply the contemplation of eternal truth, but for the acceptance and love of the created world with all its warts and bruises. To affirm God as Creator and Provider, for Augustine, meant that there was no evil in the divine realm. To disapprove of anything in creation, even of what tastes bitter to diseased senses, is to impugn the Creator, to miss the lessons of guiding Providence, and to attribute evil where none exists: "For you evil does not exist at all, and not only for you but for your created universe, because there is nothing outside it which could break it and destroy the order which you have imposed upon it."[59] His ascent from material things to their eternal cause was always accompanied by a return to those same created things in appreciation of their beauty and existence as creatures of God, in acceptance of the lessons providentially contained in them, and in reverence for the divine, sacramental assistance.

At this point in the text, the centrality of the Eucharist and the mysteries of the Church is clear, but Augustine had forecast this new mode of ascent earlier in the narrative. Augustine had criticized the practice of deferring baptism and of keeping him from being brought up in the Church and from participating in the sacraments. He affirmed that it would have been better had he been baptized and "been quickly healed and if, thanks to the diligent care of my family and my own decisions, action had been taken by which I received the health of my soul and was kept safe under the protection which you would have given me."[60] Also, lest we were inclined to mistake his encounter with Cicero's *Hortensius* as the beginning of his return to God, Augustine announced that "Return to you is along the path of devout humility," by which we are purified of evil habits. The cup of redemption is confession, not philosophy.[61] Confession means not forgetfulness but remembrance of history by which self-knowledge is met with the external teachings of doctrine leading to an inner disturbance of soul (i.e., contempt for one's sin) and conversion of the mind to God. The importance of baptism, Eucharist, and the work of ecclesial ministers is made explicit in book 13. The goal of the text from this point on is the Church, the community of believers, or the City of God whose foundation in the Trinity is most clearly laid out in the last book.

## *ILIAD*: RETURN FROM EXILE AND THE FOUNDATION OF THE CHURCH

As mentioned before, the second half for the text complements the first in mirrored fashion. The kingdom of God is quite literally in the text the reversal of the human kingdom. Books 8 to 10 concern Augustine's overcoming of self (though it would be more accurate to say Christ's overcoming of Augustine), and books 11 to 13 are about Christ's victory over the world. Thus in the first three books of the second half Augustine is both Aeneas and Turnus. For this reason, Augustine's odyssey seems to overlap his participation in the founding event.[62] No one stands between Augustine and the fulfillment of his destiny but Augustine. In the end, his war is with no one else, and his last victory is over his own will. But, ultimately, the *Confessions* is not about Augustine but about Christ, who alone is victorious over strife—through Scripture, conversion, and the ministry of the Church.

## OVERCOMING SELF

In the eighth book the Virgilian and the Pauline structures of the *Confessions* meet and the pagan narrative of virtue and peace is overturned by the Christian. It is here that Augustine begins to explain the difference between a pagan assessment of progress and a Christian notion of progress and regress within the bounds and under the control of eternal Providence.[63] What appears to be defeat is affirmed according to Pauline logic to be victory, and victory defeat. In this way the conquest of Rome, or the establishment of an eternal city solely by force of arms and law, is an example of regress. In so far as the victors relied on human power and wisdom instead of Christ's wisdom and humility, they were ultimately unable to overcome the enemies of humanity. Although Augustine quoted or drew upon Virgil at several points in the *Confessions*, almost all of the quotations and illusions are from the first half, Aeneas's odyssey. Here Augustine includes his only quotation from the second half of Virgil's work:

> Until he [Victorinus] was of advanced years, he was a worshipper of idols and took part in sacrilegious rites. At the time almost all of Roman nobility was enthusiastic for the cult of Osiris and "Monstrous gods of every kind and Anubis the barking dog, Monsters who once bore arms against Neptune and Venus and against Minerva" (Virgil, *Aeneid* 8. 698f.), gods that Rome once conquered but then implored for aid.[64]

The passage that Augustine quoted here is from the description of the legendary heroes pictured on Vulcan's shield. Augustine uses this image to contrast the pagan martial heroes who failed to overcome the monstrous gods, with Christian heroes who overcame the world and the pagan gods. Without condemning explicitly all pagan gods, Augustine points out the difficulty anyone might recognize between legend and cult. Yet, he hints here at the limitations of the Roman conquest narrated by Virgil, and Victorinus and Christian martyrs provide genuine role models.[65] What we see in book 8 is that his earlier intellectual conversion was followed by a moral conversion in which God healed his divided will and granted the gift of continence. Augustine quoted Romans 7:24–25, "Wretched man that I was, who would deliver me from this body of death other than your grace through Jesus Christ our Lord?"[66]

The eighth book stands as complement and reversal of the sixth. Where Augustine had earlier thought that virtue could be obtained by self-mastery, he wins this moral victory over self through the gift of continence. The narrative of Augustine's famous conversion scene has been the topic of some debate, since no corroborating evidence has come to light. Some critics are tempted to find here a literary device, and we might notice echoes of Virgil. There is a tantalizing parallel between Aeneas on the banks of the Tiber and Augustine in the garden. Both appear to be at an impasse, divided within themselves about how to proceed and lacking the necessary resources. In both instances a divine figure appears to show the way and to grant the needed assistance. In Augustine's case the divine figure is Lady Continence. She, Augustine learns, may be possessed only as a gift humbly sought and not by an effort of self-mastery. In the attitude of humility, Augustine was also able to overcome his negative assessment of belief narrated in book 6.

His moral conversion was followed by his religious conversion in book 9.[67] Here Augustine expressed his unrestrained love of the doctrine and Scriptures of the Church in his extended meditation on Psalm 4. Wanting to be overheard, Augustine expresses his desire to take up his new role as leader in the Church rather than as purveyor of human custom. With the beginning of his heart's detachment from secular success, Augustine also moved further away from the philosophers in book 5 who did not investigate God with a religious spirit, and was able to experience an affection for eternity in his conversation with Monica. Here his belief in eternity is no longer limited by his imagination as it was earlier. Instead, in conversation with his mother concerning heaven, Augustine let the one judgment that God creates from eternity replace all his imaginings and any ideas he might have about God's nature.[68] When his mind, freed from its own vain conceptions, was thus grounded on a true judgment and his will is open to divine assistance, Augustine experienced the joy of eternity, for which he hungered for so long but for which he only recently had a taste.

Book 10 marks a final stage in his self-overcoming. Augustine, in book 4, had attributed his earlier blindness to his attraction to created things or to thinking with the mind of the flesh. He could not love God or find in God any consolation because his god was a fantasy. By contrast, he reflected in book 10 on his own mind as drawn beyond itself by the attraction of eternity. The pattern here reflects the ascent described in book 7, only this time he moves from things remembered or the content of memory, to the power by which he judges the value of his memories and experiences dissatisfaction, to the Light that illuminates his memory and grants the dissatisfaction.[69] God illumines the mind by granting an attachment to the whole.[70] We desire to possess the whole of what we possess now only in part. In light of this attachment the mind is aware that a piece of what ought to be held together as a whole is missing. Being in possession of partial joy or happiness, we all desire the fullness of joy and happiness. The missing piece is sought after in virtue of what has been retained.[71] In this way, the will, desirous of the whole and dissatisfied with partial goods, may be convicted of error by God, who will not be possessed together with error.

On this basis, Augustine is able to offer his account of his previous mistakes and to pass judgment on himself. He contrasts his earlier blindness-caused-by-pride with illumination-revealed-in-humility, and he discovers in himself the real difference between the lust for knowing and a genuine love of truth. The lust for knowing is not simply a disease of the natural philosophers and peripatetics, it is a human disorder that is not overcome by the Platonic discovery of the transcendent immateriality of the divine or the non-existence of evil. Augustine reflected that he had been in the condition of knowing but not loving the truth, and knew that it is possible for someone even to hate the truth. From this, he observed that there is a distinction between assent and consent or between the intellectual assent to truth and the consent of the will that loves something good.[72]

The task of the moral life, then, is to bring consent in line with assent. Human beings fall by loving created things as though they were uncreated and parts of creation as if they were the whole. They rise as they learn to enjoy God not for any "reward save the joy that you are to them. This is the authentic happy life, to set one's joy on you, grounded in you and caused by you."[73] Happiness lies not in escape from material conditions and a desire to cease to be human, but in the love of what God has done, and a desire to be the kind of creatures God created, that is a community of pilgrims.[74]

The destiny of human life is not the transitory peace that is obtainable on earth. However, one does not obtain peace by escaping the transitory condition of pilgrims. Alluding to the first book of the Bible, Augustine wrote, "I have become for myself a soil which is a cause of difficulty and much sweat" (Gen 3:17ff).[75] Augustine believed that there were some temptations that he could never escape since the fulfillment of certain necessities of life and the obligations of his position brought a certain amount of satisfaction that remained as a snare for him. These dangers are a part of the requirements of justice, for the Christian vocation is not simply contemplation, but love and concern for others.[76] Augustine confessed that he longed to take flight from the temptations of the world in a life of solitude. But, this was forbidden to him, for God's gifts were given him for the sake of the community, and he found new consolation in participating and distributing Christ's body for the sake of those for whom Christ died.[77]

## FOUNDING OF THE CHURCH—BOOK 11: ETERNITY AND TIME

The problem of justice and temporality addressed in book 3 is resolved in book 11. Since the concern of the Christian life is both worship of God and the well being of others, the Christian community is rooted in justice and seeks temporal peace. This is possible only when one loves God above all else. Augustine conceived of justice in relation to God's eternity and Providence. What Augustine could not yet understand as a student at Carthage was how divine justice could remain immutable while its proscriptions differed with time and place (most notably laws regarding polygamy and unique commands to perform acts customarily deemed unjust).[78] Also, he had trouble with the relationship of justice to intention.

For instance, he affirmed that the accumulation of possessions may or may not be from greed and that the punishment of overt acts may proceed from desire for improvement of citizens or else from vengeance.[79] Both actions and intentions are understood to be a part of justice. Thus, Providence justly condemned his pursuit of moral rectitude, since it proceeded, not from a desire to love God above all things, but from impure motives—a desire for love. We see in this book how a correct understanding of time and eternity leads to a correct estimate of suffering and human happiness. Since Augustine was unable to pass judgment on his own intentions, he was unable to discover in eternity the unfailing justice according to which his own misery was a sign of God's provident care. God did not create the human heart to rest in vanities.

An appreciation of God's benevolence in the midst of suffering and temptation is founded on an understanding of God's unchanging, eternal nature. For, as we have seen, Augustine held that there is no evil in creation. Yet, justice is displeasing to the wicked who desire that what eternity has caused should be otherwise than it is.[80] Augustine offers an account of eternity from an understanding of creation. Creation is not formation, and whatever God creates undergoes a change from having no potency for existence to possessing existence. That is to say, no capacity to change preceded creation in any way. Likewise, no time as the measure of motion or change preceded creation in any way. Augustine affirmed that "everything is said in the simultaneity of eternity. Otherwise time and change would already exist, and there would not be a true eternity and immortality."[81] Yet, not everything simultaneously created exists simultaneously. What undergoes a change from non-existence to existence has a beginning and an end in time. Divine justice, therefore, is identical and simultaneous while the "times which it rules over are not identical, for the simple reason that they are times."[82]

Finally, understanding the relation of eternity and time clarifies the difficulties in book 10 concerning the promise of happiness (i.e., freedom from temptation) and inescapability of temptation in this life: "For 'by hope we are saved,' and we await your promises in patience."[83] We cannot escape the temporal unfolding of divine justice and Providence; yet, God is more intimate to us than we to ourselves, and we are never closer or further away from eternity. Ordered desire loves the temporal for the sake of the eternal and makes the mind and heart submissive to the historical events of salvation and to the details of one's personal journey out of love for the eternal end of all things. This is true humility. The pure intention to serve God means to submit to the work of Providence while "scattered in times whose order I do not understand . . . moving not towards those future things which are transitory but to 'the things which are before' me, not stretched out in distraction but extended in reach, not by being pulled apart but by concentration."[84] The soul ordered to eternity accepts in faith and hope the various times and their unity in the context of the whole of eternity and of Providence and not in opposition to these. Thus the Christian community is founded on the historical works of Providence witnessed in Scripture and graces given under the bodily form of the sacraments.

## BOOK 12: FRIENDSHIP

The constitution of a community is founded more in friendship than in law, since friendship brings about a unity of souls.[85] In the next book Augustine took up the theme of Christian friendship. Here Augustine made use of a type-antitype relationship between his youthful companions in book 2 and his fellow pilgrims in book 12. In book 2 Augustine saw himself as moving from unity into multiplicity under the misguidance of his parents and influence of his friends.[86] Book 2 is the only book in which Augustine is separated from his studies, and in which, apart from the story of Catiline, we do not see him reading any books. Even God is silent.

By contrast book 12 contains Augustine's hermeneutic for reading Scripture and presents Moses in the image of a true friend. Except for the fact that a living friend may be queried for clarification, reading Scripture is not unlike speaking to a friend. As with any conversation partner, one person is unable to see into the mind of the other and must interpret the words spoken and believe that the account is a faithful representation of the speaker's meaning.[87] Thus Augustine wrote, "It is one thing to inquire into the truth about the origin of creation. It is another to ask what understanding of the words on the part of a reader and hearer was intended by Moses, a distinguished servant of your faith."[88]

Augustine therefore argues for a generous hermeneutic. Since he cannot see in the mind of Moses what he meant when he wrote the opening verses of Genesis, at least in his love for God and his servant he was willing to impute to Moses any legitimate reading that was consonant with truth. Bringing a charitable mind to Scripture, he treats his author as a friend and tries to make sense out of the text giving the author the benefit of the doubt and attributing, as much as possible, to the author only what makes the text true: "In Bible study all of us are trying to find and grasp the meaning of the author we are reading, and when we believe him to be revealing truth, we do not dare to think he said anything which we either know or think to be incorrect."[89] Thus an author can become a friend when readers subject their minds to the rule of truth and the requirements of unity in Christian charity. Augustine brought to his reading of Genesis three truths that he affirmed on other grounds: the immutability and eternity of God, the temporal and dependent existence of creatures, and the mode by which the House of God may be conceived to be both created and immortal.

Christian friendship is founded on the recognition of the absolute goodness of the Creator and the relative goodness of all created things and on the true things narrated in the Scripture. With Moses and all Christians, Augustine shared a desire for the House of God, the true Jerusalem, which is the created and yet immutable home for pilgrims. The very nature of the House of God as created perfection sets limits to the emergence of human pride. "Pride imitates what is lofty,"[90] and Augustine saw in his theft the prideful imitation of God's power and freedom. Augustine argued that even the highest creation, that immutable realm toward which the human mind strives, is only immutable in its contemplation of God and is, in principle, dependent on God precisely because it is created. Also, the wisdom it possesses is created and has its source in God. Christians, then, should not seek to escape time and creation, but should seek to imitate the House of God. Augustine, finally, offered his text in friendship to any who would read it with a loving heart.[91]

## BOOK 13: THE CITY OF GOD

Augustine's final book recapitulates the entire work, making a new beginning.[92] In it Augustine attempted to discern the principles of the City of God or heavenly city in Genesis 1. What he presents is the reverse of what he experienced as a youth being brought up in a classical pagan culture, albeit as a catechumen with a devout mother. Pagan cultural formation never even attains its goal of virtue in so far as it fails to love God above all else and to think of God aright. Justice demands that God the source of all be loved above all and given his due. It also demands that what is of more value be esteemed above what is of less value. A culture or custom of formation that systematically excludes this fact and fails to nurture a just intention with respect to God could not attain its natural end, the education of virtue. It would be extraordinary for students to learn virtue from role models, like those in book 1, who are not themselves ordered in mind and heart to God above all else. The examples of their lives would overshadow the meaning of their words. In the heavenly city strength comes from the sacraments and the ministers who model this good intention by their ascetic lifestyle and care of the welfare of others.

As the earthly city is human custom, the heavenly city is only analogously a city. It is founded on true teaching, and it is directed by a deliberate intention to please God and so bears fruit—it is able to enjoy God.[93] It extends beyond the borders of city, nation, or race to include all those seeking Christian virtue.[94] It exists most clearly wherever a soul that has been made subject to God through ministry, baptism, and the gifts of continence and renewal of mind has "need of no human authority as a model to imitate."[95] It exists to redeem creation and shares with the earthly city the same concern for justice and "the same end of temporal and earthly felicity."[96] The heavenly city pursues, no less than the earthly, "such kindness as rescuing a person suffering injustice from the hand of the powerful and providing the shelter of protection by the mighty force of just judgment."[97] The heavenly does this more perfectly because of its foundation on Christ, the sacraments, and true friendship. The church "is not an entity distinct from the world, but the world reconciled unto itself and unto God: *mundus reconciliatus ecclesia*."[98] However this is accomplished in time, and its benefits are manifest only gradually. Christian life beginning with baptism is a long process of the healing and reformation of creation that is completed only beyond history. Yet, although it has an eschatological dimension, it does not exist apart from creation and its progress is real

## CONCLUSION

Between the time of his conversion and the writing of the *Confessions*, Augustine struggled to reconcile his place in the church with his aspirations to pursue personal virtue apart from the temptations of the world. In Augustine's *Confessions* the liberal arts as they were shaped and determined by the study of classic Roman literature are relativized by baptism and Christian ministry. The result is in no way a rejection of the human sciences, for their limited yet salutary role is preserved. But, it does indicate the role faith and confession play in the purification of reason and the will and points to the transcendent goal of human happiness beyond space and time.

Human happiness consists not in a Neo-Platonic contemplation of God and an escape from time and matter, but in a temporal return from exile. The political philosopher Eric Voegelin claimed that progress in history is always a movement away from love of self and toward the love of God. And he put Augustine's expression of that movement at the center of his philosophy of history:

> Exeunt enim multi latentur,
> et exeuntium pedes sunt cordis affectus:
> exeunt autem de Babylonia.
>
> [He begins to leave who begins to love.
> Many the leaving who know it not,
> for the feet of those leaving are the affections of the heart:
> and yet, they are leaving Babylon][99]

## NOTES

1. Gillian Clark comments that "Augustine, whose life had been shaped by the written word, acknowledges that he was looking for a text to change his life" (*Augustine: The Confessions* [Cambridge: Cambridge University Press, 1993]) p. 68.

2. That there is such a literary unity of the text is by no means the common opinion. John J. O'Meara in *The Young Augustine* (New York: Alba House, 1965) asserted that the *Confessions* lacks structure. Henri-Irénée Marrou in *Saint Augustin et la fin de la culture antique* (Paris: Boccard, 1938) supposed that if there were a unity it "is psychological and not literary." Quoted in Frederick J. Crosson, "Structure and Meaning in St. Augustine's *Confessions*," in Gareth B. Matthews, ed., *The Augustinian Tradition* (Berkley, Los Angeles, and London: University of California Press, 1999) p. 27–38.

3. James J. O'Donnell, *Augustine: A New Biography* (New York, London, Toronto, and Sydney: Harper Collins, 2005), p. 140.

4. Sabine MacCormick comments that "The playful allegory of [Vergilian] images endowed the discourses of Cassiciacum with beauty and charm, but this was not the only dimension that Vergil brought to the conversations between Augustine and his students. At times Vergil's verses articulated the very truth that was being sought by this small assemble of lovers of wisdom. Supplications that were addressed in Vergil's poem to Apollo, the god of prophecy, thus became for Augustine steps toward his own supplication of the Christian god. In a broader, more sweeping sense, the protracted wanderings, *errores*, that had led Aeneas from his native city of Troy to distant Italy exemplified for Augustine the many years he himself had spent searching for the truth whereby God might be known. Vergil's verses could accordingly direct a 'well-educated soul' to endure life's vicissitudes as steadfastly and firmly as the exemplary characters of the *Aeneid* had done: 'Firmly he stands, like a rock in the sea'" (*The Shadows of Poetry: Vergil in the Mind of Augustine* [Berkley, Los Angeles, and London: University of California Press, 1998]) p. 48.

5. "The theoretical pretext," writes O'Donnell, "for the *Confessions*, as scholars have long seen, was the upheaval in Augustine's reading of Paul that occurred in the months that followed his ordination as bishop." The *Confessions* "has three main forces running through it: first, the will to affirm the idealized, spiritual religion that he had discovered a decade earlier; second, the need to confront the ambiguities and frustrations of his Episcopal position; third, his longing for an appropriate literary and spiritual agenda, for a personal life to accompany his public one" (O'Donnell, *Augustine*, p. 78). Frances Young asserts that the text is imbued with what she calls "typological imagination" by which Augustine's own life is presented in terms of a type of the Christian life informed by his reading of Paul; see Young, "The *Confessions* of Saint Augustine: What is the Genre of This Work?" *Augustinian Studies* 30-1 (1999) 1–16.

6. MacCormick, *Shadows of Poetry*, p. 53.

7. *The Teacher* 2.3. The sentence Augustine chose for his grammatical example is instructive of his early sense of the relationship of the Christian God to the Roman empire: *Si nihil ex tanta superis placet urbe relinqui*. See J. H. S. Burleigh, ed., *Augustine: Earlier Writings* (Philadelphia: Westminster Press, 1953), p. 69–101.

8. Augustine, *Epistulae* CCLVIII.5, quoted in MacCormick, *Shadows of Poetry*, p. 38.

9. *Confessions* 9.6.14.

10. See Henry Chadwick's note in *Confessions*, p. 164.

11. Augustine, *Confessions* 5.1.1. English translations of the *Confessions* are taken from Henry Chadwick's translation (New York: Oxford University Press, 1992).

12. N. T. Wright, "Paul's Gospel and Caesar's Empire," in R. Horsley, ed., *Paul and Empire* (Harrisburg, PA: Trinity Press International, 1997) p. 160–83.

13. N. T. Wright, *Paul: In Fresh Perspective* (Minneapolis: Fortress Press, 2005), p.78.

14. The rhetorical devise of taking up difficulties in reverse order is observed by others. James J. O'Donnell notes that Augustine treated of the three lusts in this manner. From books 2 through 4 Augustine highlights his sins according to the disordered desires of the flesh (2), of the eyes or curiosity (3), and of secular ambition (4). Augustine's moral recovery "follows a reverse pattern: his zeal for his public career fades first at Milan, then his adhesion to the spirit of curiosity that had led him to the Manichees, and only last his enslavement to the desires of the flesh" (O'Donnell, *Augustine Confessions*, Vol. 1 [Oxford: Clarendon Press, 1992] p. xxxv–xxxvi). However, as will be clear, I do not think that before book 7 there is so much of any actual healing as there is indication of what would have been salutary but for the absence of Christian humility. Kenneth Steinhauser also notes a relationship of problem and solution among the beginning and concluding books of the work. He argues, "In books 11–13 Augustine once again takes up the preoccupations of his youth responding to the questions raised in *De Pulchro et apto*. However, this time Augustine is more concerned with the Creator than creation" (Steinhauser, "The Literary Unity of the Confessions," in Joanne McWilliam, ed., *Augustine: From Rhetor to Theologian* [Waterloo, Ontario: Wilfrid Laurier University Press, 1992] p. 15-30, quotation on p. 21).

15. J. W. Mackail, *Virgil and His Meaning to the World Today* (New York: Cooper Square Publishers, Inc., 1963), p. 94.

16. Virgil, *Aeneide: Testo a fronte*, trans. Rosa Calzecchi Onesti (Torino: Giulio Einaudi editores s. p. a., 1967 and 1989), book 7, lines 44–45.

17. Virgil, *Aeneide*, book 1, lines 292–296. (trans. A. Mandelbaum, *The Aeneid of Virgil: A Verse Translation* [Berkley, Los Angeles, and London: University of California Press, 1971] book 1, lines 412–17).

18. Virgil, *Aeneide* 8.626–728.

19. Virgil, *Aeneide* 8.18–33.

20. Crosson argues that Augustine made room for Providence in the narrative by attempting to the story of his life "in such a way that the sequence of events related is adequately accounted for and yet to tell that story in such a way that those events are not adequately accounted for" (Crosson, "Structure and Meaning," p. 31). Crosson also argues that book 7 is the center of the text for reasons different from my own: book 7 "neatly demarcates the two philosophical problems of God's transcendence and his acting in time, his Word becoming flesh" (Crosson, "Structure and Meaning, 36).

21. Augustine, *Confessions* 1.13.20.

22. Augustine, *Confessions* 2.9.17.

23. Augustine, *Confessions* 6.16.26.
24. Augustine, *Confessions* 2.2.2.
25. Augustine, *Confessions* 2.3.8.
26. Augustine, *Confessions* 2.3.7.
27. Augustine, *Confessions* 2.2.2; 2.3.7.
28. Martha Nussbaum points out Augustine's criticism of Platonic love as ineffective and incompatible with Christian virtue. See. M. Nussbaum, "Augustine and Dante on the Ascent of Love," in Gareth Matthews, ed., *The Augustinian Tradition* (Berkley, Los Angeles, and London: University of California Press, 1999) p. 61–90.
29. Augustine, *Confessions* 3.1.1.
30. Augustine, *Confessions* 3.1.1.
31. As a warning to those who might suppose that Augustine's ascent to God began with his reading *Hortensius*, Augustine notes that "Return to you is along the path of devout humility. You purify us of evil habit, and you are merciful to the sins we confess" (Augustine, *Confessions* 3.8.16).
32. Augustine, *Confessions* 3.8.16.
33. Augustine, *Confessions* 4.4.9; 4.7.12.
34. Augustine, *Confessions* 4.2.3.
35. Augustine, *Confessions* 4.7.12; 4.8.13.
36. Augustine, *On Free Will* 2.8.22, in J. H. S. Burleigh, trans., *Augustine: Earlier Writings* (Philadelphia: Westminster Press, 1958), p. 102–221.
37. Augustine, *Confessions* 4.15.26.
38. Augustine, *Confessions* 5.12.22.
39. Augustine, *Confessions* 5.3.4.
40. Augustine, *Confessions* 5.10.18.
41. Augustine, *Confessions* 6.3.4.
42. Augustine, *Confessions* 1.12.19.
43. Augustine, *Confessions* 2.2.4.
44. Augustine, *Confessions* 6.16.26.
45. Augustine, *Confessions* 1.6.7.
46. Augustine, *Confessions* 1.12.19.
47. Augustine, *Confessions* 1.14.23.
48. Augustine, *Confessions* 1.17.27.
49. Augustine, *Confessions* 2.2.3.
50. Augustine, *Confessions* 13.12.13.
51. Augustine, *Confessions* 5.10.19. In his commentary, James O'Donnell brings out Augustine's later recognition of the critical and dangerous character of this period in his life. He argues that Augustine's intention was not to become a "Plotinian sage" but a Christian who had no need of the walls of a Church: "He thought he was on the straight path to orthodox Christian truth; it was only in retrospect that he saw that he was not" (O'Donnell, *Augustine Confessions*, vol. 2, p. 471).
52. Augustine, *Confessions* 7.15.21.
53. Augustine, *Confessions* 7.10.16.
54. Augustine, *Confessions* 7.20.26. The position here requires greater defense in light of a possible Platonic reading. When Augustine contrasted his vision of God with his "customary condition" and the weight of his body (7.17.23), was he contrasting distinct ways of participating in God according to a Neoplatonic schema

such that Being is correlative to Intellect, but Augustine's vision of God who is beyond Being is a mode of participation that is beyond intelligence? Perhaps his slight esteem for the *Categories* suggests that God cannot be known by the intellect. However, I am to think that Augustine's concern in the *Confessions* is the importance of the sacraments and the relationship between moral virtue, especially humility, and intelligence. Pride prevents one from truly partaking of and enjoying the grace of Eucharist (7.18.24), in part, because of the consequences that Augustine's Eucharistic vision had for thinking about suffering (7.13.19). Thus, I take "customary condition" to refer not to intelligence and the desire to know God, in contrast with a *supra-noetic* ("beyond-intellectual") mode of participation, but to refer to vices and patterns of living that are in tension with the desire to know God and to enjoy God.

55. Augustine, *Confessions* 7.20.26. For the debate concerning Augustine's conversion to the humility of Christ see W. Millard, "The Incarnation in Augustine's Conversion," *Recherches augustiniennes* 15 (1980) 80–98. The theological implications of Augustine's view of a personal growth in faith are brought out in several of Basil Studer's works. He argues in "History and Faith in *De Trinitate*," *Augustinian Studies* 28-1 (1997) 7–50, that Augustine's conception of mediation "expresses a higher reflection on the *res gestae* narrated by the Gospel. ...the mediation of Christ consisted primarily in the revelation of the love of God and in a freely accepted death. In both cases, Christ appeared as what his is, the eternal Son of God: the Son who alone knows the Father, and the Son who alone perfectly accomplishes the will of God" (p. 42). Studer insists that Augustine's "model of *exercitatio mentis* is without doubt a vital one for Christian theology. First of all it includes the faith as far as it is a kind of historical knowledge. In order to believe what we cannot see, the faithful have to submit themselves with confidence and humility to the divine authority which is present in time" (p. 45–46).

56. Augustine, *Confessions* 7.11.27.

57. Augustine, *Confessions* 7.9.13-14.

58. Augustine, *Confessions* 7.18.24.

59. Augustine, *Confessions* 7.13.19.

60. Augustine, *Confessions* 1.11.18.

61. Augustine, *Confessions* 3.8.16.

62. In the *Retractationes*, Augustine described his book as ten books about himself and three on Genesis. This has led some commentators to conclude that the last three books of the *Confessions* represent an incomplete commentary on Genesis. I take Augustine at his word, but that does not mean that there may not be further designs built into the structure of the text.

63. Augustine, *Confessions* 8.5.8.

64. Augustine, *Confessions* 8.2.3.

65. Commenting on the treatment of pagan gods in the *City of God*, Ernest Fortin wondered "whether Augustine's keen sensitivity to the needs of the social life and his profound attachment to Rome 'wicked and dissolute as it was,' were not such as to induce him to temper the radicalness of his own critique by couching it in terms that remain somewhat cautious" (Fortin, "Augustine and Roman Civil Religion," in J. Brian Benestad, ed., *Classical Christianity and the Political Or-*

*der: Reflections on the Theologico-Political Problem* [New York: Rowman & Littlefield Publishers, Inc., 1996] p. 85–105, quotation on p. 97).

66. Augustine, *Confessions* 8.5.12.

67. Bernard Lonergan described these three conversions as shifts in horizon and as modalities of self-transcendence. See Lonergan, *Method in Theology* (Toronto: University of Toronto Press, 1971) p. 237–44.

68. Augustine, *Confessions* 9.10.25.

69. Augustine, *Confessions* 10.17.26; 10.25.36.

70. Augustine, *Confessions* 10.18.27.

71. Augustine, *Confessions* 10.19.28. On the way in which the whole is present to the mind Augustine wrote, "Briefly to express in words as best I can the idea of eternal law as it is stamped on our minds I should say this: it is just that all things should be in perfect order" (Augustine, *On Free of the Will* 1.6.15).

72. Augustine, *Confessions* 10.23.34.

73. Augustine, *Confessions* 10.22.32.

74. Augustine, *Confessions* 10.4.5-6.

75. Augustine, *Confessions* 10.25.25.

76. Augustine, *Confessions* 10.37.61.

77. Augustine, *Confessions* 10.43.70.

78. Augustine, *Confessions* 3.7.13.

79. Augustine, *Confessions* 3.9.17.

80. Augustine, *Confessions* 7.16.22.

81. Augustine, *Confessions* 11.7.9.

82. Augustine, *Confessions* 3.7.13.

83. Augustine, *Confessions* 11.9.11.

84. Augustine, *Confessions* 11.19.39.

85. Augustine, *Confessions* 2.5.10.

86. Augustine, *Confessions* 2.1.1.

87. Augustine, *Confessions* 12.25.35.

88. Augustine, *Confessions* 12.23.32.

89. Augustine, *Confessions* 12.18.27.

90. Augustine, *Confessions* 2.6.13.

91. Augustine, *Confessions* 12.26.36.

92. See Robert McMahon's literary study, *Augustine's Prayerful Ascent* (Athens, GA: The University of Georgia Press, 1989).

93. Augustine, *Confessions* 13.25.38 ff.

94. Fortin, "The Political Thought of St. Augustine," *Classical Christianity*, 1–29.

95. Augustine, *Confessions* 13.33.48.

96. Augustine, *Confessions* 13.17.20.

97. Augustine, *Confessions* 13.17.21.

98. Fortin, "Political Idealism and Christianity," *Classical Christianity*, p. 31–63, quotation on p. 44.

99. Augustine, *Enerrationes in Psalmos* 64.2, quoted in Eric Voegelin, "Immortality: Experience and Symbol," *Collected Works of Eric Voegelin*, Volume 12, Ellis Sandoz, ed. (Baton Rouge: Louisiana State University Press, 1990) p. 52–94, quotation on p. 78. See also Voegelin's "Configurations of History," Collected Works Vol. 12, p. 95–114.

# 5

# Theo-Semiotics and Augustine's Hermeneutical Jew, Or, "What's a Little Supersessionism between Friends?"[1]

C. C. Pecknold

## INTRODUCTION

Jewish historians have recently returned to St. Augustine's so-called witness doctrine, concerning the protected status of the Jew in a number of his works. One of the motivating factors for the interest, as made evident in Jeremy Cohen's recent *Living Letters of the Law: Ideas of the Jew in Medieval Christianity*, has been the recognition that the positive effects of Augustine's witness doctrine may outweigh some of the more anti-Jewish polemics inherent in early church discourse.[2] Augustine's own distinctive version of the witness doctrine is understood as foundational for a whole series of policy decisions in the medieval church which amounted to the protection and preservation of Jewish communities. In the light of this history of positive effects, it is perhaps surprising, as Cohen notes, that "despite limitless modern interest in Augustine, scholars have still not explicated much of the complexity in his teaching on the Jews and Judaism."[3] One of the key features of Cohen's own analysis of Augustine's reception of the Christian tradition of the witness doctrine, as well as his recognition of Augustine's distinctive development of the doctrine, resides in his awareness that the Jew of patristic discourse was not based primarily upon face-to-face encounters with actual Jews, but was based on a purpose-built or "hermeneutically crafted Jew" that was best suited for Christian self-definition. Cohen's work complements Paula Fredriksen's in reconsidering the importance of Augustine's witness doctrine, and a significant body of literature is being built which asks historians and theologians alike to reconsider "Augustine and the Jewish question."[4] This essay offers a theological contribution to these important historical reconsiderations.

In this brief essay I will suggest that the reasoning which guides Augustine is a type of scriptural pragmatism which seeks to replicate—by the way he interprets the Scriptural text—what he understands about God's incarnational and trinitarian logic. This logic can be seen in his theo-semiotics (i.e., his sacramental theory of signs), and in his biblical hermeneutic, which follows the rules of faith, hope, and love. Hence, his biblical interpretation conjoins the literal and the allegorical senses into an effective third unit of understanding because this performs an incarnational and trinitarian logic of dynamic union.

The strategic move I make is to suggest that this scriptural logic must also be operative in his construction of the hermeneutical Jew as a sign of the literal sense of Scripture in contrast to the hermeneutical Christian, who provides the allegorical sense. The effects of Augustine's logic can be seen in history: to preserve the literal sense is to preserve the Jewish people. To preserve the allegorical sense in its relation to the literal sense preserves the Christian people as well, precisely in their relation to the Jewish people.

But some critical questions also need to be asked. Did Augustine follow his own logic far enough? How far was he from seeing the deep resonance between his biblical hermeneutics and his image of the hermeneutical Jew? Is it possible to take his logic further than the tradition has done thus far? Need the historian and theologian part ways in asking such questions?

His theory of signs suggests that if his hermeneutical Jew represents the literal sense, the Christian interpretation is not supersessionist in the sense that the allegorical supersedes the literal. The literal does not pass away, it is not "cast off," nor is it even sublated. For the mature Augustine, the literal and figurative must be conjoined into an effective unit, one that leads readers into, as he puts it in *De doctrina christiana*, "the kingdom of charity."

My comments, then, fall into two parts that test the relationship between theory and practice in Augustine. In the first part I discuss Augustine's theo-semiotics to uncover what is at stake theologically in his hermeneutics. In the second part I turn to examine his "hermeneutical Jew" in *Tractatus adversus Iudaeos*. In the first part I will examine the importance of John 1:14 as a textual rule, the identity between the Word made flesh and Scripture, the mediation of scriptural signs, and the rules which Augustine implicitly follows to try (hermeneutically at least) to replicate God's redemptive plan in his scriptural interpretation. In the second part I will examine his most mature work on the Christians relationship to the Jewish people, *Tractatus adversus Iudaeos*. I discuss the structure of the document, identify the best and worst bits of it, and finally suggest the ways in which our reading of this text might be transformed by integrating Augustine's biblical hermeneutic (his theo-semiotics) with his account of the hermeneutical Jew.

## THEO-SEMIOTICS

Brian Stock notes that in Augustine's theory of sacred signs, in his theo-semiotics, "he does not attempt to fix firm conceptual boundaries."[5] There is a flexibility in Augustine's thought which makes his work of enduring significance. But he does set his theo-semiotics quite decidedly within the textual universe of the Hebrew scriptures and within that of the New Testament. His theory of signs is intimately bound to his reading of Scripture and both are bound to his incarnational and trinitarian theology.

For Augustine, reasoning consisted of those intellectual practices necessary to make sense of the sacred text because of the central place of Christ in his theology. Christ's incarnation as the Word of God, then, and not simply scripture, was "the basis for the concept of the sacred sign." His is not a biblicist approach. The scriptures are central to the degree that they "textually replicate"[6] the incarnate Word; and to this degree they are the most appropriate form of Christian discourse.

## JOHN 1:14, THE INCARNATE WORD, AND THE UNAVOIDABLE MEDIATION OF SIGNS

One of Augustine's most important semiotic innovations was to link *signum* with *sacramentum*, thus acknowledging the mediatorial role of the sign with the mysterious revelation of transcendent meaning. This innovation intensified his lifelong love of language in a way that "baptized" signs—signs became sacraments, they mediated the transcendent in language. Language, because "the Word became flesh and dwelled amongst us" (John 1:14), was inextricably bound up with the mysterious revelation of God in Christ.[7] It should come as no surprise that his major treatise on how to teach Christianity, *De doctrina christiana*, would attend to the mediatorial nature of the sign and the incarnational logic of the scriptures.[8] The link between his theory of signs and his incarnational theology is inextricable.[9] Michael Cameron, a specialist in Augustinian semiotics, agrees,

> "The Word made flesh" (John 1:14) discloses the capacity of the uncreated and supratemporal to "dwell" in the created and temporal. Because of the symbiotic relationship between Christology and language (*doc. Chr.* 1.13.12), the incarnation constitutes the basis for a renewed sacramental understanding of signification whereby the sign not only represents but contains and mediates the reality it signifies. . . . [T]he bond of sign and reality is so close that the signifying thing takes the name of the thing signified. . . . [T]he sign incarnates meaning before it is understood to point the way to meaning. Functionally speaking, for temporal beings image is intrinsic to essence, and medium is elemental to message.[10]

These insights are regulated by a crucial text in Augustine's reasoning. Hence, as Cameron suggests, John 1:14 becomes a rule for Augustine's theory of signs—his rule for faithful reading. The Word made flesh reveals to the world, by sheer grace, that the uncreated and supratemporal has the capacity to dwell within the created and temporal.[11] This affirmation is true of all reality, but since all reality is mediated to us through signs (he teaches that all "things are learned about through signs"),[12] then this reflection must be found in linguistic signification itself, and preeminently through scriptural signs which encode the divine logic in a corporate body, the Body of Israel, the Body of Christ.

## THE MEDIATION OF SCRIPTURAL SIGNS

The unavoidable mediation of signs necessitates Augustine's sacramentalism, which places Christ at the center of his interpretive process: the mediation of the Word of God made flesh in salvation history becomes the hermeneutical rule for good reading practice. This rule about what constitutes good mediation extends to all other texts, and in the prologue to *De doctrina christiana* Augustine refers to another passage in John where, "Thomas said to Jesus, 'Lord, we do not know where you are going. How can we know the way?' Jesus said to him, 'I am the way, and the truth, and the life. No one comes to the Father except *through me*'" (John 14:5–6). It is consonant with Augustine's whole approach in *De doctrina christiana* to think through the implications of this biblical reasoning about mediation, thinking hermeneutically about the "*through me*" of the incarnate Word. From the prologue to the end of book 4, Augustine's incarnational theology is reflected in his insistence upon the non-dualistic *harmonia*[13] between letter and spirit, between outer and inner, between the temporal and the eternal, between the literal and figurative senses, between sign and thing; all of that is indicative of the redemptive union of the human and divine in the Word made flesh.

Therefore, John 1:1–14 "paradigmatically encodes" this "rule of faith," a rule that is required for good reading practice. The rule teaches him a way of mediating the inner and the outer in a way that conjoins the two into a whole that does not obliterate its constituent parts. In just such a way, Stock describes the effect Ambrose had upon Augustine. He writes that what impressed Augustine was that "the bishop [of Milan] proceeded deliberately from the literal to the spiritual sense of the text: it was not the one or the other that disarmed the wary Augustine, but *their combination into an effective unit*."[14] This incarnational conjoining of the literal and spiritual into a third effective unit can also be seen in the technology of his triadic theory of signs, in which a sign (1) is a thing (2) which is known by (3) its effects upon the reader or reading community.[15]

The scriptures offer us a semiotic system that mediates "something else" to us, they are "signs used in order to signify something else," to effect something else.[16] Augustine writes, reasoning on the basis of Psalm 102, Romans 8, and John 1:14, "For you will cure all my diseases through him who sits at your right hand and intercedes with you for us. . . many and great are those diseases, many and great indeed. But your medicine [given through the scriptures and sacraments of the Church] is still more potent. We might have thought your Word was far removed from being united to mankind and have despaired of our lot unless he had become flesh and dwelt among us."[17] The divine mediation of the Word in language determines how scriptural signs both mediate and transfigure the shape of embodied reality.

The mediating words of Scripture, then, can heal humanity (even the humanity of scripture itself) to the extent that they are read *as the incarnate Word is read* and performed or made flesh "in the community of readers which is the Church." Thus the logic of the incarnation, which is the logic of Scripture itself, may provide tools for semiotic repair in communities of interpretation.[18]

## TRIADIC SEMIOTICS—LITERAL AND ALLEGORICAL CONJOINED INTO AN EFFECTIVE UNIT

The *triadic* structure implicit in Augustine's definition, that a (1) *sign* must (2) *mean something* to (3) *someone*, "is the key to Augustine's entire hermeneutic theory," according to Markus.[19] What the *triadicity* of Augustinian semiotics suggests is that the meaningfulness of the sign is received within the dynamic of human community, and that such a community of sign-users will inevitably extend the meaningfulness of signs by discovering new relationships of meaning between signs and reading communities, the fruit of which should be visible in the long run (generating a tradition). Augustine imagines an infinite process of literal and allegorical senses being conjoined into ever new effects upon readers, itself a process of replicating the reparative logic of the incarnate Word through communal interpretation.

Augustine's theo-semiotic theory, even in this embryonic form, is able to take into fuller account the role of the reading community and the effect signs have on readers. He is therefore also able to think theologically and pragmatically about the use of scripture for effecting and healing problems within the social body called to be Christ's body, the Church. Not surprisingly then, much of books 2 and 3 in *De doctrina christiana* are oriented around solving problems in the community of interpretation—repairing semiotic problems that arise in our reading through careful sacramental reasoning. In order to discern the Word in the words, Augustine says we must be sensitive to the kind of semiotic problems we will face. He divides the kinds of problems that may arise into two main categories: signs that are unknown and signs that are ambiguous.[20]

For example, solving problems with *literal* signs that are "unknown" involves increasing language skills necessary for knowing the sign-thing relation. If the problems seem related to "ambiguous" literal signs, Augustine judges that linguistic and semiotic skills, history, context, reason, and especially the *regula fidei* ("you should refer it to the rule of faith") should all play key roles in solving the interpretive problem.[21] If the problem cannot be resolved by any of these means, Augustine says that as long as it does not contradict the historical context of the text, or the incarnational, trinitarian, and charitable *regula fidei*, then the reader or reading community can interpret the text "in any of the ways that are open."[22] In principle, Augustine does not object to an infinite plurality of interpretations granting that they do not contradict the "rule of faith," and its implicit corollary, the rule of charity. That is to say, interpretive problem-solving should follow these rules of faith and love.

Similarly, when Augustine discusses problems with *figural* signs, he argues for bringing the literal-historical and the figurative-allegorical into a kind of triadic unity of letter and spirit. In other words, the truly triadic sign is the sign read or *transfigured* in the spirit to mean the (incarnational and trinitarian) transfiguration of the historical reality with the spiritual or allegorical reality. Figurative signs require *the reader* to unite the "letter" and the "spirit" of the sign-thing relation into some third effective understanding of reality, indwelling more deeply the fullness of meaning within the semiotic universe that the scriptures instantiate. Otherwise, Augustine says, we are "enslaved under signs," rather than directed toward "that reality to which all such things are to be referred," namely God.[23] Literalism is enslavement, but if the spirit is truly allowed to animate the letter, and if this third thing can become a useful sign to the reader for salvation, then, Augustine says, there is "spiritual freedom."[24]

## TEXTUALLY REPLICATING GOD'S PLAN OF REDEMPTION ENTAILS SEMIOTIC REPAIR OF THE WORLD

But what is important to notice here is that Augustine assumes that the problems of reading are to be fully engaged—they are, in a real sense, where all the action is. The majority of *De doctrina christiana* is oriented around semiotic problem-solving in the interpretive community. To make explicit the identity between Christ and Scripture, the wounds of the text, if you will, are like Christ's wounds, occasions to go deeper into the Word for healing and repair. In this sense, the identity between Christ and the Scriptures, or even Christ and the Law, means that, like Christ, the Scriptures make a reparative space for the world precisely within those textual wounds that enable semiotic problem-solving to occur within the reading community. And for Augustine, the *aporias* of Scripture are where his incarnational rules of faith and love come most clearly into focus, and his problem-solving semiotic aims at shaping the reading community through such deep engagements with Scripture.

Augustine promotes in *De doctrina christiana* a suprainstrumental view of Scripture, where Scripture is not only charitably interpreted but charitably used for the sake of the kingdom, because, as he puts it, "*love reigns supreme*," and he commends the reader to "take pains to turn over and over in your mind what you read, until your interpretation of it is led right through to the kingdom of charity."[25] For Augustine, "love of God and neighbor" is the final arbiter in solving interpretive problems in community—but again, it is a dynamic orientation rather than a static one: the entire interpretive process is judged by its ability to replicate the effects of God's Word embodied in human flesh, and this can only be judged by its fruits in the reading community, that is, over time and through a tradition.

Scripture reading, then, is an inescapably communal activity—which might be called the logic of relations, or simply triadicity, the irreducible yet dynamic relation between a text and its meaning for a particular reading community over time.[26] Augsutine's hermeneutic requires a bond of love dynamically to unite these complex relations of Scripture in tradition. Here I find in Augustine something like a *vestigia trinitatis* in the logic of scripture itself.[27] For Augustine, the Father, Son, and Holy Spirit suggest the triadicity (even the tri-unity) of the given sign (the rule of God) and its meaning (its mediation) in relation to the reading community (where inspiration resides). The relationality of the semiotic "third" is both the Gift of the Holy Spirit, which is the bond of love between the Father and the Son, but also the gift of effective meaning to a community of readers. Put differently, scriptural interpretation, if it is to be properly theological, must hermeneutically, exegetically, textually replicate the redemptive logic of the Triune God in human history.

## *TRACTATUS ADVERSUS IUDAEOS*

With this redemptive theologic firmly in place, let us return to the theological problem of Augustine's Jew. It has been said that Augustine's hermeneutical Jew seems sometimes to be a cipher for Manicheans or Pelagians, or any number of symbolically rendered heretics. There may be some truth to this, but I don't think this is Augustine's intention. The Jew has a very different status than do heretics. Augustine's constructed vision of Jewish identity is genuinely different than any consciously textual "other." Jewish otherness is internal to Christian identity in a way that heresies are not—precisely because Jewish otherness is *Hebraica veritas*. Whatever might be said positively about heretics, and their importance for shaping Christian communities *via negativa*, they are never referred to as "truth."

*Tractatus adversus Iudaeos* (ca. 429) shows us that the heart of the Jewish-Christian schism, at least in Augustine's mind, is hermeneutical.[28] It is about the interpretation of signs. Here Augustine provides Christians not so much with ready answers to questions that real or imagined Jews might ask, as he provides semiotic guidance to Christian readers of Jewish texts, and Christian readers of the Jew *as* an embodied text.

## THE GOODNESS AND SEVERITY WITHIN GOD'S LIFE

The most basic logic of Augustine's homiletical guidance in this document comes from Romans 11:22, concerning the goodness and severity of God. There are not two logics here—one good and one severe—but a single logic which holds goodness and severity in some kind of unity, bound by something like a charitably defined divine Justice. This logic then generates rhetoric about humility, which is then followed by severe judgments about Jewish hermeneutical failures to read well. The structures of these severe judgments then return to the rhetoric of humility, deferment of judgment, and finally return to a rule of love. The document as a whole places severity within the boundaries of goodness, beginning and ending with the theological virtues of faith, hope, and love.

## THE WORST BITS

It is important to consider "severity" first—that is, the worst bits of the document. Jews are stubborn and blind; they killed Christ; they can't read. Augustinian severity inherits the rhetoric of those harshest kinds of immanent criticism from the New Testament church. Augustine inhabits Paul's internal critique of Judaism and, in this sense, insinuates himself into the role of critical insider, distancing himself from his family of origin. The verb "to change" appears over twenty times in this short tract. "Cut off" or "cast off" also appears in the text at least twenty times, and if you included words such as "retire," "ceased," "the old," the "no longer," and the "passing," then a simple word count alone shows that one of the strongest motifs in this late document in the Augustinian corpus is one of supersession and fulfillment, a motif which fits within, I suggest, the general motifs announced at the outset, concerning the severity and goodness of God.

The violent severity of "cutting away" is acknowledged as violent from the beginning of the document. He writes, "By the just severity of God, therefore, the unbelieving pride of the native branches is broken away from the living patriarchal root, and the grace of divine goodness, the faithful humility of the wild olive is ingrafted."[29] However, the language of cutting away is not quite right, and Augustine knows it. The language really should be something like sublation, or the idea of penultimacy. He writes that Christ "came to fulfill, not to destroy," and he sets this fulfillment as a boundary concept around the language of severity. This is because he holds God's severity and goodness together, and also because he is concerned about what the scriptures bear witness to.

Augustine clearly has an apologetic tone, and he never wavers from pointing out the blindness of his Jews. He has a problem with how they read their texts, and he does not expect that problem is going to go away, save at the Eschaton. But at least he *imagines* an on-going conversation with Jews through the scriptures. Even with the violent biblical language of cutting and casting away, there is the language of searching the scriptures with the Jew, of *derash*. Clearly Augustine hopes on some level to transform Jewish hermeneutical existence; but even if they reject a Christian hermeneutic, he tells Christians to continue reasoning with Jews through the "testimonies" of "sacred Scripture."[30] If a hermeneutical change were to occur within Jewish reading practices, Augustine thinks that Jews could "be cured by means of this advantage offered them," but even if they will not change their reading practices, reasoning with them through the scriptures may at least convince them "by its evident truth."[31] If Christians can recognize Hebrew truth, perhaps Jews will minimally recognize Christian truth.

Nevertheless, his judgments remain severe. In chapter 7, Christ "transcends all heights," and Christians "have surpassed [Jews] in increases and have replaced them."[32] Zion and Jerusalem are themselves "a fitting witness [*adversus*, in answer to] the Jews, because from that place where they crucified Christ the Law . . . the Word of God has proceeded to the Gentiles."[33] But again, the harshness of an apparent replacement theology is set within the tempering language of fulfillment, and of fullness, which hearkens back to his sacramental theory of signs, and his view that the literal and figurative sense are both incomplete if they are not conjoined into a third. Christ not only fulfills the Law but is the Law. Though Augustine writes that the Law that proceeded from Zion and Jerusalem is now written on "tablets of the heart" rather than on "tablets of stone," the mutually exclusive logic of tablets of stone versus tablets of the heart does not cohere well with his biblical hermeneutic, in which literal and figurative senses are incomplete without each other.[34]

There is an analogy here with David Weiss Halivni's Ezra-story of a maculate text needing to be restored through the community of interpretation.[35] But here it is Christ's body which does the restoring and the fulfilling, the transforming and the transfiguring of broken tablets of stone. Here Augustine makes a subtle but clear link between Christ as the Law and the Jewish interpretation of the scriptures as Law. The importance of this claim, at least in my reading, is that the identity between Christ and the Law, and the Jew and the Law, means that the scriptures, as Law, become a meeting place for Christians and Jews. The scriptures are like scaffolding which structure and enable a mutually supersessionist conversation to build up the kingdom of charity. Just as Jesus engaged the Pharisees concerning the Law, so shall the Christian draw near to the Jew as bearer of Hebrew truth, as herself a sacred text which must be read, a text which must be argued with, a text which must be constantly consulted, yet always guided by the rule of faith, and especially the rule of love. Christ's fulfillment of the Law must also mean a kind of Christian identification with the *Hebraica veritas*, with the hermeneutical identity of the Jew. Drawing near to the Jew as sacred text, through exegetical conversation, I suggest is a kind of textual replication of the Word made flesh in community. Augustine's rule of charity requires that we read his work in this direction; and even if he himself did not get this far, the effects of his thought in the history of Jewish-Christian relations certainly did.

## THE BEST BITS

To reiterate, Augustine's Christology requires a sacramental view of the transformation of all dyadic relations with regard to scriptural semiotics.

The flesh of Christ is transfigured through a spiritual anointing. The literal sense is similarly transfigured through the spiritual sense. But what does this mean for carnal Israel? What does the "Word made flesh" mean for "Israel according to the flesh"? What does carnal Israel mean for spiritual Israel? It most certainly does not mean that there are two Israels, one human and one divine; but there is one Israel which bears witness to the way of salvation. If this is true, then the only solution is to work together towards the witness of the one God who has called one Israel. It is supersessionist, of course. That is the hermeneutic. There is a real conflict between Jews and Christians. But the supersessionism that the hermeneutic requires also preserves the *Hebraica veritas*. Any supersessionism that is true to the tradition will want genuinely to co-abide with the Jew as part of the Body of Israel.[36] Whatever conflict there may be, the hermeneutic requires a bond of trust, even a bond of love, and that bond is, in practice, the face-to-face interpretation of scripture between Jews and Christians, a scriptural bond which generates its own politics of trust. It is a pity that Augustine himself doesn't have, as far as we know, anything like these face to face conversations through scripture. But the conversation he imagines, with his straw man, the hermeneutical Jew, points toward actual conversations with Jews that Christians must have. This is why the best bits of *Tractatus adversus Iudaeos*, in my view, are the scriptures that Augustine pores over in providing guidance for exegetical conversation with Jews.

There are at least eighty-eight scriptural citations in this short document. And three-quarters of these citations are from the Hebrew Bible. Predictably his citations are largely from the Psalms and Isaiah, where his Christological hermeneutic is most effective. It is no surprise then that one of the best bits from *Tractatus adversus Iudaeos* is the scriptural one that Jeremy Cohen has made famous. I am speaking, of course, of Augustine's use of Psalm 59, "My God shall let me see over my enemies: slay them not, lest any time they forget thy law. Scatter them by thy power."[37] This, Cohen thinks, is central to Augustine's witness doctrine. And I agree that it is massively significant that Augustine, in one fell swoop of scriptural interpretation, protects Jewish identity and religious practice well into the eleventh century and creates a Christian tradition of protecting Jewish communities that can be seen in these remarkable pockets of faithful reception of the Augustinian witness doctrine, which we have seen as recently as Karl Barth's theology of Israel.[38]

However, I am more inclined to believe that Romans 11 is a better candidate for the textual rule that stands at the heart of Augustine's witness doctrine. Reference to Romans 11 both opens and closes this document, and I think it enables him to interpret Psalm 59 powerfully rather than the other way round. In agreement with Fredriksen, Romans 11:25–32 gets to the heart of the matter and also illuminates the severity/goodness dyad that dominates *Tractatus adversus Iudaeos*. The deferment of Israel's future, "until the full number of Gentiles have come in" (Rom 11:25), inevitably means a long-term engagement with Jews. The long and short of it is that if "all Israel will be saved," then we clearly want to be in conversation with those who bear textual witness, even in their own bodies, to the one Israel and the one God.

It is clear that Romans had a profound effect upon Augustine, and when it comes to thinking about Judaism, I think it does regulate his reading of the Psalms and of Isaiah. But with all the regulative power of Romans, I still think the textual rule about the Word being made flesh is more basic. This also might explain the subtle ways in which Augustine provides an advance on the Pauline doctrine of the mystery of Jewish salvation. Augustine either perceives a subtle development in Paul, or he develops Paul's thought in a new direction, displaying how this mystery of Jewish salvation is to be hermeneutically performed, partly through Christian efforts to replicate the reparative capacity of the Word made flesh in exegetical debate with Jews.

## A POTENTIAL LOGIC FOR REREADING *TRACTATUS ADVERSUS IUDAEOS* THROUGH HIS BIBLICAL HERMENEUTIC

When Augustine tries to meet the real or imagined charges that Jews might bring to Christians, charges apparently about their observance or non-observance of the Law, he does so consistently with appeal to a change that has occurred in history which has transformed the meaning of signs in the hermeneutical universe. His reply to Jews is most simply this: "Search the Scriptures." He writes, "search the sacred writings carefully; the same writings bear witness to the world about this sacrifice, which is being offered to the God of Israel, not by your nation alone from whose hands he foretold He would not take the gift; it is being offered by all nations . . . ," not in only one place, in the earthly Jerusalem, but everywhere.[39]

Augustine does view Jews instrumentally. Jewish utility, it seems, is primarily that of witnesses to the truth of Christianity (cf. *City of God* 18.36). But it is significant to recognize that this Augustinian witness doctrine, even with its worst bits, has the effect of protecting Jewish identity for centuries. Yet this is still insufficient. Reading *Tractatus adversus Iudaeos* should convince any reader that Augustine is thinking not only about a Jewish witness to Christianity but about the Christian witness to Jews; he ends his tract by commending Christians to bring their testimony to the Jews "with great love." Jewish utility is not the only reason why Augustine fashions his hermeneutical Jew. His Jew is Paul's Jew, and his Israel is

Paul's Israel—which is somehow bound up in the mystery of God's economy of salvation, which has to do with issues of time and especially the deferral of judgment. More than anything, Augustine's hermeneutical Jew is bound up with the interpretation of Scripture, and the interpretation of Scripture must be regulated by the rules of faith and love that we have discussed. It is his biblical hermeneutic which requires this mysterious love of the Jew which protects and converses and stands in a significant sociopolitical alliance with Israel's flesh. The challenge here is not to replicate Augustine's distance from real Jewish interpretive communities, but to take his logic further than he was able to by deepening the integration between his biblical hermeneutic and his hermeneutical Jew.

If Augustine's biblical hermeneutics, with the literal and figurative understood through their conjunction into an effective unit, are applied to the hermeneutical Jew, then the Pauline "mystery of Jewish salvation" takes on a pragmatic dimension. Augustine's hermeneutic suggests a kind of education with the Jew—a hermeneutical process of the community repairing semiotic problems, and via this repair of semiotic problems, repair of the world. The "problem" between the two hermeneutical traditions is to be dealt with pragmatically *and* theologically by the incarnational and trinitarian rules of faith, hope and love—using the Law lawfully for the sake of charity. This is not something that Paul explicitly offers us, but if Augustine's biblical hermeneutic becomes the basis for our understanding of his hermeneutical Jew, perhaps we will be able to detect subtle developments in the mature Augustine's thinking, and also be encouraged to develop his logic for ourselves. That is the constructive challenge, and I trust by now that it is not a challenge that leaves the historical or the literal behind. The challenge is also one for us here, for historians and constructive theologians to think together about the Augustinian tradition, and the enduring power of its effect upon future generations of readers, both readers of Augustine, and of the scriptures which shaped his reasoning.

## NOTES

1. This essay originally appeared under the same title in *Augustinian Studies* 37:1 (2006) 27–42. It appears here, in a slightly revised form, by kind permission of the journal editors.

2. Jeremy Cohen, *Living Letters of the Law: Ideas of the Jews in Medieval Christianity* (Berkeley: University of California Press, 1999).

3. Cohen, *Living Letters of the Law*, p. 20.

4. This essay is based on a paper delivered to a joint session of the Study of Judaism Section and the Augustine and Augustinianism Consultation of the 2004 annual meeting of the American Academy of Religion. I am grateful to Paula

Fredriksen's paper, "Augustine and the Jewish Question: The Witness Doctrine Reconsidered," and to Michael Signer's insightful and integrative response to both of our papers. For an excellent bibliography and introduction to the issues, see Michael Signer's "Jews and Judaism" in *Augustine through the Ages: An Encyclopedia* (Grand Rapids: Eerdmans, 1999), edited by Allan Fitzgerald, pp. 470–74. See especially, Paula Fredriksen, "*Excaecati Occulta Iustitia Dei:* Augustine on Jews and Judaism," *Journal of Early Christian Studies* 3 (1995) 299–324; "Secundum Carnem: History and Israel in the Theology of St Augustine on the Destiny of Israel," in *The Limits of Ancient Christianity. Essays on Late Antique Though and Culture in Honor of R.A. Markus*, eds. William Klingshirn and Mark Vessey (Ann Arbor: University of Michigan Press, 1999) 26–41; and "Augustine and Israel. *Interpretatio ad litteram*, Jews and Judaism in Augustine's theology of History," *Studia Patristica* 38 (2001) 119–135.

5. Brian Stock, *Augustine the Reader: Meditation, Self-Knowledge, and the Ethics of Interpretation* (Cambridge: Harvard University Press, 1996) 9.

6. The phrase belongs to David Dawson, see "Sign, Allegorical Reading, and the Motions of the Soul in *De doctrina christiana*," in D. Arnold and P. Bright, eds., *De doctrina christiana: a Classic of Western Culture* (Notre Dame: University of Notre Dame Press, 1995) 135.

7. Cf. *De doct. chr.* 1.13.12. I follow Edmund Hill's new translation in *Teaching Christianity: De Doctrina Christiana* (Hyde Park: New City Press, 1996). Augustine discusses that we are able to know God through wisdom precisely because wisdom came "by the Word becoming flesh and dwelling amongst us. . . . It is something like when we talk." Augustine's theory of language, his sign theory, is itself a work which reflects an incarnational logic working itself out in a theory of human language, and if an incarnational logic, then also a trinitarian logic (in keeping with the text which is functioning as a rule here, namely Jn 1). Also see Takeshi Kato, "*Sonus et Verbum: De doctrina christiana* 1.13.12," in *De doctrina christiana: a classic of western culture*, pp. 87–96.

8. Edmund Hill has come down strongly in favor of reading "doctrina" in pedagogical terms (thus his translation of *De doct. chr.* as "Teaching Christianity"). But see Gerald A. Press, "The Subject and Structure of Augustine's *De Doctrina Christiana*," *Augustinian Studies* 11 (1980) 99–124, esp. 123, who argues that Augustine plays on the multiple meanings associated with "doctrina": "*Doctrina* is a word with many meanings—teaching, instruction, education, knowledge, learning, culture—and of old and varied associations." Press shows that it is fruitless to fix the meaning of the word "doctrina," and much better to see the central point: Augustine is presenting a Christian *doctrina* that is worth having precisely because it promises to heal us—it is *doctrina* "for our salvation," where *doctrina* is dedicated to discovering the Word of God in a redemptive relation to everything (sacred and secular). Here I am tempted to use *doctrina* and *tractatio scripturarum* interchangeably.

9. The tide does seem to be turning. But for example, Frederick Van Fleteran reflects the flawed but widespread assumption shared by many classical scholars in an otherwise excellent and very helpful article when he writes, "Curiously, Augustine's semiotics stem from grammar and rhetoric, not the Bible, and in particular not the author of John's Gospel for whom sign was so significant": see "Prin-

ciples of Augustine's Hermeneutic: An Overview," in *Augustine: Biblical Exegete*, eds. J. C. Schnaubelt and F. Van Fleteren (New York & Frankfurt: Peter Lang, 2001) p. 13. This opinion is likely drawn from the tendency in Augustinian studies to unduly privilege classical sources and to underestimate the deepest internal reasons for Augustine's hermeneutical decisions. Whenever Augustine "absorbs" a theoretical point, whether it is from Philo, Plotinus, or Tyconius, he "repairs" it in a scriptural universe on theological grounds, and in doing so transforms the theory with the scriptures. When we think of Augustine as a "synthetic thinker," as he is often called, it is important to recognize the direction of the synthetic relation (scripture absorbs and then repairs the way we read the world).

10. Michael Cameron, "Signs," in *Augustine through the Ages: An Encyclopedia*, ed. A. Fitzgerald (Grand Rapids: Eerdmans, 1999) 795.

11. See Michael Cameron, "Signs" in *Augustine through the Ages*, 795.

12. *De doct.chr.* 1.2.2. Wittgenstein, in his view that language-use mediates reality, is indebted to Augustine in a way that often goes unrecognized.

13. Augustine does not use the word *harmonia* in *De doctrina*, but I borrow from his theological use of it in *De trinitate* 4.1.4 where he likens our participation in the Word made flesh (simultaneously partaking of both humanity and divinity) to the Greek idea of *harmonia*, clearly recalling his early work *De musica*, evidenced in his musical references to singing, tuning strings, tonometer, etc. With Catherine Pickstock I agree that Augustine actually offers a non-dualist account of reality (though I think it is the corrective pressure of the scriptures on his thought which prompt this development, owing especially to a christological and trinitarian reading). Cf. Pickstock, "Soul, City and Cosmos after Augustine," in John Milbank, Catherine Pickstock, and Graham Ward (eds.), *Radical Orthodoxy* (London: Routledge, 1999) 243–77.

14. Brian Stock, *Augustine the Reader*, p. 61, emphasis mine.

15. *De doct. chr.* 2.1.1.

16. *De doctr. chr.* 1.2.2. My understanding of this is indebted to Rowan Williams important essay, "Language, Reality, and Desire in Augustine's *De Doctrina*," *Literature and Theology* 3 (1989) 138–50.

17. *Conf.* 10.43.69.

18. Mark D. Jordan, "Words and Word: Incarnation and Signification in Augustine's *De doctrina christiana*," *Augustinian Studies* 11 (1980) 175–95, esp. 178. Cf. *De doct. chr.* 1.14.13. See also Oliver Davies, "The Sign Redeemed: A Study in Christian Fundamental Semiotics," *Modern Theology* 19:2 (April 2003) 219–41, esp. 226. Davies stresses the sacramental rite of the Eucharist, where Augustine's sacramental semiotics are first more broadly theological and scriptural before they become re-contextualized through liturgical performance.

19. Markus, "Sign, Communication, and Communities in Augustine's *De doctrina christiana*," in Arnold and Bright, eds., *De doctrina christiana: a classic of western culture* (Notre Dame: University of Notre Dame Press, 1995) 97–108, esp. 103.

20. *De doct. chr.* 2.10.15., "Now there are two reasons why texts are not understood: if they are veiled in signs that are either unknown or ambiguous."

21. *De doct. chr.* 3.2.2, 2–5.

22. *De doct. chr.* 3.2.5.

23. *De doct. chr.* 3.9.13.

24. *De doct. chr.* 3.9.13. No modern interpreter has understood Augustine on these points as well as Henri de Lubac. See, e.g., Lubac, *Scripture in the Tradition*, trans. Luke O'Neill (New York: Herder & Herder, 2000).

25. *De doct. chr.* 3.15.23.

26. See Peter Ochs, *Peirce, Pragmatism and the Logic of Scripture* (Cambridge: Cambridge University Press, 1998).

27. This *analogia* can be understood in ways that anticipate Karl Barth's famous identity between the Trinity and Revelation in his *Church Dogmatics* I.1. For more extended comment on these points, see my *Transforming Postliberal Theology: George Lindbeck, Pragmatism and Scripture* (London and New York: T. & T. Clark, 2005).

28. *Tractatus Adversus Iudaeos*, PL 42:51–64. I have relied upon the Liguori translation provided in Augustine, *Against the Jews* (*Tractatus adversos Judaeos*), in Saint Augustine, *Treatises on Marriage and Other Subjects*, Fathers of the Church, vol. 27 (Washington D.C.: Catholic University of America Press, 1969) 387–414. Hereafter *Adv. Iud.*

29. *Adv. Iud.* 1.1 (Liguori 392).

30. *Adv. Iud.* 1.2 (Liguori 392).

31. *Adv. Iud.* 1.2 (Liguori 393).

32. *Adv. Iud.* 7.9 (Liguori 404).

33. *Adv. Iud.* 7.9 (Liguori 404).

34. *Adv. Iud.* 7.9 (Liguori 405).

35. See David Weiss Halivni, *Revelation Restored: Divine Writ and Critical Responses* (London: SCM Press, 2001).

36. On "co-abiding" with the Jew, and abiding in Christ, see Graham Ward, "A Christian Act: Politics and Liturgical Practice," in Randi Rashkover and C. C. Pecknold, *Liturgy, Time and the Politics of Redemption*, Radical Tradition series (Grand Rapids: Eerdmans, 2006) 29–49.

37. *Adv. Iud.* 7.9 (Liguori 403).

38. Barth does not explicitly claim that his theology of Israel inherits Augustine's witness doctrine. But an argument may be made that Barth does indeed receive this tradition and is able to subtly extend this tradition under different historical pressures. For Karl Barth's theology of Israel, see Katherine Sonderegger, *That Jesus Christ Was Born a Jew: Karl Barth's "Doctrine of Israel"* (University Park: Pennsylvania State University Press, 1992).

39. *Adv. Iud.* 9.13 (Liguori 411).

# II

# AUGUSTINE AND NON-WESTERN RELIGIONS

6

✣

# Way and Wilderness: An Augustinian Dialogue with Buddhism

Michael Barnes

## INTRODUCTION

In a fascinating article on Buddhism and post-modernity, Stephen Batchelor reflects on the central metaphor which has been used to describe the *Buddhadharma* since its earliest days—the image of the "way" through the wilderness.[1] Walking along a footpath through a patch of woodland, he is suddenly struck by what it means for a path to be a path. A path gives a sense of direction; it allows for freedom of unobstructed movement; it is made up of the traces of those who have gone before. He then draws parallels between these three points and the "three jewels"—of *Buddha,* the embodiment of the goal; *Dharma,* the teaching; and *Sangha,* the community of disciples. "Taking refuge" in the three jewels is a formal act of initiation, a commitment to core non-negotiable values by which Buddhists attempt to make sense of human existence. But it is also, says Batchelor, "a metaphor of sustained authenticity in treading the path."[2] Writing as one of the most articulate and thoughtful advocates of a post-modern Buddhism, Batchelor is suspicious of grand totalizing narratives that seek to explain everything. The danger, he says, is that the essentially "communal endeavour" of Buddhist practice, following in the footsteps of others, becomes "institutionalized as a religion with dogmatic belief systems."[3] Batchelor is arguing for a Buddhist practice which cultivates a sensitivity to the utter contingency of things and a model of personhood based not on achieving "answers" to metaphysical questions but on the integrity of practice, thus coming to terms with *dukkha*, "suffering," the anguish and tragedy of human existence.

Such a starkly agnostic Buddhism seems light years away from the intensely intellectual ferment which Augustine provoked in his dealings with the philosophies and religions of his time. The conviction of this article, however, is that a dialogue between Buddhism and Augustinian spirituality draws attention to a particular model of "self-making," what it means to be a person, which undergirds both. Christians and Buddhists may have very different ideas of what constitutes the way itself, let alone how to speak of the end or goal. They would agree, however, that the integrity of religious practice depends on maintaining an integrity of tradition. In what follows, my intention is to bring the Augustinian tradition into dialogue with Buddhism, especially the sort of Buddhism which Batchelor advocates. I shall first introduce an early Theravadin Buddhist text, the *Samaññaphala Sutta*, which has as its central theme the "fruits of being a recluse," the stages of progress on the way to enlightenment. Although these stages appear to be no more than a series of increasingly rarefied states of mystical consciousness, I shall argue that they are better understood as steps on the path toward an interior freedom. I shall then return to Batchelor's article and consider how he deconstructs the theme of way or path and manages to retrieve it for a more authentic Buddhist practice. The point I want to take from him is that the metaphor of religion as path or way links origins and goal by enabling a practice of following. Augustine might not have used words like "deliverance" or "enlightenment" in the Buddhist sense which Batchelor develops to such effect, but the vast treatises which flowed from his pen witness to a never-ending process of coming closer to a proper sense of self—and the Trinitarian God of love who sustained him. This is a very different language from that found in non-theistic Buddhism; a religion based on the revelation of God's Word is bound to set much greater store by the "content" of faith than one which guards the value of silence and insists on maintaining a critical edge. On the other hand, the counterintuitive Buddhist account of the person as *anatman*—lacking a substantive sense of self—sounds certain resonances with the central paradox of Christianity that one must lose the self in order to find it. I shall seek to argue that what holds the two traditions together, admittedly in an uneasy tension, is the experience of elation at the overcoming of loss and the finding again of a sense of direction—an experience in which the marking and measuring of time has a crucial role to play.

## RELIGION, ENGAGEMENT, AND THE PURSUIT OF TRUTH

That great Augustinian theme of the mystery of time provides the broader context for a question which runs through these reflections. In recent years the actual experience of encounter with the religious other has transformed approaches to the theology of religions. To take just one example, the magisterium of the Roman Catholic Church speaks of four different forms of dialogue: "theological exchange," "religious experience," "common action" and "common life."[4] The emphasis is on the connotations of the word "dialogue" and the various responsibilities which Catholic Christians inherit from *Nostra Aetate*, the "Declaration of the Relationship of the Church to non-Christian Religions" of the Second Vatican Council.[5] But the *theological* issue which is raised by this seemingly innocuous word has less to do with the co-existence of "religions" than with the more pressing and more intractable question of how the self which is committed to teaching can co-exist with the self which seeks to learn from and with the other. How is that particular vision of truth which is promised in Christ to be maintained when one is *on the way*, in the middle of a sometimes confusing and threatening wilderness?

This is a question which Augustine would have relished. When he speaks of *religio*, Augustine does not have in mind "the religions" in the modern sense of discrete, historically developing traditions of belief and practice. On the other hand, what is often referred to today as "religious pluralism," the challenge of a diffuse "context of otherness" which attends the journey of faith, was as much a reality for him as it is for today's Christians.[6] *De Vera Religione* was written at that critical point in his life when the shift from purely philosophical concerns to something much more focused on theology was leading him to confront his own interiority.[7] While he has no doubt that Christian faith is the "true religion" which is superior to religious practices and philosophies of various kinds, Augustine's main aim is not to argue for "true" against "false" religion, but to expound "proper piety" or "genuine worship."[8] *Religio* is used along with *cultus*—cult or worship, what "cultivates" the relationship with God or makes it flourish. As with Aquinas, *religio* is bound up with the virtue of justice—the worship which is due to God.[9] Augustine is more concerned with describing the personal confrontation with the splendour and love of God which his Christian faith has taught him. If "religion" in this sense refers to what people *do* before it is concerned with what they say they believe, then Augustine was no stranger to Batchelor's image of the spiritual life as a way or journey.[10] The tradition of theologizing which he inspired, confronting the full complexity of human living in all its grandeur and folly, is thoroughly rooted in the experience of conversion and its implications for Christian discipleship. As Charles Mathewes has so cogently argued, Augustine was a "master of engagement" whose constant struggle with the "otherness" within himself makes him an important model for anyone committed to interreligious dialogue and the theology of religions.[11]

My starting point, therefore, is with spiritual practice and with what a modern "master of engagement," the Sri Lankan Jesuit theologian, Aloysius Pieris, refers to as "spiritual idioms."[12] For Pieris Christianity is more "prophetic" or "*agapeic*," while Buddhism is more "mystical" or, in his term, "gnostic." These idioms—differences in ethos, style, and practice—express what in their origins are very different "liberative moments," the Buddha's enlightenment and the "redemptive love" revealed in the Paschal Mystery of Christ's Death and Resurrection. Pieris' point is that the two traditions cannot be compared and contrasted as objects for a conceptual dialogue. Rather, a certain "idiomatic exchange" is required if interreligious encounter is to be properly rooted in the lived experience of communities of faith. Any dialogue, especially one which would reflect on the value of knowledge or wisdom and its relationship with love and compassion, must be grounded in the practice of prayer and meditation—which implies a "*communicatio in sacris*."[13] However, this is precisely *not* to say that the metaphor of religion as way, track or path sets a more or less straightforward set of practices apart from the pursuit of truth. Pieris and Batchelor would agree in their critique of "religion" as a system of thought, an account of "how things are." They also share a similar unease about the tendency to extract dialogue from a complex history of cultural and theological interaction.[14] Memory, whether of putatively foundational experiences or of subsequent formative engagements, is never pure and needs regular "performance," whether through liturgy or study or meditative practice, if it is to open up that vision of a life-giving fullness which the tradition promises. With Augustine's help, I hope to bring two very different but complementary religious "idioms" into a dialogue which has implications not just for Buddhist-Christian understanding but for the project of theology of religions itself.

## THE FRUITS OF BEING AN ASCETIC

The *Samaññaphala Sutta* is the second of the "long discourses" from the *Digha Nikaya* of the Theravada tradition.[15] The title means the "discourse on the fruit of being a *samana*"—a wandering ascetic or recluse. In the introduction Ajatasattu, the king of Magadha, asks his ministers: "Who is the recluse or brahman whom we may call upon tonight, who, when we shall call upon him, shall be able to satisfy our hearts?"[16] They reply by referring to this teacher and that, but these names fail to please the king.

Then it is suggested that the king should visit Gotama, the Buddha. The king and his ministers travel with a great retinue to meet the Buddha whom they find "with the brethren around him." Ajatasattu raises a question about the "visible fruits" of various crafts and professions. But what about an ascetic? What comparable fruit does the ascetical life have to show? The Buddha's response is to enter into a lengthy description of the advantages or fruits of a life spent wandering in search of enlightenment. Each section of the discourse is punctuated by a comment which picks up the context established by the original question: "Can you show me any immediate fruit, in this world, of the life of a recluse?"[17]

The Buddha's response, pointing out the "fruit, higher and greater than the last," is peculiar to the question addressed by the *Samaññaphala Sutta*. But much of the material which structures this discourse is repeated, with variations, in the following eleven sermons of the *Digha Nikaya* as well as in some of the discourses of the *Majjhima Nikaya*, the collection of discourses of "middle length."[18] The context of each discourse differs according to the questions which the Buddha addresses—characteristics of the true Brahman, ethics, wisdom, and so on. Underlying these particular topics, however, is a standard pattern which is disrupted in order to deal with various questions which come up for review. The structure behind this pattern is familiar—the eight practices of the Noble Eightfold Path.[19] Set in parallel with these eight steps, this basic text amounts to a narrative version of the Buddha's Middle Way, a graphic description of the path to enlightenment. The fact that the same basic text is repeated with variations indicates that it probably represents a formula which expresses a time-honored tradition. The sequence of paragraphs is, however, not a statement of ethics or even a guide to meditation, but a summary of the way by which the disciple may expect to make systematic progress toward the goal of enlightenment. It "personalizes" the pattern.

What may, as a shorthand, be referred to as the "Way of Deliverance"[20] begins with the appearance in the world of a "fully awakened one, abounding in wisdom and goodness, a Blessed One, a Buddha" whose teaching causes a householder to go forth to the "homeless state," in search of enlightenment. The text says that the householder "has faith in the Tathagata (the one who has found the truth)."[21] Feeling confidence in the person of the teacher the householder declares: "Full of hindrances is household life, a path for the dust of passion. Free as the air is the life of him who has renounced all worldly things. How difficult is it for the man who dwells at home to live the higher life in all its fullness, in all its purity, in all its bright perfection!"[22]

Then follows the description of the Way itself, beginning with ethical behaviour and various directions for right living. According to the *Digha Nikaya* text the ascetic should be confident of heart, without fear, seeing no danger anywhere; according to the *Majjhima Nikaya* version, he should learn to be content with little and thereby experience a perfect internal peace and happiness. After this comes an often-repeated summary of the practices of "guarding the senses" and "mindfulness and self-possession." The practice of right mindfulness (*samma sati*, in the standard formula of the Noble Eightfold Path) repeats itself at various stages on the Way. It is more than one ascetic practice among others, rather a particular attitude or sensibility which informs all actions, at all times. Thus in the *Digha Nikaya* text it is said that "in going forth or coming back he keeps clearly before his mind's eye all that is contained within it. So also in looking forward, or in looking around, in stretching forth his arm or in drawing it in again, in eating and drinking, he keeps himself aware of all it really means." [23]

Mindfulness is the key to the Buddhist Way; we will return to it in more detail shortly. Meanwhile let us finish the description of the Way and an important dimension of the practice of meditation itself. "He chooses some lonely spot to rest at on the way. And returning there after his round for alms he seats himself, when his meal is done, cross-legged, keeping his body erect and intelligence alert."[24] Various hindrances to concentration are overcome, mindfulness is strengthened by practice, feelings of joy and ease arise. Then "estranged from lusts, aloof from evil dispositions, he enters into and remains in the first rapture—a state of joy and ease born of detachment, reasoning and investigation going on the while."[25] The word "rapture" is *jhana* in Pali; very often it is translated simply as "meditation" and refers to a particular lucid trance which, as a strengthening of mindfulness, is typically Buddhist.[26] But it is important to note that what is described here in great detail is not a single practice but *a scale of progress* through the four (and, in some of the *Digha* versions of the Way, eight) meditative states or stages.

It is at this point that the refrain typical of the *Samaññaphala Sutta* reappears, as if the Buddha is keen to remind his listeners that it is here, in overcoming the various hindrances to enlightenment, that one finds "an immediate fruit of the life of an ascetic, visible in this world, and higher and sweeter than the last." Together the series of four *jhanas* amounts to a sort of bridge or passage in which the ascetic moves from the sort of "one-pointed" concentration which is typical of all yogic methods to a more attentive and contemplative wisdom. After the fourth stage of *jhana* the next sections of the text attempt to describe the realization of the Four Noble Truths, the overcoming of various obstacles, and the attainment of the final liberating insight or knowledge. Various imaginative similes are utilized, one of which takes us back to the image of the way through the wilderness with which we began. The Buddha speaks about the experience as being like that of a man who goes from one village to another and then returns:

> Then he would know: "From my own village I came to that other one. There I stood in such and such a way, sat thus, spake thus, and held my peace thus. Thence I came to that other village; and there I stood in such and such a way, sat thus, spake thus, and held my peace thus. And now, from that other village, I have returned back again home.[27]

The householder who left home is back where he began. But this is not the end. Something has changed. The familiar is now seen quite differently. It is notable that at each stage of the Way the defining qualities are clarified—or, perhaps, purified. The first *jhana* is characterized by "joy and ease, born of detachment, reasoning and investigation going on the while."[28] The second speaks about the ascetic "suppressing all reasoning and investigation" and thus entering a state "of joy and ease, born of the serenity of concentration."[29] With the third *jhana* the ascetic holds himself "aloof from joy" and becomes "equable"; that is to say he regards all mental states with a peaceful undisturbed equanimity.[30] The fourth is marked by "self-possession and equanimity, without pain and without ease." The Buddha explains:

> Just, O king, as if a man were sitting so wrapt from head to foot in a clean white robe, that there were no spot in his whole frame not in contact with the clean white robe—just so, O king, does the ascetic sit there, so suffusing his body with that sense of purification, of translucence, of heart, that there is no spot in his whole frame not suffused with it.[31]

What is then described in the text are the results of this state of "self-possession and equanimity"—various mystical states and experiences, each of which is said to be a "fruit, higher and sweeter than the last," but, more important, a growing sensitivity to the way things are:

> Just, O king, as if in a mountain fastness there were a pool of water, clear, translucent and serene; and a man, standing on the bank, and with eyes to see, should perceive the oysters and the shells, the gravel and the pebbles and the shoals of fish as they move about or lie within it; he would know: "This pool is clear, translucent and serene, and there within it are the oysters and shells, and the sand and gravel, and the shoals of fish are moving about or lying still." This, O king, is an immediate fruit of the life of an ascetic, visible in this world, and higher and sweeter than the last. And there is no fruit of the life of an ascetic, visible in this world, that is higher and sweeter than this.[32]

This is the closest the text gets to speaking of *Nirvana*, the *summum bonum* of the Buddhist way. The careful attention to the stages of *jhana,* which aim to reduce the level of emotional as well as intellectual distraction, describes not some speculative state of being but, more pragmatically, a state of pure and undivided attention which leaves the ascetic on the threshold of *Nirvana*—or, as stated earlier, back home but seeing that familiar world more precisely for what it is.

## MINDFULNESS OF THE WAY

The *Samaññaphala Sutta* gives one version of a basic text which I have called the Way of Deliverance. As an expansion of the formula of the Noble Eightfold Path, it narrates the Buddha's Middle Way, making for a particularly graphic description of Batchelor's primary metaphor of the spiritual life. Dominating the text is the *jhana* scale of progress, with its distinct stages of purification and simplification of consciousness, each a "fruit" of the ascetical life which gains an ultimate value in a clarity of vision, the overcoming of a primal forgetting or ignorance. The point being made is that the gaining of such a clarity is never straightforward; one is always likely to be distracted or led astray by a state of consciousness which, however attractive and "fruitful" in itself, is nevertheless not to be identified with *Nirvana*. Hence the insistence that the ascetic must always move forward, never resting content with one particular "fruit." Other versions of the text invoke different sets of graduated stages—some of which do seem to be interested only in identifying states of consciousness rather than in transcending them.[33] Nevertheless, the direction of the basic text is clear: what is important is constantly to purify consciousness and to aspire to a deeper concentration for the sake of *that clarity of vision without which enlightenment is impossible*.[34] The detailed description of stages is less important than the demand not to be absorbed into any particular stage, however pleasant or "fruitful," but to move beyond them all.

The fact that the description of the stages of *jhana* is the longest and most complex part of the text should not distract attention from the meditative practice which in the Noble Eightfold Path is called "right mindfulness."[35] Strictly speaking, this is not a practice as such, a particular type of meditation. It is, rather, the inner contemplative attitude or sensibility which is to be maintained throughout the time of meditation—and indeed throughout one's life as a whole. It is, to put it another way, the quality of attention which is strengthened or purified by the practice of *jhana*. In the *Samaññaphala Sutta* the word occurs in a number of different places. It is also the topic of a text, "On the Setting Up of Mindfulness," in which what is commended is a continued process of recollection, a calling to mind or being aware of certain specified facts and experiences of life.[36] Here the practice of mindfulness is concerned not so much with attending to outer experience of the world as such but with developing a lucid awareness of the *vehicles* of that experience. Thus the meditator is told that it is through the body that one should contemplate the body, through the mind one should contemplate mind, through feelings one should contemplate feelings. Or as the Buddha himself is supposed to have said: "in what is seen there should be what is seen; in what is heard only the heard; . . . in what is sensed only the sensed; in what is thought only the thought."[37] Attention is paid to whatever is given, *as it is given,* in the present moment, the "here and now."

Does that not mean, however, that what is being commended is still a particular *gnosis* or intuition? Is the fruit of mindfulness not a particular heightened state of consciousness? Walpola Rahula, in what remains one of the most lucid yet profound of popular commentaries on Buddhist meditation, says that practicing mindfulness is not a matter of learning a formal method but of attending to the everyday, and to what is given to consciousness in the present moment. "This does not mean that you should not think of the past or the future at all. On the contrary, you think of them in relation to the present moment, the present action, when and where it is relevant."[38] What is built up, with the aid of the process of *jhana,* is a discriminating understanding of the phenomenal world, a detached objectivity. The particular quality which is noted in the fourth *jhana,* the almost untranslateable quality of *upekkha*—"looking out over with peaceful equanimity"—seems to consist of total awareness and clear comprehension, a complete lack of disturbance from all negative emotional states, such as anger and ill will, but also what may be considered more positive ones, too—for joy and happiness impose their own limitations and can also be distractions from the proper apprehension of the present moment.

It is clear from an interpretation of the Buddhist Way based on mindfulness and the *jhanas* that the ultimate soteriological value is given to a purified consciousness in which the mind has become freed from its dependence on sensory objects. This is not to say that "ultimate reality" can only be grasped by a consciousness somehow "different" from everyday awareness. On the contrary, the ordinary processes of cognition have to be purified from limitation and distraction so that the characteristics of reality—understood by the Buddhist as suffering, impermanence, and insubstantiality[39]—are known with perfect clarity and equanimity. The wilderness through which the path passes is seen in a different way—not as a threat but as the source of enlightenment.

## THE WAY EVER WILDERNESS

Despite being presented as a narrative version of the Noble Eightfold Path, the *Samaññaphala Sutta* remains highly schematic in character. This is perhaps unsurprising, given that it was intended as a template for monastic practice and, to that extent, is cast very much in Pieris's "gnostic idiom."[40] However, the very fact that it has been adapted as a response to various questions makes it more than a Buddhist version of a creedal or liturgical formula. Avoided are questions of a metaphysical nature; what is described is the path, not the goal. The only way to know the latter is to practice the former. Such a practice emerges from the dialectical interplay of mindfulness and *jhanic* progress, a regular attempt not to purify the present moment *from* the past, but to bring the past *into* the present, to activate memory.[41] At this point the distinction between the "gnostic" and "agapeic" idioms opens up an important dialogue. Christian ascetical and mystical traditions have their own versions of a measured process of inner attention—or, to use the more Augustinian word, conversion. In both traditions the intention is to transcend forms of desire, whether this is expressed in more cognitive or affective terms. Only through clarity of attention, in Buddhist terms, or through the overcoming of sin, in Christian, can the goal of the path be apprehended. But visions of the end are less important than a gradual attunement to the path itself, and a growing awareness of everything which has brought the searcher from an initial relationship of trust in a teacher to a deeper sense of self-reliance and clarity of purpose. Thus, as developed in its various versions, our basic Way of Deliverance text shows how the searcher is always *on the way*—and thus each and every stage has a value in itself. This point comes out clearly in Batchelor's retrieval of a more authentic postmodern Buddhism.

Batchelor's reflections on the nature of path are based on a single, very Buddhist insight, namely that way and wilderness are correlative terms. The one cannot be understood without the other; indeed the latter needs to be examined more carefully if the value of the former is to be properly appreciated. The way, in short, is ever wilderness. Batchelor observes that this relationship of interdependence has been subverted by modernity's obsession with order and organization. Today the image which "way" conjures up is not of the meandering tracks frequented by the Buddha and his first followers but the massive motorway networks and the carefully planned grids which define the public space of our modern cities. Traces of human footprints have long disappeared under tarmac and concrete. Meanwhile "wilderness" has developed romantic connotations of a primal innocence. Rain forests, polar ice caps, river systems, and the creatures which they support no longer hide some dark force of nature which always threatens to destroy the fragile efforts of human beings to find a passage through an infernal wasteland. They are themselves the victims of human greed and exploitation. In short, while "way" as a metaphor for the spiritual life has been domesticated, "wilderness" has been turned into a place of desire and fascination. Today's spiritual searcher longs not for the security of a tried and trusted path but for that unknown world far from any "trace of marauding humanity," as Batchelor evocatively puts it.[42] For the Buddhist the key experience of "taking refuge" is still there. But in a world where paths are rather ordinary and obvious links between A and B, images of safety and sanctuary can easily dull the senses rather than inspire them. These days, suggests Batchelor, it is the experience of *losing the way* rather than finding it which is spiritually creative:

> A path is most explicitly experienced as such when you find it again after having lost it. When driving at a constant 70 mph along a motorway we are oblivious to the path-nature of the experience. Like a telephone, or a hand, we tend only to notice a path when we lost it or it breaks down. At the moment of finding it again or recovering its use, we experience exhilaration, gratitude and relief—but no sooner have these feelings surfaced than we forget the startling, gift-like nature of the thing and once more we take it for granted.[43]

Although not Batchelor's intention, it is this disarming experience of a way somehow found yet lost, a wilderness at once threatening and beguiling, which, in my opinion, brings the impersonal world of Buddhism much closer to the Christian spirituality of Augustine. Augustine knew nothing about Buddhism; the great religions of India were not part of his conceptual world. No doubt, if he had read the *Samaññaphala Sutta* with its formalized rhetoric of fruits of the Way, he would have found plenty to criticize. He would also have given scant regard to the apparent lack of attention to anything like transcendent reality. In the *City of God* Augustine speaks of the "moral teachings and disciplines of the Indians" which he sets together with the "magical spells of the Chaldaeans."[44] Here he is quoting from Porphyry, whose attempts to find some universal way to the liberation of the soul, Augustine treats with a certain lordly disdain.[45] Elsewhere, he speaks of the ideals of pagan spirituality in similarly negative terms. His demolition of the cyclical theory of world history, mocking the "merry-go-round" of "unremitting alternation between false bliss and genuine misery," is set in stark contrast to faith in the Christ who "died once for our sins."[46] For Augustine it is only through the Incarnation of God's Word that the dim intuitions of pagans and Platonists are made plain. "Thus you see," he tells them, "to some extent and from afar off and with clouded vision, the country in which we must find our home; but you do not keep to the road along which we must travel." [47]

Certainly such unambiguous polemics remind us that there are important differences between the *gnostic* Buddhist Way, in which the homeless ascetic returns to home enlightened, and Christian *agapeic* faith in the one who called himself the Way, Truth, and Life. The former has about it something of the great Indian concept of *samsara*, literally "flowing together," the cyclical pattern of emanation and return, which is reflected in the religious practice of the ascetic meditator who seeks to gather up all things into a single moment of contemplative insight.[48] The latter is a more audacious engagement with an unknown future, supported only by faith in the Christ whose Spirit goes before and guides the searcher. For Augustine the spiritual journey is no cyclical return to a familiar "home" but a constant movement of ascent toward Light and Truth, the God in whom all things will be renewed. I suspect, however, that Augustine would have appreciated Batchelor's insistence that the Buddhist finds the true meaning of the Noble Eightfold Path not by developing some conceptual scheme but by learning to value the experience of following the way, not of escaping from the wilderness but of returning to it—a point which brings the typical Buddhist imagery of the forest close to the Christian, and Jewish and Muslim, sense of the desert as the great expanse where God's majesty is to be encountered.

## PILGRIMAGE AND LOSS

As John Milbank puts it in an evocative phrase, "the Church is that paradox: a nomad city."[49] Augustinian spirituality is above all a spirituality of pilgrimage, an inner journey into the mystery of a self which is made in the image of the Trinitarian God.[50] Augustine would have been sensitive to the polemical point which Batchelor is making: it is more in the spirit of Buddhism to risk losing the way rather than turning what is essentially a spiritual practice into a "totalizing narrative that explains everything."[51] The measured paragraphs of the *Samaññaphala Sutta* do read at times like a carefully calculated assault on some distant fortress. Batchelor's critique adds flesh to the formula, rereading it for today and reminding the practitioner that progress on the Way is never straightforward, that for all the coded references to "fruits," there are also various impediments and obstructions to be negotiated. In fact the more one becomes mindful of what is given to present consciousness, the more one becomes aware of just how unpredictable the "fruits" may be—that sense of unexpected gift to which Batchelor draws our attention. My suggestion is that it is the experience of elation at recovering from loss, finding refuge and restoration after wandering without a sense of direction, which opens up an important point of dialogue between the two traditions.

The point is powerfully made in the well-known Buddhist allegory of the demoralized son and his compassionate father from the *Lotus Sutra*.[52] This is a more dramatic account of the Way, with attention paid to the typically Mahayana theme of the compassionate *bodhisattva* whose "skilful means" teaches the Way to those who have lost any sense of their original Buddha-nature. This story differs from its "Christian parallel," the Lukan parable of the prodigal son, in important ways. The former is much more focused on the gradual unfolding of a broken relationship while the latter emphasizes the joy of finding. But both speak of human fulfillment not just as the recovery of lost innocence but as the revelation of something new. Roger Corless makes the same point in his juxtaposition of the *Lotus Sutra* allegory and one of the *Showings* of Julian of Norwich, the parable of the Lord and the Servant.[53] Julian's revelations, says Corless, puzzled her because they revealed a powerful sense of the love of God which seemed so much at variance with the Church's usual teaching of the wrath of God. Similarly in the *Lotus Sutra*, it is not just that the original truth of the Buddha nature is restored but that one *becomes Buddha*. As Corless puts it, the son in the parable does not merely inherit *from* his father: "he inherits *his father*." [54]

In both traditions spiritual progress is made by confronting the fundamental "problem" of the human condition—whether this is understood in terms of human sinfulness or, in more "gnostic" Buddhist terms, as the result of ignorance or "thirst" in its various forms.[55] In both, a painful process of coming to terms with the reality of life in the wilderness results in an unexpected abundance. The restoration of a broken relationship involves more than setting things right, a return to the tried and trusted. It would not have been possible without that bitter sense of alienation which makes the relationship genuinely *new*, not just a mending of what has been broken. Putting it in the impersonal language of Buddhism, enlightenment comes not from achieving a particular level of gnostic intuition or tuning into some sort of esoteric wisdom but from cultivating a sensitivity to the radical *emptiness* of all things, their "infinite unfindability," as Batchelor puts it.[56] As the great Buddhist concept of *pratityasamutpada* teaches, all things are interdependent, intimately reliant on each other for their arising and passing away. Thus there can be no restoration without loss, any more than there can be way without wilderness, path without non-path. It is in the losing of the way, giving up the desire for the security it promises, that one finds the way; one becomes Buddha by forgetting Buddha.

The peculiarly Buddhist terms of this paradox seem at first sight to be totally at variance with the Christian vision of a new creation effected by the love of God revealed in Christ. Certainly the two are not to be aligned in any straightforward fashion. Nevertheless, the theme of loss and restoration is powerfully present in both traditions. The dialectic of way and wilderness is implicit on almost every page of the *Confessions*. There the parable of the Prodigal Son is more than a guiding metaphor for the spiritual life. It forms what the anthropologists would call the "deep structure" of human existence. Thus at the very end of book 2, Augustine soliloquizes on the sinfulness of his early life and the joy of salvation:

> With you is utter peace and a life immune from disturbance. The person who enters into you "enters into the joy of the Lord" (Matt 25.21) and will not be afraid; he will find himself in the supreme Good where it is supremely good to be. As an adolescent I went astray from you (Ps 118.76), my God, far from your unmoved stability. I became myself a region of destitution.[57]

The wilderness of the parable is identified with Augustine himself. But this is a complex self, with an "inside" and an "outside," an interiority and a set of exterior relations, which exists in a strange and unresolved tension with itself—and with God. This self is never completely at peace—until, of course, it finds itself at rest in God, the one source of all peace.

The *Confessions* tells the story of a very personal journey, away from a "region of destitution," mirrored in the social and religious conventions of an increasingly oppressive world, and a new transforming relationship made possible by the love revealed by the Word of God. What sets out as an autobiography turns into a meditation on the nature of the self and concludes with a rereading of the opening chapter of Genesis with its final astonishing vision of the Sabbath day of rest which "has no evening and no ending."[58] At this point Augustine finds some sort of resolution of his own painful experience of personal fragmentation and division, his separation from the God in whom alone all things come together in peace and harmony. But even the promise of the abundance of God's grace cannot overcome the central *aporia* which Augustine discerns all around him—and most obviously *in* himself. The capacity to track a single life across the entire span of past, present and future arouses in him a sense of the eternal mystery of things, an anticipation of the glorious fullness which the way promises. At the same time that very capacity is hung about with the experience of loss; he remains distant from the future to which he aspires. To know oneself as bound by time is both the glory and the tragedy of human beings. For all that we glimpse the timeless bliss at the end of our journey along the way, we remain always *on the way*; we may not separate ourselves from that time-bound wilderness which is our world.

## ETERNITY AND TRANSIENCE

It is time to return to the question with which we began, to the experience of a life which is always lived on the way: in Buddhist terms with constant mindfulness of what is given in the present, or—as the Christian would put it—"in Christ," who is the way, truth, and life. How are we to maintain the integrity of the self in the flow of time, past, present, future? If we ourselves are part of that flow, how can we stand apart from it? Augustine's reflections on the nature of time in book XI of *Confessions* are much more than a speculative treatise on an abstract problem. Rather he takes a conundrum of human living and opens up a fascinating meditation on how human beings are to keep their attention fixed on what is eternal and unchanging in the midst of transience and change. For Augustine himself human living is a struggle to make sense of an existence which is always on pilgrimage, yearning for a glorious future yet never confident of achieving it. In trying to express his perplexity, he muses upon the act of reciting a psalm. The words he has just heard said exist only as memory while the words still to be recited exist only as expectation:

> But my attention is on what is present: by that the future is transferred to become the past. As the action advances further and further, the shorter the expectation and the longer the memory, until all expectation is consumed, the entire action is finished, and it has passed into the memory. What occurs in the psalm as a whole occurs in its particular pieces and its individual syllables. The same is true of a longer action in which perhaps that psalm is a part. It is also valid of the entire life of an individual person, where all actions are parts of a whole, and of the total history of "the sons of men" (Ps 30.20) where all human beings are but parts.[59]

In other words, through the joint action of memory and anticipation, past and future are brought into a correlation which allows an almost godlike glimpse of all things gathered into one. The vision at Ostia is the best-known example of what Augustine understands to be only a momentary anticipation of eternity—the timeless experienced in the middle of time:

> Our minds were lifted up by an ardent affection towards eternal being itself. . . . There life is the wisdom by which all creatures come into being, both things which were and which will be. . . . And while we talked and panted after it, we touched it in some small degree by a moment of total concentration of the heart.[60]

Then he returns to the everyday, aware of this extraordinary capacity of the mind to extend itself, yet bewildered that it is so difficult to escape from time. That momentary stillness which contemplates the eternal is all but impossible to achieve.

However, as so often, in reflecting on the mystery of a life which aspires to so much and yet experiences so painfully its own fragmentation, Augustine finds salvation at the heart of his own perplexity. No sooner does he express his anguish than he finds himself asking, "Who can lay hold on the heart and give it fixity, so that for some little moment it may be stable, and for a fraction of a moment may grasp the splendour of a constant eternity?"[61] Strangely he finds that the human capacity to mark the passing of time arises from his preoccupation with the God who draws the human soul to himself. In the recognition of the problem comes the solution. He cannot escape from himself, any more than he can extract himself from the passage of a time-bound existence. But Augustine does not find God; he *is found by* God. His experience is of an eternity which has entered into and transformed the temporal, binding past and present and future together in a way beyond the power of unaided human nature to achieve.

In recognizing and becoming ever more conformed to the eternal truth which is God, the standard is Christ whose presence within the soul is the form or measure by which Augustine comes to judge and understand. Augustine's "theological aesthetic"—the God revealed in the one who calls himself way, truth, and life—is the key to all his work. But this is no revelation of an esoteric truth such as he once espoused in his Manichean days. Nor is it to be neatly set against the philosophical teaching of neo-Platonism which he found so lacking when compared with Christianity. The drama of his own conversion is the intellectual bedrock on which his commitment to Christianity as "true religion" is founded. He had no doubt about the deep intelligibility of Christian faith: not just its inner coherence and rationality, but its capacity to engage with and transform the various dimensions of "otherness" which it confronts. But conversion is more than a moment of intellectual clarity; it is also a more disarming, and more ill-defined, *process* of surrender to the God whose transforming love stands in such marked contrast to human sinfulness. "My sin was this," says Augustine, "that I looked for pleasure, beauty and truth not in [God] but in myself and his other creatures, and the search led me instead to pain, confusion and error."[62] Later he speaks of his own Pauline struggle to come to terms with the newness of Christian faith which both builds on the foundations of what has gone before—in Augustine's case, of course, the Platonism which never left him—while elaborating a form which is quite unique. In other words, this is familiar ground (Augustine never leaves the painfully familiar world which reminds him of his sinfulness), yet it is also always and ever new (he never ceases from being led onward by glimpses of eternity). It is this new life in God which has taught him to distinguish between "presumption and confession."[63] "It is one thing from a wooded summit to catch a glimpse of the homeland of peace and not to find the way to it, but vainly to attempt the journey along an impracticable route. . . . It is another thing to hold on to the way that leads there, defended by the protection of the heavenly emperor."[64]

## LIVING IN TIME

Christianity and Buddhism both teach versions of this way to the homeland of peace. The latter is more reticent about the role played by the "heavenly emperor," preferring the benign, more assuredly "gnostic" compassion of the thoughtful father. This is in line with a tradition which, as Batchelor points out, is suspicious of the totalizing power of language. Thus the Way of Deliverance begins with the personal relationship of trust established between seeker and teacher but this is only the first step, the immediate "fruit of being an ascetic." The searcher must find his own way—in line with the Buddha's final instructions that his followers should "dwell making yourselves an island (support), making yourselves your refuge, and not anyone else as your refuge."[65] Earlier I noted that the *Samaññaphala Sutta* develops its own narrative structure as it seeks to express the complex interplay between two different forms of yogic meditation, the "setting up of mindfulness" and the process of *Jhana*, the simplification of consciousness. In the later tradition these forms lead to the formation of different schools of meditation—*Vipassana* and *Samatha* in Theravada, *Rinzai* and *Soto* in Zen.[66] But these distinctions should not cause us to lose sight of the fact that such practices have to be held together. Mindfulness may, strictly speaking, be the only practice necessary; it is certainly central to the understanding of Buddhist meditation. But there is more to mindfulness than a largely passive awareness of various disconnected stimuli, episodes in one's life vaguely coalescing in the present. As Rahula insists, the aim is to see everything through attention to the present moment. This cannot be done without constant practice. The whole point of the rather tortuously expressed stages of *Jhana* is that mindfulness needs to be strengthened. Otherwise it is taken to be merely a temporary "fruit of being an ascetic" and no more. Rather, a single but differentiated practice is intended to develop the peculiarly Buddhist quality of *upekha,* or equanimity. To say that this leaves the meditator "on the threshold" of Nirvana is to follow the explicit teaching of our text, which speaks only of progress on the way and not of the end itself. The "fruits of the ascetic" describe a graduated progress in the ordering of desire and grasping in all its forms; even the desire for Nirvana itself must be purified of false images, ideas, and feelings. Thus the primary aim of Buddhist meditation is not a ruthless process of self-conquest but that quality of mindful attention to the present without which it is impossible to see things as they really are. In these terms Buddhist enlightenment is less the bright fulfilment which comes at the end of the path than a deep content, marked by qualities of wisdom and compassion, learned within the painful process of journeying itself.

Augustine's agonizings about the mystery of the marking of time, tantalizing glimpses of an eternity which always eludes him, are absent from a tradition which never presumes to "name" the eternal. His style of writing, and the *agapeic* experience he describes, reflect a personal drama which is lacking in the more abstract exhortations of the *Samaññaphala Sutta*. Where the Buddhist text illustrates the fundamental truth about human existence in an ever-repeated formula, Augustine finds himself pouring out his heart in love of a God who has saved him from himself. Where Buddhism teaches that "right effort" can only be achieved by constant practice of "right mindfulness," the Augustinian insight is that it is only *God* who can order human desire. Where Buddhism brings past and present into a correlation, but never presumes to speculate beyond what is given in the present, Christianity dares not just to remember the past but to anticipate in the present the fullness of time. It is through "confession" that one anticipates the fullness of what is to come—whether in words of praise and thanksgiving in the liturgy, or in the peculiarly Augustinian sense of a direct address toward God expressing humility and loving dependence. For Augustine it is only through the linking of this present moment to the memory of what has gone before that the hoped for future can become a reality. Through what he calls the "distension of the soul" the three dimensions of time are held together; autobiographical confession in the present moment unifies memory of the past and hope for the future in a single offering to the eternal God in whom alone time stands still. How can this be possible? How can the glimpse of eternity be a source of hope and proof against the subtle sin of presumption? Only God can grant this—as Augustine seems to suggest at the end of book XI of *Confessions:*

> Let the person who understands this make confession to you. Let him who fails to understand it make confession to you. How exalted you are, and the humble in heart are your house (Ps 137.6; 145.8). You lift up those who are cast down (Ps 144.14; 145.8) and those whom you raise to that summit which is yourself do not fail.[67]

This is a richly *agapeic* or prophetic tradition—the power of God's revealed Word provoking a response of heartfelt confession of faith. Augustine is forever looking forward to a future which is greater and better. The more *gnostic* Buddhist Way has no such vision—or, rather, it steadfastly subordinates any account of *Nirvana* to the immediate moment and to the present "fruit" of following the Way.

Clearly it is possible to set two such different traditions in opposition to each other—the one concerned with where the path is leading, the other with how the path has led to this present moment. But, if Pieris is right that we are speaking of the instantiations of complementary religious idioms, then the question is more about how what he calls *communicatio in sacris*, whether understood as liturgy or in its more interiorized version as meditation, can be understood essentially as ways of *marking the passing of time*. For a Christian the future is *anticipated* in the present, whereas for the Buddhist the past is *made real* in the present. For both traditions, however, living in the present moment is much more than the correlating of a whole series of past moments with a hoped for fulfilment. Putting it in terms of the way through the wilderness, both traditions find real spiritual value in the journey itself; it is not a matter of taking the way to *avoid* the wilderness, but of confronting the wilderness *through* the way. Thus for both engagement with suffering or pain or sin—or whatever term is used to describe the unsatisfactoriness of human living—is itself the promise of a "way out." But, to repeat: whereas the Buddhist marks the past in order to practice that equanimity without which the present is a source of unalloyed suffering, impermanence, and insubstantiality, the Christian projects that marking into the future—albeit into an eternity which confounds the human capacity to mark time at all.

## LIVING IN HOPE

The Christian, following Augustine, will ask how hope is not to become presumption. How are glimpses of eternity to sustain the life of constant pilgrimage and not become either temporary consolations or false intimations of a new dawn? For the Christian, hope is rooted in the promised Reign of God which is announced by Jesus and is therefore already coming to fruition in the world. In this sense hope is not a Buddhist virtue. Nevertheless the Buddhist still anticipates a future; however else Nirvana, Enlightenment, or Deliverance are to be described, such terms announce the goal of the Way, its final fruit. The seeker moves toward this goal without ever presuming to articulate its nature, relying only on traces of who or what has gone before. In Christianity, on the other hand, the future, the goal which is Godself, is to be understood as moving toward the seeker. As Pieris puts it, drawing on Moltmann, "the *Future comes towards the human*." [68]

We are dealing here with what Pieris calls a "homologue" rather than an exact equivalent.[69] In the more *gnostic* practice of Buddhist mindfulness attention to the present moment plays a more significant part in knitting together the myriad experiences which make up the self than is the case in the more *agapeic* devotion of Christianity. But this is not to say that the two idioms are in opposition, nor that the one cannot learn from the other. The *Samaññaphala Sutta* begins with trust being placed in the person of the enlightened teacher. The intention is then that the Buddha's followers learn how to free themselves from dependence on the teacher.

Throughout the text it is constant attention to the stages of the journey as a single process of interior intellectual and affective purification which builds toward the realization of the twin virtues of *prajña*, wisdom, and *karuna*, compassion, the primary motivating factors in all Buddhist traditions. The analogous religious practice for Augustine is the personal confession of faith which expresses his response to the loving initiative of God. Like the Buddhist this takes the form of a journey or pilgrimage, the following of the footsteps of those who have gone before. Our two traditions have at least this much in common, that uncanny capacity to mark time, the *distentio animi*. They differ less in terms of the *gnostic* or *agapeic* idioms of spiritual practice than with regard to certain presuppositions about what it is *possible* to bring into a correlation. Where Buddhists refuse to speculate about the future and seek only to learn that equanimity which comes from seeing the past through an eternal present, Christians are committed to the vision of a future which not only *can* but *must* be spoken about.

There is something important for both traditions to learn here. In daring to anticipate what has been promised, perhaps what the Buddhist most commends to the Christian is a healthy reticence; even talk of an "eternal present" risks turning the momentary experience into a thing to be possessed. A Christian properly mindful of what the present gives, some trace of God's Word, will apply that sensitivity to all aspects of experience in all their messiness and rich complexity, aware that the quality of remembrance forms the quality of hope, the anticipation of what is to come. The two movements revolve around a consciousness to self which looks, as it were, in two directions at once. Buddhist mindfulness does not anticipate any future, indeed treats such projections with a careful suspicion. Nevertheless, Christian meditators can learn from the practice of mindfulness to cultivate a dispassionate attention to the here and now. Remembering the past can, of course, be no more than an exercise in romantic self-indulgence, but an encounter with Buddhist equanimity teaches that God is not to be encountered simply because that is what is desired—for "God" all too easily becomes a projection of our unacknowledged desires. The Buddha's reticence in speaking of Ultimate Reality is a warning to Christians to listen to the Word, not to be seduced by "mere words."

Augustine's experience of coming to terms with his past is not an exercise in mindful meditation. His correlation of his own life story within the sweep of Christian revelation is an extraordinary achievement of the theological imagination. But it was brought about more by a humility learned through loss than it was by the exercise of the intellect. The *distentio animi* cannot escape or surmount its own roots in the present. Despite his efforts to order past, present, and future, he reminds us that there is no "eternal present" which surmounts the present and grants privileged access to the mystery of time. Rather, a present faithfully lived in imitation of God's act of self-giving to those who are "humble in heart" *reflects* eternity. Or, to return one more time to the terms with which we began, treading the way involves not a mechanical pursuit of a preset goal but constant attention to and valuing of what is to be known as gift precisely because it could so easily be experienced as loss. That is what gives the present moment its revelatory power: whether in Buddhism or Christianity, wilderness, forest, and desert are places of encounter. In these terms, the "*agapeic* idiom" of Augustinian spirituality may not be that far removed from Buddhism's more *gnostic* form of spiritual practice. Both traditions overcome the *aporia* of time by breaking the stranglehold which a naively *self*-centered account of the spiritual journey exercises over human living. Clearly the deconstructive strategies of the Buddhist Way of Deliverance are not to be confused with the rich interpersonal categories enunciated in the New Testament. Nevertheless, both, in their different ways, put ultimate value on a considered relationship with what is ever "other." Just as Buddhist meditators attend mindfully to whatever is given in the present moment, learning to treat all objects of experience with equanimity, so Christians grow more aware of the fullness of the mystery of human living, God mysteriously present in all its joys and tragedies. Such "mindful" Christians live with attention not to the events of their own lives as such—for they remain only as elusive memories—but to the miracle of God's love now at work within them and which alone allows them to make sense of those events.

## NOTES

1. Stephen Batchelor, "The Other Enlightenment Project," in *Faith and Praxis in a Post-Modern Age*, ed. Ursula King ( London: Cassells, 1998) 113–27.
2. Ibid., 115.
3. Ibid., 118.
4. The fourfold distinction is first noted in the 1984 document from the Secretariat for non-Christian Religions, "The Attitude of the Church Towards the Followers of Other Religions," *Bulletin* 1/2 (1984) 126–41. It is repeated in John Paul II's encyclical, *Redemptoris Missio*, para. 57 (1990), and in the 1991 joint document from the Pontifical Council for Interreligious Dialogue and the Congregation for Evangelisation, "Dialogue and Proclamation: Reflections and Orientations on Inter-religious Dialogue and the Proclamation of the Gospel of Jesus Christ," *Bulletin* 26/2 (1991) 210–50. For commentary on the relationship between the latter document and *Redemptoris Missio* see William R. Burrows, ed. *Redemption and Dialogue* (Maryknoll: Orbis, 1993), esp. "A Theological Commentary: Dialogue and Proclamation," by Jacques Dupuis, 119–58; see also Michael Barnes, "Discernere L 'Istinto

Cattolico': riflettendo, dieci anni dopo, su Dialogo e Annuncio," *Ad Gentes* (Bologna), 2001, 5.1.

5. *Nostra Aetate* states that Christians should engage in "discussion and collaboration" with members of other religions and, while witnessing to their own faith, "acknowledge, preserve and encourage" the spiritual and moral values found in non-Christian religions (para. 2). Translation from *Vatican Council II: The Conciliar and Post-Conciliar Documents*, ed. Austin Flannery (Dublin: Dwyer, 1992). The word translated as "discussion" here is "colloquia." The use of the word "dialogue" in Roman Catholic discourse is attributed to the influence of Paul VI, particularly to his first encyclical, *Ecclesiam Suam*, which speaks of dialogue as "the internal drive of charity which tends to become the external gift of charity" (para. 64). It was Paul VI who linked the inner Trinitarian dialogue with the "relationship which we, i.e., the Church, should strive to establish and foster with the human race" and spoke of the "dialogue of salvation" (paras. 70–77), later taken up by the two dicasterial documents noted earlier.

6. The phrase "context of otherness" is developed at greater length in Michael Barnes, *Theology and the Dialogue of Religions* (Cambridge: Cambridge University Press, 2002), see especially chapter 1.

7. According to Wilfred Cantwell Smith, *The Meaning and End of Religion* (Minneapolis: Fortress Press, 1991), "modern predispositions are betrayed" by translating the title *De Vera Religione* as "On the true religion"—as if it is an apologetic for Christianity. Christianity is hardly mentioned; the theme is more exactly "proper piety" or "genuine worship."

8. Augustine begins *De Vera Religione*: "The way of the good and blessed life is to be found entirely in the true religion wherein one God is worshipped and acknowledged with purest piety to be the beginning of all existing things, originating, perfecting and containing the universe" (i.1).

9. See ST 2a2ae, 81

10. See, e.g., *City of God* 19.35; 10.7; 19.26.

11. See Charles T. Mathewes, "Pluralism, Otherness, and the Augustinian Tradition," *Modern Theology* 14.1 (1998) 83–112.

12. The theme is repeated throughout a collection of essays on the Buddhist-Christian dialogue, *Love Meets Wisdom* (Maryknoll: Orbis, 1988). See especially "Christianity in a Core-to-Core Dialogue with Buddhism," 110–35. See also a more recent collection of essays, *Prophetic Humour in Buddhism and Christianity* (Colombo: Ecumenical Institute for Study and Dialogue, 2005); see especially 123–27.

13. See especially *Love Meets Wisdom*, 119–24.

14. In this regard see especially Stephen Batchelor, *The Awakening of the West: the Encounter of Buddhism and Western Culture* (London: Thorsons, 1995). Pieris has not written anything on this scale from a Christian point of view, but several of his longer articles draw attention to various points of formative historical contact between Christianity and the religions of Asia. See especially Pieris, "Western Christianity and Asian Buddhism: a Theological Reading of Historical Encounters," in A. Pieris, *Love Meets Wisdom* (Maryknoll: Orbis, 1988) 17–42; and A. Pieris, "The Place of Non-Christian Religions and Cultures in the Evolution of Third World Theology," in A. Pieris, ed., *An Asian Theology of Liberation* (Edinburgh: T and T Clark, 1988) 87–110.

15. Translation from *Dialogues of the Buddha, Part I*. Pali Text Society (London: Routledge, 1973) 56–95.

16. *Digha Nikaya* 1.47.

17. *Digha Nikaya* 1.59.

18. There are eleven suttas which follow the pattern of the *Samaññaphala Sutta*, and four in the *Majjhima Nikaya*, with rather different accounts of "sila," the initial set of ethical practices.

19. Listed in what is traditionally known as the Buddha's first sermon, the *Dhammacakkappavattana Sutta*, the "Setting in motion of the wheel of truth," (*Samyutta Nikaya*, LVI, 11) as right view, right thought, right speech, right action, right livelihood, right effort, right mindfulness, and right concentration. See text and commentary in Walpola Rahula, *What the Buddha Taught* (Bedford: Gordon Fraser, 1967).

20. The term comes from Erich Frauwallner, *History of Indian Philosophy* (Delhi: Motilal Banarsidass, 1973), 117ff.

21. *Tathagata* literally means "the one who has 'thus gone' or 'fared so'"; Buddhist tradition takes it as a title the Buddha used of himself. The word for faith here is the Pali *Saddha* (Sanskrit *Śraddha*) which has connotations of devotion to a chosen teacher.

22. *Digha Nikaya* 1.62.

23. *Digha Nikaya* 1.70.

24. *Digha Nikaya* 1.71.

25. *Digha Nikaya* 1.75ff.

26. The Sanskrit root behind the word is *Dhyai*, "to think of, imagine or contemplate," giving the noun *Dhyana*. But the word means more than "meditation." Buddhaghosa in his classic Theravada commentary, *The Visuddhimagga* (137–69), speaks of the stages of *Jhana* as a process by which the mind becomes blissfully absorbed in a high degree of mindful awareness.

27. *Digha Nikaya* 1.81.

28. *Digha Nikaya* 1.73.

29. *Digha Nikaya* 1.74.

30. *Digha Nikaya* 1.75. The word translated as "equable" is *upekhako*, which has the sense of "looking out over, seeing all things without being entranced or caught up in any particular aspect."

31. *Digha Nikaya* 1.75–76.

32. *Digha Nikaya* 1.84–85.

33. Some texts speak of four *Rupajhanas* and add four more *Arupajhanas*—distinguishing consciousness of "form" and "formlessness." Others speak of *Samapattis*, "achievements," or the four *Brahmaviharas*, the "abodes of Brahma" or "supreme abidings," which describe the four qualities of *metta, karuna, mudita*, and *upekha*—usually translated as "loving-kindness," "compassion," "sympathy," and "equanimity."

34. Thus, for example, the *Sampasadaniya Sutta, Digha Nikaya* 3.112, insists that the acquisition of psychic power (*iddhi*) must not be given any independent soteriological significance.

35. In Pali *samma sati*, the penultimate element, the *jhana* scale of progress belongs in the final stage, *samma samadhi*. Mindfulness is not, therefore, to be subsumed

within the process of *jhana*. Rather it introduces the meditator to a graduated scale of mindful attention to what is given in consciousness.

36. See the *Satipatthana Sutta, Digha Nikaya* 22, *Majjhima Nikaya* 10.

37. *Udana* 1.10, quoted in the edition and commentary on the *Satipatthana Sutta* by Nyanaponika Thera, *The Heart of Buddhist Meditation* (London: Rider, 1962) 33–34.

38. *What the Buddha Taught*, 71.

39. In the Pali terms: *dukkha, anicca*, and *anatta*.

40. The second *Pitaka*, the collection of *suttas* or "discourses," needs to be related closely to the first, the *Vinayapitaka*, which gives the origin of rules of monastic practice—again set in narrative form.

41. It should be noted that *sati*, or in Sanskrit *smrti*, comes from the root *smr*—"remember," "recollect," "call to mind."

42. Ibid., 116.

43. Ibid., 114.

44. *City of God*, 10.32.

45. For an account of Augustine's late reflections on the relationships between religious plurality and Christianity see John Vanderspoel, "The Background to Augustine's Denial of Religious Plurality," in Hugo Meynell, ed. *Grace, Politics and Desire: Essays on Augustine* (University of Calgary Press, 1990) 179–93.

46. *City of God* 12.14.

47. *City of God* 10.29.

48. This is perhaps more typical of the Upanisadic view than the strictly Buddhist approach. But both are dependent on forms of yogic practice in which the chief practice is the concentrating of the attention on one point—in Pali *cittass'ekkagata*.

49. John Milbank, " 'Postmodern Critical Augustinianism': a Short Summa in Forty Two Responses to Unasked Questions," *Modern Theology* 7:3 ( 1991) 229.

50. See "Introduction: The Spirituality of St Augustine," in Mary T. Clark, *Augustine of Hippo, Selected Writings*. Classics of Western Spirituality (Ramsey, NJ: Paulist Press, 1984)1–54.

51. Ibid., 126.

52. *The Lotus Sutra*, or *Saddharmapundarika Sutra*—the "Sutra on the White Lotus of the True Teaching"—is one of the most important Mahayana texts, dating from around 200 CE. With a certain polemical intent, it distinguishes followers of the "Great Way" from the "Lesser Way," or Hinayana. Much of the text consists of collections of parables in which the Buddha teaches people of different abilities according to a quality of compassionate *upayakauśalya*, or "skill in means."

53. Roger Corless, "The Dramas of Spiritual Progress: The Lord and the Servant in Julian's *Showings* 51 and the Lost Heir in *Lotus Sutra* 4," *Mystics Quarterly* 11.2 (1985) 65–75.

54. Ibid., 72.

55. The topic of the Second Noble Truth, *Samudaya*, "arising" or cause of *Dukkha*. Various causes are given and correlated in the concept of *paticca-samuppada*, "conditioned origination." See Rahula, op. cit., 29–34; Peter Harvey, *An Introduction to Buddhism* (Cambridge: Cambridge University Press, 1990), 53–60.

56. Batchelor, "The Other Enlightenment Project," op. cit., 120.

57. *Confessions*, 2.10.18, trans. Henry Chadwick (Oxford: Oxford University Press, 1991). Chadwick comments that here "[t]he Prodigal Son is fused with a Neoplatonic theme of the soul's destitution without God, which is taken up at the beginning of Book III and again in VII, x (16)." Destitution in the soul's distance from God is a theme in Porphyry (*De abstinentia* 3.27 and *Sententiae* 40) based on Plato's *Symposium*.

58. *Confessions*, 13.36.51.

59. *Confessions*, 11.28.38.

60. *Confessions*, 9.10.24.

61. *Confessions*, 11.11.13.

62. *Confessions*, 1.20.31.

63. *Confessions*, 7.20.26.

64. *Confessions*, 7.21.27.

65. From the last sermon of the Buddha, the *Mahaparinibbana Sutta*, translation taken from Rahula, op. cit., 59–60.

66. See Walpola Rahula, *Zen and the Taming of the Bull* (London: Gordon Fraser, 1978), esp. 15–24.

67. *Confessions*, 11.31.41.

68. Pieris, *Prophetic Humour*, op. cit., 34–35 with reference to Juergen Moltmann, *A Theology of Hope* ( London: SCM Classics, 1967), 95ff.

69. See especially *Prophetic Humour*, 107.

# 7

# Augustine, Apuleius, and Hermes Trismegistus: The *City of God* and Advice on How (Not) to Read Hindu Texts

Francis X. Clooney

## INTRODUCTION

St. Augustine had strong opinions about pagan religion and culture, and he was reasonably well informed about them.[1] He also worked with a firm conviction about the superiority of the Christian religion and culture that were replacing the pagan. Accordingly, he was confident, argumentative, stubbornly settled in his views when (in his mature period) he undertook to argue with pagan authors. He was also on occasion a dedicated reader of texts who took seriously the task of a learned apologetics, since he was convinced that he could find in pagan sources evidence for the truth of his positions and the falsity of pagan views. In his argumentative reading practices, such as we find in the *City of God*, Augustine models a kind of contested erudition; he was learned enough and specific enough that we can have respect for his project, while at the same time we can also measure the limits of that learning and interpretation, observing rather clearly where he chose to stop reading and stop taking cues from the texts in question. I suggest that the vulnerability of his reading practice lay not in the notion that he should have reached better conclusions, or adopted a posture of benign tolerance; rather, his reading was vulnerable because it was guided partly by the requirements of a careful reading and partly by settled faith positions that determined in advance what would be learned by reading. He could not merely present the views of pagan authors; he needed rather to dissect those views, assess their parts variously, often reading them against the grain of their authors' intentions. That he was actually reading pagan texts means also, however, that other readings of those texts are still possible, problematizing conclusions he had thought to have demonstrated from those pagan texts. By extension, I suggest that Augustine thus exemplifies a practice of apologetic reading that can be recognized throughout Church history, including in the period of colonial, missionary encounters with Asian religions. Today, we need to consider honestly both the attraction and problem of such readings, the mix of taking others seriously, at their word, but also claiming authority to determine what those words mean, regardless of authorial intentions.[2]

To illustrate these points, in the pages that follow I look into books 8 and 9 of the *City of God*, where Augustine reads with care, though not uncontroversially, two pagan texts, the *God of Socrates* of Apuleius and the *Apuleius* attributed to Hermes Trismegistus.[3] I have narrowed my choice to these particular texts, since (as is not the case with the texts of Varro, for instance) full versions of both are available to us, so that we can not only examine Augustine's manner of reading but also compare it with other ways of reading those same texts. How he read and learned from these sources, the extent to which he read them against the intent of their authors, and when his learning stopped and the reading was left incomplete are questions that guide the first and major portion of this essay.

In the second part, I turn to Western Christian readings of Hinduism, considering (again briefly) how three Jesuits in India in the colonial missionary period—Frs. de Nobili, Bouchet, and Meurin, respectively in the seventeenth, eighteenth, and nineteenth centuries—appropriated Hindu texts for the sake of Christian mission. Since I have not been able to determine a direct influence of Augustine's reading practice on these Jesuits, my reflections is simply a thought experiment intended to illumine a shared problematic evident in the *City of God* and in the missionary writings.[4]

## AUGUSTINE'S FIRST READING OF THE *GOD OF SOCRATES*: GOD, GODS, AND DEMONS

In the following pages, I consider the *God of Socrates* and the *Asclepius* as read by Augustine in books 8 and 9 of the *City of God*.[5] By general consensus among scholars, books 1–10 of the *City of God* are dedicated to a critique of the gods of the pagans, along with the metaphysics, theology, and social ideology underlying their cult. Augustine's argument with the pagan philosophers is in books 6–10, and includes important comments on the schools of philosophy in general, a detailed critique of Varro's theory of the gods and of kinds of religion (books 6–7) and, in book 10, a concerted attack on Porphyry. He criticizes the "natural" or "physical" gods (book 6), the "mythic" and "civil" gods (book 7), and the more sophisticated, philosophically conceived gods of the Platonic tradition (books 8–10). Books 8 and 9 are pertinent here because, as I have indicated, Augustine reads closely at least parts of the *God of Socrates* and the *Asclepius*.

In the first chapters of book 8, Augustine describes favorably the wisdom of Plato and his disciples, particularly their views of God. Speculating on whether Plato in some way knew Biblical revelation, he observes:

> But it does not matter from what source Plato learned these things—whether from the books of the ancient writers who preceded him or, rather, as the apostle says, "Because that which may be known of God has been manifested among them, for God hath manifested it to them. For His invisible things from the creation of the world are clearly seen, being understood by those things which have been made, also His eternal power and Godhead." At all events, I have, I think, sufficiently shown that it was not without good reason that I chose the Platonist philosophers to discuss with them the question of natural theology which we have here taken up: that is, whether, for the sake of the happiness which is to come after death, sacred rites are to be performed for the one God or for many. I have, indeed, chosen them especially because they surpass all others in their glory and distinction, just as they do in their doctrine that there is one God Who made heaven and earth. (8.12)[6]

With this rather positive assessment of the Platonic theology in place, Augustine goes on to criticize what he considers to be unsatisfactory aspects of it, particularly with respect to the supreme, good God in relationship to lesser, imperfect beings. He introduces Apuleius and his *God of Socrates* in order to highlight the dubiousness and incoherence of taking demons seriously as mediators between higher and more perfect deities and the human race:

> Although these things are also found in the writings of others, the Platonist Apuleius of Madaura wrote a book devoted solely to this subject, and chose to call it *De Deo Socratis*. In it, he discusses and explains what kind of divine being it was that was attached and bound to Socrates by a kind of friendship, and by which, it is said, he was warned to refrain from acting when what he proposed to do would not have had a favourable outcome. Apuleius declares clearly, and most fully asserts, that this was not a god, but a demon, and he discussed with great lucidity the opinion of Plato as to the sublimity of the gods, the lowly station of men, and the intermediate position of the demons. (8.14)

In Augustine's view, this last sentence marks the theme of the *God of Socrates* and the understanding of demons he is interested in denigrating.

His goal is simply to reveal fundamental contradictions in that work and hence too in the Platonic system Apuleius describes:

> So either Apuleius errs, and it is not in this class of divine beings that Socrates' familiar spirit belongs; or Plato's beliefs are inconsistent with one another, in that he honours the demons yet removes from the well-ordered city the things in which they take pleasure; or else Socrates is not to be congratulated on his friendship with a demon. (8.14)

To Augustine, it is symptomatic that Apuleius mistitles his treatise because he is ashamed of its content:

> After all, Apuleius was so embarrassed by this friendship that he called his book *Concerning the God of Socrates*, even though, according to the discussion in which he distinguishes between gods and demons so carefully and at such great length, he should have called it not *Concerning the God*, but *Concerning the Demon of Socrates*. He preferred to put the word "demon" into the discussion itself, rather than into the title of the book, for, thanks to the wholesome doctrine which has enlightened human affairs, all, or nearly all, men now shrink from the name of demons. (8.14)

By this discrepancy, Apuleius writes into his treatise an implicit concession that demons are flawed beings, hardly to be taken seriously as mediators:

> For Apuleius himself, though he is in many ways lenient toward the demons and considers them worthy of divine honours, is nonetheless compelled to confess that they are goaded to anger, whereas we are taught by the true religion not to be moved to anger, but, rather, to resist it. The demons are beguiled by gifts; but the true religion teaches us not to show favour to anyone on account of gifts received. (8.17)

Augustine adds, as if addressing Apuleius: "What reason is there, then, apart from folly and miserable error, for you to humble yourself to worship a being whom you do not wish to resemble in your life? And why should you pay religious homage to one whom you do not wish to imitate, when the highest duty of religion is to imitate him whom you worship?" (8.17). Apuleius is thus trapped by his own double assertion: demons are flawed and demons are the intermediaries between the perfect gods and humans. In Augustine's view, Plato would have nothing to do with demons (8.18), and can be counted a witness against Apuleius's theory of demons, gods, and mediations.

I will return to Apuleius later, as does Augustine, but for now we can at least ask whether Augustine is actually striking a serious blow against Apuleius' own belief—and point in the *God of Socrates*—in highlighting the inferiority of the demons. It is at least a peculiar reading of Apuleius' project, if we consider the fuller program of the *God of Socrates*, succinctly outlined by Stephen Harrison:[7]

Gods and Men [nn. 114–132]
astral gods [114–120]
the non-astral gods [121–124]
man and his separation from the gods [125–132]
The Account of *Daimones* [132–156]
the function of *daimones* [132–137]
the location and physical substance of *daimones* [137–145]
*daimones*, emotions, and the higher gods [145–150]
types of *daimones* [150–156]
The *Daimonion* of Socrates [157–167]
Following the Moral Example of Socrates [167–178]
encouragement to virtue and philosophy [167–169]
virtue as the only real good [169–178]

Sections 1 and 2 are relevant to Augustine's project of showing the incoherence of Apuleius's view of gods and demons. Section 3 might be useful for the sake of contrasting what Socrates and Plato intended with Apuleius's project. But the crucial section 4 is simply passed over by Augustine, whose interests lie elsewhere.

Even with respect to demons, Apuleius' agenda does not easily fit Augustine's categorization of it. After discoursing on the emotions and flaws of demons—which make them like humans—Apuleius proceeds immediately to discuss how a human may have a good demon within himself or herself, the "lemur" which is more noble than those demonic "larvae" which are lesser and deserving of punishment (nn. 152–153). Higher still are the moral demons who guide righteous human behavior:

> Hence, in Plato's view, it is *daemones* from this abundant loftier type which are assigned to individual humans as witnesses and guardians in the conduct of their lives; they are, he says, such as never to be visible as present to anyone, but are judges not only of all our actions but even of all our thoughts. But when life is done and we must return whence we came, that same *daemon* who was given to us seizes hold of us and drags us off forthwith to trial, as if his prisoners, and there stands beside us in the trial of our case, refuting any lies we make and supporting any truths; and it is on his testimony that judgement is pronounced. (nn. 154–155)

This seems a very interesting further development proposed by Apuleius, and an important step toward his real, announced goal, a consideration of Socrates' *daemon*. That Augustine stops short is noticeable; if Augustine is attacking a lesser point and overlooking a related major point, this cannot but attenuate the force of his whole argument regarding Apuleius.

## AUGUSTINE'S READING OF THE *ASCLEPIUS*: PROPHETIC DESPITE ITSELF[8]

Interrupting his argument with Apuleius in order to enlist a pagan ally against him, Augustine turns aside at the end of book 8 (8.23–26) to read sections of the *Asclepius* attributed to the mythical Egyptian seer, Hermes Trismegistus. Fascinated by what he takes to be Hermes's candor regarding the impending fall of paganism and the rise of Christianity, he quotes rather extensively from the *Asclepius*, taking it as a reluctant witness in favor of Christianity's truth and paganism's failure.

The *Asclepius* is a complicated text that remains rough in its Latin version and (presumably) in its Greek sources.[9] Key, among other themes, is the plea of Hermes for that wisdom which is distinctive to the human person. By way of clarification, Hermes spells out a theory of divinity and its presence in the world. But the *Asclepius* is famous for its seeming prophecy of coming events, the decline and fall of the culture and cult of "Egypt." Here is an approximate overview of the argument of the *Asclepius*:[10]

I. Introduction and presuppositions: 1. the initiation of the conversation of Asclepius with Tat, and Hammon, on divine topics; 2. the immortality of the soul; soul and matter; 3. the four elements, one soul, one matter, one God; 4. division of gods and demons into gods and demons; 5. combinations of divided forms;

II. Human uniqueness and capacity for change: 6. human capacity to change into a god, nourishing body and soul; 7. divine consciousness, happiness; 8. human nature on earth; 9. cherishing the things of heaven; 10. the master of eternity, the world, and humans;

III. Retrieving the higher part of the self: 11. reverence—goodness—disdain for the material; 12. restoration and reward of the higher part; 13. philosophy complicated by arithmetic, music, geometry; 14. sophists; spirit and matter; 15. rules for the division of matter; 16. avoiding evil; spirit, life, understanding; 17. interactions of spirit and matter; 18. the nature of matter; 19. the gods, head of gods; 20. sacredness, greatness, ineffability of the supreme deity; 21. sex and procreation;

IV. Vice, and the difficulty of virtue: 22. vices and corruption; 23. rarity of virtuous people; the making of gods by divine and human agency.

After elaborating the higher potential of humans and the failure of humans to live up to this potential, Hermes notes how humans are able to construct the images in which lower deities live; he laments the decline of the more vital divine-human connection, and foresees the impending doom of Egypt, where this crafting of the divine-human has occurred:

V. Image making and the doom of Egypt: 24. statues; Egypt itself as the image of heaven; the predicted downfall of Egypt; 25. the impending wickedness and doom of Egypt; 26. the old age of the world; God's providence, deliberation, goodness in renewing the world; 27. the Good; death; immortality; 28. punishment and the purification of the body.

But on still deeper analysis, the realities of human and divine nature are not perishable, and so do not pass away, for there is a necessity governing all reality:

VI. God, change, world: 29. greater punishments; the world as a living entity, 30. the world, eternity, change, God, 31. eternal stability of God, 32. God, eternity—and mobility; thanks for discourse, 33. against the notion of a Void, 34. place, context/s, 35. beings and their appearances, 36. the world's changing forms;

VII. Human skill and wisdom: 37. humans—who are rational—can master the art of making gods; medicine; the problem of anger, 38. "earthly" gods, 39.-40. the fates, necessity, order, 41. concluding comments.

These last, climactic sections, excepting the paragraphs on idolatry and the "making of imperfect gods," are of no interest to Augustine in book 8 of the *City of God*.

Major portions of the *Asclepius* expound an overall view of the world as it operates, animated by divine presence and intention. Even if the world declines into disorder, still there is an equally sure renewal:

> Then he will restore the world to its beauty of old so that the world itself will again seem deserving of worship and wonder, and with constant benedictions and proclamations of praise the people of that time will honor the god who makes and restores so great a work. And this will be the geniture of the world: a reformation of all good things and a restitution, most holy and most reverent, of nature itself, reordered in the course of time (but through an act of will), which is and was everlasting and without beginning. For god's will has no beginning; it remains the same, everlasting in its present state. God's nature is deliberation; will is the supreme goodness. (n. 26)

The nature of divine action in the world is elusive and secret, but the *Asclepius* itself contributes to helping people see the deeper plan:

> The understanding of nature, however, and the quality of the world's consciousness can be fully perceived from all the things in the world that sense can detect. Eternity's understanding, which comes next, is a consciousness gained from the sensible world, from which its quality can be discerned. But the quality of consciousness in the supreme god and the understanding of that quality is truth alone. Not a shadow, not even the faintest trace of this truth can be discerned in the world, for there is falsehood wherever one discerns anything by measuring time, and where there is geniture one finds error. (n. 32)

But it is still possible to glimpse how things really are:

> Understanding differs from consciousness in this, however: that our understanding comes to understand and discern the quality of the consciousness of the world by concentrating the mind, while the world's understanding comes to know eternity and the gods who are above the world. And thus it comes about that we humans see the things that are in heaven as if through a mist, to the extent that we can, given the condition of human consciousness. When it comes to seeing great things, our concentration is quite confined, but once it has seen, the happiness of our awareness is vast. (n. 32)

It will be no surprise that Augustine would be uncomfortable with this wisdom-cosmology; Hermes's larger schema and its key elements are of little interest, since Augustine's narrower purpose is simply to show that the gods and demons of the pagans were ill thought of by candid pagan authors such as Hermes:

> The Egyptian Hermes, whom they call Trismegistus, believed and wrote differently concerning these demons. For Apuleius denies that the demons are gods; but when he says that they occupy a certain intermediate place between the gods and men, so that they inevitably seem to men to be included among the gods, he does not separate the worship due to them from the religion of the gods on high. This Egyptian, however, says that some gods are made by the supreme God, and that others are made by me. (8.23)

Augustine approvingly notes Hermes's contrast of the supreme deity with lesser deities that are merely human fabrications: "And since our discourse concerns the kinship and fellowship of men and gods, know, O Aesculapius, the power and might of man. Just as the Lord and Father, or that which is the Supreme Being, God, is the creator of the celestial gods, so is man the maker of those gods who are content to dwell in their temples as the neighbours of mankind." (8.23) Neither demons nor lesser gods are acceptable to Hermes.

Still, though, Augustine cannot but criticize Hermes for his strange mix of insight and blindness:

> Hermes next [nn. 81ff.] expounds at great length what he says in this passage, where he seems to foretell the present time: the time when, with as much vehemence and freedom as it has greater truth and holiness, the Christian religion is overthrowing all these lying fictions, so that the grace of the most true Saviour may set mankind free from the gods which man has made, and subdue him to the God by whom man was made. (8.23)

In the Christian dispensation, Hermes is compelled to speak truths with a certain precision:

> [With respect to the error of making idols,] I do not know if the demons themselves, if called upon to make confession, would confess as much as Hermes has done. He says that his forefathers invented the art of making gods because they "erred greatly" in their conception of the gods, by reason of their unbelief and because they did not attend to worship and divine religion. Did he say that they at least erred in a moderate fashion? Or was he content to say "they erred" without adding "greatly"? No, it was because they "erred greatly" by reason of their unbelief and in not attending to worship and divine religion that men invented the art of making gods. (8.24)

Amazingly, though, Hermes grieves at this truth, as if torn between a good spirit of truth-telling and an evil spirit of disordered attachments:

> And yet it is the inevitable future loss of this art, invented by great error and by turning aside from worship and divine religion, that this wise man deplores as though it were divine religion! Consider if it is not by divine power on the one hand that he is compelled to reveal the past error of his forefathers, and by diabolic power on the other that he is led to mourn the future punishment of the demons. . . . And because the Spirit is victorious who sang these things through the ancient prophets, even Hermes himself was compelled in a wonderful manner to confess, that those very things which he wished not to be removed, and at the prospect of whose removal he was sorrowful, had been instituted, not by prudent, faithful, and religious, but by erring and unbelieving men, averse to the worship and service of the gods. (8.24)

Hermes still grieves for what is false, because he is inspired by demons, not the Holy Spirit:

> Hermes, indeed, says many things concerning the Maker of this world which have the appearance of truth. I do not know how he has been brought so low by the darkening of his heart as to desire men to be always in subjection to gods who, as he himself confesses, are made by men, and whose future abolition he

> laments. . . . The Egyptian Hermes mourned for these vain, deceitful, pernicious, sacrilegious things because he knew that the time was coming when they would be taken away; but his mourning was as impudent as his knowledge was imprudent. For it was not the Holy Spirit Who revealed these things to him, as He did to the holy prophets. (8.23)

The more sensible conclusion, in Augustine's view, is to recognize truth where it is to be found, but also to welcome and appropriate the truth. Pagan authors may be entirely in error; some will have inscribed in their works particular insights that are true and valuable; but few will respond appropriately. Christian prophets rejoice in their message; pagan prophets are grieved even by the accurate words they speak. In the end, Augustine prizes all the more highly the true prophets who are inspired, know the truth, and rejoice in it.

The cost of reading the *Asclepius* against itself is to ignore its concern for the need to cultivate the higher self and to exercise one's freedom in choosing a life of wisdom, and thus to recover the true image that survives the fall of Egypt and its artificial deities. This overall point of the *Asclepius*, not unlike that of the *God of Socrates*, should be acceptable to Augustine, but still he passes over it in silence.

Augustine feels licensed by his Christian faith to read selectively and to leave aside even key dimensions of the pagan author's intent. Insofar as texts speak the truth, they will cohere with reality as it truly is, the reality of the Christian God who has conquered all the other gods. For Augustine, errors abound in pagan texts, and are of little direct interest. It is when a truth appears unpredictably and out of place—a prediction of the doom of Egypt and its gods—in a text that otherwise mourns that decline, that a selective reading is justified, gleaning truth amidst errors. But the *Asclepius* is an extant text which we can reread; if we do so, Augustine's own selective reading is problematized by further testimonies aside from those he had found useful. Consider for instance the prayer Trismegistus offers at the end of the *Asclepius*:

> We thank you, supreme and most high god, by whose grace alone we have attained the light of your knowledge; holy name that must be honored, the one name by which our ancestral faith blesses god alone, we thank you who deign to grant to all a father's fidelity, reverence and love, along with any power that is sweeter, by giving us the gift of consciousness, reason and understanding; consciousness, by which we may know you; reason, by which we may seek you in our dim suppositions; knowledge, by which we may rejoice in knowing you. And we who are saved by your power do indeed rejoice because you have shown yourself to us wholly. We rejoice that you have deigned to make us gods for eternity even while we depend on the body. For this is mankind's only means of giving thanks: knowledge of your majesty.

> We have known you, the vast light perceived only by reason. We have understood you, true life of life, the womb pregnant with all coming-to-be. We have known you, who persist eternally by conceiving all coming-to-be in its perfect fullness. Worshipping with this entire prayer the good of your goodness, we ask only this, that you wish us to persist in the love of your knowledge and that we never be cut off form such a life as this. (n. 41)

Although this is a beautiful passage worthy of close consideration, it does not of itself serve to refute the truth of Augustine's claim about the demonic realm and the partial nature of the truth asserted in the *Asclepius*. But it makes it quite evident that the *Asclepius* has more to say than Augustine wants to notice, and so does not fit easily into the instrumental reading he has determined for it.

## AUGUSTINE'S SECOND READING OF THE *GOD OF SOCRATES*: CONFUSING THE NATURE OF DEMONS

After finishing with the *Asclepius* and cementing his idea that the gods and demons of the pagans do not live up to a proper understanding of the true God, but (as even the wiser pagan authors admit) are doomed to perish, in book 9 Augustine returns to his critique of the *God of Socrates*,[11] arguing that Apuleius cannot mount a credible effort to claim happiness and virtue for the purportedly intermediary demons:

> What, then, is the difference between good and evil demons? The Platonist Apuleius, though he discusses them in general terms and speaks at such great length of their aerial bodies, is silent as to the virtues of the soul with which, if they were good, they would be endowed. He is silent, then, as to that which might give them happiness.

By an inner compulsion that makes his writing truer than his intentions, he speaks uncomfortable truths that the Christian can embrace: "He cannot, however, remain silent as to that which shows that they are miserable" (9.3). Augustine goes on to list the vices and defects of demons admitted by Apuleius, and concludes: "Can there be any doubt that, in these words, it is not some inferior part of their souls that is said to be disturbed like a stormy sea by the tempests of the passions, but the very mind in respect of which the demons are said to be rational creatures?" (9.3). Even if one pleads that Apuleius is distinguishing good from evil demons, or claiming that the poets are the ones who wrongly made demons appear as gods, problems persist: "Someone may say that it is not all the demons, but only the evil ones, that the tales of the poets represent—not without truth—as hating and loving certain men. . . . But how are we to understand this when

. . . he then describes all the demons, and not only the evil ones, as being intermediate between the gods and men by virtue of their aerial bodies?" (9.7). The theory of mediation breaks down, since Apuleius cannot bring himself to portray the demons as adequate mediators.

Indeed, Augustine insists that Apuleius is actually making a fine case against his own position regarding demons: "For, having first spoken of the gods in heaven, he then extended his description somewhat, to include men themselves, and he said that their station is a lowly and earthly one. He said this so that, having described the two extremes, he might then speak, in the third place, of the demons who are between them" (9.8). After speaking of humans and what they have in common with gods, and more so how humans are deficient in various ways, Apuleius does not leave room for good demons, nor distinguish the good from the bad: "If, therefore, he had wished us to believe that some of the demons are good, he would have included in his description of them something by which we might see that they have some measure of blessedness in common with men. As it is, however, he has mentioned no good quality of theirs whereby the good may be distinguished from the bad" (9.8). Apuleius, despite himself, helps make the case that there is no reason to preserve an intermediary role for demons. When he is truthful, his writing subverts his own plan to take demons seriously.

It is striking how Augustine never adverts to the major theme of the *God of Socrates*: the example of Socrates as testifying to the nobility of a life of inner wisdom. Rather, having focused on distinctions Apuleius makes in preparation for that major point, he stops there. The latter part of the *God of Socrates*, which Augustine omits, is where Apuleius finally gets to his main point:

> Accordingly, all of you who are listening to this divine judgment of Plato through myself as intermediary should take care to shape your minds in approaching any action or thought on the understanding that a person can have no secret before these guardians, whether inside or outside the mind. The consequence is that such a *daemon* participates in everything with close attention, inspecting everything and understanding everything, and dwelling in the inmost sanctum of the human mind in the function of consciousness itself. (nn. 155–156)

After a discussion of the daemon of Socrates, Apuleius urges a turn within and dedication to the life of philosophizing:

> Why, then, should not we too be roused by the example and mention of Socrates, and give ourselves over to desire to follow a philosophy like his, seeking after similar divine powers? But we are dragged down from this objective for some obscure reason; there is nothing that astonishes me more

> than the fact that men do not cultivate their mind, though all desire to live as well as possible, all are aware that the mind is the sole source of life, and all know that there is no alternative to cultivating the mind in order to achieve the best existence. (nn. 167–168)

He goes on to exhort his readers to live such a life. Apuleius himself is thus using the discourse on gods and demons to make a point about human being and human wisdom.

All of this—all that is most important to Apuleius—is missing in Augustine's account. It may be disappointing, but not surprising, to readers of Augustine that he is not interested in a path of the cultivation of *pagan* wisdom. His lack of interest is rooted in his desire rather to accentuate the wisdom of his own Christian faith by summoning Apuleius as a witness to that faith. Near the end of Augustine's discussion of Apuleius at the end of book 9, we find witness to what Augustine does believe to be certainly true, as the measure by which one reads properly: "But if, as is argued much more credibly and probably, all men must necessarily be miserable while they are mortal, then we must seek a Mediator Who is not only man, but also God" (9.15). After expounding how this Mediator perfectly brings God and humans into contact—and without the clumsy and failed ruse of demonic mediation—he emphasizes that Jesus Christ is the perfect mediator because he is truly human:

> He is not, however, the Mediator because He is the Word; for, as the Word, supremely immortal and supremely blessed, He is far removed from miserable mortals. Rather, He is the Mediator because He is man; and by His manhood He shows us that, in order to obtain that good which is not only blessed but bliss-bestowing, we need not seek other mediators by whose aid, as we might suppose, we are gradually to strive towards it. We have no such need because a God Who is blessed and bliss-bestowing has become a sharer in our humanity, and so has furnished us with all that we need to share in His divinity. (9.15)

There is no need for other intermediaries, as if these could bring the pure, high gods into contact with humans. Since Christians do not need demons, there is no reason to honor such unworthy beings. In 9.17, after a repeated affirmation of the Christian faith perspective and Platonic testimonies in its favor (9.16), Augustine still more decisively distinguishes his view from that of the pagan intellectuals by pointing to Christ, who is like to both God and humans and thus a perfect mediator. Christ, who has no fear of human imperfection, makes the mediation of demons unnecessary: "Far be it from the God Who is certainly immune from contamination to fear contamination from the humanity with which He clothed Himself, or from the men among whom He dwelt in human form!" (9.17). With this confession of Christian truth already in place as his guiding principle, Augustine has to read Apuleius's project of a philosophical wisdom as a non-solution to a non-existent problem of separation from the divine: Christ is the perfect mediator, fulfilling a role that Apuleius's demons clearly could not fill. Augustine's creedal statement on the mediatory role of Christ is therefore also a norm by which to decide what to take seriously and what to ignore when reading the *God of Socrates*. Apuleius's main purpose is ignored, as Augustine fastens on a secondary, instrumental theory of demons. Apuleius's primary concern—the philosophical life that Socrates stands for—cannot on its own terms be of interest to Augustine, who fails to engage the main point of the *God of Socrates*, instead seeking only to undercut the demonology that is merely instrumental to Apuleius's major point.

To conclude this section: Augustine's reading of the *God of Socrates* and the *Asclepius* is not merely idiosyncratic or a misreading; rather, he has a coherent stance and works with it rather consistently. Insofar as texts are true, they point to reality as it is known more clearly to the Christian, in keeping with Christian faith. Texts with philosophical values, such as those of the Platonic tradition, partially represent reality, but do not reflect it fully or accurately, and the intentions of pagan authors do not matter definitively regarding the value of their own writings.

Augustine accordingly asserts a right to pick and choose, indicating which parts of non-Christian texts are to be accepted and which rejected. As a result, he declines to take the gods and demons of the pagan authors seriously, and also refuses to notice the agenda of Apuleius and Hermes, since his presuppositions already preclude openness to alternative views of reality, including those articulated in pagan texts. Jean-Claude Guy, SJ, nicely captures the interplay of Augustine's reading of the *God of Socrates* and the *Asclepius*:

> En effet, les dieux multiples, ou les démons . . . , éléments inessentiels du rapport "Dieu/dieux," peuvent devenir un élément essentiel dans le rapport "Dieu/homme," si Dieu est considéré comme inaccessible à l'homme, et que donc le rapport "Dieu/homme" exige une médiation. C'est le premier pôle, "spéculatif," de la théologie philosophique, et dont Apulée est la figure. En sens inverse, les démons peuvent être considérés comme inessentiels dans le rapport "Dieu/homme," et donc appelés à disparaître: c'est le deuxième pôle, "prophétique", de la théologie philosophique, et dont Hermès est la figure. Apulée et Hermès représentent donc les deux axes de référence de toute position historique possible de la théologie philosophique. En conséquence, si aucune de ces deux figures ne résiste à l'expérience que lui fera subir la cité de Dieu, cette dernière aura alors définitivement réfuté tous ses adversaires, puisque la théologie philosophique constitue le suprême effort du paganisme pour résoudre le problème unique de l'histoire qui est celui du rapport du contingent au transcendant, de l'homme à Dieu. (p. 65)[12] (In effect, the multi-

ple deities, or rather demons. . .[which are] non-essential elements with respect to "God in relation to gods," can become an essential element with respect to "God in relation to the human," if God is considered as inaccessible to humans, such that "God in relation to the human" requires mediation. This is the first, speculative pole of philosophical theology, and of this Apuleius is the type. Conversely, the demons can be considered as non-essential with respect to "God in relation to the human," and therefore marked as ready to disappear. This is the second, prophetic pole of philosophical theology, and of this Hermes is the type. Apuleius and Hermes therefore represent the two axes of reference for every possible historical position in philosophical theology. Consequently, if neither of these figures resists the experience to which the City of God compels his submission, then the City definitively defeats all its adversaries, since philosophical theology constitutes the supreme effort of paganism to resolve the unique problem of history, that is, the relation of the contingent to the transcendent, of the human to God.)

If a pagan author writes with some insight or honesty—as Augustine admits can be true—then it is inevitable, in Augustine's mind, that such an author will on occasion speak the truth, in what Augustine counts as pieces, fragments, or patches of texts that support what is already known to the Christian community. Such fragments are rightly read out of context. The pattern then is this:

1. As a believing Christian, Augustine already knows that there is one supreme God, and that Jesus Christ, divine and human, is the perfectly adequate intermediary between the realm of God and the realm of humans;
2. Lesser beings—gods and demons—do not and cannot serve as intermediaries between God and humans;
3. Insofar as pagan authors are reasonable and honest, defects notwithstanding, their writings will partly confirm the Christian view of God, the deficiency of gods and demons, and the need for some more perfect mediation;
4. By reading selectively, and ignoring much of what pagan authors say and intend, one can glean from their writings elements of the truth about God, the gods, and mediation.

Augustine's reading of the *God of Socrates* and the *Asclepius* thus becomes both less convincing and more interesting as an instance of interreligious learning. His choice to read the texts selectively, as it were against themselves, may well be a fruitful strategy, but it appears increasingly peculiar as one begins to attend to the authors' actual agendas and to Augustine's choices about which sections of their texts not to read. A measure of indeterminacy creeps into the discussion—where is the truth in the *God of Socrates* and the *Asclepius* and in how Augustine reads them? Who decides who is the right reader of such a text, if there is no single tradition of right reading? Something more may be added:

5. Because (in our examples) Augustine is reading texts that are extant and can be read again and differently, his determination to find in pagan writings vindication of Christian truths becomes vulnerable to contestation not merely by reasoned arguments, but simply on the basis of whether the pagan texts in question were adequately read;

And so, we are forced to a second level of reflection: if we begin with firm faith positions and bring these to bear on texts from another tradition, can we actually *read* in a plausible fashion? And how do we balance a legitimately selective Christian reading against other possible readings that lead to very different conclusions?

6. The contestation between careful but apologetic reading [nn. 1–4] and a consequent and differently configured "full reading" [n. 5] opens the way for a second-level dialogue that moves beyond the initial standoff of disagreements about texts and their meanings to reflection on how (religious committed) readers make choices to read and misread texts interestingly and comfortably.

We will now add a still more complex historical perspective, examining the "Augustinian" reading practices of three missionary authors who likewise bring forward their own theologies of truth and non-Christian texts and ground these in careful attention to texts, in which there may be operative natural self-interest and poetic fancy that run counter to reason (de Nobili), or historical connections leading back to a partially remembered Biblical revelation (Bouchet), or wrong philosophical ideas are mistakenly recorded as religious doctrine (Meurin).

## READING LIKE AUGUSTINE: THREE MISSIONARY SCHOLARS

I have chosen three Jesuit missionaries who worked in India. Roberto de Nobili (1577–1656) came to south India in 1606 and worked there for some forty years. He studied Sanskrit and Tamil, and we have a number of his treatises in Tamil. In the section of his *Report on Indian Customs* considered next, he argues that a close reading of the classic Hindu law book *The Laws of Manu* shows us that brahmins are cultural and intellectual leaders, but not—whatever their status in India might seem to indicate—priestly or intrinsically religious figures. Jean Venance Bouchet (1655–1732) worked in much the same area of south India from the 1690s to his death, as pastor, mission founder, scholar, and author of numerous highly informative letters back to Europe. In two of his letters considered later, he seeks to find in Hindu writings and teachings evidence of their Biblical roots but also their self-contradictions and unwilling testimony to superior Christian truths. Leo Meurin (b. 1825) was a prominent Jesuit, bishop, and Church leader in Bombay in the latter part of the nineteenth century. In "God and Brahm," the lecture considered later, he sought to argue both the incoherence of Hindu views of God and God's role as creator, and the evidence for erroneous Hindu views written into numerous Hindu texts.[13]

I have chosen these three because they are already familiar to me, because they connect this essay to the Indian context, and especially because they are good examples of Christian apologists who were trying to read carefully in order to use their reading in making certain points about Christian truth and what is positive and negative in Hindu learning. As conceded earlier, this essay begs the question of Augustine's actual influence on the missionaries and other Renaissance and post-Renaissance intellectuals. The three Jesuits knew Augustine's works in some fashion, and would occasionally cite him in their writings; but their references to the *City of God* are rather minimal, and they do not refer to the sections I have examined earlier. I therefore cannot say that these missionaries read the *City of God* (or others among Augustine's works) carefully, nor can I state with certainty that their own reading practice was inspired by his. Rather, by way of hypothesis, I am exploring the general theme of "missionary scholars 'in the tradition' of Augustine" or "reading missionary apologists in light of our knowledge of Augustine's reading practices." So too, the three missionaries' contexts differ among themselves and are also significantly different from Augustine's. He was making the case for Christian identity in a crumbling Roman culture, while the missionaries were seeking to gain a foothold in ancient Indian cultures to which they were newcomers and foreigners. So this parallel remains a thought experiment which, I hope, sheds light on how Christians read the texts of other traditions.[14]

## Roberto de Nobili, S.J.

Roberto de Nobili is an excellent example of learned Jesuit apologists in Asia, a pioneer and among the most erudite. He is genuinely interested in adapting himself to Indian and Hindu culture—even before the words "Hindu" and "culture" came into fashion—and worked at learning the intellectual traditions of the Indian people, in order to discern what he thought was reasonable or contrary to reason in those traditions. For example, his *Inquiry into the Meaning of "God"* begins by proposing perfections of "God" (omniscience, omnipotence, goodness, etc.) that all reasoning persons should agree on. He then shows, though without quotations and apparently on the basis of personal observations, that Hindu beliefs about deities cannot possibly live up to these perfections. Hindus who understand the meaning of "God" must necessarily agree. There can be only baser reasons why the learned would continue to insist on fealty to such gods. Scriptures discussing those gods ought not be believed without measuring what they say against what is reasonable, since such texts may well have been inspired by base motives. In the remainder of the *Inquiry*, de Nobili shows that the texts—and popular beliefs—show us that such gods do not measure up to what a reasonable person can see to be the attributes of the perfect God. As a result, open-minded Hindus will abandon belief in such gods; the rest will be exposed as unwilling to think coherently about their beliefs.[15]

The *Inquiry* is worthy of investigation as highlighting the tension between reason and scripture, and between popular and rationalized religion, but another of de Nobili's works is more pertinent to our study. In his *Report on Indian Customs* he makes extensive use of a famous (or notorious) classic, *The Laws of Manu*, a major religious law text, in order to show that Indians—and newly arrived Western observers—have wrongly interpreted as religious what are actually natural and cultural social structures. As de Nobili uses *Manu* to argue for the secular nature of Indian society and learning, and in particular, the religious neutrality of brahmins, we have what is possibly the earliest instance of a missionary's careful reading of a Hindu text. De Nobili's use is positive, since he relies on *Manu* without anywhere criticizing the law book, but still he is reading it against cultural expectations; his reading is also highly selective, and indicative of what one might call "Augustinian reading against the grain."

An example from book 6 of the *Report* shows us how de Nobili uses *Manu* and other sources to determine what it means when certain human beings are honored as "gods." He argues that this honoring is an explicable social custom, and he cites texts to prove his point. After some citations from the very ancient *Taittiriya Upanisad*, he turns to *Manu*:

> In speaking on the same subject, the *Laws of Manu* goes further. In explaining the law, at the verse which begins with *gurur agnih*,[16] the author substitutes the words *sarvasya guruh* ["guru of all"] for the word "god," i.e., he is "the one who surpasses all things.". . . In truth, *Manu* explicitly maintains that the brahmin is to be regarded as father and mother to men: "That one [i.e., the brahmin] is the apex of all races, father, mother, teacher to all mortals."[17] The following verse sets forth that [the guru] has priority over the natural father and mother, precisely because of his wisdom: "By the two fathers, namely, one according to nature and the other according to the manner of wisdom which proceeds from the brahmin, we obtain the incorruptible good of this life." (*Manu* 2.146) (6.3.1)[18]

There are no grounds in the text, he says, for postulating that "god-like brahmins" were meant to be taken as divine or even intrinsically religious figures: "It is clear, therefore, that from this appellation 'god' no conclusive argument can be derived in support of the alleged brahmin priesthood. The appellation is nothing more than an exaggerated expression of the honor which these people consider attributable to wisdom" (6.3.1).

De Nobili then draws parallels with ancient Greece, where Plato, Hermes Trismegistus, and Pythagoras were praised as gods, simply to honor them highly. He argues that while *Rg Veda* 10.90 and its retelling in the opening chapter of *Manu* say that brahmins are divine, generated directly from the original divine Person, such narratives are to be read as symbolic:

> By means of an apt emblematic narrative (indeed, the people here are constantly making use of such allegorical stories), they intended (indeed, using a shrewd literary device) to explain the different kinds of occupations devolving severally on the four social orders which I have distinguished and set forth in Chapter One [of *Manu*]. So they narrated that God produced the brahmins from his face or his head which is the seat of wisdom, the kings from his shoulder which is the sinewy center of strength, the merchants from his thigh which is the symbol of fecundity, and the plebeians from his feet which placed beneath the other parts as a base supports the whole body. That this is the true meaning of that statement is clear from the *Laws of Manu*. (*Manu* 1.31) (6.3.2)

With numerous additional detailed references to *Manu* that cannot be cited here, de Nobili goes on to argue that brahmins are not divine nor even essentially priestly, but simply wise:

> These texts substantiate two facts: the first, as we have state above, is that the brahmins are of all men the noblest. The second is that this nobility is based not on some sort of priestly function, but on the hereditary office of instructing people in wisdom, an office which is allegorically expressed by their springing from the head, or representing the head. (6.3.2)

*Manu*, the quintessential orthodox law book, is thus read as undercutting what many had thought to be an obviously religious basis for Hindu caste society. Though he is favoring and not attacking *Manu*, de Nobili is nonetheless reading it so as to disturb ordinary views of the religious and even divine status of brahmins, and thereby also to change Indian society radically, rendering it open to the Gospel.[19]

But all of this adds up to a contentious (even if possible) reading of brahminism as secular and cultural rather than essentially religious and ritual. De Nobili picks up on a possibility in *Manu*, to be sure, but seemingly without a plausible sense of the whole and without admitting the fact of other passages that speak counter to his reading of *Manu* and India. Since *Manu* is available to us and can be read as offering a unified and fundamentally religious worldview, de Nobili's bold choice actually to read *Manu* and cite it extensively leaves him open to the possibility that upon rereading, one will see that he has misread *Manu*, or read it selectively without due attention to its religious structure and frame. I cannot prove this point here of course, but at least we can ask the question that was posed regarding Augustine: how do faith and a prior commitment to certain conclusions affect how one reads a text from another religious tradition?

## Jean Venance Bouchet, S.J.: How the Hindus Confound Themselves

Jean Venance Bouchet was a missionary in south India in the late seventeenth and early eighteenth centuries. If de Nobili believed that he could bring out the best in the Indian traditions by reading *Manu*—and other such texts—according to Christian expectations, Bouchet thought that close attention would show the incoherence of Hindu beliefs and the impossibility of intelligent adherence to such views. Like de Nobili, Bouchet strove to be a scholar of Indian thought. Although he was a man of action and seemingly always on the move, he found some time to read and write. His letters show great knowledge of Indian learning and reports on a wide range of religious and cultural beliefs and practices even if, unlike de Nobili, he does not quote from specific texts.[20] Taking up a variety of themes—the gods, reincarnation, spirit possession, religious and secular law, the geography of India—he insists on reporting what is in the texts, and on showing how such texts offer a derivative and garbled form of Biblical revelation; the more one studies India, the more all this becomes clear. In his own way, therefore, Bouchet stands in the Augustinian tradition: read carefully and in detail, and you will vindicate your faith and demonstrate the weakness of theirs.

My examples here will be limited to two of his letters, written to Pierre-Daniel Huet, Bishop of Avranches and a significant figure in the European debate over religion, particularly in his *Demonstratio Evangelica*.[21] Huet's massive treatise, proceeding by the certainties of a "religious geometry," aimed to show that Jesus was the Messiah, that this truth is the indisputable true message of the Old and New Testaments, and that all human culture and religion pointed toward these Christian truths. In writing to Huet, Bouchet was seeking to aid this European theorist with confirmatory evidence from a fresh venue; describing India for Huet, Bouchet sought to detect the sources of India's wisdom in the Bible, a source for a great confidence that some truth, confirmatory of the Gospel, can be found in Indian texts.

In a 1710 letter, Bouchet wrote on parallels between the Biblical and Indian teachings:

> [These conjectures] all go to prove that the Indians have drawn their religion from the books of Moses and the prophets, that all the fables with which their books are full do not so entirely obscure the truth that it cannot still be recognized by me; and finally, beyond the religion of the Hebrew people which at least in part their commerce with the Jews and Egyptians taught to them, one can still discover among them clearly marked traces of the Christian religion, which was announced to them by the apostle Thomas, by Pantaenus, and by other great men of the first centuries of the Church. (p. 48)[22]

A prudent and agile comparativist, Bouchet admits that the parallels need not be exact, but also that no one should want them to be such:

> Be that as it may, my lord, I do not believe that to recognize in the doctrine of the Indians that of the ancient Hebrews it is necessary that everything match perfectly from one side to the other. The Indians often attribute to different persons what Scripture tells us of just one; or, instead, they collect in just one person what Scripture divides among many. But this difference, far from ruining our conjectures, must serve, it seems to me, to support them. Moreover, I believe that a resemblance pushed too far would be good only for rendering them suspect. (p. 51)

India mirrors, though obscurely and with distortion, beliefs and practices clear in the Bible and the Roman Catholic Church. Reading Hindu texts carefully offers a multitude of clues that will confirm Christian beliefs and undermine the Hindu. Because the Biblical link is still evident in Hindu writings, his reading confirms Huet's findings about the ancient world:

> Having read your learned *Demonstration of the Gospel*, my lord, I was reminded that the teaching of Moses had entered even India. Your attention to noticing in the various authors everything that one might find to be favorable to our Religion has made you in part anticipate things I would have said to you. I then add only those new things which I have discovered regarding these topics by reading the most ancient books of the Indians and by the dealings I have had with the wise men of this country. (pp. 48–49)

Bouchet knew in advance the outcome of his study—Christian truths always prevail—but he did not find in that confidence an excuse for laziness. Rather, he reports how periods of enforced leisure allowed missionaries such as himself time to study Indian texts for a salutary purpose: "However, my lord, in other seasons we find ourselves sufficiently free to be able to put aside our labors for the sake of some sort of study. Our concern then is to render even our relaxation useful to our holy religion. We immersed ourselves in this look at the sciences current among the idolaters, for whose conversion we are working" (p. 6). This careful reading pays off in uncovering errors which can then be used against the very teachings and convictions the authors presumably intended to inculcate:

> We make ourselves find, even in their errors, something with which to convince them of the truth we have come to announce to them. It is in this time, when the duties connected to my ministry leave me with some leisure, that I have gone as deeply as was possible for me into the system of religion received among the Indians. (p. 47)

On this basis, Bouchet takes up in order a series of theological topics: Indian beliefs about God; the idea of a primal God and subaltern deities; the privileged place of Brahma, Visnu, Rudra; the Goddess as the highest power. In each case he verifies various errors with evidence he himself has found in their texts, or about which he has deemed himself reliably informed.

In a second, 1714 letter to Huet, Bouchet focuses on a single topic: the origins of and rationale for belief in reincarnation. Bouchet first remarks how people keep asking him about the connections between Indian and Biblical thought—connections already explained rather extensively and impressively by Huet himself in his *Demonstratio Evangelica*. Bouchet admits that his own first-hand experience and reading confirm Huet's thesis:

> For a long time, my lord, I have in fact been aware of the opinions of the brahmins. I have read many books by wise Indians, and I have often engaged their more able teachers; from reading the former and from engagement with the latter I have drawn all that detailed information which can aid me in probing deeply their system regarding the transmigration of souls.

He is serenely self-assured that by reading he can assess Indian learning and its errors: "I was at first surprised, in reading their books, to see that there are almost no errors of the ancient authors which the Indians did not either adopt or invent" (p. 54). He admits reincarnation to be an error pervasive in many cultures, but most of the letter is devoted to exploring just the Greek-India connection, particularly how Pythagorean and to some extent Platonic ideas are operative in India.

Once he is finished with his detailed exposition of the connection,[23] in the third part of the letter[24] Bouchet takes up a further theme by which our comparison with Augustine comes into clearer focus: Hindus' ideas can be used against them. Here Bouchet demonstrates his use of the gathered information in refuting Hindus by their own testimonies: "in order to disabuse them entirely of a system that is both impious and ridiculous, we have recourse to reasons drawn from their own doctrine, their usage, and their maxims. These are the reasons by which one can make them feel the contradictions into which they have fallen, which confound them and constrain them from recognizing the absurdity of their beliefs" (p. 59).

He proceeds to list five contradictions[25]—logical conundrums—by which he can snare his brahmin interlocutors in their own thinking. Perhaps even more than Augustine, he thought that this aggressive use of pagan learning against pagan beliefs would persuade his listeners to give up on their religion. Bouchet seems not to have known of the many sophisticated arguments long debated in the Hindu traditions, and his particular interlocutors evidently did not tap into that vast learning so as to raise doubts in his mind. Rather, they end by confounding themselves and, in theory at least, having to admit their own religion to be false: "Reasons of this sort, taken from their own teachings, make an incomparably stronger impression on them than others which would be much more solid. We draw at least this advantage: after we have convinced them of the falsity of some point in their teaching, they cannot deny that a religion based on such a teaching is likewise false" (p. 61). Bouchet adds that he persisted in pointing out the absurdity of the positions which they, like the Pythagoreans, adhered to because they were stubbornly committed to the "ridiculous doctrine of transmigration" (p. 63). But he is not unhappy with the situation. Indeed, "we never cease to gain great advantage from these absurdities. As the Indians are convinced that the soul is immortal, that sins are punished, and virtue rewarded after death, we make use of the same argument that Tertullian used against Laberius,[26] to prove to him the resurrection of the dead" (p. 64). After giving examples of how Laberius turned pagan beliefs against their adherents, at the end of the letter Bouchet generalizes his insight into the harmfulness of Hindu learning and the need to disabuse Hindus of that learning:

> Mark then this true portrait of the Indians: there is no fable so grossly contrived that they do not believe it or propose it to others, as entirely worthy of belief. . . . Thus, my lord, even a lie serves us in making known the truth to these people. Once they are firmly persuaded regarding the blindness in which they have been living until now, the truth finds no more obstacles and begins to illumine their spirits; when God deigns to work in their hearts by the impressions of his grace, the work of their conversion is accomplished. (p. 63)

The rational and erudite dimension of evangelization is once again shown to include a negative attentiveness, a reading of tradition against itself: show people the contradictions in their own principles as articulated in their own texts, accentuate those contradictions, and so encourage Hindus to lose faith in their own texts and beliefs. The more familiar one is with their books, the more one will be able to use that learning to unsettle their fondest, most persistent errors. Bouchet had no doubt that this approach succeeded in demonstrating to Indians (or to Europeans who were thinking about what would convince Indians) the flawed and undesirable nature of the Hindu traditions. Hindu texts, with their Biblical roots, could become effective witnesses against Hindu beliefs.

But like Augustine and de Nobili, Bouchet had gotten himself into a complicated situation, wherein his claims seem to exceed the evidence he gives. To make his positions convincingly, more was required to show, in some particular case, that a specific Hindu text contains an absurdity, a tenet that no sensible person could entertain. Unlike de Nobili and Augustine, Bouchet makes assertions that cannot be pinned down with certainty, but his own definiteness about pagan errors makes it possible to ask for evidence regarding those errors. By claiming to use Hindu learning against Hindu beliefs, Bouchet takes up a bold task—but one that seems, after 300 years, still incomplete.

## Leo Meurin, S.J.: The Hindu Scriptures as the Documentation of Errors

At the Bombay Catholic Debating Club in 1865, Leo Meurin gave a lecture entitled, "God and Brahm"—or, as he states on its first page, "The Existence and Nature of God." We know little about the context for the lecture, other than that the Club was founded by Meurin himself for the sake of defending Catholic doctrine,[27] but it is possible to comment on the course of Meurin's argument. His lecture falls naturally into three parts. First (pp. 1–16), he offers a standard proof of God's existence, necessarily inferred from the fact that there is a world. This is a claim about the way things really are, and its implications are quite clear. Either the atheists or polytheists are right, or Christians are right; there is no middle ground. Meurin also points to the perfections of this God, who can be only one, and who is a good, omniscient and omnipotent spiritual being. By contrast, Brahman—the absolute reality of the Hindus—is a "philosophical fiction" which cannot be God. That wise people—among the Hindus too—should know all this, has been stated clearly in Romans, chapter 1 (p. 18):[28] all have natural knowledge of God and are culpable if they persist in their ignorance.

In the second part of the lecture (pp. 16-27), Meurin turns to the Hindu scripture, admitting that whatever reason might say, true revelation would have still more authority. Were the Hindu gods vouched for in a true revelation, it would have to be accepted:

> we would at once implicitly and conscientiously submit to the doctrines of the Hindu system, if their source, the Vedas with some other poetical and philosophical works, could be proved to be, what they pretend to be, a revelation or inspiration of God, or, at least, to have been written with His assistance, which would entitle them to a claim of divine infallibility, and demand from us unconditional belief. (p. 17)

But he then disposes quickly, in a few sentences, of the notion that the Hindu scriptures might be revelation—they are not evidently the oldest in the world, they do not report historical events, they are contradicted by the indubitably authoritative Bible, and they are self-contradictory.

But Meurin is still motivated to explore the content of Hindu scriptures, since he wants to demonstrate from Hindu texts that he had reliably reported the views he deemed false: "Lest we should seem to have resumed the Hindu philosophical Theology less exactly, we deem it proper to substantiate this brief sketch by quoting a few passages from the *Bhagavat-Gita*, the Vedanta [Upanisads], and the Vedas, as given by Colebrooke and Thomson" (p. 20). Hindus will be convicted by their own words, and Meurin can exonerate himself of having invented the errors he attributes to the Hindus. There follow seven pages (20–27) entirely devoted to quotations from select texts. In ascending order of importance he cites the *Gita*, Upanisads, and Vedas (20). He offers very few comments or notations, and in no case does he comment on context.[29] Thus, he begins twenty-four citations from the Upanisads simply as follows: "(God is that) whence are the birth (and continuance and dissolution of this world)" [*Taittiriya Upanisad* 3.1]; "He wished to be many and prolific and became manifold" [*Chandogya Upanisad* 6.2.3]; "He is the etherial element (*acash*), from which all things proceed and to which all return." [*Chandoyga Upanisad* 1.9.1] (pp. 23–24).

Meurin ends his long list rather abruptly, with a citation from the *Atharva Veda* that ends with the words, "The omniscient is profound contemplation, consisting in the knowledge of him, who knows all and from that, the manifested vast one, as well as names, forms and food, proceed: and this is truth" (p. 27). With a rhetorical flourish, he immediately adds,

> And this is untruth. The Hindu philosophers, ever rich and fertile in examples and similes, frequently explain the pretended illusoriness of this world besides the sole reality of Brahm by saying that all the wonderful stories which one tells of a great hero would prove false and illusory by the discovery of the sterility of the woman, whose son he is said to be . . . the Creator of heaven and earth is yet unknown to the Hindus, who are still an idolatrous creature-adoring people. (p. 27)

We do well to know the texts, since they serve as undeniable evidence of just what's wrong with Hindu thinking: "It is not very difficult to prove that Brahm is not God, and thus to show the erroneousness of the whole system of the Hindus without resorting to the very easy task of ridiculing the absurdities of their abominable mythology which is built on the foundation of their philosophy" (pp. 27–28).

Since Meurin offers no intervening comments, we cannot be sure of the depth of his knowledge of the texts he has chosen, beyond the fact that he thinks they support pantheism. But this is not certain. Even were one to stay within the bounds of Colebrooke and Thomson—apparently an anthology—the excerpts could be read with different sympathies. But Meurin, the busy vicar, seems unaware of the centuries of discussion and debate around the texts he cites. The first text he cites, for instance, from *Taittiriya Upanisad* 3—"(God is that) whence are the birth (and continuance and dissolution of this world)"—is a complex textual artifact with a past and a future. The first part of *Taittiriya* chapter 3 replicates on a cosmic scale the examination of the structure of the self introduced in chapter 2, legitimating the connection by our quotation, which states that everything (including self and cosmos) comes from a single source. In turn, the same *Taittiriya* 3 text is the reference embedded in the second verse of the vastly influential *Brahma Sutras*, the fundamental Vedanta theological text, wherein Badarayana defines Brahman, the ultimate reality, as the source and end of all beings. It is, by Vedanta reckoning, the foundation stone of a kind of natural theology that will however be contested in verse 3 of the *Brahma Sutras*, which seems to state that only scripture can offer knowledge of Brahman. In turn, generations of Vedanta theologians argue the meaning of *Brahma Sutras* verses 2 and 3, and also of the *Taittiriya* text cited by Meurin. Taken by itself, much of what is interesting about the verse is omitted. The same could be said, I think, regarding almost all of the other texts cited by Meurin in his long list.

After his list, Meurin devotes the third section of his essay (pp. 27–36) to reaffirming the inconsistencies of Hindu views of causality, the nature of Brahman as cause, and so forth. Having worked for a moment as a careful reader—or at least as a discriminating consumer of an anthology—he reasserts that Hindu views are unacceptable. It is striking that this third section does not build on the second, but is in fact connected directly back to the first and the philosophical argument that Hindu beliefs are simply wrong. After reaffirming Christian truth and Hindu error, Meurin concludes with an impassioned prayer that Hindus be soon freed from the abominable idolatry of their religion.

Meurin has sought simply to make clear by their own words that the Hindus held the views that reason shows to be false. But, as was the case with Augustine's reading of Apuleius and Hermes, Meurin's appeal to the text is not necessarily a reliable ally. The same texts can and have been read differently, and in their fuller context can be interpreted for the sake of conclusions quite different from Meurin's. Read with care for context, few of the texts testify simply to the pantheism Meurin is attacking; few fall in line with a conclusion as neatly defined as his. When recontextualized and then read more deeply in accord with tradition, the crude "pantheism" dissipates and the arguments for a proper notion of God become vulnerable to new questions, because one can read differently the texts Meurin has claimed in support of his philosophical and theological arguments. Texts were supposed to be allies, but upon rereading, they may turn out to be witnesses for the defense as well.

In their own ways, de Nobili, Bouchet, and Meurin are all in the tradition of Augustine the apologetic reader. De Nobili cites *Manu* with sufficient specificity that we can re-examine his readings; Bouchet seems to be reading both written texts and oral accounts of texts; Meurin draws on an anthology to find the passages he needs. Hinduism, vastly rich in textual materials, favors the erudite approach, just as the literary riches of ancient Rome facilitated Augustine's learned arguments. But by reading, they also made themselves vulnerable to the subsequent scrutiny of other readers who can go back and read the same texts with different expectations and for different results. The erudite apologist seems all the more credible and worthy when he cites texts carefully; but upon doing so, he also becomes all the more susceptible to unwelcome alternative readings.

## AUGUSTINE AND THE PROJECT OF READING HINDU TEXTS

While "Augustine and the world religions" and "Augustine and Hinduism" are certainly larger and more compelling topics, in this essay I have taken up only a smaller matter propaedeutic to such larger studies: a particular component of Augustine's reading practice, his enlisting of specific pagan texts as witnesses to the Christian faith and against the traditions to which those pagan texts belong. I have thus sought to trace what happens when a Christian reader takes up some body of pagan (or non-Christian, or Hindu) learning, with the determination to read it studiously—as a Christian apologist or missionary. It is well for us to be as clear as possible on what we learn by reading religious texts in traditions other than our own, and I hope to have contributed to clearer thinking on this topic.

Augustine neither ignored the pagan classics, nor read them without established expectations about what they could mean for him; he was determined to be able to point to particular passages demonstrative of his intended points, even if read at cross purposes to their seeming original intent. He was both apologist and exegete, and his reading was (at various points in his career) essential to his apologetics. This is an admirable dimension of Augustine's project; even today, theologians who state views of religions without studying the texts of those traditions would do well to imitate Augustine more closely. Although we may imagine that we can do better than Augustine, the real danger is that we will risk less, learn less, and accomplish less, because we fail to read, or read in a way that is safely distanced from our theology.

Even if his readings can sometimes be marked as "misreadings," they cannot be dismissed; Augustine's importance requires that we carefully reflect on his legacy with respect to (what is hopefully) our ongoing tradition of Christian engagement with other religious traditions. While I have not been able to show that Augustine's reading style *directly* affected the three Jesuit readers introduced here, I have argued that the selective reading practice exemplified in the *City of God* books 8 and 9 sheds a stark and honest light on a reading style adopted by these later figures. De Nobili, Bouchet, and Meurin are all vulnerable to the same phenomenon of rereading that complicates or possibly undercuts their hoped-for results. A contemporary Christian reader cognizant of the Augustinian tradition does not solve the problem of biased reading by ceasing to read, as if less reading would somehow make faith claims more secure. Nor can there be an ideal objective reading of texts that will resolve matters of faith, as if contextual study might be thought actually to undercut Christian faith claims. Reading and believing need to remain in creative tension. Our better hope then is to see if we can intentionally extend Augustine's method.

As mentioned, Augustine offers a two-stage process: first, the selection of a pagan text; second, a detailed reading of parts of the chosen text, against its pagan intent, now for the sake of confirming Christian teachings and discrediting pagan content. But since the *God of Socrates* and the *Asclepius* do not necessarily support Augustine's rhetorical points and conclusions, his reading may be chastened by a rereading that unsettles the conclusions Augustine (or any other Christian apologetic reader) sought to draw. While this third step problematizes an apologetic reading, it does not suddenly falsify the faith behind the apologetic reading. Rather, in disclosing the biases and choices of the apologetic reading and drawing in other readings pertinent to the conversation, it compels believers to explain more clearly how the texts of other religions might conceivably testify on behalf of Christian truths and against non-Christian views. This more complex pattern of readings and further readings—the choice of a text, the apologetic reading, and then, too, alternative readings that question the apology—gives fresh life to all sides of the arguments instigated by Augustine with respect to the *God of Socrates* and the *Asclepius*, as Apuleius and Hermes get to speak back to Augustine. Similarly, we can reread *Manu* as cited by de Nobili, the Vedas as cited by Meurin, and the multiplicity of Hindu texts read (aurally) by Bouchet, and require of the missionary apologists more stringent defenses of their exegesis.

What prospect does all this afford the Christian reader who imagines coming to a Christian judgment on Hinduism by studying Hindu texts? There is no reason at all why a Christian theologian cannot dedicate herself or himself to studying such texts and wagering, as did Augustine, that the texts will support Christian views and, due to their incoherence or incompleteness, undercut Hindu views. A theologian may also continue offering secondary reasons why she or he thinks close readings will testify to Christian truths and undercut Hindu beliefs. But if that project fails because the texts do not actually seem to be incoherent or incomplete, and because they can be read quite differently by other readers, then the apologetic reader will simply have to try harder to make the exegetical case—or at some point admit that Hindu texts cannot be counted on as allies in making final judgments about Hinduism, but instead remain stubborn places of resistance to any neat apologetic strategy. We might then find ourselves in a conversation about the reading of texts that seems to have no single end—that is, in a real conversation; and perhaps then we would be better off as scholars and believers. If reflection on Augustine's study of the *God of Socrates* and the *Asclepius* leaves us in this new situation, then we have found another, albeit unexpected reason to be grateful to St. Augustine.

## NOTES

1. Particularly helpful with respect to how carefully (or not) Augustine, at different points in his career, read the pagan authors he quotes, see James J. O'Donnell, "Augustine's Classical Readings," in *Recherches Augustiniennes* 15 (1980), pp. 144–74.
2. On the location of the *City of God* in the apologetic tradition, and regarding the possible influence on Augustine of earlier Christian apologists, see Gerard O'Daly, *Augustine's City of God: A Reader's Guide* (Oxford: Clarendon Press, 1999), chapter 3, "The Apologetic Tradition."
3. On the general Latin Christian attitudes toward pagan religion and literature, see "La polémique des Apologistes latin contre les Dieux du paganisme," *Recherches Augustiniennes* 17 (1982), pp. 3–128 and particularly (as background for this essay) pp. 94–102. For Augustine in particular, see the comprehensive *Augustine and the Latin Classics* by Harald Hagendahl (Studia Graeca et Latina Gothoburgensia 20.1–2; Stockholm, 1967), and (for example) William M. Green's helpful review of the same (the *Classical Journal*, January 1968, pp. 186–189). Mary Daniel Madden's "The Pagan Divinities and their Worship as Depicted in the Works of St. Augustine Exclusive of the *City of God*" (Washington: Catholic University of America, 1930) is helpful too, excepting its exclusion of the *City of God*. See also Andre Mandouze, "Saint Augustin et la religion romaine," *Recherches Augustiniennes* 1 (1966), 187–223. On the larger topic of Augustine's theory and practice of reading, see Brian Stock, *Augustine the Reader: Meditation, Self-Knowledge, and the Ethics of Interpretation*, and *After Augustine: The Meditative Reader and the Text*. In neither work, however, does Stock discuss the *City of God*.
4. Of course, we must be careful not to identify Augustine's agenda with that of later writers. The *City of God* is large and complex, and its motivations and theology grew over time; he wrote in a difficult era, within the context of a longer, ongoing dispute with pagans about true religion, and more specifically in light of various disasters that had befallen the empire, most notably the sack of Rome in 410 by Alaric and the Goths. On the purposes of the *City of God*, see O'Daly, pp. 27–38, and also R. W. Dyson's introduction, pp. xi–xv, to his edition and translation, *The City of God Against the Pagans* (Cambridge: Cambridge University Press,

1998). Likewise, it would be a mistake to conflate their purposes, related to the project of converting Hindus and finding a place for Christianity in India, with Augustine's defense of Christianity in the late Roman Empire. In general, the large question of the influence of the *City of God* on later Christian thinking about religions is only touched upon here, and will have to be left to specialists in historical theologians.

5. On the project of books 6–10, see O'Daly, pp. 101–34.

6. Throughout, I use Dyson's translation of the *City of God*. References marks book and section numbers in the *City of God*.

7. *Apuleius: Rhetorical Works*. Translated and annotated by Stephen Harrison, John Hilton, and Vincent Hunink. Edited by Stephen Harrison. Oxford: Oxford University Press, 2001, p. 192. Harrison follows his introduction (pp. 185–94) with a translation of the text (pp. 195–216), the numbering of which I have also followed. I have used his translation throughout. See also the translation of the *De Deo Socratis* by S. M. Trzaskoma found in *The Unknown Socrates: translations, with introductions and notes, of four important documents in the late antique reception of Socrates the Athenian*, by William M. Calder III et al. (Wauconda, IL.: Bolchazy Carducci Publishers, Inc., 2002. The translation is found at pp. 245–72, and the Latin at pp. 273–304.

8. There is a vast literature about the *Asclepius* and Hermes (though they are also treated separately, depending on opinions about the text's authorship). I have used the translation of the Latin *Asclepius* found in Brian P. Copenhaver, *Hermetica: The Greek* Corpus Hermeticum *and the Latin Asclepius in a new English translation, with notes and introduction* (Cambridge University Press, 1992); the translation is found at pp. 67–92, and notes at pp. 211–60. On the reception of Hermes and the *Asclepius* in Europe, see Antoine Faivre, "Figures d'Hermès Trismégiste à la fin du XVIIIe siècle," *L'Orient dans l'Histoire religieuse de l'Europe: l'Invention des origines*. Edited by Mohammed Ali amir-Moezzi and John Scheid (Turnhout, Belgium: Brepols, 2000), pp. 131–37. On the Renaissance and post-Renaissance reading of the Hermetic literature with respect to religions, including by the Jesuit Athanasius Kircher, see Jan Assmann, "The Mosaic Distinction: Israel, Egypt, and the Invention of Paganism," *Representations* 56 (Fall, 1996), 48–67. While except for stray references I have not been able to show significant links of the Jesuit missionaries (considered below) to knowleldge of the *Asclepius* and related texts, much less to root the Jesuit construction of Asian religions in their reception of Hermeticism, the possibility of making such connections, via Kircher and others, is not to be ruled out.

9. On the range of issues related to Egypt and its religion and ancient conceptions of these, the Hermetica and the speculations about the identity of Hermes Trismegistus and, finally, the problems posed by the *Asclepius* (in Greek, the "Perfect Discourse") and by its reception as a prophetic text by Lactantius, Augustine, and later readers, see Garth Fowden, *The Egyptian Hermes: A Historical Approach to the Late Pagan Mind* (Cambridge: Cambridge University Press, 1986).

10. References are to paragraph numbers, and section numbers are according to the Copenhaver translation, which I have used throughout.

11. See Guy, pp. 66–69 on the structure of Augustine's double critique of Apuleius.

12. Jean-Claude Guy, SJ, Unité de structure logique de la "Cité de Dieu" de saint Augustin (Paris: Études Augustiniennes, 1961).

13. Much is written about de Nobili, and one may best start with A. Saulière, *His Star in the East* (Madras: de Nobili Research Institute, and Anand, Gujarat: Gujarat Sahitya Prakash, 1995). On Bouchet, see my *Fr. Bouchet's India: An 18th Century Jesuit's Encounter with Hinduism*. (Chennai: Satya Nilayam Publications, 2005). Fr. Meurin, a German Jesuit who worked in India for many years, became a bishop and was Vicar-Apostolic in Bombay. Some of his writings—mostly argumentative, and mostly in argument with Anglican and Protestant Christians—are collected in *Select Writings of the Most Reverend Leo Meurin, SJ*. Edited by P. A. Colaco. (Bombay: C. M. Braganca and Company, 1909); Colaco prefaces the collection with a biography of the bishop, who was still living at the time of the first, 1891 edition. For general reflection on missionary reading practices, see my essays, "Understanding and the Refusal to Understand as Complementary Dynamics in Jesuit Missionary Learning," Contributions to Indian and Cross-Cultural Studies: Volume in Commemoration of Wilhelm Halbfass, edited by Karin Preisendanz (Vienna: Austrian Academy of Sciences Press, forthcoming), and "Francis Xavier, and the World/s We (Don't Quite) Share," in Francis X. Clooney, editor, *Jesuit Postmodern: Scholarship, Vocation, and Identity in the 21st Century* (Lanham: Lexington Press, 2006), pp. 157–80.

14. In truth, I must add, it was also difficult to find missionaries who undertook close readings of non-Christian texts. Many theorized about the sources of such texts and criticized their authority and claims, but very few have given us in writing a careful reading of a non-Christian text.

15. In another work, the *Dialogue on Eternal Life*, de Nobili argues at length that the "true Veda" remains conformable to reason even while transcending it; Hindu scriptures do not live up to this standard while, by implication, the Bible does.

16. Here and throughout, de Nobili gives the Sanskrit along with his Latin rendering, but I have omitted the Sankrit here.

17. Not in the extant text of *Manu*.

18. References are to section numbers in the *Report*.

19. For further reflection on de Nobili's use of *Manu*, see my "Yes to Caste, No to Religion? Or Perhaps the Reverse: Re-Using Roberto de Nobili's Distinctions among Morality, Caste, and Religion," for Joe Arun, SJ, editor, *Roberto de Nobili Reconsidered* (Chennai: Institute for Dialogue of Religions and Cultures, forthcoming).

20. Even in his well-respected writings on Indian legal customs, Bouchet moves back and forth between the written and oral traditions; but he does so vaguely and without documenting his observations by reference to particular Hindu texts, as de Nobili had begun doing a full century before. Bouchet repeatedly refers to what is said in the Vedas and later texts, but often enough he says that one or another brahmin has told him what a text, unavailable to him, says. It is uncertain whether his dependence on brahmins is because the "texts" were not written, or because he could not read the Sanskrit, or because they are deliberately withheld from him. See *Fr. Bouchet's India*, pp. 11–16.

21. Shelford, April. "Thinking Geometrically in Pierre-Daniel Huet's *Demonstratio Evangelica* (1679)," *Journal of the History of Ideas* (March 2003), pp. 599–617.

22. References are to page numbers of passages as cited in English translation in *Fr. Bouchet's India*.

23. The body of the letter is given over to fourteen loci of partial similarity between the Greek pagan and Indian Hindu worlds, documented with reference to Greek sources and also to Indian sources, more vaguely described.

24. Pp. 238 ff.

25. The number of points is not definitively marked, and my enumeration is tentative.

26. Laberius was refuted by Tertullian in his *Apologeticus*; see n. 48 in particular for the argument Bouchet is alluding to here.

27. See Colaco's introduction, pp. vi–vii.

28. References are to page numbers in *Selected Writings*.

29. It is not clear how Fr. Meurin would have managed this list in the lecture format claimed for "God and Brahm."

# 8

# Wisdom, Compassion, and Charity: The Lotus Sutra and Augustine

Leo D. Lefebure

The Lotus Sutra proclaims the hopeful message of Shakyamuni Buddha that "My Law [*dharma* in Sanskrit] can free you from birth, old age, sickness and death and enable you at last to achieve nirvana."[1] But it also cautions that only Buddhas can understand the dharma, and the dharma "is not something that can be understood through pondering or analysis" (ch. 2; p. 31). If only Buddhas can understand the dharma, it would seem impossible for others to benefit from the wisdom of the enlightened ones. According to the Lotus Sutra, the resolution of this difficulty comes through the use of *upaya* or, more specifically, *upaya-kausalya*, variously translated as "expedient" or "skillful" or "appropriate" means, including similes and parables.[2] The wisdom of the Buddha that cannot be captured conceptually through pondering or analysis may nonetheless be conveyed in non-literal form through concrete narratives; and the Lotus Sutra presents a number of celebrated examples. These narratives promise to transform human existence decisively, freeing humans from attachments and awakening them to wisdom (*prajna*) and compassion (*karuna*). Through wisdom and compassion the Buddha establishes skillful means in order to heal the suffering of human beings and to lead them into these virtues.

During the same time that Kumarajiva and his companions were translating the Lotus Sutra into Chinese, Augustine of Hippo proclaimed that the gospel of Jesus Christ offered humans the possibility of victory over ignorance, sin, and death, and supreme bliss in union with God in heaven. But he also insisted that God is strictly incomprehensible and the divine reality cannot be captured in any concept or image. Pondering and analysis cannot grasp the meaning of God, and so Augustine warned his congregation, "If you have comprehended, what you have comprehended is not God."[3] Despite the inadequacy of all human thought and language to comprehend God, Augustine trusted that God has used finite signs, like the narratives of the Bible, to communicate saving knowledge of God's love. Signs point to realities; even though the signs posited by God never express the divine reality adequately and literally, they can nonetheless reorient human life away from untrammeled, self-destructive desire (*cupiditas*) and toward the self-giving love that Augustine calls charity (*caritas*). The wisdom and charity of God are the origin and content of the salvific signs, whose goal is to lead humans into the wisdom and charity of God.

The Lotus Sutra and Augustine both warn that our ordinary consciousness is warped. Prior to a religious awakening, we are ignorant of who we really are and of what genuine treasures are offered to us. Both reject any claim of adequacy for a detached, speculative understanding of ultimate reality and aim instead at the practical goal of transforming human consciousness in concrete situations, teaching the true identity of human beings, liberating them from unnecessary suffering, and offering ultimate fulfillment. Both perspectives promise treasures that are our true inheritance but that come in unexpected ways.

Both Augustine and the Lotus Sutra use their theories of communication to interpret earlier forms of religious understanding and practice as legitimate in their original context but as inappropriate at the present time. Augustine interprets the Jewish beliefs and practices of the Old Testament as signs of God's love, but accuses contemporary Jews of not understanding their true significance and faults them for rejecting Jesus Christ. The Lotus Sutra, as generally interpreted, sees earlier forms of Hinayana Buddhist practice as expressions of skillful means of the Buddha appropriate for certain types of people, but it presents its own message of the One Vehicle as the only proper form for the present age.[4]

There are, to be sure, major cosmological and anthropological differences between the perspectives of Augustine and the Lotus Sutra. Perhaps most important, Augustine understands all finite reality to be created by God, who is infinite love and who becomes incarnate in Jesus Christ to redeem humankind.[5] Belief in creation shapes all of Augustine's thought. In contrast, the Lotus Sutra does not rely on a creating and redeeming God but views all realities as empty, as radically interdependent.[6] From the early Buddhist tradition to the present, many Buddhists have viewed

Shakyamuni Buddha not as God, but as a human pathfinder who points the way to liberation. In practice, however, Buddhist perspectives have varied widely. Michael Pye has commented that in the later tradition, "the Buddha is approached devotionally by many Buddhists in Asian countries more or less as God is approached, still today, by a significant number of people in Western countries."[7] While Shakyamuni states in the Lotus Sutra that he became a Buddha at a specific time in the distant past (ch. 16; pp. 225, 227, 229), many East Asian Buddhists have interpreted the narrative of his life as a representation of the eternal *dharma-kaya* (ultimate truth), "his unimaginably long life span being seen as a metaphor for the 'beginningless' truth realized by the Buddha."[8] As Burton Watson comments, "in the Lotus Sutra the Buddha, who had earlier been viewed as a historical personality, is now conceived as a being who transcends all boundaries of time and space, an ever-abiding principle of truth and compassion that exists everywhere and within all beings."[9] This perspective offers an analogue to Augustine's belief that the divinity of Christ is eternal Truth itself, transcending the limits of time and space and present to every age, yet fully incarnate in Jesus of Nazareth. Nonetheless, differences remain. Michael Fuss comments that for the Lotus Sutra, the Buddha as the "Inspired One" is the self-disclosure of the Dharma, transcendental truth; as such he is "more than a prophet, as his message claims the totality of a new religious system, invites imitation of his own way, and finally leads to the deification of the founder. Yet the 'Inspired One' is clearly distinct from a God 'incarnate' as he never claims to embody the truth and grant salvation, but merely to show the way toward its achievement."[10]

Another important difference is that the Lotus Sutra assumes that beings can be reborn in various states of existence over immense periods of time, whereas Augustine assumes that humans make a definitive decision for or against the love of God in one lifetime. Even though it may take unimaginably long periods of time, the Lotus Sutra expresses the confident hope that all sentient beings will eventually enter Nirvana; Augustine, on the other hand, starkly warns that human freedom is capable of a definitive rejection of God's love. A Christian reader of the Lotus Sutra finds therein both much that resonates deeply with the Christian tradition and also much that is profoundly different. The focus of this essay is not primarily on the important differences in the underlying cosmological assumptions but rather on the analogies in the practical strategies to transform human life in the Lotus Sutra and Augustine. For both perspectives, ultimate reality cannot be understood as a purely objective reality apart from the journey of transformation of human life. In each case, though in different ways, the practical effectiveness of skillful means or signs overcomes the epistemological impossibility of theoretically grasping ultimate reality.

## THE LOTUS SUTRA

The full title of the sutra is "The Lotus Flower of the Wonderful Law" (*Saddharmapundarika-sutra* in Sanskrit); traditionally in East Asia it has been accompanied by two shorter sutras, "Innumerable Meanings" and "Meditation on the Bodhisattva Universal Virtue."[11] However, the textual history of the Lotus Sutra is complex and conflicting, with seven different early versions surviving in Sanskrit, Tibetan, and Chinese, containing major differences among them, not to mention later translations.[12] No original text is extant, and the original language is unknown.[13] A Sanskrit version discovered in 1931 in Kashmir has been thought to go back to the fifth or sixth century C.E. and may be the oldest in this language.[14] The Chinese translations may well reflect earlier stages of transmission than any Sanskrit text available.[15] The Chinese translation of Kumarajiva and his team, completed in 406 C.E., came to be accepted as authoritative by the vast majority of the later Buddhist tradition in East Asia. This essay will discuss English translations of Kumarajiva's version of the sutra and will not attend to the important textual variations found elsewhere. The impact of the Lotus Sutra on East Asian Buddhism and culture has been immense; it was revered as the central Buddhist scripture by Tien-tai Buddhists in China and by Tendai and Nichiren Buddhists in Japan.[16]

East Asian Buddhist scholars have generally believed that the Sutra of Innumerable Meanings is the preface to the Lotus Sutra, even though the shorter sutra makes no explicit reference to the Lotus Sutra.[17] The Sutra of Meditation on the Bodhisattva Universal Virtue, by contrast, does explicitly cite the Lotus Sutra and continues the same style of teaching; thus it has been widely viewed as an epilogue.[18] Many East Asian Buddhists have revered the threefold sutra as the purest expression of the teaching of Shakyamuni Buddha.[19]

The Sutra of Innumerable Meanings begins by presenting a vast assembly on Mount Grdhrakuta before Shakyamuni Buddha. The Buddha advises the assembly that he will shortly pass into nirvana, and he invites their questions. Bodhisattva Great Adornment, however, poses the central problem: "World-honored One! The preaching of the World-honored One is incomprehensible, the natures of living beings are also incomprehensible, and the doctrine of emancipation is also incomprehensible."[20] The Buddha responds by explaining that he has preached the dharma in various ways to different beings. The Buddha goes on to promise that those who revere this sutra will find inconceivable benefits, even if they cannot realize its truth all at once.[21]

This sets the stage for the Lotus Sutra, which similarly begins with a huge assembly. Shakyamuni Buddha "sent forth from the circle of white hair between his eyebrows a ray of light, which illuminated eighteen thousand worlds in the eastern quarter, so that there was nowhere it did not reach, downward to the Avici hell and upward to the Akanishtha heaven."[22] Maitreya Bodhisattva asks what this means; and the bodhisattva of wisdom, Manjushri, explains that the Buddha "is now intending to preach the great Law" and that the rays of light represent the teaching of the Buddha, which will in time liberate all sentient beings in heaven or in hell (ch. 1; trans. by Kato, p. 42). The rest of the text consists of a series of discourses by Shakyamuni and other Buddhas and bodhisattvas about teaching the dharma, but it is not clear that any of these is actually the promised sermon. While the Sutra is quite hopeful that eventually all beings will understand its message and rejoice, it is also very clear in expecting misunderstanding and opposition from many not ready to listen.

There is, however, a paradox in the promise of the illuminating sermon; some scholars of the Lotus Sutra have argued that the Buddha never does deliver the sermon promised by Manjushri. George J. Tanabe, Jr., and Willa Jane Tanabe discover a doctrinal emptiness at the center of the text, which opens it to multiple interpretations and transformations: "The fact that the preaching remains an unfulfilled promise is never mentioned, mostly because that fact is hardly noticed, or because the paean about the sermon sounds like the sermon itself. The text is taken at face value: praise about the *Lotus Sutra* becomes the *Lotus Sutra*, and since the unpreached sermon leaves the text undefined in terms of a fixed doctrinal value (save, of course, the value of the paean) it can be exchanged at any number of rates."[23]

In the history of the later interpretations of the Lotus Sutra, however, the vast majority of East Asian Buddhists have understood the central message of the text to be the presentation of the One Vehicle and the hopeful affirmation of the capacity of all sentient beings to attain Buddhahood. The doctrinal emptiness noted by the Tanabes has historically been counterbalanced and, indeed, outweighed by the confident promise of Shakyamuni Buddha that in the long run his skillful means will draw all sentient beings to wisdom and compassion. While it is important to note the Tanabes's caveat, in this essay I will focus primarily on the dominant line of interpretation in later East Asian Buddhism.

## AUGUSTINE THE PREACHER

In or around the year 396, shortly after he had become bishop of Hippo, Augustine began writing *De Doctrina Christiana* (variously translated as "On Christian Doctrine" or "Teaching Christianity"[24]) as an educational handbook to instruct Christian teachers and preachers and bishops to interpret signs properly so that they in turn could lead the entire Christian community. The work sets forth a system of Christian eloquence and rhetoric, a way of interpreting the Christian scriptures to clarify the meaning of human existence and call humans to conversion. To accomplish this end, it offers a theory of language to clarify the way Christians speak of God and human existence. Throughout this work Augustine assumes that the signs of the Bible come from God and are God's gracious gifts to illumine our path. The message they impart cannot be proved by human reason but can be accepted in Christian faith. As Augustine explains, the first section (the first three books) discusses "a way to discover what needs to be understood," while the second part (contained in the fourth book) will present "a way to put across to others what has been understood" (DDC 1.1.1).[25]

After writing the first two books and most of the third, Augustine interrupted work on *De Doctrina Christiana* for nearly twenty years and began writing his famous *Confessions*.[26] There is a close connection between his presentation of his self-understanding as a preacher in *De Doctrina Christiana* and his presentation of the journey that led him to that position in the *Confessions*, and it has been proposed that the latter should be understood as a sequel to the former.[27] Both in preaching the scriptures and in reflecting on his own life, Augustine found that the path to knowledge passes through the interpretation of signs. The proper understanding of the images and narratives in the Bible would offer him the key to interpreting his own life's journey and the broader history of the human race.[28]

## *SIGNA* AND *UPAYA*

Both Augustine and the Lotus Sutra acknowledge fundamental problems in communication, flowing both from the distortions of human awareness and also from the incomprehensible nature of the salvific message. For Augustine, the interpretation of signs (*signa*) is crucial to following the path of the Christian life, but humans cannot communicate accurately concerning the most important matters by their power alone. There is a tragic irony in Augustine's Prologue to *De Doctrina Christiana*: he, a professional rhetorician who had earlier held a position of significant responsibility for communications at the imperial court, begins a work on how to communicate effectively by anticipating misunderstanding. To prospective critics who will not understand his rules or who will think them unnecessary, he offers a preemptive retort, using the image, familiar to Buddhists in a different context, of a finger pointing to the moon: "I am not the one to be blamed because they do not understand. It's as though they wished to see the old or the new moon, or some very dim star, which I would be pointing to with my outstretched finger; but if their eyesight was not good enough for them even to see my finger, that would be no reason why they should be indignant with me" (Prologue, p. 101).

For Augustine, ignorance and misunderstanding are pervasive in human life, and apart from God's help we do not know our true identity or situation. Our immediate understanding of ourselves and our world is systematically distorted by sin, which prevents us from seeing the signs of God's love around us. Though we are created in the image of God, with the ability to know and love, in our fallen state we mistake ourselves for the material things around us and falsely believe that our happiness and destiny lie in mastering them. As we misinterpret signs, we inevitably misread the meaning of our emotions, as well as the true significance of the persons and objects around us. Deceived in our self-understanding, we misdirect our energies and desires, making some finite object our ultimate goal. Knowing how to interpret signs accurately offers us the key to knowing ourselves, to seeing through the temptations that deceive us, to deciphering the activity of God in our lives, and to finding the true path to wisdom and happiness.[29] For Augustine, knowledge of self and knowledge of God are inseparable, but we know God and ourselves only through the indirect route of the interpretation of signs.

The Lotus Sutra is also suspicious of our ordinary self-understanding. Before learning the teaching of the Buddhas, humans do not understand the danger of their present situation, like children playing in a house that is on fire, unaware of the mortal danger they face (ch. 3), or like a son who does not know his own father and the immense inheritance which is rightfully his (ch. 4), or like children who have been poisoned but will not take the proper medicine (ch. 16). The Sutra warns that because we do not know our true situation and identity, we ceaselessly create needless suffering for ourselves and others. The predicaments of the ignorant son and the heedless children suggest that apart from the Buddha's compassionate guidance humans are powerless to awaken to their true situation. For the Lotus Sutra, knowledge of our true identity means awakening from the illusion of the false self. The Buddha compares himself to the father of the sons playing in the house on fire: "I, most venerable of the sages, am the father of this world and all living beings are my children. But they are deeply attached to worldly pleasures and lacking in minds of wisdom. There is no safety in the threefold world; it is like a burning house, replete with a multitude of sufferings" (ch. 3; p. 69). As long as humans cannot see the danger they are in, they continue in endless suffering.

The Lotus Sutra presents the teaching of Shakyamuni Buddha, but there is a paradox here. The message it presents offers hope of transforming human life, but also denies that this can be understood: "Among heavenly beings or the people of the world, among all living beings, none can understand the Buddha" (ch. 3; p. 24). The Lotus Sutra presents a series of ways to talk about what cannot be understood. The speeches of Shakyamuni Buddha offer a practical model of Buddhist rhetoric, giving examples of how to convey a transformative message that cannot literally be communicated. "The true entity of all phenomena can only be understood and shared between Buddhas" (ch. 3; p. 24), and yet the purpose of the Lotus Sutra is to share the wisdom of the Buddha with those who are not yet enlightened, assuring future Buddhahood to countless beings. Regarding those not yet enlightened, the Buddha calls for faith in his teaching to gain entrance to the wisdom of the sutra: "Even you, Shariputra, in the case of this sutra were able to gain entrance through faith alone. How much more so, then, the other voice-hearers. Those other voice-hearers—it is because they have faith in the Buddha's words that they can comply with this sutra, not because of any wisdom of their own" (ch. 3; p. 73).

In a different context, Augustine also insists that humans need faith to understand the scriptures. Faith, which is itself a gift of God, opens the way to understanding; and understanding, which remains partial and inadequate, deepens faith and leads to further questions. Augustine cites Paul's First Letter to the Corinthians as evidence that Christians live by faith: "Now we see through a mirror and in an enigma, but then we shall see face to face. Now I know in part, but then I shall know even as I am known" (1 Cor 13:12). Augustine adds his own comment: "Let no one wonder, therefore, that we must toil to see anything at all, even in this manner of seeing which has been granted in this life, namely, through a mirror in an enigma."[30]

Augustine develops his theory of communication by distinguishing between realities (*res*) and signs (*signa*). Realities are learned by signs, and so a sign is a means to an end.[31] We need signs, but we should not cling to them for their own sake. In the case of signs of God, signs should point beyond themselves to God, the ground of all true communication. Since it is not the sign that matters but the reality to which it points, to cling to the sign is to misunderstand its meaning. Elsewhere Augustine compares the words of scripture to clouds against the face of heaven: they can be luminous with the light of heaven, but they can also conceal.[32] Without a consciousness illumined by God, even divinely revealed words fail to convey their message. God illumines human minds so they can know truly: "For that light is already God Himself; the soul, on the other hand, is a creature, although in reason and intellect it is made in his image. And when the soul tries to fix its gaze upon that light, it quivers in its weakness and is not quite able to do so. Yet it is from this light that the soul understands whatever it is able to understand."[33] But even in this illumination, God remains hidden. Van Bavel comments that for Augustine, "God has the initiative in a knowledge of which the human being is not the master. What does matter is to learn how one does not know. It is not permitted to let

God disappear in our human representations. Augustine wished to do nothing other than to pave the way to the revealed Unknowable, and this requires at the same time an emptying out of every kind of representation."[34]

From the Pali canon of scripture to the present, the Buddhist tradition has long compared the teachings of the Buddha to a raft that takes one to the other shore but that should not be clung to for its own sake.[35] According to the Lotus Sutra, the words of the Buddha are pointers to a truth that cannot literally be described: "This Law [Dharma, the teaching of the Buddha] cannot be described, words fall silent before it" (ch 3; p. 25). The Buddhist tradition has also long been aware that without a transformed consciousness, the teachings of the Buddha can be misunderstood and fail to achieve their end. Augustine warns that Christians should not cling to signs, even the signs in the Bible, mistaking them for God, but must negate them by moving through and beyond them into God. Buddhists warn not to carry the raft of the Buddha's teaching around on one's head once one has reached the other shore.

The dialectic of sign and reality in communication is one of the most fascinating and paradoxical relationships in Augustine's theology. Christians need to have some sense of the reality they are interpreting in order to interpret the signs. If they do not know a reality at all, words about the reality will not help very much. But Christians learn realities through signs (*Teaching Christianity* 1.2.2; p. 106). This leaves us with the puzzle: which comes first? We can only understand the reality through the signs, but we can only make sense of the signs if we understand the reality. For Augustine, the power that undergirds this dialectic and makes it fruitful is the illumination of Christ.[36] On our own, we cannot understand either the reality or the sign, but the eternal Word both establishes the signs that lead us to itself and also gives the light by which to see clearly. The reality we are to understand is God, who is charity, and the signs that reveal God are expressions of the divine charity.

This means that for Augustine, Christian theology and preaching must proceed indirectly through the interpretation of signs, while relying on the assistance of the divine reality that is being interpreted. Where the Lotus Sutra acknowledges that we cannot state the wisdom of the Buddha directly and must use skillful means to communicate, Augustine warns that we cannot state directly what God is, and thus we make a detour through signs. Where Augustine sees the signs of the scriptures as gifts of God, the Lotus Sutra sees the parables and similes of the Buddha as gifts of his compassion. For Augustine, the illumination of Christ allows us to see signs as pointing to the divine reality.

For both the Lotus Sutra and Augustine, the stakes in interpreting are quite high. Where Augustine cautions that human understanding alone cannot grasp the divinely given signs of God's love, in the Lotus Sutra, the Buddha warns: "If persons of shallow understanding hear it [the Lotus Sutra], they will be perplexed and fail to comprehend" (ch. 3; p. 73). Where Augustine warned of harsh everlasting penalties for those who misinterpret the divinely given signs and reject God's love, the Buddha warns of severe, long-lasting consequences for the one who slanders the Lotus Sutra: "When his life comes to an end he will enter the Avichi hell, be confined there for a whole kalpa,[37] and when the kalpa ends, be born there again. He will keep repeating this cycle for a countless number of kalpas. Though he may emerge from hell, he will fall into the realm of beasts, becoming a dog or jackal, his form lean and scruffy, dark, discolored, with scabs and sores, something for men to make sport of" (ch. 3; p. 74). Augustine sees God offering wisdom and salvation freely to humans, but finds the divine invitation all too often scorned and despised. The skillful means of the Buddha reach out to all with wisdom, and the "rain of Dharma" comes down all over the world, but many are not able to accept its message and bring judgment and long-lasting suffering upon themselves for vast stretches of time.

The Lotus Sutra does, however, hold out the hope that eventually, after immense periods of time, all will understand its teaching (ch. 23; p. 286). This is one of the most far-reaching differences between Augustine and the Lotus Sutra. Where the great Christian scholar Origen had earlier expressed the Christian hope that all humans and even the devil would be saved in the end, Augustine disagreed. For Augustine, to misunderstand the signs of God is to misunderstand ourselves and God and to choose some finite reality in place of God. Unless God intervenes, this leads inexorably to everlasting separation from God. For Augustine the interpretation of signs is crucial to living the Christian life, but it is ultimately only the power of God that allows us to interpret signs correctly.

## WISDOM, CARITAS, AND KARUNA

Both Augustine and the Lotus Sutra value wisdom, though the meanings of *sapientia* in Latin and of *prajna* in Sanskrit differ in important ways. For Augustine, Wisdom is identical with God, the creating and ordering power that extends through all things. All things are always held together by the Divine Wisdom and are never separated from her. Yet in practice humans have wandered far from her; though she is present to them, they are not present to her or to their true selves. Augustine comments on the dilemma of our inability to return to our true identity and homeland: "Of this we would be quite incapable, unless Wisdom herself had seen fit to adapt herself even to such infirmity as ours, and had given us an example of how to live, in no other mode than the human one, because we too are human. . . . So since she herself is our home, she also made herself for us into the way home" (1.11.11; pp. 110–11). In one sense all created things have always been in Wisdom, but humans driven by greed had rejected her: "So she came where she already was, because she was in the world, and the world was made through her. But human beings, greedy to enjoy the creature instead of the creator, had taken on the coloring of this world . . . ; that is why they did not recognize her" (*Teaching Christianity,* 1.12.12; p. 111). In response to human ignorance, Wisdom is above all a healer binding up our wounds: "And just as when doctors bind up wounds, they do not do it untidily, but neatly, so that the bandage, as well as being useful, can also to some extent have its proper beauty, in the same sort of way Wisdom adapted her healing art to our wounds by taking on a human being, curing some of our ills by their contraries, others by homeopathic treatment" (1.14.13; p. 111). Wisdom the healer adapts herself to the needs of human beings so that they can benefit from her loving power even though they never grasp her conceptually. Augustine's Christian Wisdom does not offer a new conceptual definition but embodies herself as Jesus of Nazareth, incarnating in history the Wisdom and Love of God for the salvation of humans.

In the Lotus Sutra wisdom is the perfect insight of the Buddha, which is perfectly shared only by other Buddhas. According to the sutra, the Buddha sees that all things are originally nirvanic:[38] "The Tathagata knows and sees the character of the triple world as it really is: no birth-and-death, no going away, no coming forth, no being in the world and no extinction, no reality and no falsehood, no being thus and no being otherwise."[39] Accordingly, the Buddha advises bodhisattvas to learn, "All phenomena are empty, without being, without any constant abiding, without arising or extinction. This I call the position the wise person associates himself with. From upside-downness come distinctions, that phenomena exist, do not exist, are real, are not real, are born, are not born" (ch. 14; p. 200). As Riccardo Venturini explains, for the Lotus Sutra, "void" becomes a positive term: "Void, in fact, being emptied itself, becomes fullness. This changing and impermanent world in which we live is itself the real world. . . . The Buddha in his wisdom can affirm that the world is already saved and pure."[40]

Yet humans, through ignorance and greed, do not realize this and fall away from wisdom and spend countless eons in distress. To remedy the situation, the narratives of the Buddha's enlightenment and entry into nirvana present themselves as skillful means designed to heal human suffering. Michael Pye notes that the term "nirvana" functions in two different ways. On the one hand nirvana is "a cipher for the inexpressible," a pointer to the "nirvana-nature of all dharmas"; on the other hand, nirvana is the teaching of the Buddha, the "voice" or "sound" of nirvana, that which is "provisionally taught for the ending of ill."[41] In principle, the nirvanic nature of all reality cannot be grasped conceptually; in practice, narratives and poems present the Buddha's wisdom in a form that can transform and heal human life.

Augustine understood divine Wisdom to intervene in human life out of love for suffering humans; according to the Lotus Sutra, the Buddha sees the suffering of humans and resolves to heal them like a good physician. Chapter 16 of Kumarajiva's translation of the Lotus Sutra presents the story of a physician whose children have been poisoned; ignorant of the danger of their condition, the children will not take the medicine that can heal them. To convince them of the danger, the physician sends a message reporting his death in order to startle the children up and persuade them to take the medicine. Upon learning that his strategy has worked, the physician reveals himself to them alive (ch. 16; pp. 228–29). This offers a model for understanding the narrative of the passing of the Buddha into nirvana. The wisdom of the Buddha is timeless and everlasting. The entire narrative of the life and *parinirvana* (the passing into nirvana) of Shakyamuni is a skillful means to teach the inexpressible. John R. A. Mayer argues that in the Lotus Sutra, "though there is a fundamental singular truth, a foundation to the universe, this truth is accessible only to the Buddha. . . . While the 'foundation' is hinted at as the Void, and is characterized by the Ten Suchnesses, these are not readily assimilable concepts; indeed, they are not concepts at all; they imply the practice of compassion, the practice of self-sacrifice. It would be folly for those listening to the Buddha to think that they have a theoretical or conceptual grasp of the 'foundation' of all."[42] The wisdom that cannot be captured in concepts can be lived out in the practice of compassion.

The Buddha knows that no words can adequately express the Dharma, but he teaches out of compassion for suffering beings. Augustine knows that no words can express the reality of God, and he would prefer to be silent, but the responsibility of his office as bishop and the needs of his audience demand that he write and speak out of charity and compassion for his people. For Augustine, the fundamental principle for all interpretation and the key to the reading of all of scripture is charity (*caritas*): scripture teaches nothing but the double love of God and neighbor. Anyone who finds a different meaning in the Bible does not understand it at all (*Teaching Christianity* 1.36.40; p. 124). Anyone who finds a meaning in scripture that coheres with caritas has found a true interpretation. Even if this interpretation was not apparent to the human author of the text, it was foreseen and intended by the divine author, who is love itself. Thus Augustine can summarize the message of the entire Bible in a single sentence: "Scripture, though, commands nothing but charity, or love, and censures nothing but cupidity, or greed, and that is the way it gives shape and form to human morals" (*Teaching Christianity* 3.10.15; p. 176). Charity for Augustine "is any urge of the spirit to find joy in God for his own sake, and in oneself and one's neighbor for God's sake"; cupidity or greed is "any impulse of the spirit to find joy in oneself and one's neighbor, and in any kind of bodily thing at all, not for God's sake" (*Teaching Christianity* 3.10.16; p. 176).

Where Augustine finds his basic principle of interpretation in *caritas,* the fundamental motivation for the Buddha's skillful means is compassion. In both perspectives, the underlying virtue—Christian charity or Buddhist compassion—flows from wisdom and provides the key to interpreting the words of the scriptures. Any Christian claim to wisdom that does not lead to charity is thereby discredited; any Buddhist claim to wisdom that does not lead to compassion is similarly discredited.

Augustine further develops his principles of interpretation through a far-reaching distinction between the types of realities we interpret: (1) realities that humans are to enjoy (*frui*) and (2) realities that humans are to use (*uti*). "Enjoyment, after all, consists in clinging to something lovingly for its own sake, while use consists in referring what has come your way to what your love aims at obtaining, provided, that is, it deserves to be loved" (*Teaching Christianity,* 1.4.4; p. 107). Augustine uses the image of people in exile in a foreign land to illustrate the human situation: "And then suppose we were delighted with the pleasures of the journey, and then with the very experience of being conveyed in carriages or ships, and that we were converted to enjoying what we ought to have been using, and were unwilling to finish the journey quickly, and that by being perversely captivated by such agreeable experiences we lost interest in our own country, where alone we could find real happiness in its agreeable familiarity. Well that's how it is in this mortal life" (*Teaching Christianity,* 1.4.4.; pp. 107–108). Delight in physical pleasures leads to ignorance of who we are and perpetuates unnecessary suffering.

Augustine concludes that we should use this world and not enjoy it, so that we may enjoy God. To cling to any finite reality as our final goal is a form of illusion and idolatry. In light of this distinction, Augustine organizes all human experience around two loves: the true love (*caritas*), which is centered on God and "uses" every other reality on its path of return to God; and (2) the false self-centered and self-destructive love (*cupiditas*), which clings to finite realities for their own sake and thereby falls into idolatry. Where the Lotus Sutra finds the central problem of human existence in the ignorance of the deluded consciousness that believes in the reality of an illusory self and world, Augustine locates the fundamental problem in *cupiditas*, the choosing of some creature instead of the Creator. For both perspectives, an illusory self that makes itself or some concrete, physical object the center of its existence cannot see reality and cannot interpret language properly.

In teaching peaceful practices, the Buddha challenges those who would become bodhisattvas to focus resolutely on the one thing needful and not cling to expectations about worldly pleasures: "Clothing and bedding, food, drink, medicine—with regard to such things he should have no expectations but with a single mind concentrate upon the reasons for preaching the Law, desiring to complete the Buddha way and to cause those in the assembly to do likewise. That will bring great gain to them, an offering of peace" (*Lotus Sutra,* ch 14; p. 203). For both Augustine and the Lotus Sutra, awakening to our true identity and situation calls for a disciplining and reordering of desire and a focus on what is most important in life, the charity and compassion that flow from wisdom.

## NARRATIVES OF TRANSFORMATION

The Lotus Sutra tells the story of an impoverished, lost son who returns to find a wealthy, benevolent father (ch. 4) as a paradigm of the relation of human beings to the Buddha, who is like a kind, generous father. Augustine told the story of his own life in his *Confessions* as a reflection of the parable of the Prodigal Son in the Gospel of Luke, seeing both the gospel narrative and his own journey as paradigms of God's plan for every person.[43] According to the Buddhist story, an ignorant youth ran away from his father's home and went to another country to live. While they were separated, the son remained poor but the father grew increasingly prosperous. The father meanwhile moved to another city, settling in a magnificent home. Many years later the son came to his father's home, saw him from a distance, but did not recognize him. The father, recognizing his son, used the skillful means of hiring his son as a servant to teach him values and authentic self-knowledge. Only after years of patient, disciplined labor was the son in a fitting position to learn his true identity and receive the fortune that was rightfully his (*Lotus Sutra*, ch 4; pp. 81–86). In this narrative, the path to enlightenment is gradual, requiring patient practice to clear away the dirt and garbage that becloud our awareness. Even though the father (the Buddha) may offer immense wealth, the son (like other humans) is too deeply deceived by long-standing patterns of thought and action to awaken at once to his true identity. Once awakened to his true identity, the son realizes that all things are originally nirvanic and that he has possessed the full treasure of enlightenment all the time.

In the Gospel of Luke, Jesus presents the story of a younger son who seeks his inheritance while his father is still alive, effectively telling his father that he prefers the money to his father's presence (Luke 15:11–32). In the culture of Jesus' day, this would be a tremendous insult, deserving of disinheritance.[44] Instead, the son receives his share and promptly leaves, spending it in dissolute living until he falls into utter poverty. Reduced to the humiliating position of envying the food of pigs, he comes to his senses, literally "returning to himself" (Luke 15:17) and repents of his folly. He decides to go home, intending to seek his father's forgiveness and to ask to be a servant. The son's repentance is at the center of the drama. The father is equally prodigal in his own way. He does not wait for the son to beg forgiveness; rather, on the watch for his wayward son, the father rushes out to meet him, clothes him in a fine robe, and orders a lavish feast be prepared. In the eyes of the culture of the day, the actions of both father and son would have brought shame on the entire family. As N.T. Wright explains, the son effectively tells his father that he wishes the father were dead so he can enjoy his inheritance now. The normal social rules dictated that the father "should have thrown him out. Instead, he agrees. The son ends up doing the job beyond which it was impossible, in Jewish eyes, to sink: feeding pigs for a gentile master. He then does a further unthinkable thing: he returns home, threatening to disgrace the whole family in the eyes of the village. The father *runs* to meet him; senior members of families never do anything so undignified at the best of times, let alone in order to greet someone who should have remained in self-imposed ignominy."[45] Meanwhile, the older brother, who has diligently worked at home for many years, becomes resentful on learning of the celebration, complaining of the father's lack of appreciation for him. Filled with goods, with resentments, with himself, the older brother refuses to acknowledge his relationship to his own brother, describing him in conversation with his father as "your son." The turning point of the Buddhist story is the son's patient work over many years, a labor that culminates in awakening to the awareness of who he has been all the time. The theme of repentance for sin against the father, which is so central in the parable of Jesus, is pointedly absent from the account in the Lotus Sutra. The heart of the religious quest in the Lotus Sutra is not repentance for sin against God, but letting go of a false consciousness and awakening to one's true identity and inheritance. In both the Gospel of Luke and the Lotus Sutra, the son has to empty himself of his earlier assumptions and values in order to find himself and his father.

Augustine saw his own early life as modeled on the Prodigal Son, warped and dominated by ignorance of his true identity and by deluding desires that raged out of control. He also believed that humanity's true destiny is a state of oneness with ultimate reality, which defies description. Augustine presents his early years as a time of estrangement from his true self. He had to go through a series of disillusionments with himself, his values, his beliefs, his teachers. In retrospect, he would see the hand of God at work throughout his life; but as he was going through the very stages of his early journey, the real significance of these moments was hidden from him. A series of negations of his early beliefs makes possible the ascent to wisdom. Only later, after his conversion, could he understand the meaning of his earlier life and the role of God in it.

Where the Lotus Sutra proclaims that all things are empty, Augustine recognizes that all things cry out that they are made; they have no independent, substantial being of their own. For Augustine, recognizing the lack of independence of things is not simply an objective theory about external reality but rather a religious insight which, if appropriated, will transform humans and their relations to themselves, to other creatures, and to God.

The young Augustine cannot find his way alone, and so he needs outward guides to orient his quest.[46] Where the Lotus Sutra presents the father of the ignorant son (an image of the Buddha) as using patient, skillful means to transform the awareness of his son, Augustine retrospectively sees God constantly at work in the persons and books that he encounters along the way.

For Augustine, divine Wisdom often appears as folly to humans because God does not share the values of domination and greed that warp so much of earthly life. For the Lotus Sutra, wisdom is inexpressible, beyond the grasp of any but Buddhas, and seems foolish to those enthralled by worldly pleasures. For Augustine, it is the love of God that overcomes human obstacles, establishing signs and narratives, especially the account of the life, death, and resurrection of Jesus, to overcome human ignorance, heal the wounds of sin and ignorance, reorient the human heart, and allow human life to flourish. For the Lotus Sutra, it is the compassion of the Buddha that uses skillful means to engage humans in appropriate ways, overcoming obstacles and opening new possibilities for authentic existence. In very different ways, both Augustine and the Lotus Sutra proclaim a message of hope for assistance and aid in the process of awakening to our true identity.

## PLURALITY AND UNITY

Both the Lotus Sutra and Augustine reflect on the significance of various stages of religious practice that were appropriate for a particular time but that have now been superseded. In doing so, they formulate principles of wisdom for finding a fundamental unity amid a plurality of claims. But they accomplish this in polemical contexts that relegate earlier moments in their respective traditions to an outdated form of practice. The Lotus Sutra addresses the issue of the multiple forms of Buddhist understanding and practice, claiming to supersede all earlier forms of Buddhism and present One Vehicle for the final age of Dharma.[47] Earlier forms of Buddhism were appropriate for their period, but the Lotus Sutra proclaims that all Buddhists are now invited to the One Vehicle, which alone leads to the highest stage of fulfillment. In both the Lotus Sutra and Augustine, there are also underlying hermeneutical principles based upon charity and compassion that could be applied in contemporary interreligious discussions in ways that go beyond the horizons of the original texts themselves.

In interpreting the various stages of Buddhism, Carl Bielefeldt notes:

> Like other Mahayana texts, the *Lotus Sutra* uses the model of an unfolding religious message, or continuing historical revelation, to justify its revision of existing tradition; but, here again, it is more radical than most in its claim that it has superseded all previous Buddhism and now represents the one valid message specifically intended to guide beings in the last age of the law. In this, then, we have scriptural precedent for the hermeneutical principle of the relevance of revelation to specific historical circumstance.[48]

He comments further on "the principle of a transcendental purpose behind all immanent expressions of the religion. . . . [I]t is the Buddha's higher intention, or one great purpose, that lies behind and justifies the variety of His teachings."[49] Since the Lotus Sutra claims to be the highest and final form of the Buddha's teaching, it supersedes all earlier forms of Buddhism, which are now judged to be inadequate. Nonetheless, since the wisdom of the Buddha is incomprehensible, "the justification of the one vehicle is, by definition, beyond articulation and comprehension: it has no propositional content and cannot be judged by human standards or tested by human reason."[50] As we have seen, the Lotus Sutra warns of extremely harsh punishment for immense periods of time for those who openly oppose its teaching (ch. 3; p. 74).

Augustine also understood God to be at work in revelation in different ways at different stages. Augustine believed that God was actively at work in the history of ancient Israel inspiring Moses and other prophets, but he denied that many of the prescriptions of the Mosaic Law applied to Christians, and he argued that the revelation of God in Jesus Christ had superseded Jewish forms of religious practice. Again, everything hinges on the interpretation of signs. Augustine believed that the patriarchs and prophets and many others in ancient Israel were spiritual people who worshipped God properly by "serving under useful signs" the Law of Moses (*Teaching Christianity,* 3.9.13; p. 175). At that time, Augustine asserts, it was "not yet opportune for carnal spirits to have those signs openly explained to them"; when Christian liberty appeared, it explained these signs, "raised them [the spiritual people] up to the substantive realities, the things they were signs of, and so set them free." Unlike Jerome and many other early Christian authors, Augustine argued, as Paula Fredriksen has put it, "that both Jesus and the first generation of Jewish apostles, Paul emphatically included, were, as Christians, also Torah-observant Jews."[51]

Augustine sees Christians as living in a different stage in the history of revelation with a deeper understanding than the people of the Old Testament and with a God-given freedom from the ritual provisions of the Mosaic Law: "In this time, though, after the clearest indication of our freedom has shone upon us in the resurrection of our Lord, we are no longer burdened with the heavy duty of carrying out even those signs whose meaning we now understand" (*Teaching Christianity,* 3.9.13; p. 175). Augustine acknowledges that many Jews believed in Jesus; but concerning those who did not accept Christian claims about Jesus, he is quite harsh: "The rest of them, however, were made blind; and of them it was foretold, 'Let their table be a snare before them: and that which should have been for their welfare, let it become a trap. Let their eyes be darkened, that they see not; and make their loins continually to shake' (Ps 69:22). Thus, when the Jews do not believe in our Scriptures, their own Scriptures are fulfilled in them, while they read them with darkened eyes."[52]

Augustine argued that God's providence had scattered the Jews among the nations, partly as punishment for the crucifixion of Jesus and partly so they could bear witness to the ancient Israelite prophecies of the Christ. He concluded that Jews should be permitted to live and thought their preserving the Old Testament prophecies helped Christian efforts to convert pagans by showing that Christians had not invented the predictions of Christ.[53] Thus Augustine forbade violent attacks against Jewish communities and their synagogues. However, Jews were to be preserved in misery, in conditions of subordination to demonstrate God's wrath against them.

Where the Lotus Sutra finds unity amid the diverse forms of Buddhism in the intention of the Buddha to teach wisdom and compassion in ways pedagogically appropriate for different people, Augustine grounds the unity of scripture in the intention of God to teach charity and condemn cupidity. With this orienting principle, Augustine acknowledges a legitimate variety of interpretations. As James O'Donnell comments, "In *Christian Doctrine,* Augustine repeatedly makes another point: that when matters of strict doctrine of the faith are not involved, multiple interpretations of scripture can and should flourish side by side."[54]

## AMBIGUOUS HISTORIES OF INTERPRETATION

For better and for worse, both the Lotus Sutra and Augustine were immensely influential on later history; in particular their interpretations of the earlier moments in their respective traditions and their perspectives on different religious practices had a powerful impact on later generations. While Augustine presents one of the most beautiful and moving descriptions of divine and human love in all of Christian literature, his views concerning the divinely willed subordination of the Jewish people were prominent in shaping papal policy in this regard from Pope Gregory the Great to the twentieth century. His insistence that Jews still played a role in God's plan and that they should be allowed to live their faith has been credited with allowing them to survive as a people at all.[55] But because their religion was viewed as superseded, for over a millennium in Christian-ruled areas of Europe, Jews would repeatedly be penalized, humiliated, expelled, and, on numerous occasions, victims of physical violence.[56]

Augustine also played a major role in shaping the theology that justified persecution of heretics. In bitter conflict with Donatists in North Africa, Augustine appealed to the Roman governing authorities to imprison his opponents and destroy their churches. As scriptural foundation for this policy, Augustine interpreted Jesus' parable of the wedding banquet as a mandate for religious intolerance. When the king in the parable learns that his invitation to the feast has been widely rejected, he orders his servants, "Force them to come in" (Luke 14:23). Paradoxically, in Augustine's view, Christian wisdom and charity must demand the coercion of those who do not accept church teaching. Thus Augustine interpreted the king's command in the parable to justify the repression of Christians judged to be heretical. At his behest, the Roman Empire dissolved the Donatist Church and confiscated its property, forcing its clergy into the ranks of the Catholic Church.[57] While Augustine himself forbade physical violence against dissenters, his later followers would not always follow his restraint.[58] Augustine's theology of repression shaped a millennium and a half of Catholic history. The Catholic Church would not affirm the right of religious freedom until *Dignitatis Humanae,* The Declaration on Religious Freedom, promulgated by Vatican II in December, 1965.

The Lotus Sutra's teaching of skillful means shaped a tolerant acceptance of a variety of forms of Mahayana Buddhism in later centuries, but it also inspired the exclusivist views of Nichiren and his followers in thirteenth-century Japan. For Nichiren, the teaching of the Lotus Sutra meant that all other forms of Buddhism, including Pure Land and Zen Buddhism, were deviations that should be abolished.[59] According to Nichiren, only devotion to the teaching of the Lotus Sutra and, in particular, the chanting of homage to its title, offers hope in the present degenerate age.[60] Nichiren believed that his age was a time of corruption in which earlier forms of Buddhism were no longer appropriate. If all people would unite in chanting the title of the Lotus Sutra and placing exclusive faith in its power, then Nichiren promised that the ideal Buddha-land would come, "the wind will not thrash the branches nor the rain fall hard enough to break clods. The age will become like the reigns of [the Chinese kings] Yao and Shun."[61]

Tendai Buddhists, who also revered the Lotus Sutra, understood its message in a more inclusive manner, allowing that its wisdom could be honored by chanting the names of Amida Buddha or Bodhisattva Kannon. Nichiren fiercely rejected this position, comparing earlier Buddhist practices to medicine that has been unused for so long that it has turned into poison.[62] He attacked other forms of Buddhism so sharply that he was twice sent into exile and was threatened with execution, while followers had property confiscated and were imprisoned. Nichiren interpreted both natural disasters and military defeats as the result of neglect of the Lotus Sutra and the spread of Pure Land Buddhism. Many of his followers came from the warrior class. In later generations, Nichiren Buddhists launched bitter verbal attacks on other forms of Buddhism that sometimes led to physical violence. In 1532, Nichiren Buddhists rebelled and were able to seize control of Kyoto; but a few years later, in 1536, after a Nichiren Buddhist monk had publicly defeated a Tendai scholar in debate, Tendai Buddhist warrior monks from Mt. Hiei burned twenty-one Nichiren temples in Kyoto.[63] In the fighting that followed, an estimated ten thousand followers of Nichiren were killed; and the movement suffered a decisive defeat.[64]

The combination of reverence for the Lotus Sutra and violence continued into the twentieth century. A modern Japanese follower of Nichiren, Tanaka Chigaku (1861–1939), combined veneration of the Lotus Sutra with Japanese nationalism, a blend sometimes called "Lotus nationalism." Tanaka believed Japan had a divine mission to unify the world and reconstruct global civilization in accordance with Nichiren's interpretation of the Lotus Sutra, using violent force to bring peace if necessary.[65] For Tanaka, the Lotus Sutra not only justified the use of military force but predicted it. When war with China began in Korea in 1894, he and his followers built a prayer platform and placed a sword before a statue of Nichiren. The sword was aimed ominously at Beijing, as the community prayed three times a day for Japanese victory.

One can pose the question whether Tanaka was actually interpreting the Lotus Sutra or whether he was simply imposing his own interpretation with little or no regard for the integrity of the Sutra. George Tanabe suggests that there is a particular danger in the Lotus Sutra: because the promised sermon is not preached, the text remains empty, and this leaves it open for multiple appropriations. Tanabe warns: "Since the text is empty, it means that what Tanaka saw was not his own personal interpretations drawn in the context of the Nichiren tradition, but a clear mandate issued by a scripture whose meaning, as far as he was concerned, was as absolutely self-evident as it was absolute."[66] Of course, not all Buddhists would agree with Tanaka's reading.

## CONCLUDING HERMENEUTICAL REFLECTIONS: REREADING OUR TRADITIONS IN A PLURALISTIC AGE

Both the Lotus Sutra and Augustine have ambiguous histories of influence and both present forms of exclusivism; but both also propose hermeneutical principles for going beyond the original texts and shaping more positive forms of interreligious relations in the present situation. In each tradition there is a tension between a particular presentation of wisdom, which claims to supersede all earlier forms of the tradition, and the charity or compassion that are inextricably linked to the perspective on wisdom. Historically, the claims of Augustine and of the Lotus Sutra to present the final form of wisdom for all humankind were tremendously influential. In our contemporary context, the claims of charity and compassion may be seen as pressing toward a different possible interpretation.

As we have seen, Augustine sums up the entire teaching of the Bible in the rule: "Scripture, though, commands nothing but charity, or love, and censures nothing but cupidity, or greed, and that is the way it gives shape and form to human morals" (*Teaching Christianity* 3.10.15; p. 176). Augustine's principle that Scripture teaches nothing but charity and condemns nothing but cupidity could be applied, in a way he did not, both to the later history of Christianity and to the entire array of religious traditions. Beliefs and practices, in whatever tradition, may be seen as reflecting the will of the God revealed in Jesus Christ to the degree that they foster love and cultivate generous, healthy human relationships. Beliefs and practices, in whatever tradition, may be seen as sinful to the degree they foster cupidity and greed, thereby damaging human relationships. Augustine himself taught us that the intention of the human scriptural authors did not completely control the meaning of their texts. If an interpreter finds a reading that coheres with charity, it is in harmony with the intention of the Holy Spirit, even if the human author did not foresee it. Augustine's interpretation of other religions, particularly Judaism, stressed divine Wisdom, as enshrined in Catholic Christianity, at the cost of practical charity and led to repeated acts and attitudes that scandalously violate the call to charity.

As we have seen, Augustine was extremely critical of other religions and hoped for salvation only for those who explicitly accepted Jesus as the Son of God; but he also taught that God is *caritas*, that God loves all human beings, and that divine Wisdom entered the world for the sake of all. Vatican II, drawing out implications from Augustine's theology of God as infinite love, rejected Augustine's theology of repression of religious difference and clearly acknowledged truth and goodness in other religions (*Declaration on the Church's Relation to non-Christian Religions* 2), taught that through the incarnation the Son of God united himself to every human being (*Pastoral Constitution on the Church in the World of Today* 22), and affirmed the power of the Holy Spirit throughout all human experience offering salvation to all humanity (*Pastoral Constitution on the Church in the World of Today* 22). In light of these principles, Pope John Paul II, at the World Day of Prayer for Peace in Assisi in October, 1986, declared to the assembled religious leaders of a wide variety of traditions: "The coming together of so many religious leaders to pray. . . is the result of prayer, which, in the diversity of religions expresses a relationship with a supreme power that surpasses our human capacities alone."[67] John Paul repeatedly acknowledged the work of the Holy Spirit in other religions. Any genuine prayer is inspired by the Holy Spirit. Thus the Holy Spirit is actively at work throughout the breadth of the world's religious community.

Similarly, in light of the Buddha's teaching of wisdom and compassion for all sentient beings through the use of skillful means in the Lotus Sutra, many Buddhists have rejected the exclusivist and nationalist interpretations that have sometimes been proposed and understand the implications of the Lotus Sutra's hopeful confidence in a broader context. In particular, some Buddhists have seen Dharmakaya, the eternal, transcendent truth of the Buddha, manifesting itself in other religious traditions. Citing the Lotus Sutra's teaching on skillful means, D. T. Suzuki affirmed that Dharmakaya manifested itself in Jesus Christ: "The Dharmakaya revealed itself as Shakyamuni to the Indian mind, because that was in harmony with its needs. The Dharmakaya appeared in the person of Christ on the Semitic stage, because it suited their taste best in this way."[68] In each tradition, claims to have the final form of wisdom can lead to supersessionism and exclusivism; the insistence on charity or compassion, which is central to Christianity and Buddhism, opens up other perspectives that can transform our understanding of what it means to be wise.

## NOTES

1. *The Lotus Sutra,* trans. Burton Watson (New York: Columbia University Press, 1993) 3; p. 55. All references will be to this translation unless otherwise noted. See also: *Scripture of the Lotus Blossom of the Fine Dharma Translated from the Chinese of Kumarajiva,* by Leon Hurvitz (New York: Columbia University Press, 1976).

2. See Michael Pye, *Skilful Means: A Concept in Mahayana Buddhism* London: Duckworth, 1978), 10–17. On "skill in means" in the earliest traditions of Buddhism and Christianity, see Arvind Sharma, "'Skill in Means' in Early Buddhism

and Christianity," *Buddhist-Christian Studies* 10 (1990): 23–33. On the broader background of the term in Buddhism, see John W. Schroeder, *Skillful Means: The Heart of Buddhist Compassion,* Monograph No. 18, Society for Asian and Comparative Philosophy (Honolulu: University of Hawaii Press, 2001).

3. Augustine, Sermon 52, 16 (*Patrologia Latina* 38, 360).

4. As generally understood, the Lotus Sutra acknowledges that earlier forms of Buddhism were necessary and appropriate in their original contexts but it sees its own teaching, called the One Vehicle, as the final and highest expression of the wisdom of the Buddha. There are, however, various ways that the relation of the One Vehicle to earlier vehicles has been interpreted. The editors of *The Threefold Lotus Sutra* comment, "In this chapter [11], however, the Buddha proclaims that such teachings are all temporary and expedient, for use only until he reveals the final truth. Here the absolute One Buddha-vehicle is shown as the final truth, comprehending all temporary and expedient teachings. After this absolute One Buddha-vehicle has been revealed, none of the other vehicles is to exist independently; all Buddhism is to depend upon and be unified in it. Only this sutra contains this doctrine, and is therefore known as the One-vehicle sutra." *The Threefold Lotus Sutra: Innumerable Meanings, The Lotus Flower of the Wonderful Law, and Meditation on the Bodhisattva Universal Virtue,* trans. Bunno Kato, Yoshiro Tamura, and Kojiro Miyasaka with revisions by W.E. Soothill, Wilhelm Schiffer, and Pier P. del Campana (Tokyo: Kosei Publishing Co., 1975, reprint, 1986), p. 60, n. 14. Gene Reeves acknowledges that in the parable of the burning house, the One Buddha Way replaces the earlier ways; but he proposes a more inclusive interpretation of the sutra as a whole, arguing that the One Way integrates the earlier ways without replacing them. See Gene Reeves, "The Lotus Sutra as Radically World-Affirming," *A Buddhist Kaleidoscope: Essays on the Lotus Sutra,* ed. Gene Reeves (Tokyo: Kosei Publishing Co., 2002), 191.

5. On Augustine's understanding of creation, see Etienne Gilson, *The Christian Philosophy of Saint Augustine,* trans. L.E.M. Lynch (London: Victor Gollancz, 1961), 189–96; Eugene TeSelle, *Augustine the Theologian,* (New York: Herder and Herder, 1970), 135–46; Robert P. Kennedy, "Book Eleven: The *Confessions* as Eschatological Narrative," in *A Reader's Companion to Augustine's Confessions,* ed. Kim Paffenroth and Robert P. Kennedy (Louisville and London: Westminster John Knox Press, 2003), 167–83; and Thomas F. Martin, "Book Twelve: Exegesis and *Confessio,*" in Paffenroth and Kennedy, 185–206.

6. For the meaning of emptiness in the Lotus Sutra and a caution against identifying it with the view of the Prajna-paramita literature, see Susan Mattis, "Chih-I and the Subtle Dharma of the Lotus Sutra; Emptiness or Buddha-Nature?" in Reeves, *Buddhist Kaleidoscope,* pp. 242–44.

7. Michael Pye, "The Length of Life of the Tathagata," in Reeves, *Buddhist Kaleidoscope,* p. 165. See also sociologist Rodney Stark, who argues that non-theistic religions flourish only for the educated elite, while the masses follow more theistic paths. See Rodney Stark, *One True God: Historical Consequences of Monotheism* (Princeton, NJ and Oxford: Princeton University Press, 2001), 46–47.

8. Mattis, 245.

9. Burton Watson, "Translator's Introduction," *Lotus Sutra,* xix. On the relation between the Lotus Sutra and the development of the theory of the Buddha-body,

see Ruben L.F. Habito, "Buddha-body Theory and the Lotus Sutra: Implications for Praxis," in Reeves, *Buddhist Kaleidoscope*, 305–17,

10. Michael A. Fuss, "*Upaya* and *Missio Dei*: Toward a Common Missiology," in Reeves, *Buddhist Kaleidoscope*, 121.

11. Kato et al., ix.

12. Kato et al., xvi.

13. For a survey of the various texts and versions, see Pye, *Skilful Means*, 168–82.

14. Kato et al., xiv.

15. Watson, "Translator's Introduction," *The Lotus Sutra*, ix–x, xxiv–xxv.

16. On visual arts inspired by the Lotus Sutra, see Eugene Y. Wang, *Shaping the Lotus Sutra: Buddhist Visual Culture in Medieval China* (Seattle and London: University of Washington Press, 2005). For its influence on Japanese history and culture, see George J. Tanabe, Jr., and Willa Jane Tanabe, eds., *The Lotus Sutra in Japanese Culture* (Honolulu: University of Hawaii Press, 1989); and Jackie Stone, "Original Enlightenment Thought in the Nichiren Tradition," in *Buddhism in Practice*, ed. Donald S. Lopez, Jr., Princeton Readings in Religions (Princeton, NJ: Princeton University Press, 1995), 228–40.

17. Kato et al., xvii.

18. Kato et al., xviii.

19. Nikkyo Niwano, "The Threefold Lotus Sutra: An Introduction," in Reeves, *Buddhist Kaleidoscope*, 27. "Shakyamuni" means the sage (literally, the "silent one") of the Shakya clan, from which Siddhartha Gotama came. It is the traditional term used by Buddhists to refer to the historical Buddha, Siddhartha Gotama, after his enlightenment.

20. Sutra of Innumerable Meanings, ch. 2; trans. Kato et al., p. 13.

21. Sutra of Innumerable Meanings, ch. 3; trans. Kato et al., pp. 19–21.

22. Lotus Sutra, ch. 1; trans. Kato et al., p. 34.

23. George J. Tanabe, Jr., and Willa Jane Tanabe, "Introduction," in Tanabe and Tanabe, 2–3.

24. Augustine, *On Christian Doctrine*, trans. D.W. Robertson, Jr., Library of Liberal Arts (Indianapolis: Bobbs-Merrill Educational Publishing, 1958); Saint Augustine, *Teaching Christianity: De Doctrina Christiana*, trans. Edmund Hill, ed. John E. Rotelle (Hyde Park, NY: New City Press, 1996). All citations will be from Edmund Hill's translation unless otherwise noted. This book shaped early medieval approaches to theology in the West until the twelfth century and beyond. The classic work on this topic is Henri Irénée Marrou, *Saint Augustin et la fin de la culture antique* (1938; 2nd ed., enlarged with a *Retractatio*, Paris: Éditions de Boccard, 1949).

25. Edmund Hill, "Introduction," *Teaching Christianity*, 12.

26. On the life of Augustine, see James J. O'Donnell, *Augustine: A New Biography* New York: HarperCollins, 2005). See also Saint Augustine, *Confessions*, trans. Henry Chadwick (Oxford and New York: Oxford University Press, 1992).

27. TeSelle, p. 189.

28. For detailed discussion of and commentary on the Latin text of the *Confessions*, see James J. O'Donnell, *Augustine: Confessions*, 3 vols. (Oxford: Clarendon Press, 1992).

29. On the identification of wisdom and happiness as an orienting theme in the thought of Augustine, see Gilson, 3–10. See also Bernard McGinn, *The Foundations*

*of Mysticism,* vol. 1 of *the Presence of God: A History of Western Christian Mysticism* (New York: Crossroad, 1991), 232.

30. Augustine, *On the Trinity* 15.9.16; quoted by T.J. van Bavel, "God in between Affirmation and Negation According to Augustine," in *Augustine: Presbyter Factus Sum,* ed. Joseph T. Lienhard, Earl C. Muller, and Roland J. Teske, Collectanea Augstiniana, ed. Joseph Schnaubelt and Frederick Van Fleteren (New York: Peter Lang, 1993), 81.

31. G. R. Evans, *Augustine on Evil* (Cambridge: Cambridge University Press, 1982), 54.

32. Augustine, *Confessions* 13:15. See Robert J. O'Connell, *St. Augustine's Confessions: The Odyssey of Soul* (Cambridge, MA: Harvard University Press, 1969; reprint, New York: Fordham University Press, 1989), 163.

33. Augustine, *Thirteen Books on the Literal Meaning of Genesis,* 12.31.59; quoted by Gareth B. Matthews, "Knowledge and Illumination," in *The Cambridge Companion to Augustine,* ed. Eleonore Stump and Norman Kretzmann (Cambridge: Cambridge University Press, 2001), 180.

34. Van Bavel, 84.

35. Pye, *Skilful Means,* 120–21.

36. On Augustine's theory of illumination, see Augustine, *Against the Academicians; The Teacher,* trans. Peter King (Indianapolis: Hackett Publishing Co., 1995); and Gareth B. Matthews, "Knowledge and Illumination," in Stump and Kretzman, 180–83.

37. A kalpa is an immensely long cosmic age.

38. Pye, *Skilful Means,* 29.

39. Quoted by Pye, *Skilful Means,* 56–57.

40. Riccardo Venturini, "A Buddha Teaches Only Bodhisattvas," in Gene Reeves, ed., *A Buddhist Kaleidoscope: Essays on the Lotus Sutra* (Tokyo: Kosei Publishing Co., 2002), 334.

41. Pye, *Skilful Means,* 35.

42. John R. A. Mayer, "Reflections on the Threefold Lotus Sutra," in Reeves, *Buddhist Kaleidoscope,* 153.

43. See Leo C. Ferrari, "The Theme of the Prodigal Son in Augustine's *Confessions,*" *Recherches Augustiniennes* 12 (1977)105–18; and Kim Paffenroth, "Book Nine: The Emotional Heart of the *Confessions,*" in Kim Paffenroth and Robert P. Kennedy, eds., *A Reader's Companion to Augustine's Confessions* (Louisville and London: Westminster John Knox Press, 2003), 139–40. For another reflection on conversion in Augustine and the Lotus Sutra, see Malcolm David Eckel, "By the Power of the Buddha," in Reeves, *Buddhist Kaleidoscope,* 131–34.

44. N. T. Wright, *Jesus and the Victory of God,* vol. 2 of *Christian Origins and the Question of God* (Minneapolis: Fortress Press, 1996), 129.

45. Wright, 129.

46. Cf. Vernon J. Bourke, *Augustine's Quest of Wisdom* (Milwaukee, WI: Bruce Publishing Co., 1945).

47. See Carl Bielefeldt, "The One Vehicle and the Three Jewels: On Japanese Sectarianism and Some Ecumenical Alternatives," *Buddhist-Christian Studies* 10 (1990) 10–11.

48. Bielefeldt, 11.

49. Ibid.

50. Ibid.

51. Paula Fredriksen, "Paul," in *Augustine Through the Ages: An Encyclopedia*, ed. Allan D. Fitzgerald, (Grand Rapids, MI: Eerdmans, 1999), 622; cited by James Carroll, *Constantine's Sword: The Church and the Jews, A History* (Boston: Houghton Mifflin Co., 2001), 215.

52. Augustine, *The City of God against the Pagans*, ed. and trans. R.W. Dyson, Cambridge Texts in the History of Political Thought (Cambridge: Cambridge University Press), 18.46; pp. 891–92. On the background and context of this work, see Gerard O'Daly, *Augustine's City of God: A Reader's Guide* (Oxford, England: Oxford University Press, 1999).

53. Augustine, *City of God* 18.46; p. 891–92. On the providence of God scattering the Jews in accordance with Old Testament prophecies, see also 4.34, p. 186.

54. O'Donnell, *Biography*, 134.

55. Carroll, 218.

56. See William Nicholls, *Christian Antisemitism: A History of Hate* (Northvale, NJ: Jason Aronson, Inc., 1993).

57. See O'Donnell, *Biography*, 14–15, 220–23.

58. See Leo D. Lefebure, *Revelation, the Religions, and Violence* (Maryknoll, NY: Orbis Books, 2000), 120–29; and idem, "Authority, Violence, and the Sacred at the Medieval Court," in *Violence in Medieval Courtly Literature: A Casebook*, ed. Albrecht Classen (New York & London: Routledge, 2004).

59. Bielefeldt, 8–9.

60. See Jacqueline Stone, "When Disobedience Is Filial and Resistance Is Loyal: The Lotus Sutra and Social Obligations in the Medieval Nichiren Tradition," in Reeves, *Buddhist Kaleidoscope*, 262.

61. Nichiren, *Nyosetsu shugyo sho, STN 1:733;* quoted by Stone, "Disobedience," 263.

62. Stone, "Disobedience," 264.

63. George J. Tanabe, "The Matsumoto Debate," in *Buddhism in Practice*, ed. Donald S. Lopez, Jr., Princeton Readings in Religions (Princeton, NJ: Princeton University Press, 1995), 241–242.

64. Tamura Yoshiro, "The Ideas of the *Lotus Sutra*," in *The Lotus Sutra in Japanese Culture*, ed. George J. Tanabe, Jr., and Willa Jane Tanabe (Honolulu: University of Hawaii Press, 1989) 50.

65. George J. Tanabe, Jr., "Tanaka Chigaku: The *Lotus Sutra* and the Body Politic," in *The Lotus Sutra in Japanese Culture* ed. George J. Tanabe, Jr., and Willa Jane Tanabe (Honolulu: University of Hawaii Press, 1989), 203–206.

66. George J. Tanabe, "Tanaka Chigaku," 207.

67. John Paul II, "To Representatives of Various Religions on the World Day of Prayer for Peace," in *Interreligious Dialogue: The Official Teaching of the Catholic Church (1963–1995)*, ed. Francesco Gioia (Boston: Pauline Books & Media, 1997), 343.

68. Daisetz Teitaro Suzuki, *Outlines of Mahayana Buddhism* (New York: Schocken Books, 1907 [reprint, 1967), 159–60.

# 9

# Divine Election as *Adhikara* and *Atma-Sva-Bhava*: Rereading the *Reply to Simplicianus* in Light of a Hindu Text

Reid B. Locklin

Francis A. Sullivan's major study *Salvation Outside the Church?* lays the ground for one possible approach to the theme of the present volume.[1] In his work, after surveying a range of Augustine's works addressing the salvation of those who lived before Christ as well as various of the bishop's contemporaries, Sullivan identifies a progressive restriction of those eligible for salvation to baptized members of the Catholic Church. He writes:

> St. Augustine was firmly convinced that those who were outside the church through lack of faith and baptism could not be saved, and he knew of no alternative between salvation and condemnation to hell. . . . Reflecting on what he understood to be the certainty that infants dying without baptism and adults dying in ignorance of the Christian faith must certainly be damned, Augustine came to the conclusion that if God is just in condemning such as these, it must follow that he would be just if he were to condemn the whole human race to hell. The guilt that would justify God if he chose to do this would only be the guilt of original sin. And thus Augustine arrived at his idea that all the descendents of Adam constitute a *massa damnata*, deserving to be condemned to hell, so that if some are spared it is by the sheer mercy of God.[2]

For Sullivan, it is most important that Augustine's extremely dim view of the possibility of salvation outside the church would eventually be qualified, first by immediate followers such as Prosper of Aquitaine and eventually by the Catholic tradition as a whole.[3] Despite such later developments, the contribution of Augustine remains uncompromising and clear: there is no salvation outside of the church.

On this reading, the relation of Augustine to world religions would presumably be rather straightforward. If grace extends exclusively to Catholic faithful, then it stands to reason that there is little more of importance to say about other religious traditions. They are errors, pure and simple, and their members are destined for hell.

For many interpreters, as illustrated by the essays in this volume, such a terse formulation represents only one side of the issue, and a superficial one at that. For example, building on the work of Bernhard Blumenkranz, Paula Fredriksen has argued that Augustine's convictions about scriptural interpretation and grace in fact led him to an "original" and "uncharacteristically tolerant" view of Jews and Judaism.[4] James M. O'Donnell's controversial new biography goes a step further, situating the bishop's life and works in the pluralistic environment of Roman North Africa, in which Augustine's Caecilianist Christian sect struggled as an embattled religious minority—at least until it received the support of the Roman state. Augustine's story should not be understood as a defense of a normative tradition against various errors; it represents, instead, an original synthesis, articulated in creative and polemical dialogue with various "others," real and invented.[5] Though Fredriksen emphasizes Augustine's relative tolerance and O'Donnell his relative intolerance, both reveal how the question of religious pluralism is a complex and layered one, even for the interpretation of Augustine himself.[6]

This complexity and these layers become more pronounced if we shift our attention from *Augustine's theological understanding of religious others* to a *revised understanding of Augustine's own theology*, formulated in and through encounter with religious others.[7] Such a shift is what I attempt in the pages that follow, focusing on what may be, according to Peter Brown, "the most idiosyncratic and problematic aspect" of Augustine's thought: his doctrine of grace and election.[8] On the one hand, as Sullivan suggests, it is precisely the great bishop's uncompromising stand on the absolute necessity and complete sufficiency of divine grace that lies at the root of his similarly uncompromising attitude toward the various religious others—rival Christian sectarians, Manichees, Jews, and pagans—that inhabited his world. On the other hand, as I will endeavor to demonstrate, it is also one area of his thought that invites comparison with core affirmations of other religious traditions, in this case the non-dualist tradition of the eighth-century Hindu teacher, Adi Shankaracharya.[9]

Shankara, no less than Augustine, refused to view the final end of human life as something produced by finite means. Liberation, revealed in the scriptures and communicated through the grace of a teacher, follows from the intrinsic nature (*sva-bhava*) of God the divine self, not from any limited effort of the disciple to attain this same liberation. Yet Shankara also retains a paradoxical sense of human agency, embodied in the idea of the "fittingness" or "eligibility" (*adhikara*) that qualifies prospective disciples to receive the word of liberation in a fruitful way. Though there is much in Shankara's account that Augustine would certainly reject, the tension this Hindu teacher creates between strong affirmation and even stronger denial of human agency in the attainment of final liberation offers a useful framework within which to reconsider Augustine's own affirmations and denials as he attempts to work out the inscrutable and irresistible gift of God's grace.

## REVELATION OR REVOLUTION? GRACE AND ELECTION IN AUGUSTINE'S *REPLY TO SIMPLICIANUS*

Prior to undertaking a comparative inquiry, it would obviously be helpful to establish some interpretive parameters and historical context for Augustine's key convictions on grace and election. These convictions are spelled out in their clearest and most developed form in the Pelagian controversies that marked the bishop's final years. Yet, most scholars agree—and Augustine himself explicitly recognized—that the seed of this mature view can be found much earlier, in his reply to several questions posed to him by his old friend Simplicianus in 396 C.E. (*De diversis quaestionibus ad Simplicianum*; hereafter *Simpl.*).[10] In this reply, through a distinctive and original reading of Paul's letter to the Romans, Augustine came to a transformed understanding of the process by which human wills are converted to Christ. In so doing, he both recapitulated key themes of his earlier writings and initiated a new stage in his intellectual development.[11]

The striking novelty of the *Reply to Simplicianus* can be seen very clearly by glancing briefly at those earlier writings. A good representative example from the period is *On True Religion*, composed in Thagaste circa 390, between Augustine's baptism as a Christian in Milan and his ordination as a presbyter in Hippo (*De vera religione*; hereafter *vera rel.*).[12] Augustine attempts in this treatise to fuse a Platonic account of spiritual progress toward the One and the biblical revelation of the One God.[13] In the course of this synthesis, he makes a bold claim that sets the tone for all subsequent developments:

> the entire human race . . . is so arranged by the laws of divine providence that it appears divided among two classes. In one of these is the multitude of the

> impious who bear the image of the earthly person from the beginning to the end of the world. In the other is the succession of people devoted to the one God. . . . Those who read diligently can make out the divisions of the ages. They have no horror of tares and chaff. For the impious lives with the pious, and the sinner with the righteous, so that, by comparing the two, people may more eagerly rise to perfection (*vera rel.* 27.50).

Despite the intermingling of these two *genera*—pious and impious, sinful and righteous—in the present life, Augustine asserts that they can and should be distinguished. Together they constitute a social dynamic that perdures "from the beginning to the end of the world." A key question for Augustine's theology involves the process by which any given individual ends up in one *genus* rather than the other. That is, it turns on the content and event of conversion, on shedding the "image of the earthly person" and rising to a higher perfection. It is on this point that Augustine's thought undergoes a significant transformation in the 390s.

*On True Religion* nicely captures the essential elements of his early construction. In it, as we have already noted, Augustine presents Christianity as true religion and true philosophy, uniting the scriptures and the philosophical quest through their common orientation to the eternal God (*vera rel.* 1.1). Happiness consists in contemplation and love of this God; the unhappiness of the present human condition consists in turning away from the eternal toward the temporal world of the senses (3.3; 20.43).[14] Augustine gives such misplaced love a recognizable Christian label, "sin" (*peccatum*), and ascribes it to an entirely voluntary act of the individual soul (11.21–12.25). He states:

> If the defect we call sin overtook a person against his will, like a fever, the penalty which follows the sinner and is called condemnation would rightly seem to be unjust. But in fact sin is so much a voluntary evil that it is not sin at all unless it is voluntary. . . . And since there is no doubt that sins are committed, I cannot see that it can be doubted that souls have free choice in willing (*vera rel.* 14.27).

It stands to reason that one might recover happiness by a similarly voluntary turning away from the temporal back to the eternal. Conversion, then, would consist in this freely willed reorientation of one's love toward God.

The reality turns out to be more complex. Already in one of his earliest dialogues, Augustine's conversation partner Evodius had asked why, in most concrete instances, sinful desire seems to precede the exercise of the will rather than following from it.[15] In *On True Religion*, Augustine responds to such questions by proposing that sin attains this pervasive influence through "habit" (*consuetudo*).[16] Once begun, sinful preoccupation with temporal things gains the force of compulsive behavior, a kind of addiction to the senses. Progress toward God is still possible, however, for

> divine providence has so moderated our punishment that even in this corruptible body it is permitted to us to work toward righteousness, to lay aside all pride and submit to God alone, not to trust in ourselves but to commit ourselves to be ruled and defended by him alone (*vera rel.* 15.29).

Herein lies the special contribution of the Christian religion above mere philosophy. In the scriptures and particularly in the incarnation of divine Wisdom in Christ, God's providence provides therapy for this addiction, a gradual treatment to wean each individual of habitual sin (3.3–4, 16.30–32). Without God's providential therapy, the soul would remain prisoner to its own habitual sinfulness. At the same time, authentic conversion consists in the individual's voluntary response to this gracious offer and strenuous effort to achieve the life it prescribes.

After Augustine's ordination as a presbyter and then as a bishop, the synthesis achieved in *On True Religion* evolved in a dramatically new direction in the face of what Leo Ferrari has called his "final conversion" to Catholicism.[17] This transformation proceeded in several stages, beginning with a public debate with a Manichee named Fortunatus in 392, continuing through a sustained study of the letters of Paul in 394–395, and culminating in the *Confessions* and Augustine's massive refutation of Faustus the Manichee at the turn of the century.[18] The central event in this broader movement was the "radicalization" of his position on sin and grace in the *Reply to Simplicianus*.[19] In *On True Religion*, as we have already seen, Augustine commends Christians to set aside self-trust and place their hopes in God alone. In the *Reply to Simplicianus* he pushes this insight to its furthest extreme, identifying such self-abnegation as the major theme of Paul's letter to the Romans and indeed of the Christian gospel as a whole: namely, that "no person should glory in meritorious works" (*Simpl.* 1.2.2). If not "meritorious works," then what? The answer is grace alone, prior to any effort or intention on the part of the believer—including even faith itself.

Augustine's radical conclusion emerges only slowly across the pages of the first book of the *Reply to Simplicianus*. In the first question of this book, on Romans 7, Augustine consolidates many insights from his study of Paul in the previous two years, placing strong emphasis upon the crucial transition of the believer from a condition "under the law" (*sub lege*) to a condition "under grace" (*sub gratia*).[20] Gone is any trace of confidence that prospective Christians need only the proper education and example to turn to God: only the grace of Christ can imbue the human person with the proper disposition and authentic love to serve God aright (*Simpl.* 1.1.14–17). Human freedom has not been completely dissolved, for the soul still retains the freedom to initiate this process of conversion. "In this mortal life," Augustine writes, "one thing remains for free will, not that a person may fulfill righteousness when he wishes, but that he may turn with suppliant piety to him who can give the power to fulfill it" (1.1.14). Though some imagery has been changed and the scope of free will narrowed, the portrait here does not yet depart entirely from the account in *On True Religion*. God freely bestows grace, the "therapy" by which alone human beings can be set on the true path, but these same human agents retain the power to accept or reject this grace once it has been offered.[21]

In a second question, Augustine turns to Romans 9 and particularly to the image of the *massa*, or "lump of clay" of Romans 9:20–21, with more startling consequences. In Augustine's earlier work on Romans, this lump had signified the inclination to sin transmitted to one generation of humankind after another by the first sin of Adam. In another work from the mid-390s, this same *massa* is figured not merely as an earthly or carnal lump, but as a "mass of sin" (*massa peccati*) comprising all humanity, from which God by divine initiative brings forth both "vessels of mercy" like Jacob and "vessels of wrath" like Pharaoh, all according to what Augustine refers to in this work as their "deeply hidden merits."[22] In the *Reply to Simplicianus*, however, Augustine eclipses even deeply hidden merit in his description of humanity as *entirely* sinful, a *massa peccati* owing a "debt of unrighteousness" to God for Adam's sin (*Simpl*. 1.2.16–17, 1.2.20). From this "universal starting point" of the *massa* all members of the human race can will only their own damnation; only the grace of God can fashion them into true "human beings" capable of salvation (1.2.18).[23]

Augustine illustrates this process through the election of Jacob. In direct opposition to his own earlier interpretations, he states that the call of Jacob and of the other patriarchs preceded any merit on their part, including even God's foreknowledge of their faith.[24] Faith itself becomes a gift bestowed by God (1.2.7). To defend this position, Augustine offers an analysis of the human will. In previous works and even in the first question of the *Reply to Simplicianus*, as we have seen, Augustine maintained the freedom of the will to accept or refuse God's call. Here, by contrast, it is God who bestows both the object willed, in this case grace, and the very power to will itself (1.2.10). Thus God determines not only who receives the call but also who will be capable of response. Some, like Jacob, God calls "effectually" (*congruenter*), in a manner suited to their disposition and environment. Others, like Jacob's brother Esau, do not receive such an "effectual" call and thus remain in their sinful state (1.2.15).

Whereas Augustine had previously held to the freedom of the will to seek out God's grace, here it is precisely this impulse that God bestows upon the elected soul: "If those things delight us which serve our advancement towards God, that is due not to our own whim or industry or meritorious works, but to the inspiration of God and to the grace which he bestows" (1.2.21). Since human beings are moved to action only through delight in the objects they pursue, Augustine concludes, then this delight itself must find its source in God, not in human effort or inclination.[25] The central injunction of *On True Religion*—to place one's trust in God rather than ourselves—has been retained and even sharpened. Its voluntaristic portrait of *how* this takes place has, on the other hand, been completely transformed. "For the first time," writes Peter Brown, "Augustine came to see man as utterly dependent on God, even for his first initiative in believing in Him."[26]

Various reasons have been adduced for Augustine's intellectual shifts between 390 and 396. His pastoral activity as a newly consecrated bishop, particularly his campaigns against swearing and against the *laetitia* festivities in Hippo, may have darkened his estimation of the human condition.[27] As an interpreter of scripture, he was at the same time weaning himself of Origen's influence in favor of other exegetes such as Ambrosiaster and, more importantly, the Donatist theologian Tyconius.[28] James O'Donnell credits, among other factors, Augustine's "sheer pigheadedness" and a puzzling "inability to see beyond the literal sense of a few pages of his scriptural texts."[29] Paula Fredriksen gives credit, not to the letters of the apostle Paul themselves, but to the scriptures' portrait of that same Paul, inexplicably transformed by God from vicious persecutor into pious apostle.[30] Finally, in reconsidering his now classic biography, Peter Brown has recently questioned the novelty of Augustine's interpretation, depicting it instead as a fresh expression of the "religious experience of his world," with its pervasive sense of charismatic inspiration and divine empowerment.[31]

Whatever the true source of Augustine's doctrine of election and despite the ways in which it transposed and even reversed earlier positions, he did not entirely leave behind the insights of *On True Religion*. Humankind still stands divided between two *genera*, distinguished by their respective wills and desires. The difference is that this orientation by itself is no longer sufficient to explain the conversion from one to the other. As J. Patout Burns puts the matter,

> Augustine's analysis of the interaction of divine grace and human freedom rests on two principles: the natural desire for God, and the interaction of subjective dispositions with elements in the environment. The first provides the moving power for the entire process of conversion. The second allows a divine guidance of that power, a specification of human purposes and orientations.[32]

The election of the will by God does not appear as a bolt of supernatural light from on high and is not transferable from one person to another. It operates in and through the very particular and otherwise insignificant events of the elected individual's life. Augustine would later work this insight out in the account of his own life in the *Confessions*. Behind this rich personal account, however, lies the core conviction articulated clearly for the first time in the *Reply to Simplicianus*: namely, that salvation proceeds entirely from God's free gift, not from anything we ourselves have done.[33] If we speak at all of faith and decision, progress and achievement in becoming a Christian disciple, Augustine suggests, we do so only because of God's prior intervention on our behalf, actively creating those conditions within which alone such words represent anything more than the self-serving and self-deceptive babble of the reprobate.

## COMMENTARIES IN CONVERSATION: THE *MUNDAKA-UPANISAD-BHASYA* OF ADI SHANKARACHARYA

The conclusion to which Augustine found himself driven in the *Reply to Simplicianus* is, as we have already observed, stark and uncompromising. In fact, when confronted with this teaching in its mature form, some have found it positively immoral. John Rist, for example, offers the following assessment:

> It seems . . . that there is material in Augustine's thought from which he could have developed a theory that, although grace precedes works and "prepares" the will of fallen man, yet man could still accept or reject it. However, he chose not to develop this possibility and man is a puppet, free in the sense only of being arranged to act in a way which is not subject to external pressures. All men are thus "free"; the elect are free from serious sins, the damned are free from virtue. The elect are slaves of *caritas*; the damned are slaves of *cupiditas*.[34]

Other scholars demur, attempting to understand how Augustine might retain a robust phenomenological sense of human freedom even in the shadow of his insistence upon divine election. One such strategy looks backward to Augustine's earlier work on Romans for help, arguing that God's "effectual" calling need not invalidate the experience of free agency from one stage or condition of moral life to another.[35] A rather different strategy looks forward, showing how the radical conclusion of the *Reply to Simplicianus* actually translated into a strong basis for hope and assiduous striving in Augustine's sermons and later pastoral writings.[36]

In this section, we will look neither forward nor backward in Augustine's own career, but some distance to the side, turning our attention to an intellectual and religious world at considerable variance from that presumed by Augustine and his contemporaries. This foray will be quite modest, focusing on a single text and a single teaching tradition within the broad and diverse family of religious traditions which has come to be known as Hinduism.[37]

The selected text is, like the *Reply to Simplicianus*, exegetical in nature: a *bhasya* or commentary on the Mundaka Upanishad by the eighth-century Advaitin teacher Adi Shankaracharya (*Mundaka-Upanisad-Bhasya*; hereafter *Mu.U.Bh.*).[38] As its very name indicates, the Mundaka Upanishad is one of the Upanishads, a vast body of speculative literature that began to be compiled around the seventh or sixth centuries B.C.E.[39] This corpus is also called the Vedanta, or "end of the Vedas," because it serves as the fourth and final major component of the Vedic scriptures, which are, in turn, generally recognized as the most ancient and most authoritative Hindu sacred writings. For Shankara, as we shall see, the Upanishads can also be called "Vedanta" in a much more fundamental sense, because they alone facilitate the soteriological "end" toward which all the Vedas and indeed all humankind ultimately strain.

One basis for such a claim can be found in the verses of the Mundaka Upanishad itself (hereafter *Mu.U.*).[40] After a brief narrative introduction, this Upanishad sets out a sharp contrast between two different kinds of knowledge, one immeasurably inferior to the other:

> Two types of knowledge should be learned—those who know *Brahman* tell us—the higher and the lower. The lower of the two consists of the Rgveda, the Yajurveda, the Samaveda, the Arthavaveda, phonetics, the ritual science, grammar, etymology, metrics and astronomy; whereas the higher is that by which one grasps the imperishable.
>
> What cannot be seen, what cannot be grasped, without colour, without sight or hearing, without hands or feet;
> What is eternal and all-pervading, extremely minute, present everywhere—
> That is the immutable, which the wise fully perceive (*Mu.U.* 1.1.4b–6).

Later, the Upanishad will dismiss those who follow the "lower" knowledge of Vedic ritualism as "fools," "wallowing in ignorance," who perform the proper rites and rituals and who ascend to heavenly realms, only to return again to "this abject world" when their funds of meritorious work are exhausted (1.1.7–10). This account thus seems to presume some version of a theory of *karma* and the cycle of rebirth, which would become a fundamental tenet not only of Hinduism but also Buddhism and Jainism. According to such theories, all actions yield results, either in this life or in a future life. Particularly meritorious activity, such as the proper performance of Vedic ritual, can lead to highly auspicious rebirth in one or another heavenly realm.

Even as the Upanishad accepts such a worldview, however, it simultaneously negates it, at least as a final answer to life's questions. Thus, in this and subsequent verses, a sharp contrast is constructed between these "fools" who follow the lower path of ritual performance and those wise sages who follow the path of "higher knowledge" through which alone one comes to grasp "the imperishable"—omnipresent, immutable, and free of every imperfection. These latter are described in quite glowing terms, as for example in a passage much further along in the text:

> The seers, sated with knowledge, when they have attained [the self], become free from passion and tranquil, and their selves are made perfect.
>
> The wise, their selves controlled, when they attain him altogether, he who is present in All, they enter into that very All.
>
> The ascetics who have firmly determined their goal through a full knowledge of the Vedanta, have their being purified by the discipline of renunciation.
>
> In the worlds of *Brahman*, at the time of the final end, having become fully immortal, they will all be fully liberated (3.2.5–6).

There is a goal higher than any temporary stay in a heavenly home. There is *moksa*: final liberation, absolute freedom from this interminable cycle of births and deaths, eternal happiness, immortality. Such freedom cannot be achieved by ritual or the so-called lower knowledge, according to the authors of this Upanishad. Only the higher knowledge will suffice for this.

Though these few, somewhat cryptic verses do not nearly exhaust the varied imagery and teachings of the Mundaka Upanishad, they do offer a glimpse of its basic message. The highest end of human life, described here in terms of immortality and liberation, is not something attainable through ritual practice or worldly achievement; such a lofty goal accrues, instead, to a small group of ascetics, tranquil and self-controlled. These sages, having purified themselves through renunciation, austerity, and knowledge, enter into "that very All"—a reality identified alternately as the authentic, innermost self, *Atman*, and as the ultimate world-source that pervades and undergirds all creation, *Brahman*. "When a person comes to know that *Brahman*," the Upanishad asserts in one of its concluding verses, "he himself becomes that very *Brahman*. . . . He passes beyond sorrow, he passes beyond evil. Freed from the knots of his heart, he will become immortal" (3.2.9). Knowledge of *Brahman* and final liberation are thus drawn into a close, inextricable relation: to know *Brahman* rightly, the Upanishad suggests, is to enter into the divine existence of that same *Brahman*, beyond the constraints of sorrow, evil, birth, and death.

The exact nature of the relationship between knowledge and liberation would eventually become a matter of some controversy in Hindu tradition, as rival teaching lineages waged a battle of interpretation over the true path to *moksa*.[41] Is knowledge an accessory to the right kind of privileged action—whether this be seen as ritual performance, meditative practice or whole-hearted devotion to the true God? Does such knowledge or action culminate in some new experience of mystical union? The Advaita tradition of Adi Shankaracharya offers perhaps the simplest possible response to such questions, if also one many critics vehemently reject and some later interpreters subtly distort.[42] For Shankara advanced the claim that knowledge and liberation are not sequential at all, with one serving as a step on the way to the other. On the contrary: in the case of the liberating knowledge of *Brahman*, they are flip sides of the same coin. Truly to know the self, *Atman*, and to know the divine Being, *Brahman*, is to know oneself as this very *Brahman*, here and now. Since *Brahman* is not now nor has ever been bound by the cycle of rebirth or any limitation whatsoever, liberation consists of this simple realization.[43] The only obstacle, according to Shankara and the Advaita tradition as a whole, is *avidya*, ignorance of what is already and always the truth of one's own self.

Shankara's radical conclusion about the ultimate non-duality (*advaita*) of *Atman* and *Brahman* runs as a consistent thread throughout his authentic writings.[44] It also both arises from and significantly influences his interpretation of the Upanishads, which he considered the sole authentic means of attaining this liberating truth.[45] Hence, when commenting on how the "knot of the heart" becomes untied in Mundaka Upanishad 2.2.8, Shankara sees in this passage a précis of the essential Advaita message:

> "The knot of the heart is cut asunder". . . . The meaning is that he who perceives the Omnipotent One which is free from the cycle of rebirth, which is both "high" in its capacity as the cause [of all created reality] and [which is] "low" as the effect [i.e., created reality itself] and realizes It as "I truly am this," becomes liberated due to the destruction of the cause of the cycle of rebirth (*Mu.U.Bh.* 2.2.8).

Later, after recounting the many stages and births through which the realized sage proceeds to achieve this knowledge, Shankara places the following words in his mouth:

> "I am this, the self (*Atman*), the same in all and abiding in all beings, and not the other—the merely apparent self—conditioned by limitations arising from ignorance. Whatever glory in the nature of the universe is attached to Him alone, belongs to me who am in essence the supreme Lord" (*Mu.U.Bh.* 3.1.2).

When, finally, the Mundaka Upanishad pronounces that those with knowledge of *Brahman* become this same *Brahman*, Shankara does not interpret this in terms of physical transformation or even mystical ascent. He sees in it merely the removal of error and establishment of the truth that "I am *Brahman*," here and now, with nowhere to go and nothing left to achieve (*Mu.U.Bh.* 3.2.8–9). For this reason, not a few modern scholars have identified in Shankara's teaching a kind of "illusionistic monism," reducing the entire phenomenal order to a mere stage show projected by a single cosmic consciousness.[46]

To the degree that such interpretations ring true, they would seem to take us some distance from Augustine, from the *Reply to Simplicianus*, and especially from any sense of grace or divine election.[47] For our present purposes, however, we can observe that Shankara's understanding of final liberation does not stem primarily from a desire to construct one or another metaphysical system. It arises from his distinctive interpretation of the Vedic scriptures, as well as a strong conviction that, if final liberation is truly eternal, it cannot be something that is produced through ritual practice, ethical striving, or finite action of any kind.

A good illustration of this interpretive principle at work can be found in Shankara's account of Mundaka Upanishad 1.2.12. The original verse reads:

> When he perceives the worlds as built with rites, a Brahmin should acquire a sense of disgust—"what's made can't make what is unmade!"
>
> To understand it he must go, firewood in hand, to a teacher well versed in the Vedas, and focused on *Brahman* (*Mu.U.* 1.2.12).

True to his typical pattern, Shankara takes up each phrase of this verse in turn, expanding upon the characteristics of the authorized teacher, glossing the "disgust" (*nirveda*) of the Upanishad as "detachment" from or "renunciation" of the fruits of action (*vairagya*), and—presumably to foster precisely such detachment—dismissing the "worlds" achievable through ritual performance and indeed the entire cycle of rebirth as "filled with evils" and "impelled by evils such as ignorance and desire" (*Mu.U.Bh.* 1.2.12).

According to the great teacher, however, the central affirmation of the passage is the disciple's exclamation, "What's made can't make what is unmade!" Shankara offers an instructive paraphrase:

> Here in this cycle of rebirth there is nothing which is not a product [of action]. All the worlds indeed result from *karma* and are impermanent, since *karma* constitutes them. . . . But I yearn for something eternal, immortal, fearless, unchanging, unmoving and constant, and not its opposite. What then is the need to perform action, which requires much exertion and yields [only further] evil? (Ibid.).

The problem with ritual activity, this disciple realizes, is not that such rituals fail to achieve their intended results; it is, instead, that whatever results they achieve—precisely as "results"—necessarily fall short of the highest goal. They must therefore be left behind, at least as means to final liberation. Later Shankara will describe this transformation as a kind of conversion, with the prospective disciples "discontinuing" or "turning away from" (*ni-vrt*) a life of action and ritual performance, and taking up the "path of *moksa*" in its place (*Mu.U.Bh.* 2.2.6).

At first glance, this is very dry material for a conversion narrative. There are no dramatic garden scenes, no mysterious voices, no persecutors who become pious apostles. There is merely the calm conviction that any product of human exertion, no matter how noble the intention or faithful the performance, is by its very nature incapable of bringing about an eternal, saving result. Shankara explains this idea further in his comment on Mundaka Upanishad 3.2.6, a verse we have already encountered above. He writes:

> Any course dependent on the limitations of space and accomplished by limited means is within the pale of the cycle of rebirth. But, since *Brahman* constitutes the All, It is not to be reached through the limitations of space. If *Brahman* is [to be treated as] bound by spatial limitation, as in the case of a concrete object, then It will have a beginning and an end, will be dependent upon something else, will have parts, and will be impermanent and created. But *Brahman* cannot be any of these. Therefore Its attainment, too, cannot be bound by spatial limitation. Moreover, the knowers of *Brahman* are desirous of only such liberation as will lead to freedom from worldly bondage consisting in ignorance and the like, but not in anything that is the product of action (*Mu.U.Bh.* 3.2.6).

At issue here is the radical asymmetry between the divine Reality and those finite realities that dominate life in the here and hereafter.[48] Since *Brahman* lies, as it were, outside the entire worldly cycle of death and rebirth, action and achievement, nothing within this system can be properly said to "jump the tracks" and reach *Brahman*. There is no middle ground. Indeed, the realm of *avidya*, primordial ignorance, is no less pervasive and pernicious for Shankara than the *massa peccati* in Augustine's *Reply to Simplicianus*. It constrains, limits, and ultimately reduces all human striving to naught, including even our striving toward God.

So, we might ask, how is liberation possible at all? Only, Shankara reasons, if what we call "liberation" is really an eternal and ever-accomplished reality, against which our experiences of bondage represent a kind of anomaly to what is the more basic and enduring truth. Final liberation is not something which can be achieved in any conventional sense of that term. It can only be known, and such knowing necessarily *is* its own reward—it is, in fact, nothing less than liberation itself.

This is not an affirmation with which we would expect to discover agreement from a Christian bishop like Augustine of Hippo. It may nevertheless, and paradoxically, have something to offer an Augustinian theology of grace and election.

## THE SELF-REVEALING SELF: POSSIBLE ADVAITA READINGS OF DIVINE ELECTION

Toward the end of his life, looking back on the *Reply to Simplicianus*, Augustine summarized his essential insight as follows:

> The second question [of the first book] concerns Romans 9:10–29. In answering this question I have tried hard to maintain the free choice of the human will, but the grace of God prevailed. Not otherwise could I reach the understanding that the apostle spoke with absolute truth when he said, "Who made thee to differ? What hast thou that thou didst not receive? But if thou didst receive it, why dost thou glory as if thou didst not receive it?" This truth Cyprian the martyr too wanted to make clear, and he expressed it completely in a phrase, "In nothing must we glory since nothing is ours."[49]

Now, having touched on a few major themes of Shankara's *Mundaka-Upanisad-Bhasya*, we might read Augustine's summary along with the Hindu disciple's exclamation in Mundaka Upanishad 1.2.12: "What's made can't make what's unmade!" No work of any kind can properly be said to achieve eternal salvation. Such an achievement can only be ascribed to God. Though Augustine and Shankara differ rather profoundly about the nature of this God and many other matters, they seem to agree on at least one point: the final end of human life is not, as such or at any level, a human product. It cannot become a cause for personal glorification, but should result instead in a sustained discipline of self-abnegation, continually placing one's hope and trust beyond whatever one could construe in terms of personal accomplishment. True freedom can only be received or recognized, never achieved.

But neither Augustine nor Shankara stops with this single, shared affirmation. Augustine, as we have seen, goes on in his *Reply to Simplicianus* to elaborate distinctive understandings of the *massa peccati*, effectual calling, and the inscrutable justice of God. What analogues do such ideas have in Shankara's thought? In what ways might something like divine election be discerned in the teaching of Advaita? We turn to three possibilities, each of which adds nuance, both to Shankara's own interpretation of liberation in the Mundaka Upanishad, and to the ways in which we might read Augustine differently in light of this account.

### Grace as *Karma-phala* and *Adhikara*

One Sanskrit word often translated into English as "grace" is *anugraha*, a term which conveys a sense of personal favor, support, or acceptance. Interestingly, this term arises in the *Mundaka-Upanisad-Bhasya* in the course of a discussion, not of liberation per se, but rather of the results of ritual activity—that is, *karma-phala*, the "fruit" or "result" of action. Thus, in explaining how incorrect ritual performance can invalidate the benefits that would normally result from a householder's daily fire sacrifice, Shankara describes these same benefits as "the grace (*anugraha*) accruing from the offering of the lump of food and the like" (*Mu.U.Bh. 1.2.3*).

This passing remark nicely highlights how, though Shankara invalidates human merit as a direct means to liberation, he nevertheless maintains a highly realistic theology of *karma* when discussing worldly matters and even gives *karma-phala* an important preliminary role in shaping those rare individuals with the requisite "fitness" or "eligibility" (*adhikara*) to receive the Advaita teaching.[50] Indeed, he offers several fairly specific narratives of the course followed by the soul on the way to liberating self-knowledge. In order to become fit to receive this knowledge, Shankara writes in one place, such a soul first

> takes birth in the womb of ghost, beast, women and the like in succession and, after so many births perhaps, owing to the accumulation of the effect of virtuous deeds, he might be shown the path of yoga by some extremely compassionate teacher, on his becoming possessed of non-violence, truthfulness, continence, renunciation of everything, control of nature internal and external, and concentration (*Mu.U.Bh.* 3.1.2).

Elsewhere Shankara will expand on the list of characteristics conducive to self-knowledge, including not only virtuous practices such as self-control, equanimity, and truthfulness—alluded to here—but also detachment (*vairagya*), a discriminating intellect (*viveka*), and above all an ardent desire for freedom from the endless cycle of rebirth (*mumuksutva*).[51] Even birth as a male member of the Brahmin caste is singled out as a position of particular "fitness" (*adhikara*) to renounce worldly life in pursuit of liberation (*Mu.U.Bh* 1.2.12).[52] Such an auspicious birth, as well as the personal discipline and renunciant lifestyle that ideally go with it, is attributed to *karma-phala* as the result of virtuous actions in this or past lives and thus also, by extension, to the workings of what Shankara does not hesitate to call "grace" (*anugraha*).

Some modern interpreters, including not a few Advaitins, balk at simply identifying *adhikara* with particular castes and states of life, and rightly so.[53] Nevertheless, Shankara's insistence on such specifics reveals something of the idea's richness and complexity. Reading *adhikara* literally as "eminence" or "eligibility," for example, associates it closely with the consequences of past actions, such as personal qualities acquired in this life or a good birth acquired from past lives. Reading it with other terms sometimes used in similar contexts—such as *yogyata*, from the root *yuj*, "to join," or *samarthya*, "sameness of significance, nature, or orientation"—nuances the idea quite differently. Indeed, the contemporary Advaitin Anantanand

Rambachan suggests an approach that de-emphasizes the idiom of achievement in favor of the language of relation and conformation:

> If *brahmajnana* [i.e., knowledge of *Brahman*] is to be meaningfully and successfully attained, it is imperative that the mind enjoys a certain disposition. If the *atman* to be known is all peace and fullness, such a knowledge cannot occur in a mind which is in perpetual agitation and which entertains countless desires. . . . The significance of *brahmajnana* will [similarly] be lost to one who has not risen above the yearning and pursuit after limited ends. It is vital here, therefore, that the receptacle of knowledge *relatively conform* to the nature of the object which it seeks to know.[54]

Such a notion of *adhikara* as "relative conformity" nicely intersects with Augustine's notion of being called *congruenter*, usually translated "effectually" but more literally rendered as "suitably," "fittingly," or even "conformably." From one point of view, both *adhikara* and *congruens* speak to a coincidence or harmony of seeker and sought, lover and beloved, eternal divine Reality and the concrete personal and social conditions through which this Reality becomes an object of authentic desire.

Notwithstanding such parallels, according to Shankara this "relative conformity" to *Brahman* still arises through actions performed in this and past lives. Precisely as *karma-phala*, *adhikara* necessarily retains an element of what Augustine might have called, prior to his *Reply to Simplicianus*, "deeply hidden merit." In the experience of the Advaitin disciple, to be sure, such "election" will always retain an element of mystery, since the present life represents the culmination of innumerable past lives that—at least ordinarily—remain beyond the reach of memory. No one can say precisely what merits led to the present favorable conditions. This does not, however, render them into something other than merit . . . thus sharply qualifying *adhikara* as a final answer to the question of grace and election.

## Grace as Grace

Given these considerations, it may come as no surprise that the great Advaitin teacher also has recourse to a rather different understanding of grace under a different Sanskrit term. Highlighting the contrast between lower and higher knowledge in his introduction to the *Mundaka-Upanisad-Bhasya*, Shankara isolates "renunciation of everything of the nature of means and ends" and "the grace of the teacher" (*guru-prasada*) as, together, part and parcel of the pursuit of the higher knowledge (*Mu.U.Bh.* 1.0.0). *Prasada* can, like *anugraha*, be translated as "favor," "kindness," or even "free gift"; unlike *anugraha*, it also carries a sense of tranquility and calmness. So when Shankara speaks of "grace" in this passage, he may be drawing attention to aspects of the teacher's disposition, including equanimity, detachment, and compassion (see *Mu.U.Bh.* 1.2.12–13). Nevertheless, he also clearly indicates that liberation comes to the seeker, not as something achieved through means and ends but as a free gift.

Elsewhere, Shankara will extend this sense of the sheer gratuity of self-knowledge beyond the individual teacher to the scriptures, to the Advaita teaching tradition as a whole, and to the divine initiator of this same tradition—that is, to the Lord, described in such contexts in a highly personalistic idiom.[55] Perhaps no one has explored this aspect of Shankara's teaching more thoroughly than Bradley Malkovsky.[56] Surveying a broad range of allusions to grace, under various Sanskrit terms and across all of Shankara's authentic writings, Malkovsky identifies three major thematic clusters.[57] One of these, the bestowal of extraordinary powers by the Lord, need not detain us here. A second cluster corresponds closely to our discussion of *karma-phala* and *adhikara* earlier, for Shankara describes the just fulfillment of *karma* and maintenance of the cycle of rebirth in terms of the Lord's gracious response to human striving. "[I]n regard to the law of *karma*," Malkovsky argues, "Samkara teaches that in responding to the soul's actions the Lord dispenses the results of those actions not only according to merit, but also according to grace (*anugraha*)."[58] The cycle is not purely mechanical, then, and it does not constrain the freedom of the Lord. From one point of view, the cycle might be seen as a privileged means by which the Lord communicates divine justice and grace.

We will return to this idea later. For the moment, we should take note of a third cluster identified in Malkovsky's study: namely, Shankara's identification of grace itself as a means—indeed, the privileged means—of liberation. Malkovsky writes:

> How do we attain this experience of God as our true Self? Samkara's answer is that we have to eliminate all the false notions we have about ourselves and God. We need to hear, reflect on and interiorize the truth of scripture about these matters until complete conviction opens us in total receptiveness to the dawning of the truth from within. . . . We must have an insatiable desire to know *brahman*. We need to cultivate virtues and habits conducive to liberation, such as compassion toward others, fortitude, concentration, faith, renunciation of earthly pleasure and prestige. And, he says, we require divine grace.[59]

Just as, in his introduction to the *Mundaka-Upanisad-Bhasya*, Shankara identifies personal renunciation and the grace of the teacher as the two privileged means of liberation, so also here Malkovsky generalizes Shankara's thought to portray a broader cooperation of human effort and divine grace.[60] The grace of the Lord in granting final illumination is, it seems, what rushes in to meet the seeker after and in response to a long journey of assiduous self-cultivation.

On what *basis* would such grace be offered? One option, as we have already seen, involves *adhikara* and the fruit of innumerable past lives, which coalesce to produce the auspicious social conditions and personal characteristics conducive to self-knowledge. A second option, offered by Augustine in the *Reply to Simplicianus*, resolves the question by appealing to the "hidden equity" of God, who chooses some few from the *massa* to fashion into true human beings, capable of hearing the word of the gospel to good effect. Though Shankara places much stronger emphasis upon *adhikara*, some notion of "hidden equity" does find an echo in his thought. In another commentary, for example, he will insist that God "has independence in the matter of favouring or disfavouring all, since He is the Lord of all."[61] At the proper moments and in the proper contexts—and despite his repeated affirmation of the ultimate non-difference of self, world and God—Shankara is not averse to attributing the grace of liberation to the sovereign will of the Lord.

Neither of these two positions, however, seems to get to the heart of Shankara's teaching on this matter. To find a more secure interpretation, we will need to shift ground a bit, looking beyond explicit parallels to the inherent, gratuitous nature of liberation itself.

## Grace as *Atma-Sva-Bhava*

It is possible that the most profound meditation on divine election in the *Mundaka-Upanisad-Bhasya* arises in a place where Shankara conspicuously fails to invoke the Lord's grace at all. The Upanishadic passage which provokes this important reflection reads as follows:

> This self [*Atman*] cannot be grasped, by teachings or by intelligence, or even by great learning.
>
> Only the one [whom the *Atman*] chooses can grasp him, [the one] whose body this self chooses as his own (*Mu.U.* 3.2.3).

This famous verse, which so strongly emphasizes the freedom of *Atman* in making itself known, also appears verbatim in the Katha Upanishad. Commenting on the verse in that context, Shankara merely points out that the *Atman* comes to be known "by its own accord" —that is, presumably, not by any external constraint or finite means.[62] This minimalist interpretation leaves open the possibility of a strong doctrine of grace, as seems to be implied by the repetition of the verbal root *vr*, "to select" or "to choose," in the verse itself.[63]

Interestingly, in his comment on the same verse in the Mundaka Upanishad, Shankara shades its interpretation in exactly the opposite direction.[64] After duly noting that the Upanishad effectively removes precisely those means normally associated with the pursuit of liberation in the Advaita tradition—study of the Vedas and other scriptures, hearing the teaching and remembering it—Shankara poses the rhetorical question: "By what means then can [the *Atman*] be attained?" He answers:

> That supreme Self [*Atman*] itself which the learned one wishes to attain, by virtue of that seeking is this supreme Self attained, but not by any other means, for by nature it is ever attained.
>
> How does the realization of the Self of the learned one occur? Explanation follows: To him alone the Self reveals its own supreme form, Its true nature that was veiled by ignorance. Just as a pot and the like become manifest in light, so also the Self becomes revealed by knowledge. Therefore, aspiration after Self-realization with the abandonment of everything else alone constitutes the means of attainment of the Self. This is the meaning (*Mu.U.Bh.* 3.2.3).

In this comment Shankara appears to place his strongest emphasis, not upon divine election, but upon the appropriate kind of desire, striving, or aspiration on the part of the seeker. This authentic desire for liberation, accompanied by the renunciation of all other competing desires, alone properly constitutes the means of liberating self-knowledge.

Further on, following the lead of the Upanishad, Shankara returns to the question of *adhikara*, spelling out those personal characteristics and that state of life consonant with this rightly ordered desire (*Mu.U.Bh.* 3.2.4)—and thus directing readers' attention back to the realm of human striving. In this sense, his conclusion seems to stand in stark contrast with Augustine's doctrine of unmerited grace and even a plain sense reading of the verse itself. If there is no active willing on the part of the supreme *Atman*, no selection of some aspirants rather than others for the gift of liberation, then we cannot reasonably speak of election. Can we?

The answer, as we might expect, turns out to be both no and yes—and both at the same time, for Shankara has completely transposed the terms of the conversation. The issue turns here, as in Augustine's *Reply to Simplicianus*, upon a distinctive understanding of will and desire. How, we might ask, can desire be said to bring about final liberation? For Augustine, as we have seen, this follows from the fact that the right kind of delight is itself a gift of God, who meets the elected soul "conformably" in and through the particular circumstances of one's life. For Shankara, by contrast, the central importance of desire follows from the more fundamental reality of *Atman* itself, which can be described as "ever-attained" by its "own nature" (*sva-bhava*). As the very nature of the divine Self is *to be known*, in other words, it *comes to be known* entirely of its own accord. Hence the mere desire for this knowledge can also be called, analogously, the sole means for its attainment.

In order to illustrate this point, Shankara invokes the imagery of light. Light makes objects like clay pots known, not through any sequence of activities or accomplishments, but by virtue of its mere presence. Where there is light, Shankara observes, there we see the pot, pure and simple. Elsewhere in the commentary, he draws a further analogy to the sun: just as the sun illumines the earth without needing itself to be illumined, so also the divine Self—which is also the self of each and every conscious being—is the radiant Illuminator at the base of all possible experience, that by which we know worldly objects without itself becoming yet another such object (*Mu.U.Bh.* 2.2.7–9). Like the sun, *Atman* is self-evident and self-revealing.[65]

Since this self-revealing *Atman* is none other than *Brahman* in Shankara's teaching, some contemporary interpreters have pressed this insight further. They show how *Atman* becomes manifest, not merely in the consciousness of the individual knower, but even in the unfolding of creation itself. The entire created order, including scriptures, teacher and every worldly accomplishment, can be seen as both problem and pedagogy on the path to liberation, both the result of ignorance and the privileged means by which this ignorance is ultimately overcome.[66] We might even conclude that the *adhikara* of the seeker, and especially the desire that becomes the sole means of self-knowledge, can also be traced to this same *Atman*, the divine Lord who graciously governs the cycles of *karma* and rebirth.[67] Seeker and sought find their ultimate coherence, not in any achievement of tranquility, austerity or even desire in and of themselves, but in the all-pervasive, divine reality of the self-revealing Self.

This idea, as such, would seem to have no direct parallel in Augustine's thought. Nevertheless, an understanding of the *Atma-sva-bhava*—that is, the intrinsic nature of God the divine Self—as liberating self-communication offers a distinctive spin on the very notion of divine election. For Shankara, such "election" is not something which God *does*; it is something which God *is*, by God's own nature. God *is* the eternal electing that grounds all achievement, all seeking and all desire without itself becoming their product. Knowing this, the Advaitin disciple becomes liberated, here and now, with no further need of action and nothing further to accomplish.

Indeed, such a disciple might, with Augustine, find herself echoing the words of Cyprian: "In nothing must we glory since nothing is ours."

## CONCLUSION:
## A RICH(ER) AUGUSTINIAN THEOLOGY OF ELECTION

Having successively examined Augustine's revolutionary reading of Paul in the *Reply to Simplicianus*, Shankara's reading of the Mundaka Upanishad, and some possible correlations to divine election in this commentary and the broader Advaita teaching, we are left with at least one looming question: how might this foray into Advaita Vedanta shade or transform our reading of the great bishop of Hippo? Though neither can be fully developed in this essay, we can at least suggest two possibilities.

First of all, reading Augustine together with a Hindu interlocutor like Adi Shankaracharya reveals something of the central importance of his core insights about grace and election. If we tried to imagine that a work like *On True Religion* or Augustine's earlier commentaries on Romans somehow fell into Shankara's hands, it seems likely that the Hindu teacher would, no less than the Christian bishop, find the insistence upon free will and progress on the way to God in such works unsatisfying. Shankara's reasons for such dissatisfaction would, of course, stem from his distinctively Advaita teaching on the non-duality of *Atman* and *Brahman* and the attainment of liberation through self-knowledge. Yet, in and through this very teaching, he would also echo key elements of Augustine's later construction: that it is, above all, the right desire which disposes the seeker to receive liberation; that there is a basic congruence or conformity between this disposition and the divine fulfillment to which it aspires; that liberation does not proceed from any human achievement at all, but solely from the divine Self. Like Augustine, Shankara insists upon what one Augustinian scholar has called "ontological passivity": firm acceptance even in the midst of vigorous moral and religious striving that no such striving can ever properly be said to accomplish the salvation one seeks.[68]

Whatever contribution an Augustinian theology of grace and election might receive from Shankara's comparable reflections on grace and the self-revelation of *Atman*, it would not entail any diminishment of this core insight. In fact, if anything, it would radicalize the insight, pressing the Augustinian interpreter to speak of election less in terms of God's choice, more in terms of God's own nature as the One who freely and eternally chooses so to give.

This leads to our second observation, for behind all of the historical circumstances and exegetical problems that contributed to Augustine's theology of election lay his ever-deepening revelation of a God who reaches to human beings so far beyond our own capabilities that no human act—even faith—could be allowed to detract from the gratuity of the gift. At one level, of course, each human life invariably proceeds through striving and accomplishment, and the elect are none other than those whose life brings them to the requisite eligibility or "relative conformity" (*adhikara*) to receive God's gift aright. At another level and from a higher point of view, however, it is all grace, from beginning to end. In his own career, especially through his later controversies with the Pelagians, Augustine developed his core insight in one particular, exclusivist direction. But the development of the insight is not identical with the insight itself. If subsequent generations of Christians find themselves reflecting more deeply on the fact that the God revealed in Jesus the Christ is a God of infinite grace or even, echoing Shankara, that God's own nature (*sva-bhava*) *is* nothing other than grace and election, then quite different developments could emerge from the same fundamental insight. For the Christian theologian, such a broader and deeper application of Augustine's revelation in the *Reply to Simplicianus* will stand or fall on the employment of traditional Christian sources.[69] Yet, Shankara and other voices from outside the Christian fold may serve as useful dialogue partners for refining these insights and engaging in their creative reinterpretation.

If theologians of any stripe take up this task mindful of Shankara and Augustine, of course, we will need to make one further affirmation: namely, that the highest end of human life far transcends even the most creative such reinterpretations and will never be reached by them. All our efforts will ultimately amount to nothing, and for this—according to Hindu teacher and Christian bishop alike—we should greatly rejoice.[70]

## NOTES

1. F. A. Sullivan, *Salvation outside the Church? Tracing the History of the Catholic Response* (New York/Mahwah: Paulist Press, 1992).
2. Ibid., 37–38.
3. See ibid., 40–42 and passim.
4. P. Fredriksen, "*Excaecati Occulta Justitia Dei:* Augustine on Jews and Judaism," *Journal of Early Christian Studies* 3 (1995) 299–324. Cf. P. Fredriksen, "*Secundum Carnem:* History and Israel in the Theology of St. Augustine," in *The Limits of Ancient Christianity: Essays on Late Antique Thought and Culture in Honor of R.A. Markus*, ed. W. E. Klingshirn and M. Vessey (Ann Arbor: University of Michigan Press, 1999) 26–41; and M. Dubois, "Jews, Judaism, and Israel in the Theology of Saint Augustine: How He Links the Jewish People and the Land of Zion," *Immanuel* 22/23 (1989) 162–214.
5. J. J. O'Donnell, *Augustine, Sinner and Saint: A New Biography* (London: Profile Books, 2005), esp. 171–243. On Augustine's creative encounter with Roman society and paganism, also see R. A. Markus, *Saeculum: History and Society in the Theology of St. Augustine*, rev. ed. (Cambridge: Cambridge University Press, 1988); and J. M. Rist, *Augustine: Ancient Thought Baptized* (Cambridge: Cambridge University Press, 1994).
6. Peter Brown highlights the importance of contemporary discoveries and scholarship that illumine Augustine's religious world in the new epilogue to his classic study, *Augustine of Hippo: A Biography*, rev. ed. (London: Faber and Faber, 1967, 2000), esp. 484–87.
7. This shift can also be described more generally as a movement from a question of the "theology of religions" to a question of "comparative theology." Helpful introductions to comparative theology as a contemporary discipline include: F.

X. Clooney, S.J., "Comparative Theology: A Review of Recent Books (1989–1995)," *Theological Studies* 56 (1995): 521–50; Stephen J. Duffy, "A Theology of the Religions and/or a Comparative Theology?" *Horizons* 26 (1999): 105–15; and K. Ward, *Religion and Revelation: A Theology of Revelation in the World's Religions* (Oxford: Clarendon Press, 1994), esp. 3–49. The argument on behalf of comparative theology as distinct from theology of religions has been made particularly forcefully in two recent works by J. L. Fredericks: *Faith among Faiths: Christian Theology and Non-Christian Religions* (New York/Mahwah: Paulist Press, 1999) and *Buddhists and Christians: Through Comparative Theology to Solidarity* (Maryknoll: Orbis Books, 2004).

8. Brown, *Augustine of Hippo*, 506.

9. This is not the first time that Augustine and Shankara have been read comparatively. Previous attempts include: V. E. Devadutt, "Augustine and Sankara on Time," *Indian Journal of Theology* 33 (1984): 24–34; and Reid B. Locklin, "Sankara, Augustine, and *Rites de Passage*: Comparative Theology with Victor Turner," in *Theology and the Social Sciences*, ed. Michael Horace Barnes, Annual Publication of the College Theology Society 46 (Maryknoll: Orbis Books, 2001), 135–60; as well as the broader comparative treatments in Ben-Ami Scharfstein, "'Cogito Ergo Sum': Descartes, Augustine, and Sankara," in *Philosophy East/Philosophy West: A Critical Comparison of Indian, Chinese, Islamic, and European Philosophy*, by Ben-Ami Scharfstein, Illai Alon, Shlomo Biderman, Dan Daor, and Yoel Hoffmann (New York: Oxford University Press, 1978), 199–217; and Holmes Rolston III, *Religious Inquiry—Participation and Detachment* (New York: Philosophical Library, 1985).

10. Hereafter cited in the body of the essay. The Latin text of *Simpl.* Book 1 is available in CCSL 44 (1970), 4–56; I have followed, with some modifications, the English translation by J. H. S. Burleigh in *Augustine: Earlier Writings*, The Library of Christian Classics (Philadelphia: Westminster Press, 1953), 370–406. On the relation between the *Reply to Simplicianus* and the later Pelagian controversies, see Paula Fredriksen, "Beyond the Body/Soul Dichotomy: Augustine on Paul against the Manichees and the Pelagians," *Recherches Augustiniennes* 23 (1988): 89–105; James Wetzel, "Pelagius Anticipated: Grace and Election in Augustine's *Ad Simplicianum*," in *Augustine: From Rhetor to Theologian*, ed. Joanne McWilliam (Waterloo: Wilfred Laurier University Press, 1992), 121–32; and James Wetzel, "Predestination, Pelagianism, and Foreknowledge," in *The Cambridge Companion to Augustine*, ed. Eleonore Stump and Norman Kretzmann (Cambridge: Cambridge University Press, 2001), 49–58.

11. For helpful accounts of this early development, see F. Edward Cranz, "The Development of Augustine's Ideas on Society before the Donatist Controversy," *Harvard Theological Review* 14 (1954): 255–316, reprinted in *Augustine: A Collection of Critical Essays*, ed. R. A. Markus (Garden City: Anchor Books, 1972), 336–403; Joanne McWilliam Dewart, "Augustine's Developing Use of the Cross: 387–400," *Augustinian Studies* 15 (1984): 15–33; and Fredriksen, "Body/Soul Dichotomy," 89–105.

12. Hereafter cited in the body of the essay. The Latin text of *vera rel.* is available in CCSL 32 (1962), 187–260; I have used, with some modifications, the English translation in Burleigh, *Earlier Writings*, 222–83.

13. See Josef Lössl, "The One (*unum*)—A Guiding Concept in *De uera religione*: An Outline of the Text and the History of Its Interpretation," *Revue des Études Augustiniennes* 40 (1994): 79–103.

14. Cf. Cranz, "Development of Augustine's Ideas," 263–65; and Eugene TeSelle, *Augustine the Theologian* (New York: Herder and Herder, 1970), 67–73.

15. *De libero arbitrio* 1.11.23–12.24. Latin text in CCSL 29 (1970), 226–27; English translation in Burleigh, *Earlier Writings,* 126–27.

16. See *vera rel.* 3.3, 4.6, 34.64–35.65, 46.88, and John G. Prendiville, S.J., "The Development of the Idea of Habit in the Thought of Saint Augustine," *Traditio* 28 (1972): 29–99, esp. 31–45.

17. Leo C. Ferrari, *The Conversions of Saint Augustine* (Villanova: Villanova University Press, 1984), esp. 74–77.

18. In addition to the sources listed in note 11, see also TeSelle, *Augustine the Theologian*, 156–82; William S. Babcock, "Augustine's Interpretation of Romans (A.D. 394-396)," *Augustinian Studies* 10 (1979): 55–74; and C.P. Bammel, "Pauline Exegesis, Manichaeism and Philosophy in the Early Augustine," in *Christian Faith and Greek Philosophy in Late Antiquity: Essays in Tribute to George Christopher Stead*, ed. Lionel R. Wickham and Caroline P. Bammel (Leiden, New York, and Köln: E.J. Brill, 1993), 1–25.

19. Cranz, "Development of Augustine's Ideas," 281–82.

20. In his earlier *Propositions* on Romans, Augustine in fact proposed a four-stage schema: 1) "before the law" (*ante legem*); 2) "under the law" (*sub lege*); 3) "under grace" (*sub gratia*); and 4) "in peace" (*in pace*). See the Latin text and English translation in Paula Fredriksen Landes, trans., *Augustine on Romans: Propositions from the Epistle to the Romans, Unfinished Commentary on the Epistle to the Romans* (Chico: Scholars Press, 1982), esp. 4–7, as well as the discussion in Babcock, "Augustine's Interpretation of Romans," 58–61, and TeSelle, *Augustine the Theologian,* 156–65.

21. See TeSelle, *Augustine the Theologian*, 178.

22. *De diversis quaestionibus octoginta tribus* 68.3–4. Latin text in CCSL 44A (1975), 177–80; English translation in David L. Mosher, trans., *Saint Augustine: Eighty Three Different Questions*, Fathers of the Church 70 (Washington, D.C.: Catholic University of America Press, 1982), 160–63. For a more detailed account of the transformation of the *massa* in the early commentaries on Romans, in *div. qu.*, and in the final book of *lib. arb.*, see Fredriksen, "Body/Soul Dichotomy," 93–96.

23. Cranz, "Development of Augustine's Ideas," 263.

24. See Babcock, "Augustine's Interpretation," 65–67; and J. Patout Burns, *The Development of Augustine's Doctrine of Operative Grace* (Paris: Études Augustiniennes, 1980), 38–42.

25. On Augustine's psychology of delight and will, see especially Brown, *Augustine of Hippo*, 148–49.

26. Brown, *Augustine of Hippo*, 148.

27. See Prendiville, "Development of the Idea of Habit," 61–63; Brown, *Augustine of Hippo*, 189–202; F. van der Meer, *Augustine the Bishop: the Life and Work of a Father of the Church*, trans. Brian Battershaw and G. R. Lamb (London and New York: Sheed and Ward, 1961), 129–56, 520–26.

28. See Caroline P. Bammel, "Augustine, Origen, and the Exegesis of St. Paul," *Augustinianum* 32 (1992): 341–68, esp. 342–47; Alexander Souter, *The Earliest Latin Commentaries on the Epistles of St. Paul* (Oxford: Clarendon Press, 1927), 139–204;

and William S. Babcock, "Augustine and Tyconius: A Study in the Latin Appropriation of Paul," *Studia Patristica* 17/3 (1982): 1209–15.

29. O'Donnell, *Augustine*, 302.

30. Fredriksen, "Body/Soul Dichotomy," 102–03.

31. Brown, *Augustine of Hippo*, 506–09, quotation at 507.

32. Burns, *Operative Grace*, 51.

33. See Fredriksen, "Body/Soul Dichotomy," 103–05; and Ferrari, *Conversions*, 78–82.

34. John M. Rist, "Augustine on Free Will and Predestination," *Journal of Theological Studies, N.S.* 20 (1969): 420–47, quotation at 440. This article is reprinted in Markus, *Augustine*, 218–52.

35. See James Wetzel, "The Recovery of Free Agency in the Theology of St. Augustine," *Harvard Theological Review* 80 (1987): 101–25, as well as his more extended treatment in *Augustine and the Limits of Virtue* (Cambridge: Cambridge University Press, 1992).

36. See Brown, *Augustine of Hippo*, 508-12, and especially Carole E. Straw, "Augustine as Pastoral Theologian: The Exegesis of the Parables of the Field and the Threshing Floor," *Augustinian Studies* 14 (1983): 129–51.

37. Cf. Gauri Viswanathan, "Colonialism and the Construction of Hinduism," in *The Blackwell Companion to Hinduism*, ed. Gavin Flood (Oxford and Malden: Blackwell Publishing, 2003), 23–44, and Brian K. Pennington, *Was Hinduism Invented? Britons, Indians, and the Colonial Construction of Religion* (Oxford and New York: Oxford University Press, 2005).

38. Hereafter cited in the body of the essay. I have used the Sanskrit text and, with some alterations, the English translation in V. Panoli, trans., *Upanishads in Sankara's Own Words*, vol. 2, rev. ed. (Calicut: Mathrubhumi Printing and Publishing Co. Ltd., 1996), 107–217. I have also consulted the translation in Swami Gambhirananda, trans., *Eight Upanisads, With the Commentary of Sankaracarya*, vol. 2 (Calcutta: Advaita Ashrama, 1992), 71–166.

39. For background, see Michael Witzel, "Vedas and Upanisads," in Flood, *Blackwell Companion to Hinduism*, 68–98, and especially Patrick Olivelle, trans., *The Early Upanisads: Annotated Text and Translation* (New York and Oxford: Oxford University Press, 1998), 3–27.

40. Hereafter cited in the body of the essay, I have used the Sanskrit text and, with small modifications, the English translation in Olivelle, *Early Upanisads*, 436–55.

41. For helpful surveys of such diverse theories of liberation and their relation to Advaita Vedanta, see A. G. Krishna Warrier, *The Concept of Mukti in Advaita Vedanta*, Madras University Philosophical Series 9 (Madras: University of Madras, 1961), 7–209; and Natalia Isayeva, *Shankara and Indian Philosophy* (Albany: State University of New York Press, 1993), esp. 105–235.

42. There are many excellent introductions to the Advaita tradition and the thought of Adi Shankaracharya. The ones that have most strongly influenced this exposition are: Francis X. Clooney, S.J., *Theology after Vedanta: An Experiment in Comparative Theology* (Albany: State University of New York Press, 1993); J. G. Suthren Hirst, *Samkara's Advaita Vedanta: A Way of Teaching* (London and New York: RoutledgeCurzon, 2005); and Anantanand Rambachan, *Accomplishing the Accomplished: The Vedas as a Source of Valid Knowledge in Sankara*, Monographs of

the Society for Asian and Comparative Philosophy 10 (Honolulu: University of Hawaii Press, 1991).

43. In the Advaita tradition, this claim about "living liberation" or "liberation in life" (*jivan-mukti*) turns out to be considerably less straightforward than it initially appears, due to the difficulty of explaining why and how the liberated sage continues in the present embodied state. Excellent treatments of this complex question can be found in Mike Bos, "After the Rise of Knowledge," *Wiener Zeitschrift für die Kunde Südasiens und Archiv für indische Philosophie* 27 (1983): 165–84; and Lance E. Nelson, "Living Liberation in Sankara and Classical Advaita: Sharing the Waiting of God," in *Living Liberation in Hindu Thought*, ed. Andrew O. Fort and Patricia Y. Mumme (Albany: State University of New York Press, 1996), 17–62.

44. Hundreds of works are attributed to Shankara, only a small fraction of which are generally recognized as authentic by contemporary historical scholars. The establishment of a stable set of criteria for authenticity was initiated in the Advaita tradition by Swami Satchidanandendra and consolidated in Western scholarship by Paul Hacker and Daniel Ingalls. Due to the rigorous application of these criteria by Sengaku Mayeda, among others, a relatively fixed canon has emerged, including Shankara's commentaries on the Brahma-Sutras, the Bhagavad-Gita and the most important Upanishads, as well as the independent treatise *A Thousand Teachings* (*Upadesasahasri*). See Suthren Hirst, *Samkara's Advaita Vedanta*, esp. 4–8, 19–25; and Sengaku Mayeda, trans., *A Thousand Teachings: The Upadesasahasri of Sankara* (Albany: State University of New York Press, 1992), 3–10.

45. On the central importance of the Vedic scriptures as an independent means of knowledge (*pramana*), see Clooney, *Theology after Vedanta*, 88–102; Rambachan, *Accomplishing the Accomplished*, 31–54; Anantanand Rambachan, "Where Words Can Set Free: The Liberating Potency of Vedic Words in the Hermeneutics of Sankara," in *Texts in Context: Traditional Hermeneutics in South Asia*, ed. Jeffrey R. Timm (Albany: State University of New York Press, 1992), 33–46; and Anantanand Rambachan, "Sankara's Rationale for *Sruti* as the Definitive Source of *Brahmajnana*: A Refutation of Some Contemporary Views," *Philosophy East and West* 36 (1986): 25–40.

46. See, for example, Mayeda, *A Thousand Teachings*, 11–17; and Paul Hacker, "Sankara's Conception of Man," in *Philology and Confrontation: Paul Hacker on Traditional and Modern Vedanta*, ed. Wilhelm Halbfass (Albany: State University of New York Press, 1995), 177–85.

47. It is worth noting that such "illusionistic" interpretations of Shankara's thought, though firmly entrenched in both Advaita tradition and Western scholarship, have themselves come under a sharp critique from both inside and outside the tradition. For some representative examples of this critique, see Bradley Malkovsky, "Advaita Vedanta and Christian Faith," *Journal of Ecumenical Studies* 36/3–4 (1999): 397–422; Srinivasa Rao, "Two 'Myths' in Advaita," *Journal of Indian Philosophy* 24 (1996): 265–79; and Anantanand Rambachan, *The Advaita Worldview: God, World, and Humanity* (Albany: State University of New York Press, 2006), esp. 67–81.

48. Sara Grant has coined the term "non-reciprocal dependence relation" to describe this fundamental asymmetry. See Sara Grant, R.S.C.J., *Toward an Alternative*

*Theology: Confessions of a Non-Dualist Christian: The Teape Lectures, 1989* (Notre Dame: University of Notre Dame Press, 2002), 40–43, as well as the more extensive treatment in Sara Grant, *Sankaracarya's Concept of Relation* (Delhi: Motilal Banarsidass Publishers, 1998).

49. *Retractiones* 2.1.2. Latin text in CCSL 57 (1984), 89–91; English translation in Burleigh, *Earlier Writings*, 370.

50. Cf. Francis X. Clooney, S.J., "Evil, Divine Omnipotence, and Human Freedom: Vedanta's Theology of Karma," *The Journal of Religion* 4 (1989): 530–48.

51. More comprehensive treatments of *adhikara* can be found in Clooney, *Theology after Vedanta*, 129–41; Suthren Hirst, *Samkara's Advaita Vedanta*, 41–45; and Rambachan, *Accomplishing the Accomplished*, 85–91.

52. Clooney makes a strong case that such social restrictions of caste and gender follow from Advaita Vedanta's deep roots, as "later Mimamsa" (*uttara-mimamsa*), in the "earlier Mimamsa" (*purva-mimamsa*) of ritual exegesis from which it originally developed. According to such Vedic exegesis, women and members of the lowest caste were excluded from Vedic study. See Clooney, *Theology after Vedanta*, 134–41.

53. E.g., Rambachan, *Advaita Worldview*, 27–29; Arvind Sharma, "Sankara's Life and Works as a Source for a Hermeneutics of Human Rights," in *New Perspectives on Advaita Vedanta: Essays in Commemoration of Professor Richard De Smet, S.J.*, ed. Bradley J. Malkovsky, Studies in the History of Religions 85 (Leiden, Boston, and Köln: Brill, 2000), 109–21; and Roger Marcaurelle, *Freedom Through Inner Renunciation: Sankara's Philosophy in a New Light* (Albany: State University of New York Press, 2000).

54. Rambachan, *Accomplishing the Accomplished*, 86 (emphasis added).

55. See Suthren Hirst, *Samkara's Advaita Vedanta*, 57–59, 116–37. Cf. Bradley Malkovsky, "The Personhood of Samkara's *Para Brahman*," *The Journal of Religion* 77 (1997): 541–62; Arvind Sharma, "The Vedantic Concept of God," in *Perspectives on Vedanta: Essays in Honor of Professor P.T. Raju*, ed. S. S. Rama Rao Pappu (Leiden: E.J. Brill, 1988), 114–31; and A.G. Krishna Warrier, *God in Advaita* (Simla: Indian Institute of Advanced Study, 1977).

56. See Bradley J. Malkovsky, "Samkara on Divine Grace," in Malkovsky, *New Perspectives*, 70–83, as well as the more extensive treatment in Bradley J. Malkovsky, *The Role of Divine Grace in the Soteriology of Samkaracarya* (Leiden, Boston and Köln: Brill, 2001).

57. Malkovsky, "Samkara on Divine Grace," 73–75.

58. Ibid., 82.

59. Ibid., 76–77.

60. Cf. Ibid., 78–83, and Malkovsky, *Role of Divine Grace*, 382–87.

61. *Aitareya-Upanisad-Bhasya* 1.3.1, quoted in Malkovsky, "Samkara on Divine Grace," 82.

62. *Katha-Upanisad-Bhasya* 1.2.23, following the English translation in Swami Gambhirananda, trans., *Eight Upanisads, with the Commentary of Sankaracarya*, vol. 1, rev. ed. (Calcutta: Advaita Ashrama, 1989), 157–58. I have also consulted the Sanskrit text and English translation in V. Panoli, trans., *Upanishads in Sankara's Own Words*, vol. 1, rev. ed. (Calicut: Mathrubhumi Printing and Publishing Co. Ltd., 1995), 212–13.

63. Swami Gambhirananda, in fact, glosses Shankara's phrase "of Its own accord" as "through Its grace," in *Eight Upanisads*, vol. 1, 158n. There is some ambiguity in the manuscript tradition of this verse, with significant consequences for its interpretation. See Olivelle, *Early Upanisads*, 635n.

64. See Malkovsky, "Samkara on Divine Grace," 79–81.

65. Cf. Rambachan, *The Advaita Worldview*, 36–38, 51–52.

66. See Ibid., 91–96; Suthren Hirst, *Samkara's Advaita Vedanta*, 97–99; and Thomas O'Neil, *Maya in Sankara: Measuring the Immeasurable* (Delhi: Motilal Banarsidass, 1980), esp. 154–86.

67. See Malkovsky, *Role of Divine Grace*, 390–93.

68. Straw, "Augustine as Pastoral Theologian," 144.

69. See, for example, the penetrating discussion in George Hunsinger, "Hellfire and Damnation: Four Ancient and Modern Views," *Scottish Journal of Theology* 51/4 (1998): 406–34.

70. Warm thanks for editorial assistance on this essay are due to Jolie Chrisman and Julia Lauwers.

# 10

# Transforming the Self: Confession and Performance in the Thought of Augustine and Xunzi

Aaron Stalnaker

## INTRODUCTION

Does anyone ever really change?[1] Religions tend to answer this question with an emphatic yes. And it does seem that religions can transform people: some believers become selfless servants of the poor, or even suicide bombers. But how and why might this happen? Similar circumstances push people in quite different ways; "good intentions" alone are not sufficient for real conversion to some demanding new form of life.

More specifically, how could anyone really become more virtuous? Analogous questions were central to widespread debates in ancient China about *xiu shen* 修身 or "self-cultivation." And as Pierre Hadot has taught us, intellectually centered regimens of personal formation, which he calls "spiritual exercises," were equally essential to Greco-Roman philosophy as a shared way of life.[2] Engaging sophisticated accounts of such exercises helps to develop virtue ethics in a fruitful new direction, by stressing the intentional cultivation of character through methodical

This chapter is a revised version of the chapter entitled "Transforming the Self: Confession and Performance in the Thought of Augustine and Xunzi" which originally appeared in *Overcoming Our Evil: Human Nature and Spiritual Exercises in Xunzi and Augustine* by Aaron Stalnaker (Georgetown University Press, 2006). It is reprinted here with permission. www.press.georgetown.edu

practices. These practices can be described and analyzed in detail, just as particular virtues can, and such close analysis sheds much light on the moral psychology of character development. Whether moderns are able to cultivate virtue is, after all, one of the central issues in critiques of modernity and liberalism. If we wish to understand virtue, and perhaps even become better ourselves, it would be wise to reflect carefully on some of the most sophisticated past accounts of this process.

This leads directly to the subjects of this essay: Augustine of Hippo (354–430 C.E.), a late antique Christian of immense influence on later Western civilization, and Xun Kuang 荀況 (c. 310 B.C. 220 B.C.E.), commonly known as Xunzi 荀子 ("Master Xun"), an important early Confucian figure who shaped his tradition in profound if sometimes overlooked ways. Augustine and Xunzi both have sophisticated and insightful accounts of spiritual exercises, and both make such ethical work central to their religious visions, offering detailed analysis and advocacy of particular practices. They also build their accounts of personal formation on the basis of clear-eyed but distinctive assessments of humanity's propensities to do evil. Their analyses of "human nature" as fallen or bad profoundly shape the practical regimens they each suggest, which are tuned to restrain, ameliorate, or even transform our more questionable impulses.

Despite having no noteworthy cultural or historical connection, Xunzi and Augustine share sufficient similarities and differences to allow nuanced comparative analysis of their positions. Their prescriptions share a general shape: both have been represented in English as saying that "human nature" is "evil," and so humans need significant reformation to become good; but such translations mask important differences in anthropology, ethics, metaphysics, and understandings of what count as the most important history and texts. Interpreting each of them holistically allows nuanced, analogical comparison and contrast of their ideas around particular themes.

I have pursued a broader comparison of these figures' accounts of personal formation elsewhere in book-length form.[3] This essay, after setting the stage with general discussions of their accounts of human life, focuses more narrowly on a striking thematic difference between the two: the contrast between Augustine's "inside-out" approach to personal formation, typified by his laudatory emphasis on confessional prayer, and Xunzi's "outside-in" approach, typified by his insistence on the great value of communal ritual practice, understood expansively so as to encompass all realms of life. This fundamental contrast in strategy is then developed by exploring their differing evaluations of honesty and pretence within religious self-cultivation.

## XUNZI AND AUGUSTINE

Obviously Xunzi lived in a profoundly different culture from the modern United States, used a language unrelated to English, and was responding to a distinctive (and in certain ways quite alien) intellectual scene. With Augustine, we may be misled by the thought that he is Western, and hence "ours." Peter Brown rightly insists that "the Christianity of the . . . Middle Ages—to say nothing of the Christianity of our own times—is separated from the Christianity of the Roman world by a chasm almost as vast as that which still appears to separate us from the moral horizons of a Mediterranean Islamic country."[4] We must be alert to the distance between contemporary ideas that descend from Augustine and his own conceptions expressed in similar or even apparently identical terms, as well as to a cultural world almost as foreign as ancient China. In many ways the problems generated by historical and cultural distance are quite parallel, and similar skills are necessary to navigate both. I thus provide brief introductions to the life, context, and thought of each of our subjects.

Xunzi was born in the state of Zhao around 310 B.C.E., during the Warring States period of Chinese history, and probably lived just past the unification of China by Qin Shihuang in 221 B.C.E. This era was marked by continuing strife between several states seeking to conquer the others and succeed the clearly moribund Zhou dynasty. In this environment violence and social disruption were common, and ongoing debates over the proper ordering of self and society took on a new intensity as a "hundred schools of thought" contended for influence with rulers seeking the proper Way of human existence.

Xunzi seems to have been precocious: he left home at fifteen to go to perhaps the preeminent center of learning of his day, the Jixia "Academy" in the capital of the state of Qi, where scholars of every philosophical and religious persuasion debated each other and enjoyed the king's largesse. In such an environment Xunzi was exposed to all the major intellectual currents of his day, and distinguished himself sufficiently among the attending thinkers that he was honored three times as head libationer at the official ancestral sacrifices. Xunzi also traveled fairly widely. In between extended stays at Jixia in Qi, Xunzi spent a number of years at the court of the southern state of Chu after King Min of Qi overreached militarily and was hunted down and killed. He also visited Qin, the eventual victor in the internecine conflicts, where he was confronted with a powerful and ruthless state that impressed but saddened him. Near the end of his life he was appointed magistrate of Lanling in Chu, a post of uncertain but probably not enormous gravity, where he continued to teach his students and in all likelihood worked to put his literary legacy in order. A perhaps apocryphal story describes a very old Xunzi, having lived to see the unification of China by Qin with the help of his own turncoat student Li Si, turning down an honorary post in the new regime offered by his renegade pupil. In any case Xunzi died shortly thereafter, having failed to convince any of the kingly pretenders to adopt his Way. The future official "triumph" of Confucianism could not have been foreseen.[5]

Xunzi borrowed ideas from numerous sources to rearticulate the tradition of the Zhou dynasty passed on by Confucius and his followers; he self-consciously described himself as one of this group of *Ru* 儒, generally termed "Confucians." In particular he took issue with his Confucian predecessor Mencius over the character of human *xing* 性 or "nature." Where Mencius suggests that human *xing* is good, Xunzi argues instead that it is bad, and that any human goodness is a matter of "artifice." The innate desires that make up our *xing* often aim at real goods, Xunzi thinks, but tend to be destructively shortsighted and selfish. They disrupt our lives, gnawing at us if unsatisfied, growing without limit if we do manage briefly to fulfill them, turning families and communities against themselves in a chaotic struggle for scarce goods. Reforming these desires is the task of a demanding program of traditional Confucian ethicoreligious cultivation, centering on ritual practice, musical performance, and textual study, which Xunzi likens to straightening crooked wood in a steam press or hammering blunt metal on an anvil. If this is pursued over many years, Xunzi thinks, a complete transformation of human dispositions and desires is possible, so that even a "person in the street" can become a sage.

Xunzi's influence was most profound in shaping the Confucianism that followed him, which was officially declared orthodoxy in the Han dynasty. Xunzi's students transmitted several of the versions of key classical texts that survive today, and his general turn back to the importance of textual study was decisive in shaping later Confucianism. Nevertheless, his direct influence seems to have waned as the Han dynasty (202 B.C.E.–220 C.E.) extended, and the first extant commentary on his works dates from the Tang dynasty (618–907 C.E.), written by one Yang Liang in 818 C.E. Xunzi was further eclipsed by the ascent of Zhu Xi's Mencian-inflected "Neo-Confucianism" in the Song dynasty (960–1279 C.E.), which relegated Xunzi's position on human nature to the status of heterodoxy until the twentieth century. Nevertheless, since the eighteenth century interest in Xunzi has been growing, inspired mostly by the sophistication of his thought and the development of indigenous traditions of modern historical-critical scholarship in China and Japan, and augmented since the 1920s by a slow but steady stream of Western studies.[6]

While we know a relatively large amount about Xunzi's life when compared to other early Chinese thinkers, and can even speculate about the chronology of some of his writings, scholars know vastly more about Augustine's life, context, and works, many of which can be dated quite precisely. Augustine was born on November 13, 354 C.E., in Thagaste, a town in Roman North Africa. His parents had limited means, and managed barely to provide him with a classical literary education, at a time when mastery of the shared literary and rhetorical culture of the Roman Empire was one of few avenues for social and economic advancement. In 370 he gained sufficient support to go to Carthage to continue his studies, and while there took a mistress, with whom he had a son. In Carthage he was inspired to seek wisdom by reading a now-lost work of Cicero, and after rejecting the Christian scriptures as stylistically uncouth, became a Manichean "hearer." He became a teacher of rhetoric, first in Thagaste, then in Carthage, and finally in Rome. His fame as a rhetorician grew, and in 384 he moved to Milan, seat of the Western imperial court, where he continued to teach rhetoric, gave occasional panegyrics for famous men at court, and drifted into a circle of intellectually refined neo-Platonic Christians centered on Ambrose, bishop of Milan. His mother followed him to Milan, and arranged a marriage to a very young heiress; Augustine's long-time concubine was forced to return to Africa, although their son remained with him. Augustine admired Ambrose's sermons, first for their stylistic refinement, and later for their content; after an initial serious study of Paul's letters, Augustine converted to Christianity, which was also for him a conversion to sexual abstinence. He called off his socially advantageous marriage, resigned his post in Milan, and retired to the countryside in philosophical retreat with some like-minded friends. That spring, on Easter in 387, Augustine was baptized by Ambrose in Milan, and shortly thereafter his mother died, after they shared a vision of God.

After a delay in Rome, Augustine returned to Africa in 388 and founded a small monastic community dedicated to the shared practice of spiritual exercises; during this time his son also died, quite young. On a visit to Hippo in 391 Augustine was compelled by the local populace to be ordained as a priest. He again organized a monastic community, undertook an intensive reading of Christian scripture, and eventually succeeded Valerius as bishop of Hippo in approximately 396. As bishop Augustine had immense responsibilities. He preached numerous sermons each week, was the chief minister in the celebration of the Eucharist and the giving of baptism, and was in charge of his congregation, his clergy, the ecclesiastical property, and the administration of the church and its alms distribution. As Roman authority weakened (Rome itself was sacked in 410), he also took on increasing local authority, judging legal cases such as familial disputes over wills. He publicly debated opponents, whether Manichees, Donatists, or others, and as a Catholic in a heavily Donatist area of North Africa he was the leader of a minority religious population in a time of violent clashes between factions. He traveled frequently, attending church councils and preaching at distant churches. Despite all this he kept up a voluminous correspondence and wrote more than one hundred books, many but not all polemical, in a variety of genres. He lived a long and trying life, exercising considerable influence and power, and died on August 28, 430. While Augustine lay on his deathbed, the Vandals, who in a single year had swept across North Africa destroying much of the Roman Christian civilization Augustine had labored to rejuvenate, laid siege to Hippo, the last Roman town standing in North Africa. Hippo fell and was partly burned a year later, but Augustine's library survived.[7]

Augustine teaches that humans live in a "fallen" and "penal" state, possessing a damaged *natura* that bears only a shadowy resemblance to our "nature" as originally created by God. For Augustine this *natura* does not stand for uncultivated impulses, but is our essential being, locating us in the divinely ordered hierarchy of existence. On this account people are afflicted with "ignorance" and "difficulty," and more broadly with "concupiscence," a syndrome of covetous and ill-directed desire. With hearts darkened and chilled, we no longer have the power to love the good and act rightly. As the mature Augustine argues against his Pelagian enemies, only divine grace can heal the wound of original sin, and within this life such healing can only be partial. And yet, for Augustine, we should also seek the aid provided within the church by *exercitationes* "exercises" and *disciplina* "teaching," "training," and "discipline." By "crucifying the [fallen] inner man" and "refashioning" the divine image within our minds we can "make progress day by day" in righteousness. As the love of God is poured into our hearts, our desire for God will be kindled and our minds illuminated.

## FOLLOWING THE WAY

While many religious thinkers, including Augustine, make use of the idea of religion as a "way" of life, in early China the word *Dao* 道, aptly translated in its most basic sense by "path" or "way," was uniquely important. What the real or best *Dao* might be was the ultimate topic of political, ethical, religious, and cosmological debate, and the idea was widely understood to encompass or at least involve all of these realms. The word also provided the best way of referring to competing tendencies of thought and practice, and was the closest available analogue to Western ideas such as "religion" and "philosophy."

In lieu of a survey of the full range of early Chinese views of the *Dao*, I intend here only to give a sense of shared early Confucian presuppositions about the Way, and of how this overarching term of art shaped Xunzi's conceptions of human life and personal formation.[8] As a word, *dao* refers primarily to a "path" or "way," as noted above, but by the Warring States era (403–221 B.C.E.) *dao* had acquired more extended senses such as the manner or method for doing something (e.g., the "way" to cook), a very broad sense of the "way the world is" or should be, and the teaching or guidance that can show one "the way" in any of these senses.

*Dao* can also be used verbally to express the activity of guiding others along a path, or of following such a way oneself.

Early Confucians regarded the *Dao* in its largest sense as "nothing less than the total normative sociopolitical order with its networks of proper familial and . . . sociopolitical roles, statuses, and ranks, as well as the 'objective' prescriptions of proper behavior—ritual, ceremonial, and ethical—that govern the relationships among these roles."[9] And yet it was just as much a way of life for individuals, relating one's inner life to the broader life of the community and the natural environment, and even the cosmos as a whole. One crucial difference from the way of life promoted by Augustine must be noted immediately. For Augustine, the ultimate telos of the Christian life is a perfected, eternal life with God after the final resurrection of the dead. For Xunzi and other early Confucians the Way is its own goal—there is no ultimate telos beyond living out the Way in the world all can readily observe. While there were widespread early Chinese beliefs in some sort of spiritual afterlife (although still in communion with the living generations of a family line), early Confucians tended to downplay such speculation, and Xunzi explicitly rejects it.[10]

For Xunzi the Way is a path *through* the world we presently inhabit, which is our true and only home. The intrinsic goods made available by following the Way are their own "rewards," regardless of whether less important goods such as wealth and public acclaim accompany them or not.[11] So Xunzi claims that the Dao itself simply *is* the practice of Confucian virtues of ritual propriety, justice, deference, yielding, dutifulness, and trustworthiness (16/77/5–6).[12] The Way is very much a way of life for Xunzi, that mode of existence lived by the noble man (8/28/16) and above all the sage (8/31/5). The Dao is the sort of thing one must *ti* 體 "embody," which consists of both deep understanding and practical mastery of the Way (21/104/6).[13]

This sense that the Way itself, if properly followed, provides the best human life, and is not ordered or validated by some further ultimate destination at which it aims, was widespread in Warring States China, even among rather different ideological antagonists. Thus it is somewhat surprising to find Xunzi arguing for the superiority of his vision of the Confucian Way by stressing that his Way leads somewhere, in fact to an end or "stopping place" that is worth arriving at after long, sustained effort (2/7/8–17). He employs this novel rhetorical strategy to make three points, some of which will be further developed later: first, that sustained effort over a long period of time is necessary to reach a fully flourishing state of life; second, that concentration on that goal is necessary to ever attain it, given the difficulty of the task of self-cultivation; and third, that other purported *daos* cannot lead to such a state because they misunderstand both the goal and the path, and so lead people astray into endless disputation and fruitless practices. We should note, however, that the "goal" or "end" Xunzi here describes is still the Way itself, fully enacted in the person of the sage who spontaneously and effortlessly accords with the true Way. Xunzi is keen to encourage his readers not to give up part way along the long road of self-cultivation—but where that road leads is to the full and perfect embodiment and performance of the Way itself.[14]

One of the most famous passages in the *Xunzi* provides a wealth of evocative imagery for understanding his sense of the Confucian life. He writes:

> Those who cross water mark the deep places; if the markers are unclear people will drown. Those who govern the people mark out the Way; if the markers are unclear there will be social chaos. The rites are the markers. To go against ritual is to darken the age, and a benighted age is one of great chaos. Thus when the Way is completely clear, the difference between outside and inside is marked, and the hidden and the manifest become constant, people will at last avoid drowning. (18/82/22–18/83/1; cf. 27/127/4–5)

Lamenting his own confused and benighted age, Xunzi imagines life in the Warring States as a treacherous river or swamp, which can only be navigated via the trustworthy signs left by past Confucian sages. In his context of confusion and disagreement, Xunzi yearns for clarity regarding what is within the boundaries of the Way and what outside it, so that people can see and avoid the greatest dangers, and also find and stay on the one true path. For Xunzi, Confucian ritual provides the trustworthy guidance human beings need to navigate life successfully, by clearly marking the boundaries of the Way.

Xunzi thinks following the Way will feel very different depending on how long one pursues it, because one's mastery of it will slowly and steadily increase over time. Xunzi's gradualist conception of moral improvement is reflected in his discussions of "accumulation" and eventual "transformation" on the Confucian Way, as well as his central trope of "artifice" as the engine for personal change. These themes are integral to his sophisticated theory of ethical development, which in turn helps justify his advocacy of the spiritual exercises of study, ritual, and music.[15]

Xunzi's metaphors for this process are revealing. Instead of speaking of cultivating "sprouts" of morality into full-fledged plants, that is, virtues, as his predecessor Mencius does, Xunzi favors tougher images:

> A warped piece of wood must wait until it has been laid against the straightening board, steamed, and forced into shape before it becomes straight; a piece of blunt metal must wait until it has been whetted on a grindstone before it becomes sharp. [Similarly,] since humanity's innate endowment (*xing*

> 性 ) is bad it must wait for [the guidance of] a teacher and the model before it becomes upright, and get ritual and justice before it becomes well ordered. (23/113/9–10; see also 1/1/3–5, 23/115/16–18)[16]

For Xunzi, the process of learning from a teacher (*shi* 師 ), internalizing classical models (*fa* 法 ), and thereby *de* 得 "getting" ritual and just social norms (*liyi* 禮義 ) is most akin to the work of artisans practicing constructive crafts.[17] We must be forcibly conformed to an external model (the "straightening board"), and this requires processes akin to steaming wood and grinding metal.

In other words, Xunzi pictures moral change as a slow, arduous process of personal reformation in which we must rely for an extended period on external forms and guides to achieve what flourishing is possible for us. Like the Confucius of *Analects* 2.4, Xunzi adopts the same view that the Confucian path is lifelong (1/3/8), that it contains different stages of achievement, and that progress through the stages is slow.[18]

Such moral transformation is possible because Xunzi thinks all people, even the uncultivated, will do what they *ke* "accept" or "assent to," even when their existing desires point in another direction. This innate power of self-control makes it possible for us to decide to follow new courses of action, if we see sufficiently good reasons for doing so. Assent seems to be a natural human power for Xunzi, not something that might fail on occasion because of the strength of our desires; when desire and assent conflict, assent just trumps desires, according to Xunzi, and we suffer deprivation willingly (22/111/6, 20). On the face of it, such a position seems blind to common human experiences of "weakness of will" and internal conflict and indecision. But Xunzi is aware of such problems. He clearly believes that many people simply assent to seeking what they desire, and that all people start out this way. Only experienced difficulties can prompt us to question ourselves and our desires, and only the conscious articulation of our difficulties can open the logical possibility of overriding our desires. Since our desires do not cease to clamor for attention, on Xunzi's view, we only dissent from following them if we are convinced they will lead us into relatively greater trouble and suffering—or in other words, we dissent from them when we believe they are dangerous. This does make sense: even the vicious can usually control themselves when they think their life or some other important interest is at stake. Such a judgment of personal danger provides some foothold, Xunzi thinks, for people to judge actions to be wrong, at least in the most limited, prudential sense. And such a limited sense of personal peril will be enough, Xunzi thinks, to motivate people to try and follow the Confucian Way, despite its initial peculiarity.[19]

Xunzi gives detailed, careful accounts of three spiritual exercises central to his Confucianism. *Xue* 學 , which includes both "study" and "learning," is a combination of textual study, focused on the classical *Documents, Odes, Rituals, Music,* and *Spring and Autumn Annals*; and bodily, emotional, and intellectual appropriation of the lessons of the past into students' daily existence. It is highly dependent on authoritative teachers and a shared community of learners. Study includes wide-ranging reflection and philosophical dialogue as parts of the process of appropriation, leading ideally to deep intellectual and personal commitment to the Confucian Way.

*Li* 禮, "ritual," covers both specific ceremonial observances and a very wide range of the details of daily life, from appearance and deportment to etiquette and interpersonal morality. Ritual reorients human beings to those roots of their shared existence, Heaven and Earth, ancestors, and lords and teachers, which are not the immediate objects of our innate dispositions. It also clarifies and strengthens just social norms by highlighting social distinctions, and thus, perhaps somewhat paradoxically, reinforcing social harmony and unity in the community as a whole; this point becomes more comprehensible when we attend to Xunzi's view that ritual propriety enacts the *mutual* duties between superiors and inferiors, not merely duties of loyalty and obedience from below (e.g., 11/54/11–13). Ritual as a spiritual exercise shapes human *qing* 情 "dispositions" so that they match *wenli* 文理 "refined form and good order." This process of "cutting" and "stretching" our dispositions, of "calling up" and "tamping down" our emotional proclivities, aims to produce eventually a state Xunzi calls "the middle course where ritual flows" (19/93/1). In such a state emotions and external observances are in perfect harmony with each other, and people gracefully perform their commitments to the Confucian virtues of humaneness, justice, trustworthiness, loyalty, and reverence. But even before this "middle course" is achieved, and even without perfect understanding, ritual allows people to navigate life's transitions, however joyful or traumatic, with dignity, so that community life can continue to flourish and all enjoy peace.

Drawing on a peculiarity of classical Chinese, Xunzi argues that *Yue* 樂, "music," is also *le* 樂, "joy." According to him music has a unique power to inspire people in any number of directions, and so the sage kings carefully composed the *Odes* and *Hymns*, which use this magnetic influence in the service of refined form. By broadening and purifying listeners' intentions, and enlivening them by generating harmonious and orderly joy, music moves human beings of all sorts relatively quickly and easily to feel the rightness of the Confucian Way and develop its virtues. To discard it because of its expense would be a colossal miscalculation, Xunzi thinks, and impoverish our life together in every way.

## CRUCIFYING AND RESURRECTING THE MIND

Contrary to common misperceptions that his theology implies human passivity before an almighty God, Augustine passionately advocates what in this study I am calling "spiritual exercises." This can hardly be surprising, given the role ascetic literature and exemplars played in his conversion to Catholic Christianity.[20] Indeed, Augustine's conversion issued not only in study as a Catholic catechumen, but in philosophical retreat from the ambitious world of Milanese society and patronage. He continued to organize and lead a sequence of monastic social groupings, and risked forcible recruitment to be a presbyter in Hippo only in order to interview a prospective monastic "brother." This led to his ordination by Valerius, bishop of Hippo, who honored Augustine's wish to continue living as a monastic by permitting him to construct and head a monastery adjoining the basilica.[21] He lived for the rest of his life in a community of like-minded *fratres*, all embracing individual poverty, communal property, celibacy, daily prayer and study, and manual labor. He wrote the first monastic rule in Western Christendom, and founded other monasteries for monks and nuns.[22]

Looking simply at Augustine's views of monasticism, however, especially when contrasted implicitly or explicitly with his expectations for lay Christians, unnecessarily truncates an account of his normative ideas about practices of personal formation, which he did not think were reserved only for a few (see, e.g., *s.* 301A.8).[23] It would not be overstating the case to say that Augustine views the Christian life, in lay, clerical, and monastic forms, as consisting essentially of the practice of spiritual exercises. At various times, to various audiences, Augustine recommends practices such as sexual restraint or renunciation; voluntary poverty; almsgiving; communal ownership of property; fasting; self-examination; private and public confession of sins; various kinds of prayer, bible study and other sorts of learning (including the traditional liberal arts); philosophical dialogue; brotherly rebuke; and various forms of penance. And in his capacities as priest and bishop, Augustine of course led many through catechesis, baptism, and shared worship, which included scripture recitation, preaching, music, and celebration of the Eucharist.

Augustine uses a variety of highly suggestive traditional metaphors to convey his understanding of the Christian life. According to Augustine, for humans here on earth "the whole of our lifetime is nothing but a race towards death, in which no one is allowed the slightest pause or any slackening of the pace" (*civ. Dei* 13.10).[24] This is so in both literal and spiritual senses: we all will weaken and die physically, and in our fallen condition we are also dying spiritually, headed for the everlasting second death of divine condemnation (*civ. Dei* 13.10–11). He sometimes goes even further, saying that the unchristian life *is* death, in both soul and body, because of sin and sin's punishment; before conversion to Christianity "both soul and body [are] in need of healing and resurrection, in order to renew for the better what [has] changed for the worse" (*Trin.* 4.5).[25]

Unsurprisingly, Christ serves for Augustine as the primary model for our passage from this living death to true eternal life and felicity. More specifically, Christ is a "*sacramentum* for the inner man and an *exemplum* for the outer one" (*Trin.* 4.6).[26] By *sacramentum* Augustine does not mean "sacrament" in any post-Tridentine sense, but rather a sacred sign, something that signifies an important religious or spiritual reality (*doc. Chr.* 3.19.31; *civ. Dei* 10.5; *ep.* 138.7).[27] In a passage larded with scriptural allusions, Augustine explains what he means as follows:

> As a symbol of our inner man [Christ] uttered that cry, both in the psalm and on the cross, which was intended to represent the death of our soul: "My God, my God, why have you forsaken me" (Ps 22:1; Mk 15:34)? To this cry there corresponds what the apostle [Paul] says, "Knowing that our old man was crucified together with him, in order to cancel the body of sin, that we might no longer be the slaves of sin" (Rom 6:6). By the crucifixion of the inner man is to be understood the sorrows of repentance and a kind of salutary torment of restraint, a kind of death to erase the death of ungodliness in which God does not leave us. . . . It all takes place within, this process that the apostle refers to in the words, "Strip off the old man and put on the new" (Eph 4:22). (*Trin.* 4.6)[28]

Being carnal rather than properly spiritual, that is, oriented to love and delight in things instead of God, our inner man must be "crucified," and so suffer a "kind of death" as its carnal impulses are slowly annihilated inwardly via repentance and the "salutary torment" of restrained Christian practices. Christ's resurrection is equally a *sacramentum* "of our inner resurrection" as well, to which Augustine correlates Paul's admonition (Col. 3:1) that "If you have risen with Christ, seek the things that are above, where Christ is seated at God's right hand; set your thoughts on the things that are above." Augustine explains that to rise with Christ means "not to think carnally about Christ" (*Trin.* 4.6).[29] In other words, we are to rise with Christ and contemplate eternal realities, instead of directing our attention primarily to earthly things.

Christ's death and resurrection are also *exempla* of the outer man, that is, "patterns" or "models" for imitation. His death, Augustine thinks, encourages us not to fear those who kill the body but not the soul (Mt. 10:28), and his resurrection is a "pre-enactment" of the resurrection of the bodies of the elect at the eschaton (*Trin.* 4.6).

While the metaphor of Christlike resurrection is Augustine's dominant one, he uses many others frequently as well. A recurrent image is that of

Christ as the true doctor, healing and strengthening sick, injured humanity in the wake of our disastrous fall (e.g., *s.* 4.2; cf. *s.* 346A.8). Fallen humanity suffers from an illness so profound its sufferers cannot recognize its severity without divine illumination, which sometimes comes via tests or "exercises." We are all gravely ill, and need the medicine of grace, which is reliably present in the "wholesome treatment provided for the faithful" by and in the Church, "whereby the due observance of piety makes the ailing mind well for the perception of unchanging truth" (*Trin.* 1.4). This *medicina* or "treatment" builds up our true strength, filling us with "spiritual confidence" even to the point of martyrdom, rather than puffing us up with the vanities of worldly knowledge. Christian faith is the "medicine to heal the tumor of our pride" and "break the chains of sin" that bind us (*Trin.* 8.7).[30]

Augustine also frequently uses the vocabulary of cleaning and purification to evoke his sense of Christian life. In order to contemplate and gain full knowledge of God's substance "it is necessary for our minds to be purified," and "in order to make us fit and capable of grasping it, we are led along more endurable routes, nurtured on faith as long as we have not yet been endowed with that necessary purification" (*Trin.* 1.3). Later Augustine continues: "Our enlightenment is to participate in the Word . . . Yet we were absolutely incapable of such participation and quite unfit for it, so unclean were we through sin, so we had to be cleansed" (*Trin.* 4.4; cf. 4.24).[31] We can be cleansed from our sinfulness only by Christ, not only through His resurrection, but through baptism, to be discussed more fully below. Christ is our intercessor and mediator, the way by which we may "participate" in God's divinity.

This process of healing, strengthening, cleansing, and purification may be seen as the obverse of the "crucifixion of the inner man." Augustine summarizes this healing as the "renewal" of the inner man, or more specifically the renewal of the image of God in the mind. In an important passage, Augustine writes:

> To be sure, this renewal does not happen in one moment of conversion, as the baptismal renewal by the forgiveness of all sins happens in a moment, so that not even one tiny sin remains unforgiven. But it is one thing to throw off a fever, another to recover from the weakness which the fever leaves behind it; it is one thing to remove from the body a missile stuck in it, another to heal the wound it made with a complete cure. The first stage of the cure is to remove the cause of the debility, and this is done by pardoning all sins; the second stage is curing the debility itself, and this is done gradually by making steady progress in the renewal of this image. . . . About this [second stage] the apostle speaks quite explicitly when he says, "Even if our outer man is decaying, yet our inner man is being renewed day by day" (2 Cor. 4:16). . . . So then the man who is being renewed in the recognition of God and in justice

> and holiness of truth by making progress day by day, is transferring his love from temporal things to eternal, from visible to intelligible, from carnal to spiritual things; he is industriously applying himself to checking and lessening his greed for the one sort and binding himself with charity to the other. But his success in this depends on divine assistance; it is after all God who declares, "without me you can do nothing" (Jn 15:5). When the last day of his life overtakes someone who has kept faith in the mediator, making steady progress of this sort, he will be received by the holy angels to be led into the presence of the God he has worshipped and to be perfected by him and so to get his body back again at the end of the world, not for punishment but for glory. For only when it comes to the perfect vision of God will this image bear God's perfect likeness. (*Trin*. 14.23)[32]

This passage may be Augustine's best general description of the process of Christian discipleship he envisions. By a variety of means we are to "make progress day by day" in the renewal of the inner man, which essentially consists of the "transference" of love from earthly and temporal to heavenly and eternal things. This process is only possible on the basis of divine assistance through the many forms of grace, and is the "second stage" of healing and strengthening the Christian believer, after baptism's new beginning. The "complete cure" is received only in person before God at the resurrection, when the divine image is reformed to a final perfect likeness, and one finally moves beyond faith to the "perfect vision of God."

Whatever the metaphor Augustine chooses in any particular situation, whether it be crucifixion, healing, strengthening, purification, cleansing, renewal, or other tropes such as ascent or voyage, he generally suggests that the true and good Christian life is one of gradual progress in righteousness, supported and guided by grace as the inner man is renewed day by day. Augustine is quite clear, however, about the primary agency implied in his metaphors. He attacks neo-Platonic philosophers for thinking they can purify themselves sufficiently to contemplate God by their own power; in fact, Augustine argues, they are defiled by pride (*Trin*. 4.20). Against this, Augustine contends, human beings are "incapable of grasping eternal things, and weighed down by the accumulated dirt of our sins," caked on by love of temporal things, "so we need purifying" via faith in the humility and mercy of God's incarnation and self-sacrifice (*Trin*. 4.24).[33]

This implied combination of primary divine agency and secondary or derived human agency recurs in Augustine's occasional references to *exercitationes animi*, or "exercises of the soul," and his much more frequent references to *disciplina*, usually "instruction," "teaching," or "training," but sometimes "discipline" in the senses of a branch of knowledge, and of training in self-restraint. It is also fundamental to his treatment of the received Roman terminology for speaking of excellent character, that is, *virtus* or "virtue."[34]

Augustine believes that the Christian life, following Christ as the way toward Christ as the goal, is a collection of spiritual exercises. By this I mean that he sees Christian practices and experiences primarily as means of purification and reformation of the soul, all in order to become actually rather than merely potentially capable of cleaving to God in beatitude after the resurrection, and to a limited extent in this life. After 396, however, he is adamant and consistent that human efforts alone, no matter how committed to the power of reason and earnest effort, are insufficient by themselves to effect this reformation. Spiritual exercises must be Christian, and thus must be subsequent to baptism and performed as part of the Church, joined in loving unity to other believers in submission to Christ, as body parts submitting to their head.

Augustine thinks he has deep anthropological and theological reasons for his views of both the prerequisites and character of spiritual exercises, which follow from the essential nature of the human mind as a partly vitiated image of the divine.[35] Unless we properly understand, remember, and love this derived, creaturely nature precisely in its relation to the divine, we will misunderstand ourselves and God. But if we overestimate the actual state of our mental kinship to God, we will misapprehend our own powers and debilities, our love of self will remain idolatrous, and our practice of self-formation will be either obviously ineffective, or (even worse) will issue in counterfeit virtue of a particularly subtle kind.

Being created in the "image" of God is therefore not simply an ontological status, but also and primarily a charge, a calling, to be "refashioned to the image of God" (*Trin.* 7.5). Imaging God is not a state of being, but instead a lifelong process that essentially involves certain activities of the mind (7.12). As Rowan Williams argues, we "image" God when we understand ourselves as existing on the basis of the divine reality of love: "The image of God in us might be said to entail a movement into our createdness, because this is a movement into God's own life as turned 'outwards.' What this practically involves is . . . the life of corporate charity."[36] In other words, we are only truly human when we not only understand but embrace our status as created beings, radically dependent on God, unable to will the good apart from Him. But with God, as one of His chosen, one can participate in the outflowing life of the divine, serving as an agent of graced love for others. Of course for Augustine God does not need us to do His work, but He lovingly chooses to employ us, not as tools but as trusted servants. God includes us in the work of salvation through the activity of the body of Christ, that is, the church. The church may be the "house of *disciplina*" (*s.* 399.1) but what we learn in that school is how to further the work of redemption, the unmerited project of bringing good out of evil.

Christian spiritual exercises on Augustine's account may thus be best understood as responses to grace. Perhaps they should even be thought of as modes of grace, after an analogy to the Eucharist: such practices may be relied upon as guides and supports for the faithful on their journey home. They are not attempts to storm the gates of heaven, but to answer divine mercy and love with thankfulness, joy, and renewed commitment to the transference of love from earthly to heavenly things. All the different practices Augustine recommends are oriented to this movement from carnal to spiritual love. Such practices provide repeated occasions for grace to enter us, and "melt" our habitually hard hearts, and perhaps even begin to train the body to submit, as it should, to the soul and particularly the mind, as the mind is progressively refashioned to the image of God. This submission breaks our tendency to solipsistic unhappiness and delusion, and draws us out of ourselves into loving (rather than manipulative or desperate) engagement with others, when they are at last properly understood as finite, mortal children of God.

## RITUAL

*Li* 禮, "ritual," is many things for Xunzi. On the individual and familial levels, it is a method for personal formation; this is the aspect of ritual upon which I focus later. Ritual is also the source of genuine state power and authority, Xunzi thinks, much more effective at knitting the people and government together and generating political and military force than weapons and defenses, commands and punishments. Such tools obviously have their uses, but Xunzi finds them to be decidedly secondary to the quality of government, which rests primarily on ritual (15/72/9–12ff.). Ritual is even the key to the harmonious interrelationship and flourishing of heaven, earth, and humanity; it is the linchpin of what P. J. Ivanhoe has called Xunzi's "grand ecological vision."[37] Xunzi writes:

> Through [ritual] Heaven and Earth come together, the sun and moon shine, the four seasons follow each other, the stars and planets move, the great rivers flow, the myriad things all thrive, love and hate are moderated, and delight and anger made appropriate. If through ritual one is below, then one will be compliant; if through ritual one is above, then one will be enlightened. [Through it] the myriad things change but do not become chaotic. (19/92/4–6)

Although this might seem a burst of wild exuberance from Xunzi, verging on the magical, it should be read as a poetic evocation of Xunzi's ritualized conception of the cosmos. Different elements of the universe each have their appropriate roles, which the heavenly bodies fill with admirable regularity. The human role is to order both the human and natural worlds so that inevitable ebbs and flows do not result in chaos. This can be accomplished both through agriculture that magnifies and orders natural fecundity, and through what might be called public works projects, such as the dredging and diking of the Yellow and Yangzi rivers, traditionally credited to the sage king Yu, in order to stop destructive flooding.[38] For Xunzi, ritual is the key to harmonious and flourishing life, both human and non-human. It is thus his general prescription for the misrule, unrest and chaos of his age.[39]

It should be noted that Xunzi's term *li* 禮, translated here and by most others as "ritual" or "rites," has both narrow and wide senses. Its narrow sense covers the sorts of practices generally referred to by the English "ritual": for example, sacrifices, mourning rituals, and rites of passage into adulthood marked by ceremonial donning of the appropriate hat. His more common meaning is very wide, far beyond the usual sense of "ritual," including all matters of personal appearance, deportment, dress, speech, action, and internal and external discipline, and all interpersonal etiquette and even morality. Xunzi writes:

> When all uses of blood and vital energy, intention and purpose, understanding and reflection, follow ritual, then order will permeate [you]; if they do not follow ritual, then you will be agitated and chaotic, [or] slack and lazy. If your eating and drinking, clothing and dwelling, and movement and stillness follow ritual then they will be harmonious and moderate; if not they will be offensive and excessive, producing illness. If your expression and appearance, bearing and deportment, approaches and withdrawals, and walk follow ritual, then they will be elegant; if not they will be arrogant and obstinate, low and wicked, common and wild. Thus people without ritual will not live, affairs without ritual will not be completed, and states and families without ritual will not have peace. An Ode says: "Rituals and ceremonies completely correct, laughter and talk completely appropriate." This expresses it. (2/5/12–15)

It is hard to overstate how alien such a sensibility is to modern America with its vendors of "lifestyle choices" and "personal style." What to us seem to be optional matters of style and aesthetics are for Xunzi bound up in an integrated order encompassing personal and communal life, and the ecology of our environment. Clear and correct standards for such things are available and can be known: human existence should be *ya* 雅, "elegant," and manifest *wenli* 文理, "refined form and good order."

But how can this be? How could anyone think that attending to one's manner of walking, one's clothes and abode, could be so essential that without it we cannot live as human beings? Obviously Xunzi recognizes that many in his own day did not have correct ritual deportment and yet survived. Xunzi does appear to think that the moderation essential to a ritualized existence is much healthier, in a psychophysical sense, than a life without ritual, which would be marked by erratic excesses and deficiencies. Xunzi's deeper point, however, is more subtle. He thinks that to have a truly humane existence, that is, one properly regulated by and as far as possible incarnating ideals of goodness and beauty, we must have ritual in his wide sense. To be human in this fuller sense we need, Xunzi thinks, to live in community with others. To achieve this we must have social order, which to be orderly must involve hierarchy. In order for such an arrangement to be based on more than fear and intimidation on the one hand, and/or greed on the other, it needs to develop and rely on other emotions: respect and reverence for the truly worthy, love for one's family, and loyalty to good rulers. But since our raw dispositions are relatively better suited to being ruled by fear and greed, work must be done to heighten other sensibilities and reshape our dispositions.

This is where ritual as spiritual exercise fits into Xunzi's view. Through imitating classical models in the details of life, both personal and interpersonal, Xunzi thinks we can cultivate the refinement, sensitivity, and subtle judgment of the sagacious Zhou kings. When much of our existence is ritualized in this way, we are then sharing a far superior form of life. Our every gesture and word is pregnant with meaning, beautiful, and appropriate. This may seem counterintuitive, but when expectations for behavior are so far-reaching, greater possibilities for meaningful interaction open up, because the shared background of expectations against which people interpret each other is much fuller, allowing a wider range of variation in communication through more subtle shifts in expression, deportment, and spoken language.[40] At the same time, this habitation of classical forms serves as a training in virtue, by developing one's "taste" for the delights of good form in many aspects of life, and slowly retraining one's disposition accordingly.

## PRAYER

Augustine recommends several types of spiritual exercise. Some of the most central are learning (via listening to and reading scripture, along with secondary explanations like sermons); restriction and renunciation of sources of carnal pleasure, such as food and sex; and inspiring symbolic actions manifest in various liturgical settings. The form of such practices reflects Augustine's psychology. Because of the unity of the *mens*, techniques for self-formation must engage our memory, understanding, and love together. Only in this way can we effect the sort of "transference" of love that Augustine expects. So, for example, even when we search our memories to confess God's care for us and our own defections from that care, we come to understand our situation better and love God more deeply. Perhaps most tellingly, when we articulate our wishes in petitionary prayer, we can only give shape to our yearning with words, the "inner words" that combine memory, understanding, and love.

Augustine recommends three main types of prayer: petitionary, confessional, and contemplative.[41] Here, for reasons of space, I focus only on the first two types. Augustine's most sustained analysis of *oratio* or petitionary prayer occurs in Letter 130, to Proba, a rich Roman widow who had fled Rome with a retinue of women and was allowed to found a nunnery for them in Carthage. For Augustine prayer is a matter of great importance, and after the commandments on love he treats it before all other issues in the part of his *Rule* on monastic order (*ep*. 130.1.1, *reg*. 2.2). In the darkness of this world, walking by faith and not sight on our pilgrimage, "the Christian soul ought to regard itself as desolate, so that it does not cease to pray, and it should learn to turn the eye of faith to the words of the divine and holy Scriptures," as on a light in the darkness (*ep*. 130.2.5).[42] Prayer is thus an aspect of our earthly life, beset by temptation, suffering, and weakness, and will pass away, as does faith in deference to actual sight, in the life to come (130.2.5). In this life, though, all should pray to Christ as if they were poor, bereaved, and desolate widows, supplicating God night and day (130.3.7, 16.30).

We should pray above all for beatitude; this is an absolutely trustworthy and blameless goal, and should be the end of all our desire and striving (130.4.9, 14.27). Although the safest course, because of the corrupting influence of earthly pleasures, is to look upon possessions and worldly comforts with contempt, and give all that we have to the poor, it is still permissible according to Augustine to pray for temporal goods such as food, shelter, and clothing, for ourselves and all others, because such things are necessary for human life (130.3.7–8, 5.11, 6.13). Somewhat surprisingly, Augustine goes on to suggest that as long as we ultimately subordinate everything to love of God and the desire to cleave to Him, it is even permissible to desire and pray for honor and worldly power, and clothes and housing suitable to a high social station, as long as they are for a good end (even a subsidiary one like the welfare of offspring); such prayers are only bad if such things are asked for in themselves, to gratify pride or envy (130.6.12). We often also pray for relief from some affliction, and this is proper as well, as long as we truly subordinate our own will to God's, as Christ did during his passion. Unpleasant as they often are, the trials of this world heal the wound of pride, they exercise our patience, and punish or even eradicate sins; thus we should trust in God's mercy to discern what is truly most beneficial to us in the ultimate sense, and fear only that God will punish us by granting an unwise or vicious request (130.14.25–6; cf. *Trin*. 13.20). Thus there is a certain "learned ignorance" in prayer as we wait patiently for the great blessing to come and in the mean time learn patiently to trust the God who transcends human understanding, however inscrutable his decisions with regard to our petitions may be (*ep.* 130.15.28).

For Augustine prayer is fundamentally a matter of desire, or more precisely, of reshaping desire. We should pray with and for only one desire: to spend eternity in the presence of God (130.8.15). God asks us to pray our wishes to him, although he already knows everything, so that "our desire by which we may receive what He prepares to give is exercised through prayers" (130.8.17). In other words, prayer does not benefit or illuminate God in any way, but serves as an exercise for human beings to increase their holy desire for God. We ought to "pray always," not in the sense that we are murmuring or speaking words *ad infinitum*, but rather that "we cherish uninterrupted desire [for God] with faith, hope, and love." The effect of prayer correlates directly to the fervor of the desire behind it, and in a sense our desire itself is our prayer (*ep.* 130. 9.18, *en. Ps.* 37.14). We should, however, use words to pray at various set hours and seasons to admonish ourselves, and check our progress in holy desire; in this way we can "arouse ourselves more intensely to increase it" (*ep.* 130.9.18). Augustine writes:

> But at certain hours we recall our minds to the task of prayer from other cares and concerns, in which desire itself is in a sense cooled down, admonishing ourselves by the words of our prayer to aim at that which we desire; otherwise our desire that had begun to cool might become altogether cold, and be entirely extinguished, if it were not inflamed more frequently. (130.9.18)[43]

Prayer, then, is a way of fanning the flames of holy desire, which are all too frequently weakened by the distractions of secular existence. A "watchful and keen intention" is "indispensable in prayer," according to Augustine, and we should pray in whatever manner, long or short, with many words or few, that supports this state of alertness stretching out toward divine illumination (130.10.20). In general, "to petition much is to knock with a long and pious stirring of the heart towards Him to whom we pray. For this task is often carried out more with sighs than words, more with weeping than speaking" (130.10.20).[44]

While God does not need human words, they are nevertheless as useful to people in prayer as they are in reading, listening, and preaching. Augustine writes, "We, then, need words by which we may be reminded and may consider what we ask for, not by which we believe that we should either instruct or persuade the Lord." And moreover, after considering the Lord's prayer, Augustine concludes, "For it was necessary that the truth itself be committed to our memory by these words" (130.11.21). According to Augustine, desire can precede the words of prayer, which give it form, or "come after them and attend to them, that it may increase in fervor" (130.12.22). By using the divine words of the psalms and the Lord's prayer, especially, we admonish ourselves to desire what we must, for instance that God's name be seen as holy among people here on earth, and by these words "stir up our desire for that kingdom [of Heaven] that it may come for us, and that we may be found worthy to reign in it" (130.11.21).[45] All Christian prayer is summed up in the Lord's prayer, the paradigmatic petitionary prayer, and we should seek nothing beyond what can be subsumed under it (130.12.22). The right words, being divinely inspired, stir up the right desires in us, and refresh our memories, so that our intention toward and desire for God may be constantly reinflamed by daily prayer.

"Confession," or rather the Latin *confessio*, carries a double meaning. It does include the sense of confessing one's sins or failures (e.g., *conf.* 5.10.18), but also of acknowledging the glory or mercy of God, and especially of acknowledging God's healing action within one's own life (e.g., 1.6.10). Confession, for Augustine, is very similar in form and purpose to petitionary prayer or *oratio*, but even more intimate, a direct address to God concerning the state of one's soul and God's relations to that soul. Augustine writes:

> Accept the sacrifice of my confessions offered by "the hand of my tongue" which you have formed and stirred up to confess your name. "Heal all my bones" and let them say "Lord who is like you?" He who is making confession to you is not instructing you of that which is happening within him. The closed heart does not shut out your eye, and your hand is not kept away by the hardness of humanity, but you melt that when you wish, either in mercy or in punishment, and there is "none who can hide from your heat." Let my soul praise you that it may love you, and confess to you your mercies that it may praise you. (5.1.1)[46]

Confession should be a prayer of honest self-examination directed to God, truth-telling of the highest possible human order, based on a scrupulous accounting of inner impulses and thoughts (10.30.41ff.). God forms and stirs our voice, whether physical or mental, to acknowledge Him. Again, it is not a question of telling God anything He does not already know, but of shaping our "inner discourse," to borrow Hadot's terminology, into the proper theocentric form.[47] By reflecting on God's kindness to us we realize how great God is and how much we owe Him; by praising God in prayer we can increase our love for Him. And as the larding of the above passage with quotations from the psalms shows, a crucial aspect of confession for Augustine is to recognize how the word of God in scripture applies to and illuminates one's past and thus one's self.[48] The habits of concupiscence live on in our memories (10.30.41–34.51), but so do recollections of moments when God has "melted" our carnal hardness of heart, freeing us from the weight of habit to soar up in love for Him (10.27.38, 10.36.58). By thinking about them as we confess them, as past still present to us, we reform our memories through concentrated attention and conscious rearrangement of elements of our self-narrative (10.11.18). Because we are a mystery to ourselves, this process is not easy, and needs to continue throughout life, to persevere in some limited righteousness until the end, lest we cease to make progress but instead fall back into the abyss of sinful degradation (10.32.48, 10.35.57). And as we come to know ourselves better over time, Augustine hopes, we will come to know the God who knows us better than we ever will ourselves (10.1.1).

## SPIRITUAL EXERCISES AND THE MANIPULATION OF INNER AND OUTER

One of the striking similarities between Augustine and Xunzi is their shared conviction that learning is a foundational spiritual exercise. People cannot flourish without learning. Put another way, we do not innately possess the resources necessary to live a good life, and so must learn from others the most important, indeed salvific, facts about human existence. Moreover, learning must continue throughout our lives. It is not as if there are a few earthshaking truths we must grasp after which all is resolved. It might seem, then, that both Xunzi and Augustine would insist on the necessity of external assistance because of the paucity of internal resources available to uncultivated people. While this is true in a general sense, it obscures important differences in their treatments of what is "inner" or hidden and what is "outer" or visible, differences that help explain many of the dissimilarities between their overarching accounts of spiritual exercises.[49]

To grasp the deeper organizing principles in Augustine and Xunzi's regimes of personal formation, we need to note their partially divergent conceptions of what is morally required of human beings. In other words, what counts as a good or right action, for each of them? On this issue Augustine sits squarely within a central stream of Western ethical reflection, one which he helped shape. For Augustine, the crucial issue in evaluating human actions is whether they stem from a rightly directed will. This means they must be properly motivated by *caritas*, and properly "referred" to the right ultimate end, beatitude with God (*Trin.* 11.10). The notion of reference at play here concerns the reason or end for which an action is taken, and Augustine envisions logical links between immediate proximate intentions, intermediate goals, and the ultimate ends of beatitude, glory, or pleasure, which determine the moral quality of every particular *voluntas*, no matter how minor. This means, crucially, that for Augustine actions that seem to perfectly fulfill the requirements of some duty, at least outwardly in terms of performance, can still be fundamentally evil if they are ultimately motivated by and "referred" to some wrong end, such as personal glory.[50] An example would be doing some visibly good deed, such as helping the proverbial old lady across the street, for an ultimately selfish reason, such as gaining a good reputation so that one might be entrusted with responsibility and thus power.

A corollary of this conception is that the actual outcome of one's efforts is secondary at best, for Augustine. Indeed, because God uses all things for good, even the evil wills of sinning humans, according to Augustine *every* action will in some objective, external sense become part of God's providential design, and thus be both just and good. If one's own aims in action are thwarted, one may still rest assured that God has justly and wisely overruled one's efforts. For Augustine, in sum, moral evaluation hinges fundamentally on individual intention and motivation. As Augustine famously counsels, "Love, and do what you will. . . . Let the root of love be within. From such a root nothing but good can come forth" (*ep. Jo.* 7.8).

For Xunzi the situation is more complicated. On his account right action must be manifest in correct outward form, although to be perfect such action must be matched by appropriate emotions and desires; such is the "middle course where ritual flows." In his criticism of Mencius, Xunzi defines *shan* 善, "good," and *e* 惡, "bad," as follows: "From antiquity to the present, what all under Heaven have called good is what is correct, properly patterned, peaceful, and orderly. What is called bad is what is slanted, vicious, perverse, and chaotic" (23/115/1–2). The root meanings of goodness for Xunzi seem to concern publicly observable states of affairs, mostly involving proper social order, but the context in which this remark is made is the debate over the character of human *xing* or instincts, which suggests that the quality of human impulses is also at issue. Moreover, badness for Xunzi seems to include certain qualities of volition, such as viciousness and perversity.

To grasp what he has in mind, recall that for Xunzi the Way is "marked out" by the rituals (18/82/22–18/83/1). As discussed previously, to follow the Way one must behave in a ritually appropriate manner, which requires a certain sort of personal demeanor as well as a wide range of specific behaviors, across all spheres of human activity, including but going well beyond particular important ceremonies. Moreover, the minute details of ritual incarnate general norms of justice (*yi* 義), and so are crucial to the right ordering of society. Indeed, Xunzi says at one point that the Way is essentially a matter of creating community, by properly ordering, harmonizing, and nourishing people, so that they may flourish together (12/59/11–16). All of this suggests that right actions, on Xunzi's understanding, both *aim at* and *successfully achieve* the outward manifestation of a properly patterned society.[51]

This insistence on excellent observable form might suggest that Xunzi does not care particularly much about proper motivation and intention, but this would be mistaken. (It would also make rather mysterious his insistence on spiritual exercises designed to reform our dispositions and desires.) It is clear that Xunzi thinks we must possess the proper emotions and dispositions in order to fully exemplify the Way. One of Xunzi's more general ways of making this point is his insistence that right action (i.e., action in accord with ritual and justice, and thus the *Dao* as well) must manifest the virtue of *ren* 仁, which for Xunzi means something like "benevolence," "caring," or "humaneness" (8/28/15). Indeed, Xunzi explicitly rejects actions that are not based on ritual and justice but which accidentally hit on what is outwardly fitting, because he thinks such actions are not truly benevolent and will thus necessarily "fail," perhaps because they will fail to move their recipients appropriately (8/33/14). It appears that for Xunzi fully good actions must both be motivated by and manifest the benevolence, justice, and beautiful propriety characteristic of the Confucian Way.

This generates an interesting complication, given Xunzi's account of assent overruling our inadequate emotions and desires. To put the point briefly, Xunzi's psychology and personal formation program suggest that most people, not being sages, will need frequently to push themselves toward proper outward observances of ritual and just action in ways that pull back from or go beyond their felt emotions and desires. Such actions, for Xunzi, must in some significant sense be good, because their ultimate goal is enacting the Way, even though they are imperfect in their flawed motivation. Xunzi thus prioritizes correct outward form and performance, but relates this in complex ways to our considered intentions manifest in what we assent to, and to our initially misdirected dispositions and impulses.

These differences in their conceptions of what counts as genuinely good or right action play out in the regimes of spiritual exercises that Augustine and Xunzi each recommend, especially those that go beyond textual study and serve to help internalize or genuinely realize the lessons learned in such study. Xunzi's overarching concern with proper social order and beautiful outward form (*wenli* 文禮, "proper form and good order") leads him to devote much of his attention to what may be called performative practices like ritual and music. Such practices order persons in terms of their appearance and positioning, but also their interrelations within groups, and aim throughout to create forms and patterns that are *mei* 美, "fine" and "beautiful," as well as just. In this sort of practice individuals are pulled outward, their attention focused on timely and appropriate interactions with others. They thus cultivate alert awareness of others and their actions, and sensitivity to the numerous moral and aesthetic distinctions that ritual forms create and enforce.

When Augustine moves beyond study, by contrast, he advocates turning primarily to symbolic activities such as the Eucharist and discursive practices such as petitionary prayer, contemplation, and confession.[52] Even practices of self-restraint such as fasting and celibacy are repeatedly understood symbolically, and Augustine clearly envisions them as being simultaneous with more positive, articulate practices of prayer, mutual exhortation, and self-examination, as in the annual Easter vigil. All of these exercises encourage what Foucault has called a "hermeneutics of the self" wherein one carefully scrutinizes one's inner impulses and thoughts, even when these concern seemingly outward activities such as partaking in the bread and wine, or refraining from eating for a period of time.[53] Because the mind for Augustine is a trinity of memory, understanding, and will/love, which exists as an ongoing stream of "inner words," the crucial issues in personal formation are to discern the quality and "direction" of one's inner discourse at any given moment, and to do all one can to reshape it and properly direct it toward its true end. These goals may be accomplished by refusing consent to sinful internal words before they issue in action, by as it were "reciting" inwardly the discourse one wishes to adopt, and by using the proper terms to analyze and articulate one's own conception of self and world. Instead of finding one's rightful place in beautiful and just harmonization with other ritual actors, for Augustine we are to find our true self by correctly discerning our own deep inner relation to God. By locating and relying on this divine fountain within we may confidently go forth to love neighbor and even enemy, but without it we are lost, both inwardly and outwardly.

To put the contrast schematically, Augustine pursues an "inside out" model of personal formation, while Xunzi pursues an "outside in" model.[54] In other words, Augustine's exercises focus as much as possible on the mysterious source of our actions in our inward "heart of hearts." By working to restrain concupiscent impulses so that God's love and wisdom may enter in and inspire us to righteous action, spiritual exercises *directly* address what is most inward in order to change what generates our outward behavior. Xunzi instead suggests that the most potent strategy for effecting lasting inward change is to focus on what we can control reasonably well, that is our outward movements, gestures, and speech, and by working to perfect these observable actions we will slowly and *indirectly* reform the impulses that move us spontaneously, until at last they lead just as surely to outwardly perfect action.

This contrast helps explain some of the striking differences between Augustine's and Xunzi's programs for personal formation. Xunzi gives remarkably little attention to the sorts of meditations that seem so integral to the various forms of Augustinian prayer, for instance. Xunzi makes exercises such as the memorization and recitation of classical poetry subsidiary and introductory parts of his account of Confucian study and learning, and explicitly warns against making them more central than ritual practice under the personal guidance of a wise teacher (1/3/7–1/4/4). And while Xunzi does mention self-examination occasionally in his writings, it occupies nothing like the central place confession and self-scrutiny do for Augustine (1/1/5, 1/4/16–19, 2/5/3–6, 2/6/12, 11/54/13; cf. 1/1/12–15). Xunzian self-examination seems to be a self-interrogation concerning one's treatment of close and distant human beings, and whether one has conscientiously enacted what one teaches and purports to follow, rather than a careful sifting and interpretation of thoughts and desires in order to ferret out hidden sinfulness.

Furthermore, in contrast to the relatively direct pageantry of Xunzian ritual, Augustinian rituals such as the Eucharist are shot through with symbolism, and are meant to be occasions for the contemplation of symbols. As Robert Dodaro has argued, "behind [Augustine's] enthusiasm for liturgical symbolism lies a Platonic sensitivity to the movement from visible to invisible orders of reality."[55] According to Augustine, as we move mentally from the physical reality of the bread and wine, to their Christian symbolic meaning, to the *spiritus* or inner meaning of those Christian symbols, our minds are excited and drawn "upward and inward" to God's eternal truths in a way that would be difficult to achieve without allegory and symbolism (*ep.* 55.21). For Xunzi, the details of the rituals he discusses have meaning in that they are commonly understood to express certain feelings and thoughts, but the mode of this meaning is not in any obvious sense symbolic, but rather conventional and somewhat literal, as when the grave goods are all in some way incomplete or unusable, to mark the fact that, although mourners wish the dead person were simply moving to a new abode, he or she will not actually be using any of these implements (19/95/6–13).

Let us pursue one such issue in greater depth. The basic contrast between inside-out and outside-in strategies of personal cultivation helps explain an intriguing and deep disagreement between Augustine and Xunzi concerning the value of pretence in self-formation. Consider first Augustine's absolute proscription of lying, which he discusses in two separate treatises, and which was a departure from earlier, somewhat less strict Christian reflection on the topic (*mend.*, *c. mend.*).[56] For Augustine, lying appears to be essential to most forms of sin, which except in unusual cases (e.g., the unevangelized who are "before the law") require that we lie to ourselves about the relative goodness of the end we pursue, such as human companionship, by semiconsciously overvaluing it relative to God's unchanging hierarchical ordering of reality (e.g., *conf.* 2.3.7, 2.6.14, 2.8.16,

*Gen. lit.* 11.42.59). Since God for Augustine *is* the Truth (*conf.* 3.6.10, *c. mend.* 40), lying is at root a defection from God and God's ordering of reality, and so may never be excused under any circumstances, no matter what other evils might be avoided by doing so (*mend.* 42). Indeed, for Augustine, the worst sort of deception is a lie about matters of religion; he views any sort of lying in the midst of religious instruction or training, purportedly for someone's spiritual good, as particularly heinous (*mend.* 17).

This absolutist conception of truthfulness led Augustine to exalt a vision of the religious life as a continuing confession of the truth, both inwardly and outwardly, so that the Christian life can be seen as a contest between truth-telling and lying as general modes of existence. According to Augustine, "Every proud person is an impostor. . . . any proud person pretends to be what he is not; he cannot do otherwise." In contrast to this, the "true Israelite" or genuine believer who "ascends to Jerusalem" is one "in whom no guile [*dolus*, lit. 'artifice'] is to be found." Augustine concludes: "Why do they ascend? How do they ascend? To confess to your name, oh Lord. It cannot be more splendidly said. Just as pride presumes, humility confesses. The presumptuous wants to appear to be something they are not; just so someone who confesses does not want to appear other than they truly are, and loves what He [i.e., God] is" (*en. Ps.* 121.8). On Augustine's account it appears that pretense or outward artifice is always a mark of human pride, which seeks to dissemble about its true state as subject to God. This world-oriented guile is radically opposed to the truth-confessing love of God. The need for humble confession of dependence on God becomes only greater when one takes up exalted positions within the community, such as ecclesiastical office or consecrated virginity. Indeed, a great danger in such a state is pretending to be humble outwardly, while inwardly one begins to revel proudly in the graces one has already been given, which destroys from within like a spiritual cancer (*virg.* 43.44).

Needless to say, such a vision of the dangers of pretence is dramatically opposed to both the rhetoric and, to a lesser degree, the real position of Xunzi, who provocatively chooses *wei* 偽 or "artifice" as his summary term for both the process of personal formation and good character itself (22/107/24). On Xunzi's account, we must meet objective moral standards, which often take the form of observable public performances, despite the fact that our inadequately cultivated dispositions do not spontaneously make us feel like doing so. We thus, in a very real sense, pretend to be more virtuous than we yet are, by imitating the clothes, gestures, words, and general demeanor of a noble man, even though this does violence to our true feelings.

Is Xunzi guilty of advising all aspiring Confucians to lie about their true character? The charitable answer must be no, because a Xunzian aspirant is not deceiving himself, or even others, about what he is doing, which is learning to become good by trying to act the part. More precisely, when someone engages in "artifice" in Xunzi's technical sense, they are *ke* 可, "assenting," to some particular plan of action based on preceding *lü* 慮, "deliberation," about what is best, that is, what matches the Way in the current situation, or if they are true beginners, by assenting to directions given by their teacher, whom they respect and trust even though they do not yet understand him well. While the aspirant will suffer the frustration of thwarting some of his desires, he will be achieving, however clumsily and imperfectly, what he aims for, which is a ritually correct performance. Even in the case of an educated man, Xunzi's partly cultivated Confucian, who assents to acting properly in public on the basis of his own assessment of some matter despite his countervailing desires, this cannot really be counted as deception, because of the essential role of his assent in making such an action possible. Such Confucians are neither deceived about their own internal states, because they overrule their inappropriate desires and emotions, nor do they deceive others, because they honestly cherish the values conveyed by their performances.

Xunzi's psychological separation of assent from the responsive system of dispositions governing spontaneous desire and emotion thus makes possible a fundamentally different form of pretence from anything envisaged by Augustine. But even a very charitable Augustinian might wonder why exactly Xunzi thinks "acting the part" of goodness will eventually make one good. Might it not simply cultivate acting skill, while leaving one's heart and mind as corrupt as ever?

Xunzi's reply to such a query would be multi-faceted. First, there are very important dissimilarities between "acting" as a contemporary artistic practice and Xunzian ritual as a spiritual exercise. Acting does not intrinsically relate to some higher goal, and can be pursued for any number of reasons, in pursuit of goods internal to the practice such as producing splendid dramatic performances, or further cultivating one's skill as an actor; or goods external to the practice, such as earning a paycheck, becoming famous, or running away from one's own troubled existence.[57] By contrast, Xunzian ritual is supposed to be performed in order to follow the Way by making just and beautiful both everyday existence and important occasions. Moreover, acting covers any and all sorts of behavior—believable simulation of the full range of human conduct is included. But Xunzian ritual is focused on only one sort of character, that of the ancient sages, and is meant to encode and vivify their mode of life in as much detail as possible, so that the aspiring Confucian is not learning to imitate in general, but to imitate the mode of life of the wisest and best human beings.[58] Thus the skill at ritual an aspirant cultivates by following the advice of his teacher would be skill only at acting like a sage. Moreover, skill at acting in the contemporary sense is a specialized craft that one might exercise or not exercise whenever one felt like it. But for Xunzi, and for Confucians generally, "skill" at ritual is equivalent to increasing mastery of the overarching art of living as a human being, which covers all aspects of life and is not something one sets aside, or even could set aside if sufficiently cultivated, based on whim or circumstance.[59] In other words, for Confucians like Xunzi, genuine skill at ritual is identical to virtue itself, in their conception.

Moving to the vocabulary of "skill" recalls Aristotle's famous discussion of cultivating virtue through practicing it, where he distinguishes sharply between virtue and skill in order to defeat the objection that one could not learn to be virtuous by doing virtuous actions, since such actions must have the proper intention already to be truly virtuous.[60] Aristotle suggests that while excellent outward form is sufficient to judge the goodness of craft products, it is not enough to judge the skill of the artisan. Moreover, it is insufficient for virtuous actions to merely possess the right qualities; such actions must be done by a person in the right state, i.e., one who knows what he is doing and why (something good, because it is good), and furthermore does it out of a "firm and unchanging" state of character. On this basis he distinguishes between just actions, which are the sort that a just person would do, and performing such actions in the right way, in the manner that a truly just person would. Aristotle at this point simply asserts that the only way one can move toward actually possessing steady states of virtuous character is to frequently perform actions that outwardly manifest the good ("just actions"), as a way of practicing the deliberation that decides on what is good for its own sake, and of training emotions, desires, and discernment in order to see and judge in a consistently just manner.

Xunzi, however, can go well beyond this sort of account, given his view of the centrality of ritual skill to moral virtue. For him, this special sort of skill is much closer to virtue, and indeed essential to its full possession. Where Aristotle distinguishes sharply between virtue and skill, Xunzi conspicuously fails to make such a sharp distinction, although we should note the disanalogies mentioned above between acting and ritual mastery.

Although the two sorts of practice do differ, Xunzian personal formation seems to share significant commonalities with the process of becoming an excellent musician or dancer.[61] In such practices one must learn many basic rules, and learn how actually to execute certain sorts of movements and, eventually, performances, so that they are beautiful and good, according to the standards of the practice in question.[62] Several related things happen as practice deepens. As one gains greater expertise, one begins to understand the rationale for aspects of the practice that initially seemed arbitrary, painful, or irritating. Skill of this sort, however, is just as much physical as mental—one learns how to play the violin beautifully with one's fingers and hands as much as one's mind; one learns with both body and mind how to move smoothly and easily through various sorts of ritually regulated interactions. One also comes to appreciate better the subtleties that differentiate poor, middling, and fine performances. In tandem with this growing sensitivity, one gradually develops what can only be called artful style in one's own practice, although here there would presumably be room for a range of achievement. Indeed, Xunzi's near-assimilation of virtue with a certain sort of skill at living extends to his treatment of the sage, who may be distinguished from the noble man not only by his greater understanding of the Way and his perfected dispositions, but by his extraordinary skill at politically effective moral leadership (8/30/15–17). Perhaps most crucially, as ritual mastery increases one gradually delights more and more in the beauty of the art one is creating through performance, and in one's own and others' abilities to perform so well.

This last point is essential to the plausibility of Xunzi's Confucianism. One might wonder whether Xunzi can adequately explain how those he calls "petty people" can come to be motivated by love for the Way itself, rather than the benefits they might perceive to "playing along" with it. Xunzi's ritual reformation model hinges on the characteristics of performative skill training just discussed, combined with the process of Confucian learning. As this regimen is pursued over time, one will become aware of new sources of satisfaction, new values, that will relativize all that went before, and show that one's previous concerns were indeed "petty" or "small," as Xunzi puts it. Profit or personal benefit is not evil, on Xunzi's reckoning, but it is dramatically less important and valuable than the Confucian form of life marked by social justice, benevolent communal harmony, and the ritual and aesthetic culture that makes these possible. Confucian learning, ritual, and musical practice thus promise a transformation of our understanding and scheme of evaluation, our sensibilities, our capabilities and habits, and our tastes and desires. Xunzi's Confucianism is a comprehensive art of living well, shorn of the contemporary associations of that phrase with self-indulgent pleasure-seeking.

On Xunzi's account, almost everything that makes life good grows on the basis of learning, considered broadly. In the same way that we might justifiably say that someone who never learned to read at all has missed all that comes from loving literature, and lived a stunted and deprived existence, Xunzi thinks that the culture of Confucian learning and practice opens up the most important human goods, without which human beings are barely distinguishable from animals.[63]

A critic could certainly persist, however, and question whether this has just moved the problem of "faking it" to a new level. Why couldn't one view the whole Confucian system as merely an excellent method for personal advancement, as many throughout pre-modern Chinese history undoubtedly did? Xunzi, like the circle of Confucius's followers who produced the *Analects*, is fully aware of this problem, and in the end thinks there can be no foolproof certainty that going through the "wood straightening" process of submitting to a Confucian teacher will automatically lead to true inner goodness. Only if that process genuinely opens new horizons of life, which kindle awareness of and taste for previously unimagined goods, will Xunzian virtue become possible. A story in one of the late chapters of the *Xunzi* probably put together by his students presents Confucius talking to a Duke about how to choose worthy ministers. Confucius first suggests choosing those who follow the ancient ritual codes, including dress and demeanor, to which the Duke responds: "Is anyone who dons court robes and court shoes and tucks an official tablet into his sash a worthy person?" Confucius replies that this is not necessarily so, and then clearly relates the excellence of Confucians to the way they focus their *zhi* 志, "intentions," (i.e., direct their heart/mind) on the ways of the ancients, and care little about food, which seems to stand in here for personal interests in wealth and pleasure. He concludes, "even if there should be some who abide by these [ways of the ancients] and still do wrong, they would be few indeed, would they not?" To which the Duke can only reply: "Well spoken!" (31/144/27–31/145/5)[64]

The idea seems to be that it would be extraordinarily difficult to pursue Confucian training long enough to become observably excellent at ritual without being changed inwardly. If one never came to delight in the Way, one's dedication would flag and one would simply give up, or one would betray continuing pettiness through "slips" of the tongue or body. (This suggests that corrupt, lazy, or irreducibly "petty" students would eventually by expelled from a Xunzian teaching group.) Xunzi thinks that the practices of learning, ritual, and music are themselves very potent, and when guided by a capable teacher and accompanied by other serious students one will be "rubbed" daily by good influences that only heighten these exercises' effectiveness. But since the root issue is the transformation of the self-commanding human heart/mind, Xunzi must allow for all-too-explicable failures of cultivation, due to the intransigent pull of instinctive desires. Such failures may take the form of "apostates" from Confucianism who advocate some other Way, or the *su Ru* 俗儒, "vulgar Confucians," whom Xunzi describes with scorn as those who ape the manner of a true ritualist, spout pointless quotations from the *Odes*, all for the purpose of enriching themselves at the expense of others (8/32/17–21).

Might the aesthetic delights of Confucian ritual become a sort of idol, so that the adept who sees and enjoys his growing mastery of ritual might fall prey to a final sort of immoral seduction, caring only about the beauty of ritual performance and forgetting the value of justice and benevolence? While Xunzi does not explicitly entertain this possibility, it seems clear that he could understand this as a case of obsession by ritual. While ritual is a fine thing, essential to personal formation and the conduct of a good life, for Xunzi, it is not the only or uniquely supreme human value. Apparent "mastery" of ritual without a deeper understanding and love for the Way, manifest in equal possession of the virtues of benevolence and justice, would be rigid and misguided (2/7/18–19). In other words it would be merely counterfeit propriety.

To sum up, Xunzi thinks "artifice" is both necessary and saving because it allows us to learn, as embodied actors, how to live like sages. Such artifice is more like learning an art of performance than it is like pretending to be something one is not, because beginners cannot effectively pretend to be ritual masters, any more than I can pretend to be a concert violinist. Early stage Confucians aspire to ritual mastery, but they only gradually approach such a state. In so doing they are genuinely transformed, so long as they persevere with a heart/mind focused on the Way, because ritual for Xunzi is not something that one engages in occasionally, but rather a style or mode of existence which permeates all of our activities and social interactions. As one gradually grasps what is truly at stake, one will even *shen qi du* 慎其獨, "be watchful over oneself when alone," so that one never departs from ritual even for a moment (3/11/7).

One might even say, then, that Xunzi allows for something like inspiration, and even demands it. Where Augustine solves the problem of sincerity and moral purpose decisively by insisting on the primacy of divine agency in enabling true human agency and virtue, Xunzi "solves" the problem with much less finality. For Xunzi we come to experience a new sincerity, if we ever do, when we find ourselves to be changed by our ongoing practices of learning and performance, when the Way we sought in order to find safety and a more impressive and pleasant form of life turns out to be something altogether richer than we had initially imagined possible, and we find that the desires that once moved us have been joined by new desires, subtly changing the whole constellation of our emotional life, in gradually better accord with our increasingly sophisticated understanding of what life is about.

## PERSONAL TRANSFORMATION IN COMPARATIVE PERSPECTIVE

Augustine and Xunzi both aim ultimately at perfection, although how they conceive of such a state differs dramatically. They also focus on rather different issues as they chart the path toward this perfection, which reflect their distinctive worries about the gravest spiritual dangers. Examining their differing interests in mapping these "stages of development" helps to prepare the way for comparing their complex regimes of personal formation. Early on in his authorship Augustine develops his sequential account of the seven gifts of the Holy Spirit, but under the pressure of his debate with Pelagianism he later submerges this account in favor of the simpler scheme of law and grace that he discerns in Paul's epistles.[65] Xunzi, for his part, appears not to change his conception of a ladder of ethical development that stretches from the vast category of "pettiness," up through becoming "educated," and then "noble," to the final goal of sagehood.[66]

Over the course of his embattled episcopate Augustine becomes more and more convinced that the dangers of spiritual elitism and religious arrogance generally outweigh the goods to be attained through in-depth analysis of the real differences between beginning and advanced believers. He thus gravitates toward a scheme that draws a sharp line between those true believers who are "under grace" and those "pagans" and "heretics" who are outside the fold, still "under the law," whether they realize it or not. This scheme also draws a second sharp distinction between the living and the dead: it places all good Christians into the same fundamental status, dependent "under grace" on God's mercy, continuing to yearn for a time when their inner struggles will cease and they will be fully healed for eternal life "in peace." Xunzi, by contrast, gives all of his attention to this period of religious discipleship which Augustine seeks to level out.[67] Why this difference?

Augustine's growing resistance to distinguishing a hierarchy of spiritual achievement stems from his alarm over the extreme danger posed by *superbia*, "pride" or "arrogance," to all who attempt to make progress in righteousness.[68] Such arrogance afflicts not only proud Roman traditionalists, but even some outwardly exemplary Christians such as Pelagius. Augustine's scheme of law and grace underlines the absolutely fundamental distinction he sees between a life rooted in love of self and one rooted in love of God.[69] Even the distinction between being "under grace" and "in peace" serves to cultivate humility in believers by reminding them that perfection is impossible in this life, no matter how great their efforts to avoid sin and cleave to God. All aspects of the schema are designed to prod Christians to cast their hopes on God, instead of relying on their own strength. For us in this life, according to Augustine, no one can know his or her own spiritual state with perfect clarity, although presumably one can discern evidence of the presence of grace whenever one is genuinely moved to take some holy, loving action. But beyond such wondrous signs of new life growing in the wake of baptism, even those who have been given the grace of a superior calling such as virginity have no way of knowing if their hearts have become pure enough to willingly accept martyrdom, the ultimate test of faith for Augustine, which is most certainly open to those who are married, if God grants it (*virg*. 44.45, 47).

Xunzi shares this concern about arrogance only in the derivative sense that it conflicts with his central virtues of benevolence, ritual propriety, and justice. Pride is not a special or uniquely potent danger, in Xunzi's reckoning. The most obvious human difficulties stem from ignorant impulse-following and the chaos and misrule that stem from and exacerbate this sort of life. The more subtle danger of obsession shares some similarities with *superbia*, at least in the after-effects of self-satisfaction and preference for illusion over uncomfortable truth (21/102/5ff.). But instead of being centered on the "mimetic desire" for God-like sovereignty provoked by Satan's promise to Adam and Eve that "you shall be as gods," Xunzian obsession must be a partial apprehension of the truth, wrong only in its limited scope and failure to comprehend the larger patterns of existence.[70] Xunzi in fact thinks that every person desires to have the authority and lavish pleasures of an emperor, but he seems to see this as fundamentally a point about the strength and range of human desire, not its secret deviousness in deflecting moral self-cultivation into self-aggrandizement. Indeed, he appears to use the prospect of becoming a glorious emperor as rhetorical enticement in recommending Confucianism to the aspiring rulers of his day. This at least implies that pursuit of such a vision will not automatically plunge a ruler into evil; it also implies that Xunzi is quite confident in his abilities as a wise counselor, and in the power of virtuous ministers to steer an ambitious king rightly (11/53/12–25; note also 4/16/18ff.). Despite this seeming nonchalance about the dangers of the quest for supreme power and position, Xunzi's own program of ritual reformation centers on the need for aspiring Confucians to incessantly practice their deference as a corrective for human self-assertion, which suggests that he takes the ethical problem of arrogance more seriously than it might at first appear.

These differences in Augustine's and Xunzi's estimation of human desires for power and mastery point toward their importantly distinct understandings of subjection. By "subjection" I mean the sense of human agency as ordered toward and in important respects constituted by some authoritative standard or entity. Both Augustine and Xunzi are too frequently saddled with rather stupidly authoritarian interpretations, wherein the "best" human life is the one marked by the most thorough groveling before extant religious and even political powers.[71] Both do reject untutored self-guidance as profoundly misguided, but much of their respective bodies of work can be read as efforts to explain the sort of "tutoring" necessary for a truly humane and just life to be possible. Augustine and Xunzi are concerned to make true human moral agency possible, despite difficulties, not to derail or jail it.

For Augustine, the ultimate authority is of course God, and more specifically the triune Christian God as properly understood by the Catholic Church. Human beings cannot comprehend themselves, nor live well, unless they understand themselves in relation to God, Christ (including his body here on earth, the church), and the Holy Spirit (e.g., *en. Ps.* 121.8). Such a relation must be subordinate, in the sense that Christ's word to believers, "even if obscure, is better and truer than any insights that we can gain by our own efforts" (*doct. Chr.* 2.7.9). Such subordination and dependence is distasteful to fallen humanity, precisely because we have been rendered rebellious, riven internally by lusts for dominance, covetous possession, and selfish enjoyment. In our zest to "be like gods" we create prisons for ourselves out of habit, making ourselves ever more wretched. "Conversion" is the process of breaking these chains, of a gain in freedom, power, and even self-control, and the ongoing process of "making progress in righteousness" continues this increase in true agency. For Augustine, then, agency that is derived from and appropriately dependent on the divine is true, good, and potent; all other "agency" is in the end only a simulacrum, still subject to God's authority, but struggling fruitlessly against this fact rather than accepting and indeed loving it.

Turning to Xunzi the situation is not quite as clear, at least at first. *Tian* 天, or "Heaven" does occupy the supreme ritual position in the cosmos, but it is not the sort of entity that issues moral commands or insures the ultimate justice of events, nor is it the source of the authority of the *Dao*, for Xunzi. On his account we must be careful not to confuse the human Way with the very different Way of Heaven, each of which involves very different tasks. It might appear that Confucian tradition, especially as accumulated in the classics, would be the ultimate authority for Xunzi, but he makes it clear that the real authority rests with the human beings who carry on the Confucian tradition. Only they know how to interpret the classic texts, which are confusing and opaque to the uninitiated, Xunzi thinks (1/3/20–1/4/4). Moreover, only the best and wisest human beings have fully mastered Confucian ritual in such a way that they may teach it to others. This practical, fully articulate ritual mastery is the ultimate ground of their authority, and the ultimate source for aspiring Confucians. As Xunzi says:

> Ritual is the means by which to rectify yourself. A teacher is the means by which to rectify [your practice of] ritual. . . . When your dispositions are at peace in ritual and your understanding is like that of your teacher, then you have become a sage. Hence to oppose ritual is to be without a model; to oppose your teacher is to be without a teacher. To refuse to accept your teacher and the model and instead prefer to govern yourself: this is like relying on a

> blind person to distinguish colors, or relying on a deaf person to distinguish sounds; you have no way to abandon chaos and foolishness. (2/8/1–4)

Without reliance on a teacher and the external models he provides, people have no way to gain a sense of what is truly good. At first we are all morally "blind" and "deaf," Xunzi thinks. Only with carefully guided practice can we develop an understanding of and taste for the Way, which is what the rituals themselves "mark out" (17/82/22–17/83/1).[72] And eventually, after many years of practice our tastes or desires will become "transformed," Xunzi thinks, so that we can as sages continue the tradition ourselves without painful strain, and without error. Thus for Xunzi true human agency is found in service as the "ministers" or indeed "agents" of the *Dao*, that is, in actively governing ourselves and the world so that justice and beauty might prevail everywhere.

Clearly both Augustine and Xunzi require individually chosen subordination to just authorities as the necessary precondition for true human agency, although they conceive the particulars rather differently. Before moving on to more specific comparisons, however, we can sharpen some of the differences between them by noting the distinctive "spiritual geographies" imagined by Xunzi and Augustine as the spaces defining human agency.

Augustine conceives of desire, and indeed all love, as having a vertical dimension that relates it to God, presumed in this image to be "above" us and other worldly things.[73] The *voluntas*-aspect of each of our mind's "inner words" is striving either "up" toward God or "down" toward various changeable physical realities. This radical disjunction explains many very basic features of Augustine's understanding of the religious life. First, it means that at the basis of any human life is a fundamental orientation, either correctly ordered to God, or incorrectly away from him, which in this spatial scheme must be an opposite orientation. Second, this explains Augustine's strong interest in conversion, literally "turning around" to face God as one should. Sin is not missing the target occasionally, as implied by Xunzi's formulation of fine character as "hitting the target" one hundred times out of one hundred (1/4/12); for Augustine sin does not even aim at the target, but away from it. Augustine does use a goal or target metaphor in the sense that beatitude in the presence of God is the end of all of our striving; what is unique is his insistence on how radically misguided sin must be, as well as the difficulty implied by the image of rising up to the heavens against the pull of our carnal "gravity" dragging us back to earth.

In contrast to this picture, the space implied by Xunzi's conception of moral agency is, first of all, fundamentally horizontal: we are lost, and seek a way through the world, with travel through space serving as an image for travel through time. There is no different realm to ascend to in Xunzi's Confucianism. Xunzi does use the metaphor of a fork in the road to underline the gravity of choosing the right path to follow, and insists that a seemingly small error at the start can lead to terrible results later on (11/53/25–6). And as noted previously, he yearns for a clear distinction between what is "within" the Way and what "outside" it. But his conception of obsession as focused on partial truths that obscure our awareness of broader issues suggests that it is at least logically conceivable for Xunzi that even non-Confucians might make "errors" without being radically misguided. Of course Augustine distinguishes between more and less serious sins, as does Xunzi, and Xunzi does not hesitate to denounce the grievous errors of numerous opponents, including fellow Confucian Mencius, so it would be easy to overstate their differences here. The key issue is simply to note that Augustine's imagination of moral space drives him frequently to quite radical diagnoses of sin and evil, as in his disputes with, for example, the Donatists and Pelagians.

This difference in imagining the nature of the moral life also plays out in Xunzi's lack of interest in conversion.[74] According to Xunzi, we start out lost and ignorant, lacking reliable orientation. Our "bad" innate impulses do misguide us, but mostly because they overreach and thereby conflict with important values (to which we start out insensible), not because they direct us absolutely contrary to the good. Xunzi's followers, at least, seem to have thought that lifelong Confucian education, beginning in childhood, was the ideal (27/134/16). There would in any case seem to be no religious value, on Xunzi's account, in going wrong by following one's own devices, in order to see the bankruptcy of one's own resources for self-direction and to turn dramatically back to God, as with Augustine.

## CONCLUSION: THE PROBLEM OF COMPARATIVE EVALUATION

Leaving aside global theological judgments as either quixotic, if pursued from putatively neutral grounds, or unilluminating, if they simply reflect previous confessional commitments, what can a contemporary student of these ancient ethical vocabularies conclude about their strengths and weaknesses, with regard to personal formation? Numerous arguments are possible here, but I will concentrate on only a few, and even these can only be sketched rather than fully developed. Xunzi's account seems particularly capable of addressing the everyday struggle to domesticate and train our first-order desires, and thus better illuminates gradual progress in cultivating virtue; he also, for related reasons, articulates a fuller and more positive role for human embodiment in the moral and religious life.

Augustine's ethical vocabulary, on the other hand, seems better suited to addressing our on-going, second-order tendencies to rebel against the very idea of this sort of work on ourselves. He also provides a much better account of what can be called radical evil as a continuing human potential.

Xunzi's psychological model makes a rather sharp distinction between two kinds of motivation: the first and most basic type is desire, *yu* 欲, which he conceives as a spontaneous reaction of our relatively stable disposition, *qing* 情; the second is assent, *ke* 可, which is fundamentally a form of judgment about what is possible, permissible, or best in some situation. This two-source model makes it rather easy to envisage how second-order evaluations of our first-order desires could be brought to bear on those desires, at least insofar as Xunzi thinks assent always trumps desire when the two come into direct conflict.[75] The crucial point here is that Xunzi's moral psychological vocabulary makes it easy to theorize the common human phenomenon of impulse control, simply by separating a controlling power from our spontaneous impulses. Moreover, the terminology of "dispositions" gives him a straightforward way to fill out the psychology of long-term character formation, which he describes metaphorically as "artifice," and the "accumulation" of many actions consciously assented to over time, which slowly "cut" and "pull" our dispositions into new and better forms. Like crooked wood that has been steamed and forced to become straight, after the process has been completed, our dispositions have taken on a new form, which means that we no longer desire the "petty" things we once craved; instead we genuinely delight in good actions, and find them as satisfying as a fine meal.[76] "Virtue" in the fullest sense, for Xunzi, would then seem to imply both a wise grasp of the *Dao* considered as a comprehensive "scale" for evaluating possible actions, which allows the good Confucian to deliberate well, and also a refashioned set of dispositions, both achieved through persistent Confucian practice of study, ritual, and music.

Part of what makes this seem achievable for Xunzi is the nature, and not just the form, of the moral demands he thinks are imperative. Xunzi thinks it is impossible for anyone to extirpate basic desires for food, sex, safety, rest, and respect, so the ethical challenge is to create a form of life that can satisfy everyone's desires in a beautiful, harmonious, and just way—this grand cultural achievement is the *Dao* itself, the artful creation of past sages who have properly discerned the best way to order human life. It is no small matter that Augustine thinks the best Christian life is celibate, with very restricted food intake, and that this leads him to experience the continuing presence of sexual desire and hunger in the way he does. Xunzi never even entertains celibacy as a desirable option, let alone a possibility, and he makes lavish feasting a central religious ritual (compare, of course, the Eucharistic "meal" of small amounts of bread and wine). As argued previously, Xunzi understands ritual as to some extent a restraint, but just as much it is a way of "nourishing" and "adorning" our desires so that they take on the proper forms—forms which lead to social harmony rather than destructive competition and mutual predation. The degree of change to our dispositions that Xunzi aims for is considerably less radical than Augustine's "crucifixion" of our carnal loves, and so his expectation of the possibility of success in this endeavor, at least for some, seems achievable.

Xunzi thus possesses a relatively benign characterization of the nature of spontaneous human desires as blind and ignorantly selfish, not to be trusted by themselves to guide the self, but still aiming at basic human goods in a way that needs to be reshaped and ordered but not razed and replaced. This conception relates rather directly to his anthropology, which conceives of us as our bodies in their entirety. He thinks the *xin* 心 "heart/mind," is the ruler of the self, and needs to be well trained to fulfill this function properly, but he never imagines that there might be some locus of the self that is separable from the body. In other words, he does not identify with a soul, let alone an immortal soul, that vivifies the body and is categorically superior to it, in the way Augustine does, like almost everyone in the ancient Mediterranean world. Not surprisingly, then, the role of embodiment in full ethical personhood for Xunzi is rather different than it is for Augustine. Although Augustine's most considered image of the soul-body relation is of a marriage, understood of course in a late antique Roman way as a relationship of stark inequality that ought to be characterized by strict obedience of lower to higher, he can also imagine our bodies as an "unruly mount" that is being ridden against its will toward our true goal, beatitude. Augustine's sense of the body as at least partly "other" to ourselves, as something that needs to be ruled because it can never be trusted, is considerably more extreme, and even self-alienating, than Xunzi's views.[77] For Xunzi, the body should be beautifully adorned in appropriate clothing, and it should also be trained to become an expressive medium almost equal to our own voice, through the performative "language" of Confucian ritual, which allows us to express our concern for each other in every daily interaction, no matter how minor. Bodily skill is essential to ethical virtue, for Xunzi.

This may all have a surprising whiff of blithe Apollonian confidence, at least from an Augustinian point of view. Xunzi's account of steady work to reform oneself seems to presume both the desirability and the possibility of achieving transparent self-understanding, so that we can work steadily on our weak points in order to slowly but surely whittle them away. In particular, Xunzi's vocabulary and ethical theory seem relatively limited in their resources for articulating ongoing resistance to self-formation as anything other than frustrated first-order desire. At best, Xunzi can speak about using the wrong ethical categories to guide our deliberations, as for instance the way "petty people" "see things only in terms of personal benefit" (4/15/14). This would be one very common form of "obsession" by one consideration to the detriment of many others that form part of the Way. But vicious behavior stemming from erroneous categories of deliberation is not a case of internal resistance to self-formation, so much as an example of successful but misguided self-formation; this is a serious danger precisely because of our long-term capacities to reshape ourselves.

In comparison to this, Augustine's starkly antagonistic account of good and evil, as manifest in what I earlier called his "spiritual geography" of desire and intention, helps him to articulate resistance to personal formation as something more fundamental and deep within human beings. Even more importantly, his structurally unified account of the *mens* or mind makes the contest between divergent desires, both first- and second-order, a real case of self-division, of vacillation and even personal incoherence as competing inner discourses swirl within us, debating or talking past each other. What is truly striking in Augustine's account, in comparison with Xunzi's, is how this incoherence can be mitigated with divine aid, but not finally resolved until the "complete cure" that comes with resurrection. Self-knowledge, like knowledge of God, remains elusive and imperfect for human beings in this life, according to Augustine; God always knows us better than we know ourselves.

Because he thinks self-preference, and the grasping, covetous desires it spawns, remain as active potentials within our minds, whispering tempting inner words that continence must vigilantly reject, Augustine is also much more capable than Xunzi of articulating a robust account of corruption and self-deception. Augustine's vocabulary makes it easy to speak about how rebellion against the good can start in seemingly innocuous ways. Loving a friend, seeking to govern justly as a public official, even striving for virtue can all serve as projects of human pride instead of divine service, and inward confusion about what one really intends can cover these beginnings of sin all too effectively.

Augustine thus views the challenge of personal formation as more daunting than even Xunzi; indeed Augustine views it as completely unmanageable were it not for God's merciful love guiding us back to goodness. The success of the venture to live righteously remains unsettled throughout this life for Augustine; unless God grants us the grace to persevere to the end we will not succeed. We simply do not know what tests we might be ready to pass, on Augustine's account, although we can trust that with God all things are possible. In contrast to this, Xunzi appears to believe that even before sagehood, which forms the distant summit of personal formation in any case, noble men can be sure of their own commitment to the Way. Inward struggles of a sort continue for such men, but these are much less grievous than those that can afflict the Augustinian believer, who continues to harbor at least occasional sinful doubts about the entire project of submitting to God.

This suggests that on an Augustinian account genuine evil remains a "live option" for everyone, even the holiest, who retain the possibility of defecting from God throughout earthly existence. While Xunzi's understanding of human propensities for thoughtless self-gratification, avaricious personal aggrandizement, and obsessive pursuit of a merely partial good together provide an account of how some humans commit truly horrible crimes, Augustine's account goes further, in several helpful ways. It rules out thinking of one's own group or even self as purely good, untainted by sin, and instead instructs us to searchingly question our own motives and plans in order to test their good faith and loving intentions. Falsely localizing evil in some other social group seems to be a precondition for true atrocities, such as genocide; but Augustine's anthropology and theology stop this move decisively, while giving as well an explanation for why it tempts us (we love to see ourselves in the best possible light, even if this is blatant self-deception). Moreover, his understanding of the continuing frailty and weakness of the seemingly law-abiding, and even the genuinely virtuous, suggests that his understanding of sin can account very well for the shocking but "banal" evils of the twentieth century, perpetrated in significant part by bureaucrats and functionaries who loved their families and home communities. Lastly, Augustine argues powerfully that the human lust for power manifests itself in a perverse imitation of divine omnipotence, which drives us to assert ourselves precisely through manipulation and destruction of other things and people. This incisive charge provides a much stronger account of the sometimes baffling cruelty we routinely visit upon each other than is possible to construct out of Xunzian worries about bad impulses, distracting desire, and misguided self-formation.[78]

While in certain respects it might be possible to combine the insights of both of these figures while avoiding any respective difficulties, for example by importing some of Augustine's points about the nature and dangerousness of the human will to power into a Xunzian ethical position, in other respects it is not clear how such a synthesis could ever be achieved. Beyond their obvious and fundamental disagreements over metaphysics, sacred history, and sacred texts, one basic problem of ethical theory is that Xunzi's separation of desire from assent proves powerful when addressing issues of the gradual formation of character through sustained practice, but weak when trying to address deep self-division of the sort that Augustine charts. Conversely, Augustine's picture of a structurally unified but nevertheless disintegrated *mens*, which remains to some extent mysterious to itself, provides an excellent way of articulating the self's continuing resistance to its own highest aspirations. (This is only furthered by Augustine's contention that consent cannot overrule our strongest loves, unless we are defecting from God's providential order through sin.[79]) But this same picture makes it relatively more difficult for Augustine than Xunzi to account for the gradual development of virtue over time. It appears that there is no easy way to harmonize these two types of moral psychological pictures.[80]

A more intriguing and less clear-cut challenge would be presented by an effort to integrate a Xunzian account of the positive role of embodiment, concerning both typical "desires of the flesh" and embodied ritual action as an expressive medium for human relations, into an Augustinian Christianity. Could performance practices as an "outside-in" approach to formation supplement Augustine's more familiar symbolic and discursive spiritual exercises? I pursue such speculations no further here, but merely flag the issues involved as the sorts of thought-provoking perplexities that are generated by comparative ethical studies that take seriously the details of the religious visions they compare.

## NOTES

1. Diane Yeager asked me this question when I first discussed this project with her.

2. Hadot, *Philosophy as a Way of Life: Spiritual Exercises from Socrates to Foucault*, ed. Arnold I. Davidson, trans. Michael Chase (Oxford: Blackwell, 1995); Hadot, *The Inner Citadel: The "Meditations" of Marcus Aurelius*, trans. Michael Chase (Cambridge: Harvard University Press, 1998); Hadot, *What is Ancient Philosophy?* trans. Michael Chase (Cambridge, MA: Belknap Press of Harvard University Press, 2002).

3. Aaron Stalnaker, *Overcoming Our Evil: Human Nature and Spiritual Exercises in Xunzi and Augustine* (Washington, D.C.: Georgetown University Press, 2006).

4. Brown, *The Body and Society: Men, Women, and Sexual Renunciation in Early Christianity* (New York: Columbia University Press, 1988), xvii.

5. On Xunzi's life and influence, see John Knoblock, "The Chronology of Xunzi's Works," *Early China* 8 (1982–1983): 28–52; and Knoblock, trans., *Xunzi: A Translation and Study of the Complete Works*, 3 vols. (Stanford: Stanford University Press, 1988–1994), 3–49.

6. For fuller discussion and bibliography, see Knoblock, *Xunzi*, vol. 1, 105–20.

7. The classic biography of Augustine is Peter Brown, *Augustine of Hippo* (Berkeley: University of California Press, 1967; expanded edition published 2000).

8. The best such surveys are Benjamin Schwartz, *The World of Thought in Ancient China* (Cambridge, MA: Harvard University Press, 1985); and A. C. Graham, *Disputers of the Tao: Philosophical Argument in Ancient China* (La Salle, IL: Open Court, 1989).

9. Schwartz, *The World of Thought in Ancient China*, 62.

10. On early Chinese views of the spirit world, see Mu-chou Poo, *In Search of Personal Welfare: A View of Early Chinese Religion* (Albany, NY: State University of New York Press, 1998); and Michael Puett, *To Become a God: Cosmology, Sacrifice, and Self-Divinization in Early China* (Cambridge, MA: Published by the Harvard University Asia Center for the Harvard-Yenching Institute, Distributed by Harvard University Press, 2002). For Xunzi's views, see especially *Xunzi* 17/82/6–8, and chapter 17 generally. I discuss his use of the rhetoric of *shen* 神, "spirit," in Stalnaker, "Aspects of Xunzi's Engagement with Early Daoism," *Philosophy East and West* 53.1 (March 2003): 87–129.

11. I do not mean to imply that Augustine counsels a way of life focused on external rewards of some sort, which would be a grotesque reading of his understanding of life after the resurrection. Eternal life in the presence of God fulfills and perfects the highest goods of the Christian life here on earth, according to Augustine (*civ. Dei* 22.29–30).

12. Citations of Xunzi's works are to D. C. Lau, ed., *A Concordance to the Xunzi* (Hong Kong: Commercial Press, 1996). All citations of this will take the form chapter/page/line, so for example 19/97/9 would mean chapter 19, page 97, line 9. Unless otherwise noted, citations for Augustine's works refer to Jacques-Paul Migne's commonly accessible *Patrologia Latina,* now widely available via the Internet as a searchable database. Translations are my own unless otherwise noted.

13. Xunzi also speaks of the Way as something that can be known in such a way that it can serve as the "scales" in which diverse alternatives may be "weighed" and properly assessed (21/103/16–22). Rather than being a vague stab at some model or calculus for practical rationality, Xunzi seems to use this metaphor because it allows him to sum up the comprehensiveness of the Dao, which unites and properly relates all significant values within a single vision that can correctly guide anyone in any situation.

14. I discuss Xunzi's account of the stages of personal development in the third section of chapter six of Stalnaker, *Overcoming Our Evil*. For a fine account that analyzes his various metaphors for this process with insight, and which also stresses the effortless, *wuwei* character of Xunzi's fully realized sage, see Edward Slingerland, *Effortless Action: Wu-Wei as Conceptual Metaphor and Spiritual Ideal in Early China* (New York: Oxford University Press, 2003), 217–64.

15. There are several excellent studies of Xunzi's views of these topics. Probably the best are Philip J. Ivanhoe, "Thinking and Learning in Early Confucianism," *Journal of Chinese Philosophy* 17 (1990): 473–93; Ivanhoe, "A Happy Symmetry—Xunzi's Ethical Thought," *Journal of the American Academy of Religion* 59 (1991): 309–22; Ivanhoe, "Human Nature and Moral Understanding in Xunzi," *International Philosophical Quarterly* 34.2 (June 1994): 167–75; T. C. Kline, "Ethics and Tradition in the Xunzi" (Ph.D. diss., Stanford University, 1998); and Jonathan Schofer, "Virtues in Xunzi's Thought," *Journal of Religious Ethics* 21.4 (1993): 501–21.

16. Translation adapted from Burton Watson, trans., *Hsün Tzu: Basic Writings* (New York: Columbia University Press, 1963), 157–58.

17. For insightful discussion, see Kline, "Ethics and Tradition in the Xunzi," 205–50, and Slingerland, *Effortless Action*, 217–64.

18. In *Analects* 2.4 Confucius declares: "When I was fifteen I set my heart/mind on learning, at thirty I was established [on this Way], at forty I had no confusions,

at fifty I understood Heaven's decree, at sixty my ear complied, and at seventy I followed my heart's desires without overstepping the bounds."

19. Xunzi thinks anyone who is exposed to Confucian practices will find them strange at first, but if they go ahead and try them they will recognize their beauty and excellence, and be attracted to them, just as an impoverished rustic would, after initial bewilderment, come to love fine food if he could only have some, because of his attraction to its flavor, fragrance, and healthfulness (4/15/14–4/16/3). On Xunzi's account such attraction is not overwhelming, however. It would not guarantee acceptance if other forces intervened, such as a particularly arrogant or obstreperous disposition, or any sort of material or social disruption, such as famine or war.

20. George Lawless, *Augustine of Hippo and his Monastic Rule* (Oxford: Clarendon Press, 1987), 10, 57, and throughout.

21. Lawless, *Augustine of Hippo and his Monastic Rule*, 29–57; *s*. 355.2.

22. Lawless, *Augustine of Hippo and his Monastic Rule*, xii, 62.

23. Lawless, "Augustine's Decentering of Asceticism," in *Augustine and His Critics: Essays in Honor of Gerald Bonner*, ed. Robert Dodaro and George Lawless, 142–63 (New York: Routledge, 2000); see especially 148–52. This is the best recent essay on "asceticism" in Augustine's thought and life.

24. Translation Henry Bettenson, *Concerning the City of God Against the Pagans* (London: Penguin, 1984), 518.

25. Translation Edmund Hill, *The Trinity*, The Works of Saint Augustine, Part I, vol. 5 (Brooklyn, NY: New City Press, 1991), 155.

26. Translation Hill, *The Trinity*, 156.

27. For discussion and a fuller bibliography, see Emmanuel J. Cutrone, "Sacraments," in Allan D. Fitzgerald, ed. *Augustine through the Ages* (Grand Rapids, MI: William B. Eerdmans Publishing Company, 1999). Note especially the excellent recent treatment of *sacramentum* and *exemplum* in Robert Dodaro, *Christ and the Just Society in the Thought of Augustine* (Cambridge: Cambridge University Press, 2004), 147–59. As Edmund Hill points out (*The Trinity*, 178 n. 18), Augustine frequently sees Christ as the deeper signified reality pointed to by the many *sacramenta* of the Bible and Church, but he here interprets Christ Himself as the sacred sign, one which suggests hidden truths about human salvation.

28. Translation adapted from Hill , *The Trinity*, 156–57.

29. Translation adapted from Hill , *The Trinity*, 157.

30. Translations Hill , *The Trinity*, 67 (adapted), 247.

31. Translations Hill , *The Trinity*, 66, 154–55.

32. Translation Hill , *The Trinity*, 389–90.

33. Translation Hill , *The Trinity*, 169.

34. The best comprehensive account of virtue in Augustine is now Dodaro, *Christ and the Just Society*. See also John M. Rist, *Augustine: Ancient Thought Baptized* (Cambridge: Cambridge University Press, 1994), 148–202.

35. For fuller discussion see Stalnaker, *Overcoming Our Evil*, chapters 4, 7, and 8.

36. Rowan Williams, "Sapientia and the Trinity: Reflections on the *De Trinitate*," in *Collectanea Augustiniana: Mélanges T.J. Van Bavel*, ed. B. Bruning, M. Lamberigts, and J. Van Houtem (Leuven: Leuven University Press, 1990), 317–32.

37. Ivanhoe, "A Happy Symmetry."

38. For a brief discussion of Yu's achievements, see Knoblock, *Xunzi*, vol. 2, 13–14.

39. Shari Epstein, "Social Malaise/ Ritual Remedy: A Comparative Study of Durkheim and Xunzi," essay manuscript, n.d., helpfully discusses this aspect of Xunzi's view of ritual.

40. A classic, although in certain respects deservedly controversial, statement of the meaning of ritual in Confucianism is Herbert Fingarette. *Confucius: The Secular as Sacred*, (New York: Harper Torchbooks, 1972). A fine discussion of ritual in Xunzi is Lee Yearley, "Hsün Tzu: Ritualization as Humanization," essay manuscript, n.d.

41. I thus under the heading of "prayer" survey Augustine's accounts of *oratio*, *confessio*, and *contemplatio*, and their cognates. Augustine at times also highlights the importance of *laus*, or "praise," in prayer, as an expression of our love for and hope in God, and as a pleasant foretaste of the activity of the redeemed in Heaven, who will praise God unceasingly (*s*. 252.9, 255.1).

42. Translation Roland J. Teske, *Letters 100-155* (The Works of Saint Augustine, Part II, vol. 2. Hyde Park, NY: New City Press, 2003), 186.

43. Translations adapted from Teske, *Letters*, 192.

44. Translations adapted from Teske, *Letters*, 193.

45. Translations adapted from Teske, *Letters*, 194, 194, 193.

46. Translation Henry Chadwick, *The Confessions* (Oxford: Oxford University Press, 1991), 72.

47. Hadot uses this phrase to analyze Marcus Aurelius's Stoicism. See Hadot, *The Inner Citadel*, 125 and passim.

48. On this theme see Brian Stock, *Augustine the Reader: Meditation, Self-Knowledge, and the Ethics of Interpretation* (Cambridge, MA: Harvard University Press, 1996), 207–32, 273–78.

49. I comparatively analyze their views of learning in more detail in Stalnaker, *Overcoming Our Evil*, chapter 8.

50. As Augustine writes: "You know, then, that the virtues are to be distinguished from the vices, not by the duties [performed], but by their ends. A duty is what one ought to do, but an end is that on account of which one ought to do it. Therefore, when persons do some action in which they seem not to sin, if they do not do it on account of that for which they ought to do it, they are found to be guilty of sinning" (*c. Jul*. 4.21). Translation adapted from Teske, *Answer to the Pelagians II: Marriage and Desire, Answer to the Two Letters of the Pelagians, Answer to Julian*, The Works of Saint Augustine, Part I, vol. 24 (Hyde Park, NY: New City Press, 1998), 393.

51. For Xunzi's "'success' conception of the virtues" see Eric Hutton, "Virtue and Reason in Xunzi" (Ph.D. diss., Stanford University, 2001), 180. (Note also his illuminating general discussion of the interrelation of benevolence, ritual propriety, and justice in Xunzi on pp. 168–79, from which I draw here). Hutton takes this term from Terence Irwin, "Disunity in the Aristotelian Virtues," in *Oxford Studies in Ancient Philosophy*, Supplementary Volume (New York: Oxford University Press, 1988), 61–78.

52. I have no interest in contributing to the long-standing and anachronistic debate, along predictable lines, between those who would enlist Augustine on the side of Christ's "real presence" in the Eucharist and those who see him as advocating a "purely symbolic" reading of the Eucharist. For an example of evidence

seemingly supporting both interpretations side by side, see *ep.* 98.9. For a "Protestant" reading, see *doc. Chr.* 3.9.13, for a "Catholic" one, *s.* 229.1.

53. Michel Foucault, *The Use of Pleasure*, trans. Robert Hurley (New York: Pantheon Books, 1985), 6.

54. I draw these terms and the general sort of contrast from Kline, "Ethics and Tradition in the Xunzi," 51–52, who uses them to contrast Mencius and Xunzi. Note also Slingerland's (*Effortless Action*, 12ff. and *passim*) developed contrast between self-cultivation "internalism" and "externalism." As Slingerland rightly notes (*Effortless Action*, 291 n. 32), this contrast is not to be confused with current philosophical debates over motivational and epistemological internalism and externalism. The danger of such general slogans is that they can run together certain topics that can and should be kept distinct, specifically: (1) having or lacking various internal moral resources (2) whether, when, and why effort or striving may be required in the moral life, and (3) various approaches to spiritual exercises. Here I am using the terms "inside-out" and "outside-in" only to refer to two differing strategies of personal formation, exemplified by Augustine and Xunzi, that support different sorts of spiritual exercises.

55. Dodaro, *Christ and the Just Society*, 124, and 115–81 generally.

56. On the background to Augustine's treatment, see Boniface Ramsey, "Mendacio, De/Contra Mendacium," in Allan D. Fitzgerald, ed. *Augustine through the Ages* (Grand Rapids, MI: William B. Eerdmans Publishing Company, 1999), 556.

57. The distinction between goods internal and external to a practice comes from Alasdair MacIntyre, *After Virtue: A Study in Moral Theory*, 2nd ed. (Notre Dame, IN: University of Notre Dame Press, 1984), 187–91.

58. Hutton, "Virtue and Reason in Xunzi," 221, makes this point nicely.

59. See Xunzi's contrast between the comprehensive skill of a noble man as political leader and *Dao*-follower with that of various artisans with more specialized sorts of expertise (21/104/16–21/105/3). On this issue see Joel Kupperman, "Confucius and the Problem of Naturalness," *Philosophy East and West* 18.3 (July 1968): 175–85, esp. 181.

60. Aristotle, *Nicomachean Ethics* 1105a16–1105b20. For insightful discussion, see Irwin, trans., *Aristotle: Nicomachean Ethics*, 2nd ed. (Indianapolis, IN: Hackett Publishing, 1999), 22, 193, 195–96, who notes the logical parallel to the problem about how one could learn something one did not already know in Plato, *Meno* 80a–e. Pace Slingerland, *Effortless Action*, 259–64, Aristotle thinks he has resolved the issues regarding the cultivation of virtue by distinguishing between outward form, intention, and stable "state" or virtuous disposition. Xunzi too is much more successful in resolving these apparent difficulties than Slingerland allows.

61. These ideas are hardly original; on these issues I have learned most from conversation with Jack Kline. For other accounts that make similar points, see e.g., Karyn Lai, "Confucian Moral Cultivation: Some Parallels with Musical Training," in *The Moral Circle and the Self: Chinese and Western Approaches*, edited by Kimchong Chong, Sor-hoon Tan, and C. L. Tan, 107–39 (Chicago and La Salle, IL: Open Court, 2003); Kline, "Ethics and Tradition in the Xunzi;" Ivanhoe, *Confucian Moral Self-Cultivation*, 2nd ed. (Indianapolis, IN: Hackett Publishing, 2000), 6–7, 29–37; Kupperman, "Confucius and the Problem of Naturalness," and Kupperman, "Naturalness Revisited: Why Western Philosophers Should Study Confucius," in

*Confucius and the Analects: New Essays*, ed. Bryan W. Van Norden, 39–52 (New York: Oxford University Press, 2002).

62. On the relation of practices and virtue, see MacIntyre, *After Virtue*, 181–203.

63. Counter-arguments could certainly be provided to the literacy example, but note that it would be genuinely hard to imagine someone living without storytelling or significant shared human culture as living a good human life.

64. I owe this reference to Hutton, "Virtue and Reason in Xunzi," 222, and adapt his translation.

65. For discussion and textual sources see Stalnaker, *Overcoming Our Evil*, chapter 7.

66. For discussion and textual sources see Stalnaker, *Overcoming Our Evil*, chapter 6.

67. On the ways in which Augustine does and does not engage in such "leveling" of believers, see Elizabeth A. Clark, "Distinguishing 'Distinction': The Uses of a Bishop's Authority," paper presented at "Reconsiderations: A Conference on Contemporary Augustinian Scholarship," Villanova, PA, Dec. 2003.

68. Augustine does of course make such distinctions, for example between married and celibate, and clerical and lay Christians. He believes these differences are real and important but nonetheless tempt our tendencies to pride.

69. The classic studies of this theme in Augustine are John Burnaby, *Amor Dei: A Study of the Religion of St. Augustine* (London: Hodder & Stoughton, 1947); and Oliver O'Donovan, *The Problem of Self-Love in St. Augustine* (New Haven: Yale University Press, 1980).

70. The term "mimetic desire" comes from René Girard, *Violence and the Sacred*, trans. Patrick Gregory (Baltimore, MD: Johns Hopkins University Press, 1977), 145–49, and is applied fruitfully to Augustine in the sense I intend by Dodaro, *Christ and the Just Society*, 68–69.

71. For an egregious example, see Homer H. Dubs, "Mencius and Sün-dz on Human Nature," *Philosophy East and West* 6 (1956): 213–22, esp. 218. For a serious attempt to address concerns of some modern despisers of Augustine, and in the process to articulate an "Augustinian liberalism," see Eric Gregory, "Politics and the Order of Love: Modern Variations on Augustinian Themes," book manuscript, n.d.

72. Note also the revealing discussion of the priority of wise people to good *fa* 法, "models" and "standards," which cannot implement themselves, and which are both created and "corrected" by those who possess an enlightened understanding of the *Dao* that lies behind all such models (12/57/1–7). See Hutton, "Virtue and Reason in Xunzi," 82ff. for discussion.

73. For fuller discussion, see Stalnaker, *Overcoming Our Evil*, chapter 5.

74. For discussion see Stalnaker, *Overcoming Our Evil*, chapters 5 and 6.

75. For discussion of some complications to this seemingly simple position that make it more believable, see Stalnaker, *Overcoming Our Evil*, chapter 5.

76. This is somewhat inexact. For Xunzi, the noble man no longer desires certain basic goods such as food or social acclaim in a petty way, but only as properly understood parts of the *Dao*.

77. Of course Augustine is relatively positive regarding the body when judged in his own context, as many commentators have remarked, and he is notable in his

insistence that the body will be fully redeemed at the resurrection, so that eternal life will be embodied, in some mysterious and flawless way. None of this, however, vitiates the comparison with Xunzi regarding our experience of the body in this life. For fuller discussion, see Stalnaker, *Overcoming Our Evil*, chapters 4 and 7.

78. For a fine recent exploration of these and related themes, see Charles T. Mathewes, *Evil and the Augustinian Tradition* (Cambridge: Cambridge University Press, 2001). For an insightful parallel argument comparing Augustine with the early Confucian Mencius, see Bryan Van Norden, "Mencius and Augustine on Evil: A Test Case for Comparative Philosophy," in *Comparative Approaches to Chinese Philosophy*, ed. Bo Mou, 313–336 (Aldershot, Hants, England and Burlington, VT: Ashgate, 2003).

79. For discussion, see Stalnaker, *Overcoming Our Evil*, chapter 5.

80. The challenging test case to this claim would be someone like Aquinas, who develops a faculty psychology much more complex than Xunzi's separation of assent from desire, yet still wishes to save central Augustinian insights.

# Bibliography


Augustine. *Against the Academicians; The Teacher*. Trans. Peter King. Indianapolis: Hackett Publishing Co., 1995.

———. *Against the Jews (Tractatus adversos Iudaeos)*. In *Saint Augustine, Treatises on Marriage and Other Subjects*. Fathers of the Church, vol. 27. Washington D.C.: Catholic University of America Press, 1969. Pp. 387–414.

———. *Answer to the Pelagians II: Marriage and Desire, Answer to the Two Letters of the Pelagians, Answer to Julian*. Trans. R. J. Teske. The Works of Saint Augustine, Part I, vol. 24. Hyde Park, N.Y.: New City Press, 1998.

———. *The City of God*. Trans. Marcus Dods. New York: Random, 1999.

———. *The City of God Against the Pagans*. Trans. R. W. Dyson. Cambridge: Cambridge University Press, 1998.

———. *Concerning the City of God against the Pagans*. Trans. H. Bettenson. London: Penguin Books, 1984.

———. *Confessions*. Trans. M. Boulding. New York: Vintage Books, 1998.

———. *Confessions*. Trans. Henry Chadwick. Oxford and New York: Oxford University Press, 1992.

———. *The Confessions of St. Augustine*. Trans. F. J. Sheed. New York, 1943.

———. *De Dialectica*. Trans. B. D. Jackson. Dordrect & Boston: Synthese Historical Library, 1975).

———. *Earlier Writings*. Ed. J. H. S. Burleigh. Philadelphia: Westminster Press, 1953.

———. *Expositions of the Psalms 51-72*. The Works of Saint Augustine: A Translation for the 21st Century III/17. Trans. Maria Boulding, O.S.B., ed. John E. Rotelle, O.S.A. New York: New City Press, 2001.

———. *Faith in the Unseen*, in *Saint Augustine On Christian Belief*. The Works of Saint Augustine: A Translation for the 21st Century I/8. Trans. Matthew O'Connell, ed. Boniface Ramsey. New York: New City Press, 2005, 175–94.

———. *In Answer to the Jews*. In *Saint Augustine, Treatises on Marriage and Other Subjects*. Fathers of the Church vol. 27. Ed. Roy J. Deferrari. New York: Fathers of the Church, 1955, 385–414.

———. *Letters 100-155 [Epistulae]*. The Works of Saint Augustine: A Translation for the 21st Century II/2. Trans. Roland Teske, S.J., ed. Boniface Ramsey. Hyde Park: New City Press, 2003.

———. *Of True Religion*. Translated by J. H. S. Burleigh. Chicago: Henry Regnery Company, 1959.

———. *On Christian Doctrine*. Trans. D.W. Robertson, Jr. Library of Liberal Arts. Indianapolis: Bobbs-Merrill Educational Publishing, 1958.

———. *On Romans: Propositions from the Epistle to the Romans, Unfinished Commentary on the Epistle to the Romans*. Trans. P. Fredriksen Landes. Chico: Scholars Press, 1982.

———. *Sermons on the Old Testament, 1-19*. The Works of Saint Augustine: A Translation for the 21st Century III/1. Trans. Edmund Hill, O.P., ed. John E. Rotelle, O.S.A. New York: New City Press, 1990.

———. *Saint Augustine: Eighty Three Different Questions*. Trans. D. L. Mosher. Fathers of the Church 70. Washington, D.C.: Catholic University of America Press, 1982.

———. *Teaching Christianity: De Doctrina Christiana*. Trans. Edmund Hill. Ed. John E. Rotelle. Hyde Park, NY: New City Press, 1996.

———. *The Trinity (De Trinitate)*. Trans. Edmund Hill. Brooklyn: New City Press, 1991.

———. *Selected Writings*. Trans. Mt. Clark. Ramsey, NJ: Paulist Press, 1984.

## OTHER WORKS

Alfaric, P. *L'Évolution intellectuelle de saint Augustin*. Paris, 1918.

Apuleius. *Apuleius: Rhetorical Works*. Trans. and annotated by S. Harrison, J. Hilton, and V. Hunink. Ed. Stephen Harrison. Oxford: Oxford University Press, 2001.

Aristotle. *Nicomachean Ethics*. Trans. T. Irwin. 2nd ed. Indianapolis, IN: Hackett Publishing, 1999.

Arnold, D., and P. Bright (eds.), *De Doctrina Christiana: a Classic of Western Culture*. Christianity and Judaism in Antiquity, vol. 9. Notre Dame: University of Notre Dame Press, 1995.

Assmann, J. "The Mosaic Distinction: Israel, Egypt, and the Invention of Paganism." *Representations* 56 (Fall 1996) 48–67.

Babcock, W. S. "Augustine and Tyconius: A Study in the Latin Appropriation of Paul." *Studia Patristica* 17/3 (1982): 1209–15

———. "Augustine's Interpretation of Romans (A.D. 394–396)." *Augustinian Studies* 10 (1979): 55–74.

———. "Caritas and Signification in De doctrina christiana 1–3." In D. Arnold and P. Bright, eds., *De Doctrina Christiana: a Classic of Western Culture*. Notre Dame: University of Notre Dame Press, 1995. Pp. 140–57.
———. *Tyconius: The Book of Rules*, Society of Biblical Literature Texts and Translations (Atlanta, 1989).
Bammel, C. P. "Augustine, Origen, and the Exegesis of St. Paul." *Augustinianum* 32 (1992) 341–68.
———. "Pauline Exegesis, Manichaeism, and Philosophy in the Early Augustine." In *Christian Faith and Greek Philosophy in Late Antiquity: Essays in Tribute to George Christopher Stead*, ed. L. R. Wickham and C. P. Bammel. Leiden, 1993. Pp. 1–25.
Barnes, M. *Theology and the Dialogue of Religions*. Cambridge: Cambridge University Press, 2002.
Barth, K. *Church Dogmatics* I.1. London: T & T Clark, 2004.
Batchelor, S. *The Awakening of the West: the Encounter of Buddhism and Western Culture*. London: Thorsons, 1995.
———. "The Other Enlightenment Project." In Ursula King, ed., *Faith and Praxis in a Post-Modern Age*. London: Cassells, 1998. Pp. 113–27.
Bavel, T. J. van. "God in between Affirmation and Negation According to Augustine." In *Augustine: Presbyter Factus Sum*. Ed. Joseph T. Lienhard, Earl C. Muller, and Roland J. Teske, 73–97. Collectanea Augustiniana. Ed. Joseph Schnaubelt and Frederick Van Fleteren. New York: Peter Lang, 1993.
Beard, M., J. North, and S. Price, *Religions of Rome*. Cambridge: Cambridge University Press, 1998.
Betz, H. D. "Paul in the Mani Biography (Codex Manichaicus Coloniensis)." In *Codex Manichaicus Coloniensis: Atti del Simposio Internazionale . . . 1984*, ed. L. Cirillo and A. Roselli. Cosenza, 1986. Pp. 215–34.
———. "Magic and Mystery in the Greek Magical Papyri," in C. A. Faraone and D. Obbink, eds., *Magika Hiera* (Oxford: Oxford University Press, 1991).
Bey, H. "Media Hex." In R. Metzger, ed. *The Book of Lies*. New York: Disinformation, 2003. Pp. 334–40.
———. *T.A.Z.* Autonomedia, 2003.
Bielefeldt, C. "The One Vehicle and the Three Jewels: On Japanese Sectarianism and Some Ecumenical Alternatives." *Buddhist-Christian Studies* 10 (1990) 5–16.
Blumenkranz, B. "Augustin et les juifs: Augustin et le judaisme." *Recherches Augustiniennes* 1 (1958) 225–41.
———. *Die Judenpredigt Augustins*. Paris, Études augustiniennes, 1973; orig. pub. 1946.
———. "Géographie historique d'un theme de l'iconographie religieuse: les representations de *Synagoga* en France." In Pierre Gallais and Yves-Jean Riou, eds., *Mélanges offerts à René Crozet à l'occasion de son soixante-dixième anniversaire*. Poitiers: Société d'Études Médiévales, 1966. Pp. 1141–57.
Bonner, G. *St. Augustine of Hippo: Life and Controversies*. Rev. ed. Norwich, 1986.
Bookchin, M. *Social Anarchism or Lifestyle Anarchism*. Oakland: AK Press, 1995.
Bos, Mike. "After the Rise of Knowledge." *Wiener Zeitschrift für die Kunde Südasiens und Archiv für indische Philosophie* 27 (1983): 165–84.
Bourke, V. J. *Augustine's Quest of Wisdom*. Milwaukee, WI: Bruce Publishing Co., 1945.
Boyarin, D. *A Radical Jew: Paul and the Politics of Identity*. Berkeley and Los Angeles, 1993.

Boys, Mary C. *Has God Only One Blessing? Judaism as a Source of Christian Self-Understanding*. New York: Paulist Press, 2000.

Braarvig, J. "Magic: Reconsidering the Grand Dichotomy." In D. R. Jordan, H. Montgomery, and E. Thomassen, eds. The world of ancient magic: papers from the first International Samson Eitrem Seminar at the Norwegian Institute at Athens, 4–8 *May 1997*. Athens: Norwegian Institute at Athens, 1999. Pp. 21–54.

Brown, P. *Augustine of Hippo: A Biography*. Berkeley and Los Angeles, 1967.

———. *The Body and Society: Men, Women, and Sexual Renunciation in Early Christianity*. New York: Columbia University Press, 1988.

Burnaby, J. *Amor Dei: A Study of the Religion of St. Augustine*. London: Hodder & Stoughton, 1947.

Burns, J. P. *The Development of Augustine's Doctrine of Operative Grace*. Paris: Études Augustiniennes, 1980.

———. "On rebaptism: social organization in the third century church." *Journal of* Early Christian Studies 1 (1993) 367–403.

Burrows, W. R., ed. *Redemption and Dialogue*. Maryknoll: Orbis, 1993.

Cagnat, R., and A. Merlin with the collaboration of L. Châtelain, *Inscriptions latines d'Afrique (Tripolitaine, Tunisie, Maroc)*. Paris: E. Leroux, 1923.

Calder, W. M., III., et al. The Unknown Socrates: Translations, with Introductions and Notes, of Four Important Documents in the Late Antique Reception of Socrates the Athenian. Wauconda, IL: Bolchazy Carducci Publishers, Inc., 2002.

Cameron, M. "Signs." In *Augustine through the Ages: An Encyclopedia*. Allan D. Fitzgerald, ed. Grand Rapids: Eerdmans, 1999. Pp 793–98.

Carroll, J. *Constantine's Sword: The Church and the Jews, A History*. Boston: Houghton Mifflin Co., 2001.

Castelli, E. Martyrdom and Memory: Early Christian Culture Making. New York: Columbia University Press, 2004.

Chrysostom, John, *Discourses against Judaizing Christians*. Fathers of the Church vol. 68. Trans. Paul Harkins. Washington, D.C.: Catholic University of America Press, 1979.

Clark, E. A. "Distinguishing 'Distinction': The Uses of a Bishop's Authority." Paper presented at "Reconsiderations: A Conference on Contemporary Augustinian Scholarship," Villanova University, Dec. 2003.

Clark, Gillian. *Augustine: The Confessions* (Cambridge: Cambridge University Press, 1993).

Clark, M. T. *Augustine*. London: Chapman, 1994.

Clark, Mary T., *Augustine of Hippo: Selected Writings*. Classics of Western Spirituality (Ramsey, NJ: Paulist Press, 1984).

Clooney, F. X. "Comparative Theology: A Review of Recent Books (1989–1995)." *Theological Studies* 56 (1995): 521–50.

———. "Evil, Divine Omnipotence, and Human Freedom: Vedanta's Theology of Karma." *The Journal of Religion* 4 (1989): 530–48.

———. "Francis Xavier, and the World/s We (Don't Quite) Share." In *Jesuit Postmodern: Scholarship, Vocation, and Identity in the 21st Century*. Ed. F. X. Clooney. Lanham: Lexington Press, 2006. Pp. 157–180.

———. *Fr. Bouchet's India: An 18th Century Jesuit's Encounter with Hinduism*. Chennai: Satya Nilayam Publications, 2005.

———. *Theology after Vedanta: An Experiment in Comparative Theology*. Albany: State University of New York Press, 1993.

———. "Understanding and the Refusal to Understand as Complementary Dynamics in Jesuit Missionary Learning." In *Contributions to Indian and Cross-Cultural Studies: Volume in Commemoration of Wilhelm Halbfass*. Ed. Karin Preisendanz. Vienna: Austrian Academy of Sciences Press (forthcoming).

———. "Yes to Caste, No to Religion? Or Perhaps the Reverse: Re-Using Roberto de Nobili's Distinctions among Morality, Caste, and Religion." In *Roberto de Nobili Reconsidered*. Ed. J. Arun, SJ. Chennai: Institute for Dialogue of Religions and Cultures (forthcoming).

Cohen, J. *Living Letters of the Law: Ideas of the Jews in Medieval Christianity*. Berkeley: University of California Press, 1999.

———. "'Slay Them Not': Augustine and the Jews in Modern Scholarship." *Medieval Encounters* 4 (1998) 78–92.

Cole-Turner, R. S. "Anti-heretical Issues and the Debate over Galatians 2:11–14 in the Letters of St. Augustine to St. Jerome." *Augustinian Studies* 11 (1980) 155–65.

Copenhaver, B. P. Hermetica: The Greek Corpus Hermeticum and the Latin Asclepius in *a New English Translation*. Cambridge: Cambridge University Press, 1992.

Corless, R. "The Dramas of Spiritual Progress: The Lord and the Servant in Julian's *Showings* 51 and the Lost Heir in *Lotus Sutra* 4," *Mystics Quarterly* 11.2 (1985) 65–75.

Courcelle, P. *Recherches sur les Confessions de Saint Augustin*. Paris, 1950.

Cranz, E. "The Development of Augustine's Ideas on Society before the Donatist Controversy." *Harvard Theological Review* 14 (1954): 255–316.

Cutrone, E. J. "Sacraments." In Allan D. Fitzgerald, ed. *Augustine through the Ages*. Grand Rapids, MI: William B. Eerdmans Publishing Company, 1999.

Davies, O. "The Sign Redeemed: A Study in Christian Fundamental Semiotics." *Modern Theology* 19:2 (April 2003) 219–41.

Dawson, D. "Sign Theory, Allegorical Reading, and the Motions of the Soul in *De doctrina Christiana*." In D. Arnold and P. Bright, eds. *De Doctrina Christiana: a Classic of Western Culture*. Notre Dame: University of Notre Dame Press, 1995. Pp. 121–39.

Decret, F. *Aspects du manichêisme dans l'Afrique romaine: Les controverses de Fortunatus, Faustus et Felix avec saint Augustin*. Paris, 1970.

———. "L'utilisation des épîtres de Paul chez les Manichéens d'Afrique." In *Le epistole paoline nei Manichei, i Donatisti e il primo Agostino*. Ed. J. Ries et al. Rome, 1989. Pp. 29–83.

Devadutt, V. E. "Augustine and Sankara on Time." *Indian Journal of Theology* 33 (1984) 24–34.

Di Cesare, M. A. *The Altar and the City: A Reading of Vergil's Aeneid*. New York and London: Columbia University Press, 1974.

Diehl, E. *Inscriptiones Latinae Christianae Veteres*. 3 vols. Berlin: Weidmann, 1925–1931.

Dodaro, R. *Christ and the Just Society in the Thought of Augustine*. Cambridge: Cambridge University Press, 2004.

Dods, M. *The Writings of Justin Martyr and Athenagoras,* vol. 2 of the *Ante-Nicene Christian Library*. Ed. A. Roberts and J. Donaldson. Edinburgh, 1867.

Dolbeau, F. "Sermons inédits de saint Augustin prêchés en 397 (2e série)." *Revue Bénédictine* 102 (1992) 44–74.

Douglas, M. *Purity and Danger*. Oxford: Routledge, 1966.

Dubois, M. "Jews, Judaism and Israel in the Theology of Saint Augustine: How He Links the Jewish People and the Land of Zion." *Immanuel* 22/23 (1989) 162–214.

Dubs, H. H. "Mencius and Sün-dz on Human Nature." *Philosophy East and West* 6 (1956): 213–22.

Dufault, O. "Magic and Religion in Augustine and Iamblichus." In E. Digeser and R. Frakes, eds. *Religious Identities in Late Antiquity*. Campbellville: Edgar Kent, 2006. Pp. 63–91.

Duffy, S. J. "A Theology of the Religions and/or a Comparative Theology?" *Horizons* 26 (1999) 105–15.

Eckel, M. David. "By the Power of the Buddha." In *A Buddhist Kaleidoscope: Essays on the Lotus Sutra*. Ed. Gene Reeves, 127–48. Tokyo: Kosei Publishing Co., 2002.

Efroymsen, D. "The Patristic Connection." In *Antisemitism and the Foundations of Christianity*. Ed. A. Davies. New York, 1979. Pp. 98–117.

*Epistle of Barnabas*. In *Early Christian Writings: The Apostolic Fathers*. Ed. and rev. trans. Andrew Louth. London: Penguin Books, 1987. Pp. 155–84.

Epstein, S. "Social Malaise/ Ritual Remedy: A Comparative Study of Durkheim and Xunzi." Essay manuscript, n.d.

Evans, G. R. *Augustine on Evil*. Cambridge: Cambridge University Press, 1982.

Faivre, A. "Figures d'Hermès Trismégiste à la fin du XVIIIe siècle." In *L'Orient dans l'Histoire religieuse de l'Europe: l'Invention des origines*. Ed. M. A. amir-Moezzi and J. Scheid. Turnhout, Belgium: Brepols, 2000. Pp. 131–37.

Ferrari, L. C. *The Conversions of Saint Augustine*. Villanova: Villanova University Press, 1984.

———. "The Theme of the Prodigal Son in Augustine's *Confessions*." *Recherches Augustiniennes* 12 (1977) 105–18.

Fingarette, H. *Confucius: The Secular as Sacred*. New York: Harper Torchbooks, 1972.

Fitzgerald, A. D., ed. *Augustine through the Ages: An Encyclopedia*. Grand Rapids: Eerdmans, 1999.

Flannery, E. H. *The Anguish of the Jews: Twenty-Three Centuries of Antisemitism*. Rev. and updated ed. New York: Paulist Press, 1999; orig. pub. 1965.

Fletcher-Louis, C. H. T. "Wisdom Christology and the Partings of the Ways between Judaism and Christianity." In Stanley E. Porter and Brook W. R. Pearson, eds., *Christian-Jewish Relations through the Centuries*. London: T & T Clark, 2000. Pp. 52–68.

Flood, G., ed. *The Blackwell Companion to Hinduism*. Oxford and Malden: Blackwell Publishing, 2003.

Fortin, Ernest. *Classical Christianity and the Political Order: Reflections on the Theologico-Political Problem*. De. J. B. Benestad. New York: Rowman & Littlefield Publishers, Inc., 1996.

Foucault, M. *Histoire de la folie à l'âge classique*. Paris: Gaillimard, 1972.

———. *The Use of Pleasure*. Trans. Robert Hurley. New York: Pantheon Books, 1985.

Fowden, G. *The Egyptian Hermes: A Historical Approach to the Late Pagan Mind.* Cambridge: Cambridge University Press, 1986.

Frauwallner, E. *History of Indian Philosophy.* Delhi: Motilal Banarsidass, 1973.

Fredericks, James L. *Buddhists and Christians: Through Comparative Theology to Solidarity.* Maryknoll: Orbis Books, 2004.

———. *Faith among Faiths: Christian Theology and Non-Christian Religions.* New York/Mahwah: Paulist Press, 1999.

Fredriksen, P. "Apocalypse and Redemption in Early Christianity: From John of Patmos to Augustine of Hippo." *Vigiliae Christianae* 45 (1991) 151–83.

———. "Augustine and Israel. *Interpretatio ad litteram*, Jews and Judaism in Augustine's Theology of History." *Studia Patristica* 38 (2001) 119–35.

———. "Beyond the Body/Soul Dichotomy: Augustine on Paul against the Manichees and the Pelagians." *Recherches Augustiniennes* 23 (1988) 87–114.

———. "Divine Justice and Human Freedom: Augustine on Jews and Judaism, 392–398." In Jeremy Cohen, ed., *From Witness to Witchcraft: Jews and Judaism in Medieval Christian Thought.* Wiesbaden: Harrassowitz Verlag, 1996.

———. "*Excaecati Occulta Iustitia Dei*: Augustine on Jews and Judaism." *Journal of Early Christian Studies* 3 (1995) pp. 299–324.

———. "Paul." In *Augustine Through the Ages: An Encyclopedia.* Ed. Allan D. Fitzgerald, et al. Grand Rapids, MI: Eerdmans, 1999. Pp. 621–25.

———. "*Secundum Carnem*: History and Israel in the Theology of St Augustine on the Destiny of Israel." In *The Limits of Ancient Christianity. Essays on Late Antique Though and Culture in Honor of R.A. Markus.* W. Klingshirn and M. Vessey, eds. Ann Arbor: University of Michigan Press, 1999. Pp. 26–41.

———. "Tyconius and the End of the World." *Revue des Études Augustiniennes* 28 (1982) 59–75.

Frend, W. H. C. "The Early Christian Church in Carthage." In J.H. Humphrey, ed., *Excavations at Carthage 1976 conducted by the University of Michigan*, vol. 3. Ann Arbor, MI: University of Michigan Press, 1977. Pp. 21–40.

———. *The Early Church.* Minneapolis: Fortress Press, 1982.

———. "Jews and Christians in Third Century Carthage." In *Paganisme, Judaïsme, Christianisme: Influences et affrontements dans le monde antique. Mélanges offerts à Marcel Simon.* Paris: Éditions E. de Boccard, 1978. Pp. 185–94.

Fuss, M. A. "*Upaya* and *Missio Dei*: Toward a Common Missiology." In *A Buddhist Kaleidoscope: Essays on the Lotus Sutra.* Ed. Gene Reeves. Tokyo: Kosei Publishing Co., 2002. Pp. 115–25.

Gager, J. G. *The Origins of Anti-Semitism: Attitudes toward Judaism in Pagan and Christian Antiquity.* Oxford: Oxford University Press, 1983.

Gardner, G. *Witchcraft Today.* New York: Citadel Press, 2004.

Garnsey, P. "Religious Toleration in Classical Antiquity." In W. Shiels, ed. *Persecution and Toleration.* Studies in Church History 21. Oxford: Blackwell, 1984. Pp. 24–25.

Gilson, E. *The Christian Philosophy of Saint Augustine.* Trans. L.E.M. Lynch. London: Victor Gollancz, 1961.

Girard, R. *Violence and the Sacred*, trans. Patrick Gregory. Baltimore, MD: Johns Hopkins University Press, 1977.

Gordon, R. L. "Imagining Greek and Roman Magic." In B. Ankarloo and S. Clark, eds. Witchcraft and Magic in Europe: Ancient Greece and Rome. The Athlone

History of Witchcraft and Magic in Europe 2. London: Athlone, 1999. Pp.159–276.

Graf, F. "Augustine and Magic." In J. N. Bremmer and J. R. Veenstra, eds. *The Metamorphosis of Magic from Late Antiquity to the Early Modern Period*. Leuven: Peeters, 2002. Pp. 87–104.

———. La magie dans l'Antiquité gréco-romaine. Paris: Belles Lettres, 1994.

Graham, A. C. *Disputers of the Tao: Philosophical Argument in Ancient China*. La Salle, IL: Open Court, 1989.

Grant, S. *Sankaracarya's Concept of Relation*. Delhi: Motilal Banarsidass Publishers, 1998.

———. *Toward an Alternative Theology: Confessions of a Non-Dualist Christian: The Teape Lectures, 1989*. Notre Dame: University of Notre Dame Press, 2002.

Grayzel, S. "The Papal Bull *Sicut Judeis*." In M. Ben-Horin, B. D. Weinryb, and S. Zeitlin, eds., *Studies and Essays in Honor of Abraham A. Neuman*. Leiden: E.J. Brill, 1962. Pp. 243–80.

Green, W. M. "Review of Augustine and the Latin Classics." In *Classical Journal* (January 1968) 186–189.

Gregory, Eric. "Politics and the Order of Love: Modern Variations on Augustinian Themes." Book manuscript, n.d.

Grodzynski, D. "Superstitio." *Revue des études anciennes* 76 (1974) 36–60.

Guy, J. C. *Unité de structure logique de la "Cité de Dieu" de saint Augustin*. Paris: Études Augustiniennes, 1961.

Habito, R. L. F. "Buddha-body Theory and the Lotus Sutra: Implications for Praxis." In *A Buddhist Kaleidoscope: Essays on the Lotus Sutra*. Ed. Gene Reeves. Tokyo: Kosei Publishing Co., 2002. Pp. 305–17.

Hacker, P. "Sankara's Conception of Man." In *Philology and Confrontation: Paul Hacker on Traditional and Modern Vedanta*. Ed. Wilhelm Halbfass. Albany: State University of New York Press, 1995. Pp. 177–85.

Hadot, P. *The Inner Citadel: The "Meditations" of Marcus Aurelius*. Trans. Michael Chase. Cambridge, MA: Harvard University Press, 1998.

———. *Philosophy as a Way of Life: Spiritual Exercises from Socrates to Foucault*. Ed. Arnold I. Davidson. Trans. Michael Chase. Oxford: Blackwell, 1995.

———. *What is Ancient Philosophy?* Trans. Michael Chase. Cambridge, MA: Belknap Press of Harvard University Press, 2002.

Hagendahl, H. *Augustine and the Latin Classics*. Studia Graeca et Latina Gothoburgensia 20.1–2. Stockholm, 1967.

Halivni, D. W. *Revelation Restored: Divine Writ and Critical Responses*. London; SCM Press, 2001.

Harkins, F. T. "*Historia*, Reading, and Restoration in the Theology of Hugh of St. Victor." Ph.D. dissertation, University of Notre Dame, 2005.

———. "Nuancing Augustine's Hermeneutical Jew: Allegory and Actual Jews in the Bishop's Sermons." *Journal for the Study of Judaism* 36 (2005) 41–64.

Harvey, P. *An Introduction to Buddhism*. Cambridge: Cambridge University Press, 1990.

Heath, J. and A. Potter, *Nation of Rebels*. New York: HarperCollins, 2004.

Hirschberg, H. Z. *History of the Jews in North Africa*. 2 vols. Leiden: E.J. Brill, 1974.

Horsley, R., ed. *Paul and Empire*. Harrisburg, PA: Trinity Press International, 1997.

Hunsinger, G. "Hellfire and Damnation: Four Ancient and Modern Views." *Scottish Journal of Theology* 51/4 (1998) 406–34.

Hutton, E. "Virtue and Reason in Xunzi." Ph.D. diss., Stanford University, 2001.

Hutton, R. "Paganism and Polemic The Debate over the Origin of Modern Pagan Witchcraft." *Folklore* 111.1 (2000) 103–17.

———. *The Triumph of the Moon*. Oxford: Oxford University Press, 1999.

Irwin, T. "Disunity in the Aristotelian Virtues." In *Oxford Studies in Ancient Philosophy*, Supplementary Volume. New York: Oxford University Press, 1988. Pp. 61–78.

Isayeva, N. *Shankara and Indian Philosophy*. Albany: State University of New York Press, 1993.

Ivanhoe, P. J. *Confucian Moral Self-Cultivation*. 2nd ed. Indianapolis, IN: Hackett Publishing, 2000.

———. "A Happy Symmetry—Xunzi's Ethical Thought." *Journal of the American Academy of Religion* 59 (1991) 309–22.

———. "Human Nature and Moral Understanding in Xunzi." *International Philosophical Quarterly* 34.2 (June 1994) 167–75.

———. "Thinking and Learning in Early Confucianism." *Journal of Chinese Philosophy* 17 (1990) 473–93.

Janowitz, N. *Icons of Power*. University Park: Pennsylvania State Press, 2002.

———. *Magic in the Roman World: Pagans, Jews and Christians*. Oxford: Routledge, 2001.

John Paul II, "To Representatives of Various Religions on the World Day of Prayer for Peace." In *Interreligious Dialogue: The Official Teaching of the Catholic Church (1963-1995)*. Ed. Francesco Gioia. Boston: Pauline Books & Media, 1997. Pp. 343–45.

Johnson, L. T. *The Writings of the New Testament: An Interpretation*. Philadelphia: Fortress Press, 1986.

Jordan, M. D. "Words and Word: Incarnation and Signification in Augustine's *De doctrina Christiana*." *Augustinian Studies* 11 (1980) 175–95.

Juster, J. *Les Juifs dans l'Empire Romain*. 2 vols. Paris, 1914.

Justin Martyr, *Dialogue avec Tryphon*. 2 vols. Ed. G. Archambault. Paris, 1909.

Kato, T. "*Sonus et Verbum: De doctrina christiana* 1.13.12." In D. Arnold and P. Bright, eds. *De Doctrina Christiana: a Classic of Western Culture*. Notre Dame: University of Notre Dame Press, 1995. Pp. 87–96.

Kelly, A. *Crafting the Art of Magic*. Woodbury: Llewellyn Publications, 1991.

Kelly, J. N. D. *Golden Mouth: The Story of John Chrysostom—Ascetic, Preacher, Bishop*. Grand Rapids: Baker Books, 1995.

Kennedy, R. P. "Book Eleven: The *Confessions* as Eschatological Narrative." In *A Reader's Companion to Augustine's Confessions*. Ed. Kim Paffenroth and Robert P. Kennedy. Louisville and London: Westminster John Knox Press, 2003. Pp. 167–83.

Kline, T. C., III. "Ethics and Tradition in the Xunzi." Ph.D. diss., Stanford University, 1998.

Knoblock, J. "The Chronology of Xunzi's Works." *Early China* 8 (1982–3) 28–52.

———. *Xunzi: A Translation and Study of the Complete Works*. 3 vols. Stanford: Stanford University Press, 1988–1994.

Kupperman, J. "Confucius and the Problem of Naturalness." *Philosophy East and West* 18.3 (July 1968) 175–85.

———. "Naturalness Revisited: Why Western Philosophers Should Study Confucius." In *Confucius and the Analects: New Essays*, ed. Bryan W. Van Norden. New York: Oxford University Press, 2002. Pp. 39–52.

Lai, K. "Confucian Moral Cultivation: Some Parallels with Musical Training." In *The Moral Circle and the Self: Chinese and Western Approaches*, edited by Kim-chong Chong, Sor-hoon Tan, and C. L. Tan. Chicago and La Salle, IL: Open Court, 2003. Pp. 107–39.

Lau, D. C., ed. *A Concordance to the Xunzi*. Hong Kong: Commercial Press, 1996.

Lawless, G. *Augustine of Hippo and his Monastic Rule*. Oxford: Clarendon Press, 1987.

———. "Augustine's Decentering of Asceticism." In *Augustine and His Critics: Essays in Honor of Gerald Bonner*, ed. Robert Dodaro and George Lawless. New York: Routledge, 2000. Pp. 142–63.

Lefebure, L. D. "Authority, Violence, and the Sacred at the Medieval Court. In *Violence* in Medieval Courtly Literature: A Casebook. Ed. Albrecht Classen, New York & London: Routledge, 2004. Pp. 37–66.

———. *Revelation, the Religions, and Violence*. Maryknoll, NY: Orbis Books, 2000.

Lim, R. *Public Disputation, Power, and Social Order in Late Antiquity*. Berkeley and Los Angeles, 1995.

Linder, A. *The Jews in Roman Imperial Legislation*. Detroit, 1987.

Locklin, Reid B. "Sankara, Augustine, and *Rites de Passage*: Comparative Theology with Victor Turner." In *Theology and the Social Sciences*. Ed. Michael Horace Barnes. Annual Publication of the College Theology Society 46. Maryknoll: Orbis Books, 2001. Pp. 135–60.

Lonergan, B. J. F. *Method in Theology*. Toronto: University of Toronto Press, 1971.

Lössl, J. "The One (*unum*)—A Guiding Concept in *De uera religione*: An Outline of the Text and the History of Its Interpretation." *Revue des Études Augustiniennes* 40 (1994) 79–103.

*The Lotus Sutra*. Trans. Burton Watson. New York: Columbia University Press, 1993.

Lubac, Henri de, *Scripture in the Tradtion*, trans. Luke O'Neill (New York: Herder & Herder, 2000).

Lund, J. "A Synagogue at Carthage? Menorah-lamps from the Danish Excavations." *Journal of Roman Archaeology* 8 (1995) 245–62.

MacCormick, S. *The Shadows of Poetry*: *Vergil in the Mind of Augustine*. Berkley, Los Angeles, and London: University of California Press, 1998.

MacIntyre, A. *After Virtue: A Study in Moral Theory*. 2nd ed. Notre Dame, IN: University of Notre Dame Press, 1984.

Mackail, J. W. *Virgil and His Meaning to the World Today*. New York: Cooper Square Publishers, Inc., 1963.

MacQueen, D. J. "Augustine on Superbia: The Historical Background and Sources of His Doctrine." *Mélanges de science religieuse* 34 (1977) 193–211.

Madden, M. D. "The Pagan Divinities and their Worship as Depicted in the Works of St. Augustine Exclusive of the *City of God*." Dissertation, Catholic University of America, 1930.

Malkovsky, B. "Advaita Vedanta and Christian Faith." *Journal of Ecumenical Studies* 36/3–4 (1999) 397–422.

———, ed. *New Perspectives on Advaita Vedanta: Essays in Commemoration of Professor Richard De Smet, S.J.* Studies in the History of Religions 85. Leiden, Boston, and Köln: Brill, 2000.

———. "The Personhood of Samkara's *Para Brahman*." *The Journal of Religion* 77 (1997) 541–62.

———. *The Role of Divine Grace in the Soteriology of Samkaracarya*. Leiden, Boston, and Köln: Brill, 2001.

Mandouze, A. "Saint Augustin et la religion romaine." *Recherches Augustiniennes* 1 (1958) 187–223.

Marcaurelle, R. *Freedom through Inner Renunciation: Sankara's Philosophy in a New Light*. Albany: State University of New York Press, 2000.

Marcus, J. R. *The Jews in the Medieval World: A Sourcebook: 315-1791*. Rev. ed., M. Saperstein. Cincinnati: Hebrew Union College Press, 1999.

Markus, R. A., ed. *Augustine: A Collection of Critical Essays*. Garden City: Anchor Books, 1972.

———. "Augustine on magic: A neglected semiotic theory." *Revue des Études Augustiennes* 40 (1994) 375–88.

———. *Saeculum: History and Society in the Theology of St. Augustine*. New York: Cambridge University Press, 1970.

———. "Sign, Communication, and Communities in Augustine's *De doctrina Christiana*." In D. Arnold and P. Bright, eds. *De doctrina christiana: a Classic of Western Culture*. Notre Dame: University of Notre Dame Press, 1995. Pp. 97–108.

Marrou, H. I. *Saint Augustin et la fin de la culture antique*. 2nd ed. Paris: Éditions de Boccard, 1949 (originally 1938).

Martin, T. F. "Book Twelve: Exegesis and *Confessio*." In *A Reader's Companion to Augustine's Confessions*. Ed. Kim Paffenroth and Robert P. Kennedy. Louisville and London: Westminster John Knox Press, 2003. Pp. 185–206.

Mathewes, C. T. *Evil and the Augustinian Tradition*. Cambridge: Cambridge University Press, 2001.

———. "Pluralism, Otherness, and the Augustinian Tradition." *Modern Theology*, 14.1 (1998) 83–112.

Matthews, G. B., ed. *The Augustinian Tradition*. Berkley, Los Angeles, and London: Universtiy of California Press, 1999.

———. "Knowledge and Illumination." In *The Cambridge Companion to Augustine*. Ed. Eleonore Stump and Norman Kretzmann. Cambridge: Cambridge University Press, 2001. Pp. 171–85.

Mattis, S. "Chih-I and the Subtle Dharma of the Lotus Sutra; Emptiness or Buddha-Nature?" In *A Buddhist Kaleidoscope: Essays on the Lotus Sutra*. Ed. Gene Reeves. Tokyo: Kosei Publishing Co., 2002. Pp. 241–59.

Mauss, M. *Sociologie et anthropologie*. Paris: Presses Universitaires de France, 1950.

Mayeda, S., trans. *A Thousand Teachings: The Upadesasahasri of Sankara*. Albany: State University of New York Press, 1992.

Mayer, J. R. A. "Reflections on the Threefold Lotus Sutra." In *A Buddhist Kaleidoscope: Essays on the Lotus Sutra*. Ed. Gene Reeves. Tokyo: Kosei Publishing Co., 2002. Pp. 151–59.

McGinn, B. *The Foundations of Mysticism*. Vol. 1 of *The Presence of God: A History of Western Christian Mysticism*. New York: Crossroad, 1991.

McMahon Robert. *Augustine's Prayerful Ascent*. Athens, GA: The University of Georgia Press, 1989.

McWilliam, J., ed. *Augustine: From Rhetor to Theologian*. Waterloo, ON: Wilfrid Lourier University Press, 1992.

McWilliam-Dewart, J. "Augustine's Developing Use of the Cross: 387–400." *Augustinian Studies* 15 (1984) 15–33.

Meeks, W. A. "Breaking Away: Three New Testament Pictures of Christianity's Separation from the Jewish Communities." In Jeremy Cohen, ed., *Essential Papers on Judaism and Christianity in Conflict: From Late Antiquity to the Reformation*. New York: New York University Press, 1991. Pp. 89–113.

Melito of Sardis, "On the Passover." In *The Christological Controversy*. Trans. and ed. Richard A. Norris, Jr. Philadelphia: Fortress Press, 1980. Pp. 33–47.

Merlin, A. *Inscriptions latines de la Tunisie*. Paris: Presses Universitaires de France, 1944.

Meurin, L. *Select Writings of the Most Reverend Leo Meurin, SJ*. Ed. P. A. Colaco. Bombay: C. M. Braganca and Company, 1909.

Meynell, H., ed. *Grace, Politics and Desire: Essays on Augustine*. Calgary: University of Calgary Press, 1990. Pp. 179–93.

Migne, J. P., ed. *Patrologiae Cursus Completus, Series Latina*. Paris, 1844–64.

Milbank, J. "'Postmodern Critical Augustinianism': a Short *Summa* in Forty Two Responses to Unasked Questions." *Modern Theology*, 7:3 (1991) 225–37.

Milbank, J., C. Pickstock, and G. Ward, eds. *Radical Orthodoxy*. London: Routledge, 1999.

Millard, W. "The Incarnation in Augustine's Conversion." *Recherches augustiniennes* 15 (1980) 80–98.

Minerbi, S. I. *The Vatican and Zionism: Conflict in the Holy Land, 1895-1925*. Trans. A. Schwarz. Oxford, 1990.

Moltmann, J. *A Theology of Hope*. London: SCM Classics, 1967.

Morrison, G. "Pop Magic!" In *The Book of Lies*. Trans. Richard Metzger. New York: Disinformation, 2003. Pp. 16–25.

Murray, M. *The Witch-Cult in Western Europe*. Oxford: Clarendon Press, 1921.

Nelson, L. E. "Living Liberation in Sankara and Classical Advaita: Sharing the Waiting of God." In *Living Liberation in Hindu Thought*. Ed. A. O. Fort and P. Y. Mumme. Albany: State University of New York Press, 1996. Pp. 17–62.

Nicholls, W. *Christian Antisemitism: A History of Hate*. Northvale, NJ: Jason Aronson, Inc., 1993.

Niwano, N. "The Threefold Lotus Sutra: An Introduction." In *A Buddhist Kaleidoscope: Essays on the Lotus Sutra*. Ed. Gene Reeves. Tokyo: Kosei Publishing Co., 2002. Pp. 27–49.

Ochs, P. *Peirce, Pragmatism and the Logic of Scripture*. Cambridge: Cambridge University Press, 1998.

O'Connell, R. J. *St. Augustine's Confessions: The Odyssey of Soul*. Cambridge, MA: Harvard University Press, 1969; reprint, New York: Fordham University Press, 1989.

O'Daly, G. *Augustine's City of God: A Reader's Guide*. Oxford: Oxford University Press, 1999.

O'Donnell, J. J. *Augustine: A New Biography*. New York: HarperCollins, 2005.

———. *Augustine. Confessions*. 3 vols. Oxford: Clarendon Press, 1992.

———. "Augustine's Classical Readings." *Recherches Augustiniennes* 15 (1980) 144–74.

O'Donovan, O. *The Problem of Self-Love in St. Augustine*. New Haven: Yale University Press, 1980.

Olivelle, P., trans. *The Early Upanisads: Annotated Text and Translation*. New York and Oxford: Oxford University Press, 1998.

O'Meara, John J. *The Young Augustine*. New York: Alba House, 1965.

O'Neil, L. T. *Maya in Sankara: Measuring the Immeasurable*. Delhi: Motilal Banarsidass, 1980.

Origen. *Contra Celsum*. Trans. H. Chadwick. New York: Cambridge University Press, 1953.

Paffenroth, K. "Book Nine: The Emotional Heart of the *Confessions*." In *A Reader's Companion to Augustine's Confessions*. Ed. Kim Paffenroth and Robert P. Kennedy. Louisville and London: Westminster John Knox Press, 2003. Pp. 137–54.

Panoli, V., trans. *Upanishads in Sankara's Own Words*. Vol. 1. Rev. Ed. Calicut: Mathrubhumi Printing and Publishing Co. Ltd., 1995.

———, trans. *Upanishads in Sankara's Own Words*. Vol. 2. Rev. Ed. Calicut: Mathrubhumi Printing and Publishing Co. Ltd., 1996.

Parkes, J. *The Conflict of the Church and Synagogue: A Study in the Origins of Antisemitism*. New York: Atheneum, 1985; orig. pub. 1934.

Parsons, W. *Saint Augustine: Letters*, vol. 1. New York, 1951.

Pecknold, C. C. *Transforming Postliberal Theology: George Lindbeck, Pragmatism and Scripture*. London and New York: T & T Clark, 2005.

Pennington, B. K. *Was Hinduism Invented? Britons, Indians, and the Colonial Construction of Religion*. Oxford and New York: Oxford University Press, 2005.

Pickstock, C. "Soul, City and Cosmos after Augustine." In J. Milbank, C. Pickstock, and G. Ward, eds. *Radical Orthodoxy*. London: Routledge, 1999. Pp. 243–77.

Pieris, A. *An Asian Theology of Liberation*. Edinburgh: T. &. T. Clark, 1988.

———. *Love Meets Wisdom*. Maryknoll: Orbis; 1988.

———. *Prophetic Humour in Buddhism and Christianity*. Colombo: Ecumenical Institute for Study and Dialogue, 2005.

Poo, Mu-chou. *In Search of Personal Welfare: A View of Early Chinese Religion*. Albany, NY: State University of New York Press, 1998.

Prendiville, J. G. "The Development of the Idea of Habit in the Thought of Saint Augustine." *Traditio* 28 (1972) 29–99.

Press, G. A. "The Subject and Structure of Augustine's *De Doctrina Christiana*." *Augustinian Studies* 11 (1980) 99–124.

Puett, M. *To Become a God: Cosmology, Sacrifice, and Self-Divinization in Early China*. Cambridge, MA: Published by the Harvard University Asia Center for the Harvard-Yenching Institute, Distributed by Harvard University Press, 2002.

Pye, M. "The Length of Life of the Tathagata." In *A Buddhist Kaleidoscope: Essays on the Lotus Sutra*. Ed. Gene Reeves. Tokyo: Kosei Publishing Co., 2002. Pp. 165–75.

———. *Skilful Means: A Concept in Mahayana Buddhism*. London: Duckworth, 1978.

Rahula, W. *What the Buddha Taught*. Bedford: Gordon Fraser, 1967.

———. *Zen and the Taming of the Bull*. London: Gordon Fraser, 1978.

Rambachan, A. *Accomplishing the Accomplished: The Vedas as a Source of Valid Knowledge in Sankara*. Monographs of the Society for Asian and Comparative Philosophy 10. Honolulu: University of Hawaii Press, 1991.

———. *The Advaita Worldview: God, World, and Humanity*. Albany: State University of New York Press, 2006.

———. "Sankara's Rationale for *Sruti* as the Definitive Source of *Brahmajnana*: A Refutation of Some Contemporary Views." *Philosophy East and West* 36 (1986) 25–40.

———. "Where Words Can Set Free: The Liberating Potency of Vedic Words in the Hermeneutics of Sankara." In *Texts in Context: Traditional Hermeneutics in South Asia*. Ed. J. R. Timm. Albany: State University of New York Press, 1992. Pp. 33–46.

Ramsey, B. "Mendacio, De/Contra Mendacium." In Allan D. Fitzgerald, ed. *Augustine through the Ages*. Grand Rapids, MI: William B. Eerdmans Publishing Company, 1999.

Rao, S. "Two 'Myths' in Advaita." *Journal of Indian Philosophy* 24 (1996) 265–79.

Rashkover, R., and C. C. Pecknold, eds. *Liturgy, Time and the Politics of Redemption*. Radical Tradition Series. Grand Rapids: Eerdmans, 2006.

Reeves, G. "The Lotus Sutra as Radically World-Affirming." In *A Buddhist Kaleidoscope: Essays on the Lotus Sutra*. Ed. Gene Reeves. Tokyo: Kosei Publishing Co., 2002. Pp. 177–99.

Ries, J. "Saint Paul dans la formation de Mani." In *Le epistole paoline nei Manichei, i Donatisti e il primo Agostino*. Ed. J. Ries et al. Rome, 1989. Pp. 7–27.

Rist, J. M. "Augustine on Free Will and Predestination." *Journal of Theological Studies, N.S.* 20 (1969) 420–47.

———. *Augustine: Ancient Thought Baptized*. Cambridge: Cambridge University Press, 1994.

Rives, J. B. "Magic, Religion, and Law." In C. Ando and J. Rüpke, eds. *Religion and Law in Classical and Christian Rome*. Potsdamer Altertumswissenschaftliche Beiträge 15. Stuttgart: Franz Steiner, 2006.

Rolston, H., III. *Religious Inquiry: Participation and Detachment*. New York: Philosophical Library, 1985.

Saulière, A. *His Star in the East*. Madras: de Nobili Research Institute; Anand, Gujarat: Gujarat Sahitya Prakash, 1995.

Scharfstein, B. A. "'Cogito Ergo Sum': Descartes, Augustine, and Sankara." In *Philosophy East/Philosophy West: A Critical Comparison of Indian, Chinese, Islamic, and European Philosophy*, by B. A. Scharfstein et al. New York: Oxford University Press, 1978. Pp. 199–217.

Schofer, J. "Virtues in Xunzi's Thought." *Journal of Religious Ethics* 21.4 (1993) 501–21.

Schroeder, J. W. *Skillful Means: The Heart of Buddhist Compassion*. Monograph No. 18, Society for Asian and Comparative Philosophy. Honolulu: University of Hawaii Press, 2001.

Schwartz, B. *The World of Thought in Ancient China*. Cambridge, MA: Harvard University Press, 1985.

*Scripture of the Lotus Blossom of the Fine Dharma Translated from the Chinese of Kumarajiva*. Trans. Leon Hurvitz. New York: Columbia University Press, 1976.

Seiferth, W. *Synagoge und Kirche im Mittelalter*. München: Kösel-Verlag, 1964.

Sharma, A. "'Skill in Means' in Early Buddhism and Christianity." *Buddhist-Christian Studies* 10 (1990) 23–33.

———. "The Vedantic Concept of God." In *Perspectives on Vedanta: Essays in Honor or Professor P.T. Raju*. Ed. S. S. Rama Rao Pappu. Leiden: E. J. Brill, 1988. Pp. 114–31.

Shelford, A. "Thinking Geometrically in Pierre-Daniel Huet's *Demonstratio Evangelica* (1679)." *Journal of the History of Ideas* (March 2003) 599–617.

Shuck, G. "The Myth of the Burning Times and the Politics of Resistance in Contemporary America." *Journal of Religion and Society* [http://purl.org/JRS] 2 (2000).

Signer, M. "Jews and Judaism." In *Augustine through the Ages: An Encyclopedia*. Grand Rapids: Eerdmans, 1999. Pp. 470–74.

Simon, M. *Verus Israel. Étude sur les relations entre chrétiens et juifs dans l'empire romain (135-425)*. Paris: Éditions E. de Boccard, 1964; originally, 1948.

Slingerland, E. *Effortless Action: Wu-Wei as Conceptual Metaphor and Spiritual Ideal in Early China*. New York: Oxford University Press, 2003.

Smith, J. Z. "Trading Places." In M. Meyer and P. Mirecki, eds. *Ancient Magic and Ritual Power*. Leiden: Brill, 2001. Pp. 13–27.

Smith, W. C. *The Meaning and End of Religion*. Fortress: Minneapolis, 1991

Sonderegger, K. *That Jesus Christ Was Born a Jew: Karl Barth's "Doctrine of Israel."* University Park: Pennsylvania State University Press, 1992.

Souter, A. *The Earliest Latin Commentaries on the Epistles of St. Paul*. Oxford: Clarendon Press, 1927.

Stalnaker, A."Aspects of Xunzi's Engagement with Early Daoism." *Philosophy East and West* 53.1 (March 2003) 87–129.

———. *Overcoming Our Evil: Human Nature and Spiritual Exercises in Xunzi and Augustine*. Washington, D.C.: Georgetown University Press, 2006.

Stark, R. *One True God: Historical Consequences of Monotheism*. Princeton, NJ and Oxford: Princeton University Press, 2001.

Stock, B. *After Augustine: The Meditative Reader and the Text*. Philadelphia: University of Pennsylvania Press, 2001.

———. *Augustine the Reader: Meditation, Self-Knowledge, and the Ethics of Interpretation*. Cambridge, MA, and London: Belknap Press, 1998.

Stone, J. "Original Enlightenment Thought in the Nichiren Tradition." In *Buddhism in Practice*. Ed. Donald S. Lopez, Jr. Princeton Readings in Religions. Princeton, NJ: Princeton University Press, 1995. Pp. 228–40.

———. "When Disobedience Is Filial and Resistance Is Loyal: The Lotus Sutra and Social Obligations in the Medieval Nichiren Tradition." In *A Buddhist Kaleidoscope: Essays on the Lotus Sutra*. Ed. Gene Reeves. Tokyo: Kosei Publishing Co., 2002. Pp. 261–81.

Stothert, R. *Writings in Connection with the Manichaean Heresy*. Vol. 5 of *The Works of Aurelius Augustinus*. Ed. M. Dods. Edinburgh: T & T Clark, 1872.

Straw, C. E. "Augustine as Pastoral Theologian: The Exegesis of the Parables of the Field and Threshing Floor." *Augustinian Studies* 14 (1983) 129–51.

Stroumsa, G. G. "From Anti-Judaism to Antisemitism in Early Christianity?" In O. Limor and G. G. Stroumsa, eds., *Contra Iudaeos: Ancient and Medieval Polemics between Christians and Jews*. Tübingen: J.C.B. Mohr, 1996. Pp. 1–26.

Studer, B. "History and Faith in *De Trinitate*." *Augustinian Studies* 28–1 (1997) 7–50.

Sullivan, F. A. *Salvation Outside the Church? Tracing the History of the Catholic Response*. New York/Mahwah: Paulist Press, 1992.

Suthren-Hirst, J. G. *Samkara's Advaita Vedanta: A Way of Teaching*. London and New York: Routledge Curzon, 2005.

Suzuki, D. T. *Outlines of Mahayana Buddhism*. New York: Schoken Books, 1907 [reprint, 1967].

Swami Gambhirananda, trans. *Eight Upanisads, with the Commentary of Sankaṛacarya*. Vol. 1. Rev. Ed. Calcutta: Advaita Ashrama, 1989.

———, trans. *Eight Upanisads, With the Commentary of Sankaracarya*. Vol. 2. Calcutta: Advaita Ashrama, 1992.

Synan, E. A. *The Popes and the Jews in the Middle Ages*. New York: Macmillan, 1965.

Szerszynski, B., and E. Tomalin, "Enchantment and its uses: religion and spirituality in environmental direct action." In J. Purkis and J. Bowen, eds. *Changing Anarchism*. Manchester: Manchester University Press, 2004. Pp. 199–229.

Tanabe, G. J., Jr. "The Matsumoto Debate." In *Buddhism in Practice*. Princeton Readings in Religions. Ed. Donald S. Lopez, Jr. Princeton, NJ: Princeton University Press, 1995. Pp. 241–48.

———. "Tanaka Chigaku: The *Lotus Sutra* and the Body Politic." In *The Lotus Sutra in Japanese Culture*. Ed. George J. Tanabe, Jr., and Willa Jane Tanabe. Honolulu: University of Hawaii Press, 1989. Pp. 191–208.

TeSelle, E. *Augustine the Theologian*. New York: Herder and Herder, 1970.

*The Threefold Lotus Sutra: Innumerable Meanings, The Lotus Flower of the Wonderful Law, and Meditation on the Bodhisattva Universal Virtue*. Trans. Bunno Kato, Yoshiro Tamura, and Kojiro Miyasaka with revisions by W.E. Soothill, Wilhelm Schiffer, and Pier P. del Campana. Tokyo: Kosei Publishing Co., 1975, reprint, 1986.

Thera, Nyanaponika, *The Heart of Buddhist Meditation* (London: Rider, 1962).

Torchia, N. J. "St. Augustine's Treatment of Superbia and Its Plotinian Affinities." *Augustinian Studies* 18 (1987) 66–80.

van der Meer, F. *Augustine the Bishop: the Life and Work of a Father of the Church*. Trans. B. Battershaw and G. R. Lamb. London and New York: Sheed and Ward, 1961.

Van Fleteren, F. "Principles of Augustine's Hermeneutic: An Overview." In *Augustine: Biblical Exegete*, eds. J. C. Schnaubelt and F. Van Fleteren. New York & Frankfurt: Peter Lang, 2001.

Van Norden, B. "Mencius and Augustine on Evil: A Test Case for Comparative Philosophy." In *Comparative Approaches to Chinese Philosophy*, ed. Bo Mou. Aldershot, Hants, England and Burlington, VT: Ashgate, 2003. Pp. 313–36.

Venturini, R. "A Buddha Teaches Only Bodhisatvas." In *A Buddhist Kaleidoscope: Essays on the Lotus Sutra*. Ed. Gene Reeves. Tokyo: Kosei Publishing Co., 2002. Pp. 333–36.

Vermander, J.–M. "La polémique des Apologistes latin contre les Dieux du paganisme." *Recherches Augustiniennes* 17 (1982) 3–128.

Virgil. *Aeneide: Testo a fronte*. Rosa Calzecchi Onesti. Editor. Torino: Giulio Einaudi editores s. p. a., 1967 and 1989. English translation by Allen Mandelbaum. *The Aeneid of Virgil: A Verse Translation*. Berkley, Los Angeles, and London: University of California Press, 1971.

Voegelin, Eric. *Collected Works of Eric Voegelin* Volume 12. Ed. E. Sandoz. Baton Rouge and London: Louisiana State University Press, 1990.

Wahlde, U. C. von, "The Johannine 'Jews': A Critical Survey." *New Testament Studies* 28 (1982) 33–60.

Wang, E. Y. *Shaping the Lotus Sutra: Buddhist Visual Culture in Medieval China*. Seattle and London: University of Washington Press, 2005.

Ward, G. "A Christian Act: Politics and Liturgical Practice." In R. Rashkover and C. C. Pecknold, eds. *Liturgy, Time and the Politics of Redemption*. Radical Tradition Series. Grand Rapids: Eerdmans, 2006. Pp. 29–49.

Ward, K. *Religion and Revelation: A Theology of Revelation in the World's Religions*. Oxford: Clarendon Press, 1994.

Warrier, A.G. Krishna. *The Concept of Mukti in Advaita Vedanta*. Madras University Philosophical Series 9. Madras: University of Madras, 1961.

———. *God in Advaita*. Simla: Indian Institute of Advanced Study, 1977.

Watson, B., trans. *Hsün Tzu: Basic Writings*. New York: Columbia University Press, 1963.

Wax, M. and R. Wax. "The Notion of Magic." *Current Anthropology* 4 (1963) 495–518.

Wetzel, J. *Augustine and the Limits of Virtue*. Cambridge: Cambridge University Press, 1992.

———. "Pelagius Anticipated: Grace and Election in Augustine's *Ad Simplicianum*," In *Augustine: From Rhetor to Theologian*. Ed. J. McWilliam. Waterloo: Wilfred Laurier University Press, 1992. Pp. 121–32.

———. "Predestination, Pelagianism, and Foreknowledge." In *The Cambridge Companion to Augustine*. Eds. E. Stump and N. Kretzmann. Cambridge: Cambridge University Press, 2001. Pp. 49–58.

———. "The Recovery of Free Agency in the Theology of St. Augustine." *Harvard Theological Review* 80 (1987) 101–25.

Wilken, R. L. *John Chrysostom and the Jews: Rhetoric and Reality in the Late 4th Century*. Berkeley: University of California Press, 1983.

———. *Judaism and the Early Christian Mind: A Study of Cyril of Alexandria's Exegesis and Theology*. New Haven: Yale University Press, 1971.

Williams, A. L. *Adversus Judaeos: A Bird's-Eye View of Christian Apologiae until the Renaissance*. Cambridge: Cambridge University Press, 1935.

Williams, R. "Language, Reality, and Desire in Augustine's De Doctrina." *Literature and Theology* 3 (1989) 138–50.

———. "Sapientia and the Trinity: Reflections on the *De Trinitate*." In *Collectanea Augustiniana: Mélanges T.J. Van Bavel*, ed. B. Bruning, M. Lamberigts, and J. Van Houtem. Leuven: Leuven University Press, 1990. Pp. 317–32.

Wilmanns, G., and R. Cagnat, J. Schmidt, and H. Dessau, eds. *Inscriptiones Africae Latinae. Corpus Inscriptionum Latinarum*, vol. 8. Berlin: G. Reimerum, 1881–1959.

Wright, N. T. *Climax of the Covenant: Christ and the Law in Pauline Theology*. Minneapolis: Fortress Press, 1992.

———. "Jesus and the Victory of God." Vol. 2 of *Christian Origins and the Question of God*. Minneapolis: Fortress Press, 1996.

———. *Paul: In Fresh Perspective*. Minneapolis: Fortress Press, 2005.

Yearley, L. "Hsün Tzu: Ritualization as Humanization." Essay manuscript, n.d.
Yoshiro, T. "The Ideas of the Lotus Sutra." In *The Lotus Sutra in Japanese Culture*. Ed. George J. Tanabe, Jr., and Willa Jane Tanabe. Honolulu: University of Hawaii Press, 1989. Pp. 37–51.
Young, F. "The *Confessions* of Saint Augustine: What is the Genre of This Work?" *Augustinian Studies* 30–1 (1999) 1–16.

# Index

# Contributors

**Michael Barnes** is a Jesuit priest of the British Province. He has lectured in Buddhist studies at the Gregorian University in Rome and currently teaches at Heythrop College in the University of London where he is responsible for a master's program in interreligious relations. He has written several books on the theology of religions, notably *Theology and the Dialogue of Religions,* (Cambridge University Press, 2002), and various contributions to collections and symposia on interreligious spirituality. A frequent visitor to India, he lives in a multicultural town in West London where he runs a small dialogue center which seeks to combine theological reflection with the pastoral practice of interreligious dialog.

**Brian Brown** is an associate professor of religious studies at Iona College in New Rochelle, New York. He teaches classes in Buddhism, Chinese Religious Traditions, Religion and Cosmology, and Religion and the Constitution. He holds doctoral degrees in the history of religions from Fordham University and in law from New York University. He is the author of *The Buddha Nature: A Study of the Tathagatagarbha and Alayavijnana* (Delhi: Motilal Banarsidass, 1991, 1994), which examines the fundamental tenet of Mahayana Buddhism that all sentient beings have the inherent potentiality to attain the supreme and perfect enlightenment of Buddhahood. He is also the author of *Religion, Law and the Land: Native Americans and the*

*Judicial Interpretation of Sacred Land* (Westport: Greenwood Press, 1999) which analyzes a series of court decisions regarding the legal claims of various Native American tribes who attempted to protect ancestrally revered lands from development schemes by the federal government. Dr.Brown's otherwise diverse studies in global religious traditions and the law converge in his consistent interest in the legal, moral, and spiritual dimensions of humanity's relationship with the natural world.

**Francis X. Clooney** is the Parkman Professor of Divinity and professor of comparative theology at Harvard Divinity School. He has written widely on Hindu religious traditions and their implications for Christian theology. He taught in the theology department at Boston College for over twenty years, and from 2002 to 2004 was Academic Director of the Centre for Hindu Studies at Oxford University. First president of the International Society for Hindu-Christian Studies, he is the author of numerous books, including *Seeing the Texts* (1996), winner of the Best Book Award in Hindu-Christian Studies; *Hindu God, Christian God* (Oxford University Press, 2001); *Divine Mother, Blessed Mother: Hindu Goddesses and the Virgin Mary* (Oxford University Press, 2005); *Father Bouchet's India* (2006); and most recently, editor of *Jesuit Postmodern: Scholarship, Vocation, and Identity in the 21st Century* (Lexington Books, 2006). His current books are a study of the spiritual theologies of Vedanta Desika (Hindu, fourteenth century) and Francis de Sales (Catholic, seventeenth century), and a Christian commentary on the three holy mantras of the Srivaisnava tradition.

**John A. Doody** is Robert M. Birmingham Chair in the Humanities at Villanova University where he is associate dean for curriculum in the College of Arts and Sciences. He also directs the Core Humanities program. He has taught at Haverford College and the University of Notre Dame, where he received his degree in philosophy. His interests are in social and political philosophy and he has published work on Habermas and MacIntyre.

**Olivier Dufault** was born in Montréal, Québec, Canada, where he obtained a master's degree in history at McGill University, under the supervision of Elizabeth Digeser. After studying at *l'École Pratique des Hautes Études* in Paris, he has now begun Ph.D. studies in history at the University of California at Santa Barbara. His interest lies in the intersection of the religious, the philosophical, and the political in antiquity.

**Paula Fredriksen** is the William Goodwin Aurelio Professor of the Appreciation of Scripture at Boston University. Her degrees are from Wellesley College (B.A., 1973), Oxford University (Theol. Diploma, 1974), and Princeton University (Ph.D., 1979). She has previously taught at Stanford, the University of California at Berkeley, and the University of Pittsburgh. She has published numerous books on Augustine, Jesus, Paul, conversion, apocalypticism, and Jewish/gentile relations in late antiquity.

**Franklin T. Harkins** received his Ph.D. in theology from the University of Notre Dame (2005). He was a Lilly Fellow and Lecturer in the Humanities and Theology in Christ College at Valparaiso University, and is now an assistant professor of theology at Fordham University. His primary area of expertise is the history of Christianity in the patristic and medieval periods. Harkins is particularly interested in the history of Jewish-Christian relations from antiquity to the present. He received the 2006 North American Patristics Society Best First Article Prize for his piece, "Nuancing Augustine's Hermeneutical Jew: Allegory and Actual Jews in the Bishop's Sermons," which appeared in the *Journal for the Study of Judaism* in 2005.

**Paul LaChance** is assistant professor of theology at the College of Saint Elizabeth. He wrote his dissertation (Boston College) on Boethius and has authored articles on Boethius and Christology.

**Leo Lefebure** is the Matteo Ricci, S.J., Professor of Theology at Georgetown University and a priest of the Roman Catholic Archdiocese of Chicago. He is the author of four books, including most recently *Revelation, the Religions, and Violence*, which received the Pax Christi U.S.A. 2001 Book Award and which was translated into Indonesian and published in Jakarta. He is a long-time participant in dialogues with Jews, Muslims, and Buddhists. He is a member of the board of directors for the Society for Buddhist-Christian Studies, convenor of the Comparative Theology Group of the Catholic Theological society of America, associate editor of *Chicago Studies*, and editor-at-large for *The Christian Century*.

**Reid Locklin** serves as assistant professor of Christianity and the Intellectual Tradition in the Christianity and Culture Programme at the Centre for the Study of Religion at the University of Toronto. He completed his Ph.D. in systematic and comparative theology at Boston College, focusing on the religious pedagogies of Augustine of Hippo and Adi Shankaracharya. He is the author of *Spiritual but Not Religious? An Oar Stroke Closer to the Farther Shore* (2005), as well as various articles and essays. He is currently writing a Christian theological commentary on Shankara's independent treatise, *A Thousand Teachings*.

**Kim Paffenroth** is associate professor of religious studies at Iona College. He is the author of several books on the Bible and theology. Lately his interests have turned to considering the interface of religion and popular culture, authoring *Gospel of the Living Dead: George Romero's Visions of Hell on Earth* (Baylor, 2006), and co-authoring (with T. Bertonneau) *The Truth Is Out There: Christian Faith and Classic Sci-Fi Television* (Brazos, 2006). The former book won the 2006 Bram Stoker Award in the nonfiction category, and was nominated for the International Horror Guild Award. Paffenroth has since embarked on a career writing horror fiction, with the publication of his first horror novel, *Dying to Live* (Permuted Press, 2007). He lives in Cornwall-on-Hudson, New York, with his wife and two children.

**C. C. Pecknold** (Ph.D., University of Cambridge) teaches in the department of theology at Loyola College in Maryland. He is the author of *Transforming Postliberal Theology* (T & T Clark, 2005) and has most recently edited *Liturgy, Time and the Politics of Redemption* (Eerdmans, 2006), in the respected *Radical Traditions* series.

**Aaron Stalnaker** is assistant professor of religious studies at Indiana University. He received his Ph.D. from Brown University. His interests are in the ethics and philosophy of religion, with attention to both Chinese and Western theories and practices. He founded and is currently the chair of the Comparative Religious Ethics Group of the American Academy of Religion.